Amsterdam's People of the Book

JEWISH SOCIETY AND THE TURN TO SCRIPTURE IN THE SEVENTEENTH CENTURY

Amsterdam's People of the Book

JEWISH SOCIETY AND THE TURN TO SCRIPTURE IN THE SEVENTEENTH CENTURY

Benjamin E. Fisher

HEBREW UNION COLLEGE PRESS

HEBREW UNION COLLEGE PRESS

Cover design by Paul Neff Design LLC
Set in Arno Pro by Raphaël Freeman MISTD, Renana Typesetting

Printed in the United States of America

Library of Congress Cataloging-in-Publication Data

Names: Fisher, Benjamin E., 1981- author.
Title: Amsterdam's people of the book : Jewish society and the turn to scripture in the 17th century / Benjamin E. Fisher.
Description: [Cincinnati, Ohio] : Hebrew Union College Press, [2020] | "The book had its genesis during my doctoral studies in the Department of History at the University of Pennsylvania"--Acknowledgements. | Includes bibliographical references and index. | Summary: "An investigation of the primacy of Scripture to the 17th-Jewish Portuguese community in Amsterdam, as opposed to the more common emphasis on rabbinic works. Shows how the influence of surrounding Christian culture, scientific discovery, and the Portuguese Jews' converso background all contributed to this emphasis"--Provided by publisher.
Identifiers: LCCN 2019058450 (print) | LCCN 2019058451 (ebook) | ISBN 9780878201884 (hardback) | ISBN 9780878201891 (ebook)
Subjects: LCSH: Jews--Netherlands--Amsterdam--History--17th century. | Bible. Old Testament--Criticism, interpretation, etc., Jewish--History--17th century. | Bible. Old Testament--Study and teaching--Netherlands--Amsterdam. | Bible--Influence. | Judaism--Relations--Christianity--History--17th century. | Amsterdam (Netherlands)--History--17th century.
Classification: LCC DS135.N5 A5334 2020 (print) | LCC DS135.N5 (ebook) | DDC 949.2/352004924009032--dc23
LC record available at https://lccn.loc.gov/2019058450
LC ebook record available at https://lccn.loc.gov/2019058451

This book is dedicated to Goldie Kurtz,
the one person who journeyed with
Amsterdam's People of the Book
from beginning to end.

Table of Contents

Acknowledgements ix

Introduction:
Centering the Bible in Jewish and European Culture 1

1. Amsterdam's People of the Book: From Classrooms to Confraternities 27

Part I. The Educational Infrastructure: Officials, Schools, and Confraternities 31

Part II. Education and the Bible in Seventeenth-Century Amsterdam 42

Part III. Adult Education in Early Modern Amsterdam: The Bible Beyond the Schools. 63

2. Centering the Bible in Jewish Theology: Salvation and Scripture 85

Part I. The Christian and Converso Prologue to Jewish Perspectives on Scripture 88

Part II. Scripture and Salvation: The Connection under Assault 103

Part III. Saul Levi Morteira and Jewish Salvation: Between the New Testament and the Hebrew Bible 111

3. "One of the Greatest Problems That There Is in Scripture": Menasseh ben Israel, Mathematics, and the Authority of the Bible. 125

Part I. Biblical Contradictions and Infallibility: Jewish and Christian Contexts 133

Part II. Old Miracles and the New Philosophy 143

Part III. The Challenges of Biblical Chronology 148

Part IV. One of the Greatest Problems That There Is in Scripture 155

4. Opening the Eyes of the *Novos Reformados*: Rabbi Saul Levi Morteira, Radical Christianity, and the Jewish Reclamation of Jesus, 1631–1660 167

Part I. Jewish Readers of Christian Bibles 175

Part II. From the *Preguntas* to the *Tratado*, 1631–1660 180

Part III. Medieval Precedents 185

Part IV. Morteira and the Socinians: The Discovery of Judaizing Christians 188

5. Polemic and Scholarship in Seventeenth-Century Amsterdam: Rabbi Saul Levi Morteira and the History of the New Testament. 205

Part I. Medieval Precedents 209

Part II. Jesus and the New Testament in a Rabbinic Context 212

Part III. The New Testament and Its Greco-Roman Context 225

Part IV. New Testament Origins 232

Epilogue: Jewish Biblical Studies in Amsterdam: Spinoza's Origins and the Horizon of Modernity 253

Bibliography 281

Index 301

Acknowledgements

AMSTERDAM'S PEOPLE OF THE BOOK BENEFITED GREATLY FROM THE assistance, support, and encouragement of many experts, colleagues, institutions, friends, and family members, and it is a pleasure to have the opportunity now, as the project reaches its conclusion, to express my sincere appreciation.

The book had its genesis during my doctoral studies in the Department of History at the University of Pennsylvania, where I studied medieval and early modern Jewish history with two of my most important advisors and mentors, David Ruderman and Talya Fishman. Throughout my years at Penn, in academic seminars, lectures, and meetings both formal and informal, I learned to read historical texts both modern and ancient, to think and write about Jewish history's big ideas, and to appreciate its minute details. These wonderful scholars' advice, attention, and questions helped me think through the place of Amsterdam's Portuguese Jews in the wider lens of medieval and early modern Jewish history, and their approaches to scholarship continue to inspire my work today. Anthony Grafton was also a deeply valued advisor, and was constantly generous with his time, advice, insights, and guidance. My first forays into the world of Sephardi biblical studies took place in seminars with Roger Chartier, and I am grateful to him and to John Pollock for pointing me in this exciting direction. The Herbert D. Katz Center for Advanced Judaic Studies at Penn was another early home for the project, and conversations with many fellows and visiting scholars including Michela Andreatta, Shlomo Berger, Theodor Dünkelgrun,

Elliott Horowitz, Yosi Israeli, Yosef Kaplan, Amnon Raz-Krakotzkin, Adam Shear, Adam Sutcliffe, Joanna Weinberg, and Carsten Wilke were a source of inspiration and ideas. Joseph Gulka and Judith Leifer helped me navigate the Katz Center library's holdings. Arthur Kiron provided valuable assistance with the Katz Center's rare books, and his insights helped shape my thinking about early modern Jewish books and readers. Miriam Bodian, and Harm den Boer, Matt Goldish, Julia Lieberman, and Peter Stallybrass also shared their insights and advice and provided generous assistance. During my years at Penn, I benefited from the support of a Benjamin Franklin Fellowship, and grants from the Memorial Foundation for Jewish Culture and the Doris G. Quinn Foundation, for which I am extremely grateful and without which this book could not have been completed.

Towson University was the next home for my research on *Amsterdam's People of the Book*. As a new Assistant Professor of Medieval and Early Modern Jewish History, the opportunity to design and teach graduate seminars and undergraduate courses provided valuable arenas for reflecting on key themes, readings, and questions with students. In addition, the opportunity to present works in progress with colleagues led me to think through and sharpen questions, ideas, and arguments. Rita Costa-Gomes has been especially selfless with her advice, always willing to discuss all things related to the world of medieval and early modern Spain and Portugal, and the linguistic nuances of this time period. During my first years at Towson, Daniel Fisher read parts of several chapters, and organized conference panels for the UC Berkeley Memory and Identity Group, where early versions of ideas and arguments in this book were presented. A tireless scholar and advocate for the humanities, Daniel was always ready to listen to, discuss, and debate my ideas and I am very grateful for his efforts. Terry Cooney has been a supportive and encouraging Dean at Towson, and Christian Koot and Ronn Pineo have been most supportive department chairs.

Towson generously allowed me to continue work on *Amsterdam's People of the Book* beyond the university. In 2013–2014 I spent an invigorating semester at Harvard University's Centre for Jewish Studies as a Starr Fellow during the "Historical Consciousness and the Jewish

Historical Imagination" project. The opportunity to present my work, and discussions with Peter Gordon, Rachel Greenblatt, Jonathan Gribetz, Sarit Kattan Gribetz, Michael Miller, and Eugene Sheppard were stimulating and thought provoking. I was also privileged to spend the Trinity Term, 2015, as a Dorset Visiting Fellow at the Oxford Centre for Hebrew and Jewish Studies, as part of the Jewish Books in Amsterdam seminar led by Shlomo Berger and César Merchán-Hamann. The projects of all the participants made a significant contribution to my thinking about Jewish readers, books, libraries, and thought in early modern Amsterdam. Shlomo Berger, the driving force behind the seminar, passed away tragically mere weeks after the concluding conference – depriving the world of a wonderful scholar and an even better *mensch*, whose advice, insights, and support were critical during the growth of my book.

This book project owes an immense debt to institutions, colleagues, and friends in the city of Amsterdam. The human dimension to this project is significant. My good friends Esther and Karel Weener, and Marcelo Bendahan, invited me into their homes with sincere warmth, as though I were a longtime friend rather than a recent acquaintance from a café, or the synagogue. Their hospitality and friendship over the years have made research in their city such a joy and pleasure. Jetze Touber, then at Utrecht University and now at Ghent University, took an interest in my work, shared his expertise and encouragement enthusiastically, and provided valuable feedback and support. Several institutions in Amsterdam were also critical in the completion of this project. The Bibliotheca Rosenthaliana was a central resource during many visits to the city, and its director Emile Schrijver provided helpful advice about the collection. My explorations of the Amsterdam Municipal Archive would have been much less fruitful without the expert guidance of Odette Vlessing. And the writing of *Amsterdam's People of the Book* would simply not have been possible without the expertise and assistance of the staff and librarians of the Ets Haim – Livraria Montezinos, who made their rich collection of print and manuscript materials available to me, even during a frenzied and chaotic period of renovations and relocation. I am endlessly grateful for their assistance and guidance.

I am also deeply grateful for the enthusiasm and support of Jason

Kalman at Hebrew Union College Press, the two external reviewers, and for Sonja Rethy's expert suggestions and attention to details both large and small throughout the editing process. Their guidance was invaluable in bringing this project to fruition.

As *Amsterdam's People of the Book* nears completion, I wish also to thank my teachers and mentors who first inspired my interest in early modern history and Jewish history at the University of Toronto: Natalie Zemon Davis, Mark Meyerson, Derek Penslar, and Nicholas Terpstra, whose advice, efforts, support, and encouragement have been have been so important. Last but not least, I am grateful to Sarah Fisher, for being a compassionate friend and true humanitarian; to Goldie Kurtz, who read the chapters of this book many times, listened to my ideas, and asked penetrating questions; and to Oren and Ilan, who although very young, have already begun asking questions about "Daddy's Book."

Benjamin E. Fisher
Towson University

INTRODUCTION

Centering the Bible in Jewish and European Culture

ON AUGUST 27, 1649, THE SPANISH AMBASSADOR TO THE NETHERlands, Antoine Brun, sent a report to Madrid in which he described the departure from Spain of a Christian merchant, banker, and financier named Tomás Rodrigues Pereyra.[1] Brun noted that Pereyra had left Madrid three years previously, that he had allegedly stolen a significant amount of money from the Spanish king, and that he was now living in the Dutch city of Rotterdam as a Jew.[2] While we may never know whether Pereyra truly absconded with wealth stolen from King Philip IV, Brun was unquestionably correct about Pereyra's religious transformation. After arriving in the Netherlands, Tomás Pereyra joined the community of Portuguese Jews that had existed there since the late sixteenth century.[3] The transformation of Tomás Pereyra the New Christian into

1. Regarding Tomás Rodrigues Pereyra/Abraham Israel Pereyra, see Henry Méchoulan, *Hispanidad y Judaismo en Tiempos de Espinoza. Edición de La Certeza del Camino de Abraham Pereyra* (Salamanca: Ediciones Universidad de Salamanca, 1987).
2. Jonathan Israel, "Spain and the Dutch Sephardim, 1609–1660," *Studia Rosenthaliana* 12, no. 1–2 (1978): 49–50.
3. Regarding the earliest settlement of Portuguese Jews in the Low Countries, see Daniel Swetschinski, *Reluctant Cosmopolitans: The Portuguese Jews of Seventeenth-Century Amsterdam*. The Littman Library of Jewish Civilization (London and Portland: Liverpool University Press, 2000), 167–70; Miriam Bodian, *Hebrews of the Portuguese Nation: Conversos and Community in Early Modern Amsterdam* (Bloomington and Indianapolis: Indiana University Press, 1997), 25–53; and Aron di Leone Leoni, *The*

Abraham Israel Pereyra the ex-converso was observed and described by Moshe Raphael d'Aguilar, one of the leading rabbis in the community. Aguilar remarked about Pereyra that,

> The esteemed gentleman arrived from Spain with only such simple and hazy information about the veracity of our holy Torah that those lands make obtainable. He came here, where [Torah] can be upheld and taught in adequate freedom, but [he came] at an adult age, when the study of the holy tongue was difficult and wearying for him. Nonetheless, since piety is part of his inner nature, he began first of all to participate consistently in academies of learning, to listen attentively to the words of Torah spoken there, and to learn from the books of faith; and so he accumulated a priceless treasure of holy wisdom . . . But this kindly man did not make do with acquiring knowledge himself, and tried to involve others in his devout learning.[4]

Aguilar is no doubt referring here to Pereyra's activities as a patron within the Jewish community. Although Abraham Pereyra devoted himself to the study of Judaism, like many adult émigrés to Amsterdam, he never truly mastered the skills required for working independently in Jewish legal and theological texts, and viewed patronage as a prestigious alternative.[5] As Menasseh ben Israel wrote only a short time after Pereyra's arrival in the Netherlands, Pereyra used the "considerable wealth" that he had taken with him from Spain in order to establish a yeshivah, and to pay the salaries of many Torah instructors.[6] Abraham Pereyra also

Hebrew Portuguese Nations in Antwerp and London at the Time of Charles V and Henry VIII (Jersey City, NJ: KTAV, 2005).

4. Yosef Kaplan, "From Apostasy to Return to Judaism: The Portuguese Jews in Amsterdam," in *Binah: Studies in Jewish History, Thought, and Culture*, ed. Joseph Dan (New York: Praeger, 1988), 99–117.
5. Miriam Bodian, *Hebrews of the Portuguese Nation*, 97.
6. Menasseh ben Israel, *Thesouro dos denim que o povo de Israel he obrigado saber e observar*, vol. 5 (Amsterdam, 1645–1647), Dedicatoria [unpaginated]. "Vieraõ Vs. Ms. De Espanha; e avendo tirade hua taõ consideravel riqueza, lhes pareceo que esta seria tanto mais acreditada e noble, quanto mais empregada em bens vsos. Instituem Vs. Ms. logo hua illustre Iessiva, e com muytos salarios a enriquecem de Baalé Tora. Della para Presidente faze[m] Vs. Ms. Eleiçaõ de minha pessoa; e desde aquelle tempo, me [h]aõ enchido de tantos favores."

participated in the founding of the *Honen Dalim* (*Apiada al pobre*; "He who pities the poor") poor relief society, and the *Tora Or* academy of scholars, both of which organized regular Bible study meetings.[7] At the *Tora Or* confraternity, members met for thirty minutes each day to discuss passages from the "Book of Rabbi Moses," probably the *Mishneh Torah*, and for an hour on Sabbaths and festivals they debated questions regarding the weekly Torah portion. At the *Honen Dalim*, Pereyra and other members met once a week in order to discuss "some faithful comment upon the Bible" and the "ideas that occur to the reader."[8]

Later in life, Pereyra reflected upon and wrote about his experiences, and counselled other recent neophytes in the community about how most effectively to immerse themselves in the practice of Judaism and the study of its texts. Pereyra believed very firmly that the study of Scripture, both independently and in confraternities, was an essential element in the process of transitioning from the Christian world into Jewish society. He writes that,

> When you leave the synagogue and come to your house, you must take a copy of the Bible and read it... and, when studying, give it all your attention... Note every difficulty and ask about it, fixing for yourself a specific time at one of the academies of learning, for this is the true remedy and through it will you learn, by presenting your doubts... and listening to the learned answers. Thus, at the set time, you will heal your soul... and in this way you will benefit from the constancy and attention that you devote to study of the Torah and to reading of other books... It was in this way that I myself studied at the Torat Or Yeshivah at the feet of our faithful shepherd, the noble gentleman, the scholar, Rabbi Isaac Aboab.[9]

7. Daniel Levi de Barrios, *Triumpho del govierno popular* (Amsterdam, 1683), 69. "En el dia primeiro se discurre sobre algun fiel comento de la Biblia." See also pp. 81, 86. "Y la Yesiba de Tora Hor camina cada dia de los seis de la semana media hora, con los que explican el libro de Rabenu Mosseh, teniendo sus quince grados en los quinze Academicos con la luz del Divino Sol, que cada Sabado, y cada Pasqua la esparce una hora sobre los que assisten a la Yesiba, y los que en esta Hora responden a las proposiciones que se ofrecen sobre la Parasa de la semana."
8. Daniel Levi de Barrios, *Triumpho del govierno popular*, 265–66.
9. Yosef Kaplan, "From Apostasy to Return to Judaism," 110–11.

Abraham Pereyra's experience of conversion from Christianity to Judaism was powerfully shaped by his adopted community's engagement with the Hebrew Bible. Personally, he placed great emphasis on reflecting upon the Bible; he perceived Scripture as being central to the Jewish education of returning conversos, and he helped to create institutions that facilitated and perpetuated the study of Scripture by adults within the Portuguese Jewish community long after their initial transition to the world of Judaism.

Amsterdam's People of the Book argues that Scripture played a central role in the education of ex-conversos and their descendants in Amsterdam as well as in the cultural life and rabbinic scholarship of this community, and that the prominence of the Bible in such diverse areas of this society resulted from the ongoing resonance of the converso experience, as well as from the Protestant environment in which they converted to Judaism.

Origins of the Portuguese Jewish Community in Amsterdam

The Jewish community that Abraham Pereyra joined in the mid-1640s was composed overwhelmingly of individuals who were descendants of Jews who had fled Spain in 1492, and who found refuge – temporarily – in the Kingdom of Portugal, across Spain's western border. Estimates vary widely regarding the number of Jews who made this journey, from 30,000 individuals all the way to 85,000 or even 115,000.[10] However large, it is clear that a very substantial number of Spanish immigrants augmented the existing population of Portuguese Jews, which is estimated at 30,000 on the eve of Spain's edict of expulsion.[11] The reprieve from Ferdinand and Isabella's edict was brief. According to the Portuguese chronicler Damão de Góis, in 1496 King Manuel I of Portugal signed his own edict of expulsion in an effort to arrange a marriage with a Spanish princess that would make him heir to the throne of Castille and Aragon. Princess Isabella, according to de Góis, would not accept his proposal

10. António José Saraiva, *The Marrano Factory: The Portuguese Inquisition and its New Christians, 1536–1765*, ed. and trans. H.P. Salomon and I.S.D. Sassoon (Leiden and Boston: Brill, 1991), 1–19; Daniel Swetschinski, *Reluctant Cosmopolitans*, 57.
11. António José Saraiva, *The Marrano Factory*, 1.

while Jews remained in Portugal.[12] In March 1497, Manuel ordered all Jewish children under the age of fourteen to be baptized and placed in the care of Christian families, and in June thousands of Jews preparing to leave from Lisbon were forcibly converted as well.[13]

Whereas in Spain the edict of expulsion came with the option of exile or conversion, in Portugal forced conversion was universal, virtually inescapable, and specifically affected highly committed Jews who had resisted conversion and fled from Spain. Furthermore, despite the intent to create a religiously homogenous society in Portugal, conversion left communal, religious, and family connections intact, since exile was not initially an option. And because the Portuguese Inquisition was not established until 1536, there was little disincentive to the practice of Judaism in secret.[14] It is this population of Portuguese and Spanish forced converts that forms the core of the émigré community of ex-conversos established at Amsterdam in the late sixteenth century.

Amsterdam may appear at first to be an unusual choice as a place of refuge for New Christians during this period. There were only small numbers of Jews in the Netherlands as a whole, and there was no history of Jewish settlement in Amsterdam. At the same time, there were well-established communities of ex-conversos and Iberian Jews in Venice, Salonika, Safed, and Constantinople. However, a variety of political, economic, and diplomatic developments provided both opportunities and motivation for many New Christians to flee, and to select Amsterdam as their destination. In the first years of the seventeenth century there was a confluence of three important events: an agreement in 1601 arranged by Philip III and the Duke of Lerma that permitted New Christians to emigrate from the Iberian Peninsula in return for a large payment; the emergence of the United Provinces as a stable, independent, and internationally recognized state following the revolt against Spain; and the lifting of the Spanish-Dutch trade embargo in the last years of the sixteenth century, which created lucrative commercial opportunities and made

12. António José Saraiva, *The Marrano Factory*, 11.
13. António José Saraiva, *The Marrano Factory*, 12–13.
14. Yosef Hayim Yerushalmi, *From Spanish Court to Italian Ghetto. Isaac Cardoso: A Study in Seventeenth-Century Marranism and Jewish Apologetics* (Seattle and London: University of Washington Press, 1981), 4–8.

Amsterdam a leading entrepôt for trade in sugar and spices.[15] These factors stimulated a wave of emigration that provided the nucleus for the initial ex-converso community in Amsterdam. Further waves followed in the 1630s and 1640s, stimulated by a significant spike in Inquisitorial activities; a dramatic wave of negative sentiment against Portuguese New Christians following the successful rebellion of Portugal in 1640; and the 1643 fall of Count-Duke Olivares, a leading patron of New Christians.[16] The crumbling of Spanish finances and a major economic crisis of October 1647 likewise led to an exodus of wealthy New Christian financiers and bankers, including Tomás Rodrigues Pereyra and many other figures who would become leading members of the Portuguese Jewish community in Amsterdam.[17]

The Biblical Culture of Portuguese Jewish Amsterdam

Like Abraham Pereyra, modern historians have recognized the important place of the Hebrew Bible in the culture and intellectual life of Portuguese Jews as they reconnected with Judaism. Daniel Swetschinski, one of the leading scholars of the Portuguese Jews in Amsterdam, has remarked upon the centrality of the Bible in Portuguese Jewish society and culture in Amsterdam. Neophyte Jews in the community established their Jewish identity by reconnecting with the biblical past. They adopted the names of the patriarchs, modeled the *Esnoga* (synagogue), their monumental architectural achievement, on Solomon's Temple in Jerusalem, and adorned their tombstones with ornate biblical motifs.[18] Harm den Boer has drawn attention to the central place of the Spanish-language 1553 Ferrara Bible in the Portuguese Jewish community, which was produced by Iberian exiles and conversos. The Ferrara Bible, reprinted ubiquitously during the seventeenth century and into the eighteenth century, helped ex-conversos rediscover their medieval Sephardic heritage and

15. Miriam Bodian, *Hebrews of the Portuguese Nation*, 25–30.
16. Yosef Hayim Yerushalmi, *From Spanish Court to Italian Ghetto*, 105, 120, 165, 177; Daniel Swetschinski, *Reluctant Cosmopolitans*, 70–78.
17. Jonathan Israel, "Spain and the Dutch Sephardim," 44–47.
18. Daniel Swetschinski, *Reluctant Cosmopolitans*, 320–22.

Jewish identity, and served as the foundation for much of the community's literary productivity and rabbinic scholarship.[19]

Despite recognizing that the Bible played a prominent role in ex-converso education and culture, historians have not studied the biblical education or scholarship of this community systematically, as subjects worthy of specific inquiry and analysis. Yet, one need not dig very deeply into the archival sources of this community, and the rabbinic scholarship of its religious leaders, for the importance of the Hebrew Bible and the New Testament to become readily apparent. Amsterdam's rabbis were prolific writers of biblically-centered scholarship. Menasseh ben Israel devoted nearly twenty years of his life to reconciling contradictory biblical verses in the *Conciliador* [Reconciler], which he published in four separate volumes between 1632 and 1651.[20] Saul Levi Morteira's *magnum opus*, the *Tratado da verdade da lei de Moisés* [Treatise on the Truth of the Law of Moses] (1660), is a four-hundred-folio treatise proving the superiority of the Hebrew Bible over the Gospels and subjecting the New Testament to a rigorous historical analysis. Jacob Judah Leon's oeuvre is composed almost entirely of biblically-oriented texts, including separate works on the construction and design of Solomon's Temple, the Cherubs, and the Ark of the Covenant in which the tablets of the Law were carried.[21] Isaac Aboab da Fonseca's major work, *Parafrasis comentado sobre el Pentateuco* [Paraphrased commentary upon the Pentateuch]

19. Regarding the reprinting of the Ferrara Bible in Amsterdam, see especially Harm den Boer, "La Biblia de Ferrara y otras traducciones españolas de la Biblia entre los sefardíes de origen converso," in *Introducción a la Biblia de Ferrara: Actas del Simposio Internacional*, ed. Iacob M. Hassán (Sevilla, 1991), 251–96, esp. 251–54. See also Harm den Boer, "Los salmos de David (Abenatar Melo)," in *Die Sefarden in Hamburg: zur Geschichte einer Minderheit. Teil 2*, ed. Michael Studemund Halévy (Hamburg: Helmut Buske Verlag, 1997), 753–80.
20. Regarding Menasseh ben Israel and the *Conciliador*, see Chapter 3.
21. Jacob Judah Leon, *Retrato de Templo de Selomo* (Middleburg, 1642); *Tratado de la Arca del Testamento* (Amsterdam, 1653); and the *Tratado de los Cherubim* (Amsterdam, 1654). Regarding Leon and his biblical writings, see A.K. Offenberg, "Dirk van Santen and the Keur Bible: New Insights into Jacob Judah (Arye) Leon Templo's Model Temple," *Studia Rosenthaliana* 37 (2004): 401–22, and *idem*, "Jacob Jehuda Leon (1602–1675) and his model of the Temple," in *Jewish-Christian Relations in the Seventeenth Century: Studies and Documents*, ed. J. van den Berg and Ernestine van der Wall (Dordrecht: Kluwer Academic Publishers, 1988), 95–115.

(1681) is a blended commentary on and translation of the Pentateuch that he hoped would replace the Aramaic *targumim* as the text read by members of his community on Sabbaths, in order to fulfill the precept of reading the Torah portion twice each week.[22] Aboab was one of the leading rabbis of the Portuguese Jews in Amsterdam, over a period of more than four decades. He was a director of multiple confraternities, a regular preacher, and an instructor in the highest levels of the community's school system. It is an interesting and significant fact that his single most extensive treatise focused on the Pentateuch, and on making the text accessible to diverse members of his community.[23] Toward the end of the seventeenth century, Rabbi Yosseph Franco Serrano printed his own paraphrase of the Pentateuch, *Los cinco libros de la sacra Ley* [The Five Books of the Holy Law],[24] a significant work of biblical scholarship and the most extensive known text written by Serrano. While several Amsterdam rabbis also wrote on theological topics, the preponderance of lengthy biblical commentaries among the most important writings of Amsterdam's leading Portuguese rabbis demonstrates the significance of Bible study in the eyes of the community's religious scholars.[25]

22. Isaac Aboab da Fonseca, *Parafrasis comentado sobre el Pentateuco* (Amsterdam, 1681). "[E]s obligacion leer la Parassa todas las semanas cada verso dos vezes, y una por el Paraphrasis Caldaico, y dize mas, que quien leyere el comento de Rasi, (nuestro gran Comentador) cumple con la dicha obligacion, en lugar del Paraphrasis Caldeo, y por quanto ni todos saben leer ni lo uno, ni lo otro, porque no lo aprendieron, yo fio todos los Hahamim convengan co[n]migo, que la lectura de nuestro PARAPHRASIS, y comento haga el mismo efecto."
23. On the *Parafrasis comentado*, see Cecilia Amparo Alba, "Isaac Aboab de Fonseca: Parafrasis Comentado Sobre el Pentateuco," in *Los Judaizantes en Europa y la Literatura Castellana del Siglo de Oro*, ed. Fernando Díaz Esteban (Madrid: Letrúmero, 1994), 19–27.
24. Yosseph Franco Serrano, *Los cinco libros de la sacra Ley* (Amsterdam, 1695).
25. See, for instance, Menasseh ben Israel's *De la resurreccion de los muertos* [On the resurrection of the dead] (Amsterdam, 1636), his *De fragilidad humana, y inclinacion del hombre al peccado* [On human weakness, and the proclivity of men to sin] (Amsterdam, 1642), and the *Nishmat Ḥayyim*, an attack on atheism and religious skepticism grounded in a demonstration of the demonic and supernatural. On the *Nishmat Ḥayyim*, see J.H. Chajes, *Between Worlds: Dybbuks, Exorcists, and Early Modern Judaism* (Philadelphia: University of Pennsylvania Press, 2003), 119–38. Marc Saperstein has also demonstrated that Saul Levi Morteira wrote a treatise on the immortality of the soul that is no longer extant. Marc Saperstein, "Saul Levi Morteira's

It is not intuitively obvious why the Bible in particular was such an important focus of religious, intellectual, and cultural life in Amsterdam, or why Scripture became the portal through which ex-conversos integrated into the Jewish world and the subject of their emphatic and sustained reflection. Why focus on the Bible specifically, instead of other branches of Jewish literature? Scholars have long appreciated the breadth of Jewish texts translated into Spanish and Portuguese for ex-conversos during the sixteenth and seventeenth centuries. As Yosef Haim Yerushalmi remarked in an address at the University of Cincinnati in 1980, "the returning converso was essentially an autodidact and, like all autodidacts, he needed books to read."[26] Yerushalmi identified a broad range of biblical, liturgical, halakhic, ethical, philosophical, historical, and messianic Jewish texts circulating in Spanish, Ladino, and Portuguese translations during this period. Spanish translations of the Bible were popular. There were also Hebrew liturgical works translated into Spanish, such as the *Libro de oraciones de todo el anno . . . traducydo del Hebrayco de verbo a verbo* [Book of prayers for the entire year . . . translated word for word from the Hebrew] (Ferrara, 1552). Translations of the Aramaic *targum*, the Song of Songs, and the Mishnah tractate *Pirkei Avot* [Ethics of the Fathers] were also highly popular.[27] Furthermore, numerous halakhic works were translated into Spanish, Portuguese, and Ladino during the sixteenth and seventeenth centuries, and were seen as crucial to providing a practical foundation for the practice of Judaism by ex-conversos. Works such as Isaac Athias's *Thesoro de preceptos* [Treasury of Precepts] (Venice, 1627; Amsterdam, 1649) provided comprehensive discussions of the 613 commandments.[28] There were also editions of Joseph Karo's *Shulhan Arukh* [The Set Table] (Venice, 1564) available to

Treatise on the Immortality of the Soul," *Studia Rosenthaliana* 25, no. 2 (1991): 131–48. Regarding the general importance of this key theological topic in Amsterdam during the early and mid-seventeenth century, see Alexander Altmann, "Eternality of Punishment: A Theological Controversy within the Amsterdam Rabbinate in the Thirties of the Seventeenth Century," *Proceedings of the American Academy for Jewish Research* 40 (1972): 1–88.

26. Yerushalmi, *The Re-education of Marranos in the Seventeenth Century* (Cincinnati, OH: University of Cincinnati, 1980), 1.
27. Yerushalmi, *The Re-education of Marranos*, 7.
28. Yerushalmi, *The Re-education of Marranos*, 7.

recent converts to Judaism. In 1568 a Judeo-Spanish edition of Karo's text was printed, and in 1609 an abridged edition was printed in Venice by Moses Altaras under the title *Libro de Mantenimiento de la Alma* [Book on the care for the soul].[29]

But why not begin the Judaic education of ex-conversos with a manual of basic Jewish laws, such as Menasseh ben Israel's Portuguese-language *Thesouro dos denim que o povo de Israel he obrigado saber e observar* [A Treasury of Precepts that the People of Israel should Know and Observe], which was printed in Amsterdam between 1645 and 1647? Using this type of vernacular manual, Abraham Israel Pereyra could have studied basic Jewish dietary laws, an extensive list of blessings, funerary rituals, practices associated with Jewish holidays and festivals, Jewish perspectives on sin and forgiveness, as well as laws concerning commerce and finance, among many others. Menasseh's guide was designed to provide practical and spiritual instruction to members of the community – from their morning prayers to their evening prayers and everything in between. Theoretically, such a text could have been the focus of Pereyra's earliest studies when he joined the Jewish community. However, this does not appear to have been the case.

It is even more notable that Scripture remained central to the religious and cultural life of these individuals long after their integration into Jewish society. Theoretically, we might understand the early focus on biblical texts as an initial didactic choice, and a convenient place to begin the Jewish education of recent converts and their descendants. Why was it the case, however, that in so many different ways the Bible continued to be a prominent focus of intensive study long after adults and their children were integrated into the community? Why, when the community designed its educational curriculum, was Scripture the overwhelming focus? Why was so little effort made to expose students to legal and theological texts at earlier stages of their education? Why defer the study of these topics and works to the end of the process, restricting them to the most advanced students? Furthermore, why is it the case that when many of Amsterdam's leading rabbis were "off the clock," finished

29. Miriam Bodian, *Hebrews of the Portuguese Nation*, 106. See also Yerushalmi, *The Re-education of Marranos*, 8–10.

with their official teaching and preaching duties, they tended to write sophisticated biblical commentaries, rather than commentaries on the Talmud and legal compendia?

Jewish Biblical Studies in the Early Modern World

While specific studies on Jewish biblical scholarship in Amsterdam and approaches to engaging with the Bible among the Spanish and Portuguese Jews are limited, there have been several studies of sixteenth-century Italian and Mediterranean Jewish approaches to reading the Bible that advance our understanding of early modern Jewish engagements with sacred texts. Among the most recent and extensive, Andrew Berns' *The Bible and Natural Philosophy in Renaissance Italy* investigates "the reciprocal relationship" between natural philosophical and biblical inquiry in the sixteenth century, in central and northern Italy, where Jewish and Christian scholars appealed to knowledge from natural philosophy in order to clarify questions of biblical exegesis, and to studies of Scripture to resolve medical and natural philosophical questions.[30] Focusing on one of the classic figures of pre-modern Jewish biblical scholarship, Eric Lawee's comprehensive analysis of Isaac Abravanel's approach to biblical commentary illuminates the fundamentally liminal character of Abravanel's commentaries, which combine a traditional emphasis on the literal veracity of the Bible's miracles and an insistence on regarding every biblical commandment as a necessary dogma with an innovative historicist approach to reading the text. Abravanel has a sharp sense of the distance between the prophets and the events they narrate, asks important questions about the authorship of biblical texts, and views certain biblical texts as having been based on multiple original sources.[31] Jordan Penkower has explored Elijah Levita's relationship with Christian Hebraists and his arguments that the vowels of the Hebrew Bible were a late accretion to the text; he has also studied the printing of Jacob ben Ḥayyim ibn Adoniyah's 1525 Rabbinic Bible.[32] Additionally,

30. Andrew Berns, *The Bible and Natural Philosophy in Renaissance Italy* (New York: Cambridge University Press, 2015).
31. Eric Lawee, *Isaac Abarbanel's Stance Toward Tradition: Defense, Dissent, and Dialogue* (Albany: State University of New York Press, 2001).
32. Jordan Penkower, "New Perspectives on Sefer Massoret ha-Massoret of Elijah Levita.

Joanna Weinberg has demonstrated Azariah de' Rossi's contributions to sixteenth-century Christian debates about the translations of the Vulgate and Septuagint through his study of the Syriac New Testament,[33] and B. Barry Levy has written about the growing sophistication of Jewish efforts to correct the texts of Torah scrolls and Bibles during the Renaissance.[34] In her doctoral dissertation, Neta Ecker-Rozinger studies the biblical commentaries of Eliezer Ashkenazi (1513–1586), who was born and educated in Salonika and served as a rabbi in Egypt before traveling broadly in Italy and eastern Europe.[35] There is thus a growing body of scholarship on Jewish encounters with Scripture in Italy and the Mediterranean in the fifteenth and sixteenth centuries. There has been relatively less systematic work on Jewish approaches to reading and studying the Bible in northwest Europe during the period between the seventeenth century and Moses Mendelssohn in the mid-eighteenth century – a time period and geographic region in need of further research.

This is the case despite the fact that the intervening period of time witnessed significant developments in European – and, I argue – Jewish approaches to reading Scripture. Amsterdam's Portuguese Jews lived in a biblically-obsessed age in which diverse European societies turned to the Bible for models of political and social organization, and for information about the imminent arrival of the Messiah. Scholars and theologians applied increasingly sophisticated philological methods in order to reconstruct the most accurate possible representation of God's Word, a project that led them into the linguistic worlds of ancient Greek, Latin, and Hebrew, and that resulted in the publication of the monumental polyglot Bibles of Alcalá, Antwerp, Paris, and London,

The lateness of the Vowel Points and Criticism of the Zohar." *Italia* 8 (1989): 7–73 and *idem*, "Ya'akov ben Hayim u-tsemihat mahadurat ha-mikra'ot ha-gedolot," 2 vols. PhD diss., Hebrew University of Jerusalem, 1982.

33. Joanna Weinberg, *Azariah de Rossi's Observations on the Syriac New Testament: A Critique of the Vulgate by a Sixteenth-Century Jew* (London, Turin: Warburg Institute, 2005).
34. B. Barry Levy, *Fixing God's Torah: The Accuracy of the Hebrew Bible Text in Jewish Law* (New York: Oxford University Press, 2001).
35. Neta Ecker-Rozinger, "Universalistic Tendencies in Rabbi Eliezer Ashkenazi's Teachings," PhD diss., University of Haifa, 2010.

which presented Scripture not just in Hebrew, Greek, and Latin, but also in the languages used by early Christians: Aramaic, Syriac, Arabic, and Ethiopic.[36] Many of the most heated and controversial disputes between Protestants and Catholics centered on problems of biblical interpretation, the relationship between Scripture and other potential *loci* of spiritual authority, the accuracy of the received Latin biblical text, and the issue of who had the freedom to interpret God's Word. Catholics were no less preoccupied with Scripture during this period. In the decades following Luther's challenge and the Council of Trent, leading Catholic theologians devoted vast energies to defending the Vulgate as the authoritative translation, and to editing a new, corrected version of the text, culminating with Clement VIII's edition of 1592.[37]

As Debora Shuger has demonstrated, during the late sixteenth and seventeenth centuries a new approach to humanist biblical scholarship emerged, based on an acute sensitivity to the social and cultural contingencies that shaped the teachings and practices described in the New Testament.[38] The biblical scholarship of figures like Joseph Scaliger, Isaac Casaubon, Hugo Grotius, and others, is characterized by a serious awareness of the "historical discontinuities" that separated the Near Eastern culture of Jesus and the earliest Christians from the ecclesiastical institutions and traditions subsequently established and defended by sixteenth-century Catholic scholars. During the later part of this period, European biblical scholars viewed the New Testament as a text that had to be understood in the context of ancient rabbinic Jewish legal practices and customs, as well as those of the Roman and Hellenic world, which shaped the societies in which Jesus and the Apostles lived.[39] Increasingly, many learned Christians came to see the

36. Regarding the London polyglot Bible, see Peter Miller, "The 'Antiquarianization' of Biblical Scholarship and the London Polyglot Bible (1653–57)," *Journal of the History of Ideas* 62, no. 3 (July, 2001): 463–82. See also Jerry Bentley, *Humanists and Holy Writ: New Testament Scholarship in the Renaissance* (Princeton, NJ: Princeton University Press, 1983).
37. Joanna Weinberg, *Azariah de' Rossi's Observations on the Syriac New Testament*, 1.
38. Debora Kuller Shuger, *The Renaissance Bible: Scholarship, Sacrifice, and Subjectivity* (Berkeley: University of California Press, 1994), 22–23.
39. Anthony Grafton and Joanna Weinberg, *I Have Always Loved the Holy Tongue: Isaac Casaubon, the Jews, and a Forgotten Chapter in Renaissance Scholarship* (Cambridge,

New Testament, as well as church institutions and doctrines as a whole, as being authoritative and true specifically because they were grounded in a demonstrable historical reality.[40] Delving into the New Testament's Jewish, Roman, and Greek substrata enabled Christian interpreters to resolve seemingly contradictory teachings and statements, thus strengthening the coherence and integrity of the text. It also allowed learned Protestant scholars to subvert Catholic understandings of key doctrines and sacraments, and was furthermore useful in depriving Jews and other non-believers of arguments for mocking and subverting Christianity, offering a stronger foundation for Christian polemics against Judaism.[41] Historicist biblical scholarship had political valences as well, providing models for the reform of society and government that juxtaposed the ancient world of Jesus with the contemporary world of the seventeenth century.[42] *Amsterdam's People of the Book* shows that some Portuguese Jews in Amsterdam were as committed to historicist biblical criticism of the New Testament as were their learned Christian contemporaries, although for very different reasons. The view that Christian Scriptures needed to be read against the background of Greco-Roman and ancient Jewish social practices was a shared assumption among Jews and Christians.

Jews and Christians also shared a deep interest in questions of biblical chronology during this period. During the sixteenth and seventeenth

MA and London: The Belknap Press of Harvard University Press, 2011), 164–226; Debora Kuller Shuger, *The Renaissance Bible: Scholarship, Sacrifice, and Subjectivity*, 22–58.

40. See the discussion of Socinian and Remonstrant biblical hermeneutics in Kestutis Daugirdas, "The Biblical Hermeneutics of Socinians and Remonstrants in the Seventeenth Century," in *Arminius, Arminianism, and Europe. Jacobus Arminius, 1559/60–1609*, ed. by Th. Marius van Leeuwen, Keith D. Stanglin, and Marijke Tolsma, 89–114 (Leiden: Brill, 2009), 89–114. Also Anthony Grafton and Joanna Weinberg, *I Have Always Loved the Holy Tongue*, 164–231, and Irena Backus, *Historical Method and Confessional Identity in the Era of the Reformation (1378–1615)* (Leiden and Boston: Brill, 2003).

41. However, note John Selden's use of historicist New Testament interpretation to complicate, and even to exonerate Jews from responsibility for Jesus's death. Jason Rosenblatt, *Renaissance England's Chief Rabbi: John Selden* (New York: Oxford University Press, 2006), 192–96.

42. Deborah Shuger, *The Renaissance Bible: Scholarship, Sacrifice, and Subjectivity*, 39.

centuries, Jewish writers like Isaac Abravanel and Azariah de' Rossi, and Christian scholars like Giovanni Maria Tolosani, Joseph Scaliger, Cesare Baronio, Gerardus Vossius, and many others, intensely debated questions of biblical chronology. Abravanel struggled to disentangle the chronology of ancient Israel's judges and kings, but found that the biblical data were contradictory and did not add up correctly. As Joanna Weinberg has demonstrated, de' Rossi systematically examined and critiqued rabbinic Jewish chronology, demonstrated that the chronological calculations received from the ancient rabbis were inaccurate, and showed that a comparison of the Bible's historical data with ancient Jewish and non-Jewish sources required a reevaluation of the collectively accepted *anno mundi* (age of the world). Within the Christian world, this was a period in which issues of calendar reform, the implications of Copernicus's astronomical discoveries for chronological studies, and debates about the integrity of the Bible's numerical information divided scholars and provoked intense debates. Tolosani participated in debates about reforming the Christian calendar at the Fifth Lateran Council (1512–1517) and published a large chronological tract called the *Opusculum de emendationibus temporum* (Venice, 1537) that contributed significantly to the 1582 Gregorian reform and the establishment of the modern calendar.[43] Like de' Rossi, Tolosani also wrestled with the dizzyingly contradictory biblical dates for ancient Israelite rulers without arriving at a satisfying resolution.

Scaliger's pioneering work in historical chronology raised and highlighted deeply unsettling problems for readers of both the New Testament and Hebrew Bible. Scaliger found unsolvable chronological contradictions in the Septuagint that he believed resulted from deliberate intervention in the text by later writers, and he confessed his inability to resolve inconsistencies in the chronology of Jesus's genealogies and execution. Above all, Scaliger's work in comparative chronology led him to the unsettling discovery of ancient Egyptian chronicles that predated the creation narrative in Genesis by centuries. The difficulties that Scaliger raised would plague the minds of many successors in

43. Edward Rosen, "Was Copernicus' Revolutions Approved by the Pope?" *Journal of the History of Ideas* 36, no. 3 (July-Sept, 1975): 531–33.

subsequent decades. In short, serious problems of biblical chronology preoccupied many scholars during the seventeenth century, Jewish and Christian, and threatened the very integrity of the Bible's authority and textual coherence. *Amsterdam's People of the Book* shows that Jews in seventeenth-century Amsterdam continued to grapple with these problems and questions out of deep concern about the implications of contradictory numerical, mathematical, and chronological information on the authority of the Bible.

Portuguese Jews in seventeenth-century Amsterdam were influenced by another topic of intense discussion and debate in the Christian world: biblical infallibility. During this period, orthodox Protestant and Catholic theologians frequently emphasized the complete infallibility and divine inspiration of the Bible, although they differed sharply on the question of who had authority to interpret Scripture. In light of the Protestant belief that the Bible was the sole authority for judging religious controversies in the church, it became especially important for Protestant scholars to emphasize the infallibility of the entire Bible. Disputes with Catholics over the question of whether the Bible was a self-sufficient tool for its own interpretation, and for deciding controversies in the church, or whether ecclesiastic institutions such as the papacy and councils were necessary to interpret the Bible, provoked Protestant theologians to sharpen their defence of biblical infallibility.

In addition, at least three other phenomena stimulated vigorous defences of biblical infallibility. First, as we have already seen, Scaliger's chronological scholarship raised questions about the reliability of the Bible's information that threatened to subvert its claims to truth and authority, and subsequent scholars tried desperately to resolve challenges to the chronological problems that he raised in a way that would preserve the Bible's integrity. Second, there were many groups within Dutch society that questioned the total infallibility of the Bible. Moderate Calvinist movements, such as the Arminians and Remonstrants, sought to limit the indisputable inerrancy of the Bible by arguing that there were different levels of truth in Scripture, and that the authors of the Bible could and did err in some instances.[44] Orthodox Reformed theologians saw

44. Richard Muller, *Post-Reformation Reformed Dogmatics: The Rise and Development of*

suggestions that Scripture could err in certain places as a direct threat to its status as a divine work, and as the basis for Christian theology and the achievement of salvation. An error in a part jeopardizes the whole. Accordingly, opponents of these movements reconciled contradictory biblical verses in order to demonstrate the Bible's complete internal consistency – and therefore its infallibility.[45]

Third, the infallibility of Scripture was challenged by Protestant and Catholic thinkers who were sympathetic to the new astronomy of Copernicus and Galileo.[46] Just as certain moderate Calvinist thinkers sought to limit the Bible's claims to infallibility on the grounds that some issues were less important theologically, so too proponents of the new science and their opponents debated whether or not certain parts of the Bible were less authoritative because they dealt with mathematical and astronomical matters, and whether the Bible's information on these topics could be erroneous or contradictory. Cardinal Robert Bellarmine (1542–1621) and the Reformed theologian Gisbert Voet (1589–1676) lived in dramatically different settings and were members of rival confessional movements, but could agree that the new science was a threat to their spiritual worldviews, which depended upon the infallibility of Scripture. They believed that the conflict between scientific findings and certain biblical verses suggested fundamental errors in Scripture that subverted its claims to divine and infallible truth. If Scripture erred in philosophical and scientific matters, then the Bible was inherently false and misleading, and the ultimate authority of Scripture would be subverted.[47] Accordingly, it was again necessary for these theologians to reiterate the belief that each and every word in Scripture was divinely inspired, that no error was possible, and that what was written in the Bible was infallibly true. The ubiquitous debate over biblical infallibility thus shaped many dimensions of Dutch cultural and intellectual life,

Reformed Orthodoxy, ca. 1520–1725 (Ada, MI: Baker Academic, 2003), 2:306.

45. Richard Muller, *Post-Reformation Reformed Dogmatics*, 2:307–10.
46. Richard Blackwell, *Galileo, Bellarmine, and the Bible* (London: University of Notre Dame Press, 1991) and Kenneth Howell, *God's Two Books: Copernican Cosmology and Biblical Interpretation in Early Modern Science* (Notre Dame, IN: University of Notre Dame Press, 2002).
47. Kenneth Howell, *God's Two Books*, 169.

and it left its mark on Amsterdam's Portuguese Jews as well. This book illustrates how concerns about defending the status and authority of the Bible led certain rabbis to compose elaborate works dedicated to proving the infallibility of Scripture.

* * *

Amsterdam's People of the Book is divided into five chapters. Collectively, these chapters are linked by a common thread: they demonstrate that from the early decades of Jewish settlement in Amsterdam, the Bible served as one of the central foci of communal identity and culture. Scripture was a central prism through which the ex-conversos defined their Jewish identity, disentangled their Christian past from the Jewish present, and navigated their relationship with diverse Christian movements in the United Provinces. Yet what they understood the Bible to be, and how it should be understood, transformed over time. The assumptions about Scripture that the ex-conversos brought with them to Amsterdam were gradually – but significantly – influenced by literary genres, theological approaches, educational practices, and scholarly perspectives drawn from the Dutch culture and intellectual world in which they were immersed. Over the course of the seventeenth century, the ex-converso perspective on Scripture adapted to the way the Bible was studied, read, and written about by different Christian communities in the Netherlands. The following chapters trace the development of this process.

Amsterdam's People of the Book begins by establishing the centrality of the Bible in the culture and minds of the Portuguese Jews. Nowhere is the primacy of the Bible in the outlook of the conversos so evident as in the realm of children's and adult education, the focus of the opening chapter, which is devoted to the place of the Bible in the education of Portuguese Jewish children and adults in seventeenth-century Amsterdam. It shows that – for many in the ex-converso community – the experience of integrating into the Jewish world truly meant becoming "people of the book." Through an examination of manuscript archival sources, this chapter shows that the Bible emerged as the central focus of the educational system in the Portuguese Jewish community during this period. From the founding of the community's Talmud Torah school system in 1616, through the unification of the three Portuguese Jewish congregations in 1639, and into the later decades of the seventeenth century, Bible study was *the* primary activity in most classes. Study of the Talmud and rabbinic literature was deferred to later stages of the educational system that most students never reached. Furthermore, charitable societies and confraternities offered adults opportunities for deepening their familiarity with Scripture, even after completion of their formal education. This chapter shows that the pedagogical choices of the community were shaped by a combination of diverse factors: the place of the Bible in converso and crypto-Jewish religious perspectives in Spain and Portugal; Dutch theories of education; and Spanish models of cultural and confraternal organization. The result was an educational system that struck foreign Jewish visitors as deeply anomalous, yet praiseworthy, and which they had never encountered before in the Jewish world. There were – I argue – unintended consequences to this educational approach. By raising generations of Jewish students who were expert in the study of Scripture, but severely limited in their understanding of Talmud and Jewish law, this educational system also contributed to a disconnect between Amsterdam's Portuguese Jews and early modern rabbinic Judaism and its religious authorities. Amsterdam has long been recognized as a hotbed of heterodox thought, the breeding ground for unorthodox figures like Uriel da Costa, Juan de Prado, and Benedict Spinoza, and for repeated conflicts with rabbis like Jacob Sasportas from more traditional corners of the Jewish world. Amsterdam's "halakhic problem," its relatively lax and even flippant attitude toward some areas of rabbinic law, resulted from – and was perpetuated by – an educational system and culture that prioritized Bible study rather than rabbinics.

The anomalous centrality of the Bible's status in Amsterdam's Jewish educational curriculum was not an accident. It was the result of decisions made by members of the community who were shaped by the lingering influence of converso beliefs about the centrality of Scripture for achieving individual salvation, and by Protestant perspectives that regularly stressed this connection. This pedagogic choice grew out of the theological centrality of the Bible in the minds of the rabbis, communal leaders, and teachers who oversaw the school system and the community's broader affairs. Here, we see that many Portuguese Jews saw engagement with the Bible, its teachings, and commandments as playing an instrumental role in their quest to attain an eternal reward, or salvation. This perspective, as we will see, originated in the culture of the Iberian conversos but was also shaped in crucial ways by the Protestant environment in which the Portuguese Jews were now immersed. For many Portuguese Jews, the conviction that Scripture and salvation were linked possessed the status of received wisdom within the community, a concept that did not necessarily require any special elaboration or explanation because its truth was self-evident to all. Yet the Bible's relevance for Jewish efforts to attain salvation were questioned by some in the community – most famously by Uriel da Costa. And in these cases, leading rabbis like Menasseh ben Israel came aggressively and vociferously to the defense of a doctrine that they viewed as a central and crucial component of their Jewish identity. To a degree, there were Jewish precedents for this thinking about the close relationship between the Bible and salvation in medieval Jewish thought, and in the perspectives of Iberian New Christians. These models however cannot account for the striking similarity between the views about salvation and Scripture expressed by Reformed theologians and Amsterdam's rabbis in the seventeenth century. Furthermore, these earlier Jewish approaches to linking salvation and Scripture do not explain why Jews turned to specifically Christian theological concepts – such as "justification" – in order to think through the process by which Jews would attain their eternal reward. Ultimately, it is the Protestant environment in which Amsterdam's Jews lived, and the reverberations of the Iberian world that they had left behind, that explain the extraordinary emphasis that they placed on the Bible theologically – in the effort to attain salvation – and the central place of the Bible in children's and adult education.

After explaining why the Bible attained such a central role in Jewish education and thought, *Amsterdam's People of the Book* explores how the Jewish approach to studying the Hebrew Bible and New Testament was shaped and influenced by the intellectual environment of the seventeenth-century Netherlands, and European culture more broadly. In Amsterdam, there emerged a new type of Jewish obsession with errors and contradictions in the Bible, and persistent, unresolvable doubts about the Bible's perfection. Jews, of course, had always believed that the Torah was flawless, often drawing on Psalm 19:7: "The law of the Lord is perfect, restoring the soul." Rabbinic sages and medieval commentators had, at various times, grappled with substantial problems and contradictions that might have threatened this assumption. Amsterdam's Jews shared this belief and conviction, but living in the world of the seventeenth-century Netherlands, saw their convictions shaken in new ways by a burgeoning demand for knowledge of all varieties that could be proved mathematically. As a fierce debate raged around them regarding the Bible's infallibility on matters of mathematics and science, Amsterdam's Jews turned to new methods and literary genres in order to defend this most traditional, conservative, and core belief. The intersection of scientific thought and biblical studies in the Netherlands changed the way the Bible was seen and understood by some learned Jews in the Portuguese Jewish community. These developments left an especially deep impression on Menasseh ben Israel's approaches to reading the Hebrew Bible. For more than twenty years, spanning nearly his entire professional career, Menasseh was obsessed by contradictory verses in the Bible, and wrote the most encyclopedically comprehensive pre-modern Jewish text ever produced reconciling these biblical contradictions and inconsistencies. No biblical inconsistency vexed Menasseh more than the mathematical, numerical, and chronological inconsistencies in the narratives of ancient Israelite judges and kings. These inconsistencies were especially challenging because of the mathematically rigorous solution that they demanded. Yet as Menasseh soon learned, the Bible's numerical information was often insufficient to satisfactorily answer his questions, and he was unable to disentangle the deeply conflicting chronological information that the Bible provided regarding these judges and kings. Menasseh's concern about the infallibility of the Bible, and his preoccupation with the mathematical problems of biblical chronology, demonstrates the presence of religious uncertainties at the center of the Portuguese Jewish community in Amsterdam, and the ways in which Protestant models of biblical exegesis helped to shape Jewish ways of thinking about Scripture. As much as these contradictions were feared by orthodox members of the Portuguese Jewish community, they were embraced and celebrated by Amsterdam's most famous Jewish heretic – Spinoza. Spinoza capitalizes upon many of the same biblical contradictions that Menasseh struggled to reconcile, in an effort to recast how the Bible should be understood and read. Fully appreciating the preoccupation with biblical contradictions in Amsterdam's orthodox Jewish scholarship is fundamental to understanding Spinoza's revolutionary impact on modern Jewish thought.

The ex-converso turn to Jewish life meant not only a serious and deep engagement with the Hebrew Bible. It also required an equally introspective, profound dialogue with the New Testament. For Iberian conversos and their descendants, Christian Scriptures were too deeply engrained in their education, culture, and perspectives to simply be ignored, or casually dismissed. The reorientation of Amsterdam's Portuguese Jews from the universe of the Gospels to that of the Hebrew Bible required an ongoing commitment to thinking about – and revising – what the pages of the New Testament meant to members of the community. Accordingly, *Amsterdam's People of the Book* also explores how Amsterdam's ex-conversos became Jews, in part, by continuing to read and think about Christian Scriptures – but in a drastically different fashion. No Jewish scholar in Amsterdam wrote about Christian Scriptures as extensively and in such depth as Rabbi Saul Levi Morteira – whose changing perspectives on Christianity and the New Testament are explored and traced.

The ex-converso understanding of the Gospels was most dramatically influenced, and transformed, by their immersion in the Netherlands and especially in the intellectual environment of Amsterdam. The arc of this transformation can be seen lucidly through the trajectory and development of Morteira's views on the New Testament during the course of his career as a rabbi in Amsterdam, from the 1630s until his death in 1660. Morteira's interpretation of identical New Testament passages in his early and later writings can be traced in order to show that his views toward Christianity and the New Testament underwent a substantial and dramatic transformation over the course of his career. From a perspective of inveterate hostility early in his career, Morteira shifted later in life to a more conciliatory tone, attempting to identify areas of common ground between Jewish and Christian Scriptures, resolving contradictory verses in the New Testament, and proving Jesus to have been a faithful follower of biblical and rabbinic law. This transformation is linked to Morteira's encounter with the mainstream Reformed church in the Netherlands, and with radical movements like Socinianism, which rejected central Christian beliefs about the Trinity and the divinity of Jesus, and which in Morteira's eyes were approaching tantalizingly close to the boundaries of Judaism. Accordingly, Morteira sought to urge them closer toward the adoption of Jewish perspectives regarding the Sabbath, Passover, God, and the canon of Scripture. Morteira's encounter with both mainstream and extremist Reformation movements demonstrates the degree to which immersion in the Protestant culture of the Netherlands could influence Jewish perspectives on Christian Scriptures, and the way these should be presented to a Jewish audience.

New Testament scholarship had a seductive appeal to Morteira in many ways. However, there were limits on the degree to which Morteira could embrace Christian Scriptures. In a community of Jewish converts from Christianity, drawing too near to the New Testament and emphasizing too much its similarities with the Hebrew Bible could provoke an unwelcome question about the very importance of membership in the Jewish community. Furthermore, Morteira was highly concerned about Christian efforts to convert Jewish members of his congregations. Accordingly, despite the moderate tone in which he often addresses the figure of Jesus, there remained a need for Morteira to demonstrate the clear superiority of the Hebrew Bible over the Gospels. *Amsterdam's People of the Book* shows that in order to prove the superiority of the Hebrew Bible and Judaism, Morteira subjected the New Testament to an extensive historical analysis. By demonstrating the historical development of Christian Scriptures, Morteira sought to dislocate the New Testament from the sphere of theological inquiry to the realm of historical analysis. In particular, Morteira believed that Christian Scriptures needed to be situated within two historical contexts: the environment of Greco-Roman and Egyptian religious beliefs that were prevalent in the ancient Mediterranean, where Christianity first emerged; and the rabbinic Jewish society in which Jesus and his earliest followers lived. Furthermore, Morteira was attentive to how parts of the New Testament developed over time, and to the ways in which non-canonical ancient Christian texts could illuminate the transformation of the canon during the first centuries after Jesus's lifetime. Morteira's efforts to trace the lineage of idolatry supposedly embedded within the pages of Christian Scriptures show Amsterdam's leading rabbi to have been part of a much broader seventeenth-century scholarly movement that historicized Sacred Scriptures, traced the genealogy of ancient religious practices, and polemically differentiated virtuous, true religion from perilous false facsimiles. The methods that Morteira adopted in his historicist critique of the New Testament and the questions that he explores show that he was deeply influenced by the historical biblical exegesis practiced by figures like Vossius, Scaliger, Hugo Grotius, Selden, and other scholars in the Netherlands and northwest Europe. Exploring the historical origins of the New Testament in this fashion, Morteira believed, would show his coreligionists that for true religious guidance it was necessary to become "people of the book" – the Hebrew Bible – as it is interpreted by Jews, and used to guide their lives and thought.

In any study of early modern biblical scholarship, the figure of Benedict Spinoza looms large. The specter of Amsterdam's most famous Jewish heretic is especially ubiquitous in a study of biblical scholarship in Amsterdam's Portuguese Jewish community, where he was born, raised, and educated. After leaving this community, Spinoza wrote one of the most impactful, programmatic seventeenth-century works about the nature of the Bible and how it should be read, the *Theological-Political Treatise,* a work that excited and enraged intellectuals across Europe from the seventeenth century onward. It has been studied from countless directions, but never from the perspective of the culture of Jewish biblical studies prevalent in Amsterdam's Portuguese Jewish community. Therefore, an Epilogue maps Spinoza and his treatise onto the topics explored in *Amsterdam's People of the Book* in order to illuminate the nexus between Spinoza's approach to biblical scholarship and that of rabbis in the ex-converso community. The Epilogue reveals that there are connections between practices of biblically-oriented education, preoccupations with the link between Scripture and salvation, the importance of biblical contradictions and inconsistencies, and the turn to historical and cultural study of biblical texts that are shared by Spinoza and the community's rabbis, suggesting that there is a closer relationship between 'heterodoxy' and 'orthodoxy' in Amsterdam than is commonly appreciated.

Finally, the Epilogue concludes with remarks about the relationship between Amsterdam's biblically-oriented culture, and the movement of the Bible toward the center of other European Jewish communities during the eighteenth and nineteenth centuries. In England, France, and Germany an increasing focus on the Bible in education and scholarship is evident, along with – in some instances – a conscious desire to shift emphasis away from the dominant role of the Talmud in Jewish intellectual life. I ask whether there is any common denominator that connects the movement of the Hebrew Bible toward the center of Jewish religious culture in Amsterdam in the seventeenth century to similar developments in diverse settings across Europe in the eighteenth and nineteenth centuries. While the existing literature does not support a direct pattern of reception linking the biblical scholarship of Portuguese Jews and Jewish communities in the eighteenth and nineteenth centuries, there is nevertheless a shared experience of deep acculturation to the biblically-oriented values and religious models of Christianity that is worthy of further study.

Together, the chapters of *Amsterdam's People of the Book* illustrate how, for the Portuguese Jews of seventeenth-century Amsterdam, the Bible became a fundamentally *early modern* text – a sacred text that was at once a heritage of the ancient past and medieval worlds, but which was in the process of becoming something different, a text that was just beginning to be understood, studied, and thought about in new ways. In many respects, readers of the Bible in seventeenth-century Amsterdam were deeply connected to and shaped by medieval Jewish traditions and exegetical interpretations. They were certain that the Bible was flawless and infallible. They fervently believed that the Bible would play a role in attaining God's eternal reward. And they shared with Jews from earlier times a conviction that their Bible and traditions were superior to those of their Christian neighbors. At the same time, the ways in which Amsterdam's Portuguese Jews thought and wrote about the Bible serve as a barometer measuring the influence of new approaches to biblical scholarship that shaped European engagement with the Bible in the sixteenth and seventeenth centuries. And, influenced by the early modern environment in which they lived, traditional Jewish concepts came to take a dramatically different shape and meaning for many of the Portuguese Jews in Amsterdam. Because of their immersion in the Protestant culture of the Netherlands, their encounters with new religious communities and movements, and their intellectual engagement with European scholarship about the Bible and the ancient world, the Bible became something new and different for this community. By becoming obsessed with the thousands of contradictions in the Bible; by internalizing Protestant theological concepts; by adopting new Protestant literary genres to express their views and commitments about the Bible; by softening the traditional Jewish polemic against Jesus; and by embracing the historical study of Scripture in a way that appreciated the multidimensional roles of ancient cultures and societies in forming present-day religious traditions, the Bible became a fundamentally early modern text, something that it had not been before. The Bible-centric culture and critical, historical approach that the Portuguese Jews cultivated in Amsterdam also incubated and helped to shape the contours of modern perspectives on the Bible, by influencing the thought and development of Spinoza, and his revolutionary views on the reading, structure, and history of the Bible, which would play such a vital part in modern political and religious thought.

The ex-conversos who created a Jewish settlement in Amsterdam in the late sixteenth century, and who built the infrastructure that supported the establishment of a permanent, self-sustaining community, did not know about the role the Bible would play in future discussions about the direction of Judaism. They constructed a biblically-oriented culture that responded to their needs within the particular context of seventeenth-century Amsterdam, and which grew out of their New Christian past, medieval Jewish traditions, and early modern European approaches to thinking about Scripture. As we see in the next chapter, the community's schools and confraternities were the incubators where this Bible-centered culture was nurtured, cultivated, and transmitted to generations of Portuguese Jews in Amsterdam.

ONE

Amsterdam's People of the Book: From Classrooms to Confraternities

IN HIS *EXEMPLAR HUMANAE VITAE* [EXAMPLE OF A HUMAN LIFE], Uriel da Costa, one of Amsterdam's most famous heterodox Jews, reflected on the process that had led him to abruptly abandon a life of comfort and status in Portugal for the uncertain vicissitudes of a dangerous journey at sea and the unknown world of Jewish society in Amsterdam. Uriel recalled that as a young twenty-year-old who had received a rigorous Catholic education preparing him for an ecclesiastic career, he began to question the path to salvation taught by the church and the New Testament. Accordingly, as he writes:

> I continued some time, and at last came to this settled persuasion that salvation was not to be obtained in the [faith] that I was in... I went through the books of Moses and the Prophets, wherein I found some things not a little contradictory to the doctrines of the New Testament, and there seemed to be the less difficulty in believing those things which were revealed by God himself... Hence I was induced to become a convert to the Law of Moses, and as he declared himself only to be a deliverer of what was revealed by God himself... I thought it my duty to make the law the rule of my obedience. Having entered upon this resolution, and finding it unsafe to profess this religion in that country

> [Portugal], I began to think of changing my habitation and leaving my native home.[1]

Uriel da Costa's hopes of practicing a Judaism that was completely synonymous with the Old Testament were ultimately dashed along the banks of the Amstel. The community of Jews established in Amsterdam in the early seventeenth century practiced rabbinic Judaism, which involved study of the Bible along with the Talmud and other post-biblical Jewish legal traditions.

Historians have described many points of contact that New Christians and crypto-Jews maintained with the religion of their ancestors between the fourteenth and seventeenth centuries. These include the inversion of traditional Catholic rituals, the secret observance of Jewish practices, the quiet – but deliberate – observance of the Sabbath and Jewish fasts, the oral transmission of Jewish prayers, conscious emphasis on the Old Testament rather than the New Testament, and the search for information about the Talmud and rabbinic Judaism in Christian literature.[2] However, recent scholarship has illuminated the particular and unique importance of the Bible – and especially the Law of Moses – in the religious identity of Iberian conversos. While Uriel da Costa is one of the most famous converso biblicists, he was by no means alone in emphasizing an extreme attachment to the Old Testament as the embodiment of Judaism. Numerous other conversos, Judaizers, and crypto-Jews combined a commitment to the Pentateuch and Bible with a characteristically Catholic theological framework. They saw the performance of biblical commandments and adherence to the Law of Moses as essential for their salvation. Even the preparation of unleavened bread during Passover was, in the words of a conversa from Trancoso in

1. Uriel da Costa, *Exemplar humanae vitae*, trans. John Whiston (London, 1740), in Uriel da Costa, *Examination of Pharisaic Traditions*, ed. and trans., H.P. Salomon and I.S.D. Sassoon (Leiden and New York: Brill, 1993), 557.
2. See Gretchen Starr-Lebeau, *In the Shadow of the Virgin: Inquisitors, Friars, and Conversos in Guadalupe, Spain* (Princeton, NJ: Princeton University Press, 2003), 53–99; Yosef Kaplan, *From Christianity to Judaism: The Story of Isaac Orobio de Castro*, trans. Raphael Loewe (Oxford and New York: Oxford University Press, 1989), 6, 42–45; Yerushalmi, *From Spanish Court to Italian Ghetto*, 183–89, 221–41.

1574, crucial "for the salvation of her soul."[3] Furthermore, Miriam Bodian has shown that a handful of conversos and Judaizers – some with no apparent Jewish ancestors – demonstrated religious convictions that resulted in their death by burning, and that their faith was informed to a significant degree by experiences of Bible study and commitment to a Scripture-based version of Judaism.[4] Iberian conversos were by no means completely severed from access to information about rabbinic Judaism and its legal texts; but the Old Testament and the Law of Moses nevertheless remained one of the most easily accessible and prominent forms of Jewish knowledge available to New Christians during the sixteenth and seventeenth centuries.[5]

The converso emphasis on Scripture as the embodiment of Judaism had a lasting impact in the ex-converso community of seventeenth-century Amsterdam, and these perspectives resonated powerfully in the community's educational system. Ex-converso Jews in Amsterdam constructed a network of schools and confraternities that was self-consciously designed to emphasize the systematic study of Scripture by children and adults alike. The school system stressed the reading and chanting of the Bible, translation of Scripture from Hebrew to Spanish, and the comprehensive study of the Pentateuch, Prophets, and Writings. Apart from some attention to Rashi, there was almost no exposure to medieval Jewish biblical commentators. Study of the Talmud and legal texts was deferred to the pinnacle of the educational process, the final

3. Miriam Bodian, *Hebrews of the Portuguese Nation*, 101.
4. Miriam Bodian, *Dying in the Law of Moses: Crypto-Jewish Martyrdom in the Iberian World* (Bloomington and Indianapolis: University of Indiana Press, 2007), xi, 37, 157–58, 166–67.
5. It has been emphasized by Yosef Hayim Yerushalmi, Yosef Kaplan, Miriam Bodian, Gretchen Starr-Lebeau, and others that New Christians were never completely cut off from the rabbinic Jewish texts and traditions. Prior to the expulsion of practicing Jews in 1492, it was relatively easy to maintain contact with traveling Jewish merchants and rabbis, as well as to acquire Jewish texts, as Starr-Lebeau demonstrates in *In the Shadow of the Virgin*, 90–98. Yerushalmi has demonstrated that Fernando/Isaac Cardoso successfully mined Patristic Christian texts for information about the Talmud and rabbinic Jewish traditions, and that these remained an important source for his scholarship long after converting to Judaism. See Yerushalmi, *From Spanish Court to Italian Ghetto*, 271–300.

two years of study in advanced religious academies that not all students could aspire to attend. As a result, Portuguese Jews raised generations of children whose direct experience of Judaism and Jewish education was informed primarily by the Bible, rather than by Judaism's legal texts. This biblical focus was not accidental, but intentional – recognized and lauded by leading members of the community. In a sermon on the Torah portion *Mi-qetz* that Saul Levi Morteira delivered in 1628, one of the leading rabbis of the community reflected on the school system and asked his audience rhetorically, "Is this not the goal of the Talmud Torah society, to impart knowledge of God's Word?"[6]

The main argument of this chapter is not that the Bible was the exclusive focus of education and religious culture in Portuguese Jewish Amsterdam, but rather that Scripture was the central focus of the curriculum *relative* to the time and attention given to Judaism's legal texts. The challenge that this chapter confronts is the need to capture the profound commitment to biblical education in Amsterdam, which was shaped to a significant degree by the emphasis on Scripture in converso culture, while at the same time remembering that the Amsterdam community was composed of rabbinic Jews deeply committed to observing post-biblical Jewish law.

Part I of this chapter provides an introduction to the Talmud Torah educational confraternity, which organized and administered the school system for the Portuguese Jewish community during the seventeenth century. This section locates the establishment of the confraternity within the project of community-building in which the Portuguese Jews engaged during the first decades of settlement in Amsterdam, and surveys the roles and responsibilities of its different functionaries. Part II shows how the resources and infrastructure of the community were used to create institutions for the education of children in which the Bible played a pivotal role, illustrating the ongoing resonance of converso perspectives on the relationship between Scripture and Judaism. This section also examines the ways in which the biblical educational practices of the Portuguese Jewish community were blended with

6. Marc Saperstein, *Exile in Amsterdam: Saul Levi Morteira's Sermons to a Congregation of New Jews* (Cincinnati, OH: Hebrew Union College Press, 2005), 40.

seventeenth-century Dutch pedagogical theories and the Iberian framework of confraternity-based social and cultural organizations. Part III explores adult education, and the opportunities available in confraternities and public sermons for adults to deepen their familiarity with Scripture, even after completing their formal education.

Part I: The Educational Infrastructure: Officials, Schools, and Confraternities

During the first decades of the seventeenth century, a community of Portuguese Jews emerged in Amsterdam. As a city with no prior history of organized Jewish settlement, the original cadre of Iberian New Christians who converted to Judaism during this period were required to establish a wide variety of institutions to serve the new community's religious needs. The early Portuguese New Christians and ex-conversos needed human resources: rabbis and cantors to provide leadership and instruction in the correct observance of Jewish customs and beliefs; they needed books, both basic liturgical and biblical works, as well as the theological and legal works upon which the observance of rabbinic Judaism was based; and they needed to create a social and cultural infrastructure that could support their community in the long term, and that would fulfill their religious needs – synagogues, a cemetery, schools, organizations to provide poor relief, medical services, and funerary rites. Assembling these communal building-blocks took time and money.

With the exception of Moses Uri Halevy, an early spiritual guide who introduced Portuguese New Christians to the practice of Judaism,[7] most of the community's religious leaders came from Italy and the Ottoman Empire, and had already gained extensive experience living in Sephardi or ex-converso communities. The Beth Jacob congregation, established before 1610, was led by Joseph Pardo, a Sephardi rabbi born in Salonika who settled in Venice, and who moved to Amsterdam in 1608 following the collapse of his finances in that city.[8] A second congregation, the Neve

7. Daniel Swetschinsky, *Reluctant Cosmopolitans*, 165–70.
8. Miriam Bodian, *Hebrews of the Portuguese Nation*, 45; Daniel Swetschinsky, *Reluctant Cosmopolitans*, 172; Cecil Roth, *A Life of Menasseh ben Israel: Rabbi, Printer, Diplomat* (Philadelphia, PA: The Jewish Publication Society of America, 1934), 17.

Salom, was established around 1612 by Samuel Palache, a Sephardi Jew from Fez and a member of a distinguished rabbinic family,[9] and was led by Rabbi Isaac Uziel, also from Fez.[10] The third Portuguese synagogue in Amsterdam, Beth Israel, was founded in August 1619 following a split within the Beth Jacob congregation, and was initially led by Joseph Pardo.[11] During this period, the community acted very aggressively to hire additional rabbis from Italian and Sephardi communities, signing contracts with Rabbi Josef Salom on April 22, 1619, and Rabbi Saul Levi Morteira on April 25, 1621.[12] Salom, originally from Salonika, had been living in Amsterdam since at least 1616. In order to entice Salom to remain in the Amsterdam community, he was offered a generous salary, and a communally subsidized house.[13]

In addition to these learned rabbis, the Amsterdam community sought to build the institutions necessary for maintaining a Jewish community in the longer term. When Jewish public worship became recognized by the authorities in 1614, the Portuguese Jews purchased land for a cemetery at Ouderkerk.[14] The following year they created a dowry society for poor brides, the *Santa Companhia de dotar orphas e donzelas pobres*.[15] This period also saw the emergence of a political-economic organization that oversaw certain aspects of the three congregations' affairs. The Twelve Year Truce between the United Provinces and Spain (1609–1621) facilitated the flow of trade between the Iberian Peninsula and the Low Countries, as well as the immigration of wealthy Portuguese

9. Miriam Bodian, *Hebrews of the Portuguese Nation*, 46.
10. Cecil Roth, *A Life of Menasseh ben Israel: Rabbi, Printer, Diplomat*, 22–23.
11. Daniel Swetschinski, *Reluctant Cosmopolitans*, 172–73.
12. *Termos de Talmud Torah e de Ets Haim* GAS [Gemeente Amsterdam Stadsarchief] 334 1051 Fol. 6a–8b. The recent and most authoritative work is Marc Saperstein, *Exile in Amsterdam: Saul Levi Morteira's Sermons to a Congregation of New Jews*. Morteira was a close confident and spiritual guide to the ex-converso physician Elijah Montalto and accompanied Montalto to Paris in the early seventeenth century.
13. GAS 334 1051 Fol. 7b. Julia Lieberman, "Educational Institutions among the Western Sephardim in the Seventeenth Century," 16–17. Julia Lieberman generously shared a preliminary version of her forthcoming article on the Talmud Torah educational systems established in the Western Sephardi diaspora.
14. Miriam Bodian, *Hebrews of the Portuguese Nation*, 46.
15. Miriam Bodian, *Hebrews of the Portuguese Nation*, 46–47.

New Christian merchants.[16] In light of the growing size and wealth of the community, in 1622 leading members of the congregations created the *Imposta* board, which was comprised of two elected members from each of the three congregations, and which acted as a political, economic, and religious superstructure for the community. The board collected duties on brokerage fees, insurance policies, and commercially valuable goods bought and sold by Portuguese Jews, such as precious stones and gold.[17] The *Imposta* board also, in ensuing years, became responsible for supervising the slaughtering and sale of kosher meat and administering the cemetery.[18]

The earliest Portuguese Jews in Amsterdam were thus engaged in a project of community-building that involved establishing, mostly from scratch, religious, political, and economic institutions. There was also a need to establish an educational framework for children in the community. It is within this context that we should see the spring 1616 meeting of leading members of the Beth Jacob and Neve Salom congregations who gathered to establish the Talmud Torah confraternity. In its initial incarnation, the Talmud Torah was a relatively modest institution created in order to pay the community's rabbis, and to purchase liturgical and educational texts for individuals too poor to acquire their own books.[19] It was governed by three elected members, two parnassim and one gabbai.[20] Later, during the course of the seventeenth century, the number

16. Daniel Swetschinski, *Reluctant Cosmopolitans*, 182.
17. Miriam Bodian, *Hebrews of the Portuguese Nation*, 50–51.
18. Daniel Swetschinski, *Reluctant Cosmopolitans*, 182–84.
19. GAS 334 1051 Fol. 1a–1b. "Os parnassim egabaj nam despenderam mais q[ue] ordim[en]to do seu anno... eprincipalmente em pagar os Robissim q[ue] tomarem p[ara] meldar... segundariamente em comprar liuros assi os necessaries p[ara] aliuros de resguardo q[ue] estauas sempre neste kahal como os para dar de deprimido e... dar aos talmedim pobres q[ue] os nam tiuerem... como ja dar liuros de rezao e tefilim aos pobres q[ue] os nam tiuerem nem poner pa[ra] os compraren."
20. The parnassim and gabbai were lay leaders elected from among the community. See Daniel Swetschinski, *Reluctant Cosmopolitans*, 190–96. Each new board of governors was elected by its predecessor. Swetschinski has shown that (at least at the level of the overall communal governors) parnassim tended to be around forty years of age, while the gabbai was normally between twenty-eight and thirty-eight years old. The wealthiest percent of the community provided the largest proportion of elected officials.

of officials was expanded from three to six, and their responsibilities grew to include the purchase of texts for the schools, and the creation and maintenance of a communal library. It was also the responsibility of elected officials to inventory communal property (financial resources, books, ritual objects, records, chests, cabinets, etc.) at the end of each one-year term.[21]

In 1624, perhaps motivated by the controversy over Uriel da Costa, the elected officials of the *Mahamad*, who governed the community as a whole, intervened in the administration of the confraternity, "in order to consult regarding some matters pertaining to the good governance of the Talmud Torah."[22] Seizing on the opportunity presented by the presence of the directors of the Talmud Torah and the community, the senior officials "ordered, with unanimous approval, [that] three worthy individuals of the community shall be elected from the *Mahamad*... and from the Talmud Torah to serve as the parnassim and gabbai of the said Talmud Torah for one year." It was further decided that the salaries of rabbis could not be paid, enlarged, or diminished without the collective agreement of officials from both boards.[23] Henceforth the Talmud Torah was not entirely autonomous in its decision-making and in its election of officials.[24] Beginning around 1636, a treasurer was appointed annually in order to supervise the finances of the confraternity.[25] In order to create institutional continuity, the treasurer was normally selected from among the parnassim of the previous year so that the position was filled by an individual familiar with the confraternity's financial affairs.[26]

21. GAS 334 1051 Fol. 1b.
22. GAS 334 1051 Fol. 14a. "Estanda juntos os senores do mahamad juntamente com os senores parnassim egabaj de Talmud tora para consultarem sobre alguas cousas toquantes ao bom gouerno de talmud tora."
23. GAS 334 1051 Fol. 14a. "Ordenaraõ de comun comsentimento q[ue] entre maamad de sedaqa eode talmud tora se elejaõ tres pesoas benemeritos do kaal para seruirem de parnassim egabaj de ditto talmud tora 'hu anno'."
24. Miriam Bodian, in *Hebrews of the Portuguese Nation*, 109, has observed that the *Mahamad* pursued a policy of supervising the religious education of the Portuguese Jewish community from at least 1639. From the 1624 entries in the communal record books, it is evident that this pattern began even earlier.
25. GAS 334 1051 Fol. 17b.
26. GAS 334 1051 Fol. 18b. The text, from 1639, relates that "que aja de fiquar hu' parnas

A major responsibility of the community officials was the creation and administration of a library. Book collecting was an important activity from very early in the history of the Portuguese Jewish settlement in Amsterdam. It provided essential resources for the educational and religious needs of the community, and also provided a significant foundation for rabbinic scholarship and the composition of sermons. Inventories of communal property from between 1618 and 1624 reveal the extent to which the communal officials played a key role in collecting the resources necessary for religious activities. These inventories show that the officials had purchased hundreds of liturgical works, and books of customs providing instructions on the correct observance of fast days, festivals, and other important dates in the Jewish calendar. These texts typically appear in the records without a formal title; they are referred to generically as "books of the month" (*liuros de mes*), "books of fasts" (*liuros de taniot*), and "books of prayers" (*liuros de tefila*). These works were acquired in a variety of formats: some were purchased as loose sheets of paper, while others were already bound. The 1621 inventory records that the Beth Jacob community possessed 478 unbound copies of *liuros de taniot e mes*, 124 bound copies, and 26 unbound copies of these works in Hebrew. Apart from these *liuros de mes y taniot*, the community lent an additional 118 copies to Isaac Milano, a wealthy Portuguese Jewish merchant living in Hamburg.[27] At an early stage, Amsterdam's rabbis were collecting works to support both their own community and other ex-converso centers.[28] Within Amsterdam, leading rabbis and teachers

de T.T. seruindo outro anno" shall be elected as treasurer, and that thus "se aura de eleger en cada anno sinco parnassim de nouo eo tizoureiro passado fas o numero de 6."

27. GAS 334 1051 Fol. 9b–10a. See also Fol. 13b–14b for the records of 1622–1624. The community continued to amass these liturgical and customs books. In 1622 there were 730 such texts; in 1623 there were only 575; and in 1624 there were 681. On Isaac Milano, see Yosef Kaplan, *From Christianity to Judaism: The Story of Isaac Orobio de Castro*, 208.

28. The genre to which these books belong had a strong precedent in Sephardi and ex-converso Jewish societies. See Aron di Leone Leoni and Siegfried Herzfeld, "The *Orden de oraciones de mes arreo* (Ferrara, 1555) and a *Bakasah* composed by Abraham Usque," *Sefarad*, 62 (2002), 99–124. One of the earliest examples of this genre in Spanish is the *Libro de Oracyones de Todo el año* [Book of Prayers for the Whole Year], printed by Yomtob Atias at Ferrara in 1552. In 1555, Abraham Usque printed

frequently drew upon the resources of the library for use in their scholarship and for their students.

What sources of income financed the collection of texts, and the Talmud Torah educational confraternity as a whole? In its earliest years, it is clear that the funds available to the Talmud Torah were rather limited. Its original guidelines in 1616 called for individuals to donate only one half-florin per year as a requirement for membership.[29] Donations made by men who were called to the Torah added an additional source of revenue.[30] During the middle decades of the seventeenth century, however, the revenue available to the Talmud Torah educational society grew dramatically and provided the opportunity for members to pursue a much wider variety of initiatives. During the 1640s and 1650s there was an unprecedented immigration of wealthy Portuguese and Spanish New Christian bankers and royal financiers to the Netherlands.[31] As Jonathan Israel shows, a number of factors served to greatly increase the concentration of affluent Portuguese Jews in Amsterdam: the collapse of Dutch Brazil between 1646–1655, which led roughly 200 Jewish families to return to the United Provinces; the Treaty of Munster (January, 1648), which facilitated the movement of conversos between the Iberian Peninsula and the Netherlands; the collapse of Spanish finances in October 1647; the adoption of royal policies in Spain designed to push conversos out of positions of financial influence; and the intensification of Inquisitorial activity.[32] This combination of developments led some of

his much more influential *Orden de oraciones de mes*, which offers an easier-to-follow vernacular translation of daily prayers, liturgies for specific holidays, blessings for various occasions, and rites for the burial of the dead. New editions based on Usque's model were printed in ex-converso communities throughout the seventeenth century. The Beth Jacob congregation in Amsterdam specifically financed its own edition of Usque's *Orden de oraciones de mes* in 1618, and it is likely that many of the liturgical texts catalogued in these early inventories belong to this edition.

29. GAS 334 1051 Fol. 1b. Compare this with the twenty-florin entry fee paid by members of the *Aby Yetomim* confraternity for fatherless children later in the seventeenth century. See Julia Lieberman, "Adolescence and the Period of Apprenticeship among Western Sephardim in the Seventeenth Century," in *El Prezente: Studies in Sephardic Culture* 4, ed. Tamar Alexander, Yaakov Bentolila, and Eliezer Papo (2010): 18.
30. GAS 334 1051 Fol. 14a.
31. Jonathan Israel, "Spain and the Dutch Sephardim, 1609–1660," 1–61.
32. Jonathan Israel, "Spain and the Dutch Sephardim, 1609–1660," 29–49.

the Portuguese Jewish community's most important members – Diego Teixeira de Sampayo (Abraham Senior), Gil Lopes Pinto (Abraham de Pinto), Rodrigo Alvares (David de Pinto), Tomás Rogriuez Pereyra (Abraham Pereyra), and many others – to leave Spain for Holland and other Sephardi centers.[33]

The Talmud Torah confraternity benefited greatly from the increasing size and affluence of the Portuguese Jewish community. The growing resources of the community also enabled the creation of a second educational confraternity, the Ets Haim, which provided stipends to advanced Talmud students.[34] The inventories of both confraternities customarily made at the end of each governing board's term reflect a spike in communal wealth. Whereas inventories in the early 1620s report the possession of books, liturgical items, and a few chests and cabinets,[35] inventories in the 1640s could report significant wealth and real estate. In 1644 the inventory reports a reserve of 1,324 florins. The endowment of the confraternity grew steadily during these years, and by 1648 had reached well over 5,000 florins.[36] This growth in resources was driven by large donations made by individuals who gave significant sums of money to the Ets Haim confraternity in commemoration of deceased family members. Some of these donations were truly enormous. In 1644, Sara Cahanet, the widow of the famous scholar and kabbalist Abraham Cohen Herera, donated 1,000 florins to the Ets Haim.[37] The record books are filled with smaller – but still substantial – gifts ranging normally between 50–300 florins.[38] The community was also able to make use of revenues that came from renting out two communally owned houses that had been purchased by the Talmud Torah.[39] The growing revenues of this period enabled the expansion of the number and types of students who could be supported by communal stipends. Originally, the Ets Haim

33. Jonathan Israel, "Spain and the Dutch Sephardim, 1609–1660," 43–48.
34. See *Termos de Talmud Torah e de Ets Haim* GAS 334 1052 Fol. 1–3.
35. GAS 334 1051 Fol. 24a. Cf. GAS 334 1051 Fol. 14a–14b.
36. GAS 334 1051 Fol. 24a, 27a, 28a.
37. GAS 334 1052 Fol. 9b–10a.
38. See the entries on Fol. 19b and 26b as examples.
39. GAS 3340 1052 Fol. 12a. "Termo dacompra de duas moradas de casas por conta desta misuat de Es chaim e do alguel que dellas sefes como abaixo se declara."

society was intended to support only the most advanced students who had already been studying Talmud for a full year.[40] However, a large surplus of revenue in 1652 (1,200 florins) led the board of the Talmud Torah to expand its sponsorship to include less advanced students who were studying Rashi, "and others."[41]

The records of the Talmud Torah educational confraternity show that it was the parnassim and gabbai, rather than the rabbis themselves, who were the primary decision-makers about many important educational matters, such as the hours and subjects of instruction and the promotion of students. The authority of the lay officials is demonstrated by the contract they signed with one of the first rabbis hired to teach in the community, Josef Salom. Salom's contract is recorded in an entry of April 22, 1619, three years after the founding of the confraternity. With great flourish, it is said to be an agreement between Salom, the parnassim, and the gabbai, "with the consent" of all members of the community" (*todos os yehidim do kaahal kados*), and the members of the Talmud Torah.[42] Salom's teaching responsibilities are included among his many obligations, which are meticulously recorded over three folios. He was initially expected to provide introductory lessons and to cover the Pentateuch comprehensively "until the Prophets."[43] The following term Salom was required to teach students who were specifically assigned to him by the Talmud Torah officials, and would "not be permitted to teach any student without the license and permission of the said *senores* parnassim and gabbai who are serving that year."[44] Occasionally, as the records show, educated members of the community were fined for providing unauthorized lessons.[45] In general, religious teaching outside of the

40. GAS 334 1052 Fol. 2. "Bem entendido que nao se podera dar estipendio a nenhun talmid que pello menos nao haja meldado hun ano guemara."
41. GAS 334 1052 Fol. 13b.
42. GAS 334 1051 Fol. 6a–8a.
43. GAS 334 1051 Fol. 6b.
44. GAS 334 1051 Fol. 6a–6b
45. GAS 334 1051 Fol. 18b. In 1640, R. Jacob Gomes was found to be teaching students at night during the customary sermon or lesson without communal authorization. Although in this case the board agreed to pay him a small amount (12 florins) for his services, Gomes was admonished to cease his activities and was warned that he would not be compensated similarly in the future.

formal school system or supervision of the Talmud Torah governors was not tolerated.

Not only did Salom have little choice regarding whom he taught; the communal governors also stipulated that "he shall not be permitted, without the same license and permission, to transfer any student from one class to another."[46] This prohibition as well was typical of the way the educational confraternity functioned. Regulations from 1616 and later consistently show that elected officials were required to be present at students' examinations, and that these lay officials even had ultimate authority over the promotion of students. The founding document of the Talmud Torah confraternity states that the presence of the two parnassim and gabbai, along with the rabbi, was required for the examination of students beginning their study of the Pentateuch.[47] In 1631, an entry was made in the record books to show that "On Rosh Hodesh Sivan, the *senores* parnassim of the Talmud Torah signed below joined together in order to examine the boys, to see if they were able to pass to the higher classes."[48] An entry made in 1646 shows that sometimes parents disregarded the authority of the communal authorities and the rabbi to make decisions on the promotion of students. Officials needed to remind parents and, apparently, some parnassim, "who are also obliged to observe this rule . . . concerning not promoting any students from one school to another, except according to merit, determined by his masters." This included the rabbi, but in addition to the rabbi's endorsement, the parnassim were required to vote unanimously on these promotions, or, at the very least, four votes were necessary. Officials who violated this

"Em 15 de Adar pagou o tezoureijro Ishak Salom por hordem dos senores parnassim de talmutora ao Ruby Jacob gomes doze florins por hauer meldado de noyte com os mossos tode otempo que durou a darsa dizendolhe se lhe daua por esta ves, e que nao tomasse disso motivuo para pedir, nem pretender nos anos seguintes, se lhe conseda meldar de noyte, para por isso lhedarem cousa algua, e pore star assi de acordo, firmou oje este termo."

46. GAS 334 1051 Fol. 6b "Nao podera ensignar nenhum talmid sem licence eordem dos dittos senores parnassim, e gabay que seruirem cada anno em odito talmud thora, eassim nao podera sem amesma licence e ordem mudar nenhum talmid de hua licao aoutras e que ensinara emeldara aos talmedim de cada licao da sobreditas."

47. GAS 334 1051 Fol. 2b.

48. GAS 334 1051 Fol. 15a.

rule were to be fined twenty florins, payable to the educational confraternity itself.[49]

In the years following the unification of the three congregations, the responsibilities of the parnassim were expanded from supervision of examinations to include the supervision of classes themselves.[50] The second ordinance of these reforms states that "So that the Parnassim of the Talmud Torah can most conveniently attend the schools without hindering their business affairs, it is ordered that the *senores* of the *Mahamad,* together with those of the Talmud Torah, will elect six [parnassim] to serve [...] each one of whom shall be allotted a day of the week on which he shall attend all of the lessons being taught."[51] The fourth clause of

49. GAS 334 1052 Fol. 7b. "De parte dos senores parnassim de T.T. tiverao os senores do mahamad queixas em nao se obseruauao as ascamao no. 9: e 25 escritas neste liuro com que talmut tora padece algum detrimento, e ser de cargua aos que sao eleitos por parnasses pelo que ossenores domahamad procurando remedealo ordenao que entudo se obseruen eproybem que ninhum parente se ara de entremeter notocante a T[alud] T[orah]." Parents were apparently disatisfied with the punishments given to students at the schools, and also appear to have been attempting to advance their children into higher classes: "Os quais teraõ tambem obrigacaõ de observar esta ascama... toca naõ passando de uma escola aotra amnhun [a nehum] talmid, se naõ por merito com parecer de seus mestres eaquem mais parecer aos parnassim de todos unanimamente o, ao menos, pelos quatro vottos dos parnasses que entao seruirem, com pena que o parnas q[ue] sair de ista regla paguara vinte florins aplicados aes hain." See also a similar complaint in GAS 334 1052 Fol. 11a. This note, from 1644, states that "Vendo os senores parnassim o disturbo... que se lhe pasen seus filhos de hua escola aoutra sen que fazen capazes nalicao pera que ao adiante se euiten os muitos enconuinientes... acordan que por niua causa se posa mudar hum moso de hua escola aoutra, efeito aqueles que omereseren por escrita, easin ordenan aos senores Hahamin e ao Resim que naõ asisten asua licao nihum moso... sen algun does senores parnassim que seruiren o licencia [?], efazendo ocontrario, des florins para abolsa desta irmandade."

50. GAS 334 1052 Fol. 23a–25b. The dating of these ordinances is unclear, but appears among items that were entered in 1646. These rules and regulations included in the list are presented as amendments to those enacted immediately following the unification of the communities.

51. GAS 334 1052 Fol. 23a. "Que para mais comodamente possao os Parnassim de Talmud Thora sisstir nas escolas sem impedimento de seus negoceos se ordenou que os senores do maamad juntamente com os dittos parnassim de T.T. elejao seis cada anno por Sebuot para auere de seruir os quais se repartirao cada hu seu dia na semana no qual assistira atodas as licoes fazendo meldar, edoutrinar os mocos ate ahora de Arbit da quelle dia que seruir."

these terms states that "On Sabbaths, after the evening meal, the parnas of that day shall go to the schools and teach the *parashah* [weekly Torah reading] . . . until the hour of *minḥa* [the afternoon prayers], starting one hour beforehand, so that there will be sufficient time, and after *minḥa* he shall attend the *yeshivot* [religious academies] or debates that take place over the *parashah,* as is the custom."[52] The community's elected officials were expected to supervise regular classes in the schools, to lead discussions about the Torah portions on Sabbaths, and to participate in discussions that took place on Sabbath evenings. The community thus came to expect its parnassim and gabbaim to be able financial administrators, as well as competent, Judaically educated leaders in the educational process itself.

The broad authority of the administrators of the Talmud Torah over education, the promotion of students, and the teachers themselves reflects contemporaneous developments in both Jewish and Christian society. On the one hand, the subordination of rabbis to the communal authorities in matters of education reinforces the conclusions of Robert Bonfil, Adam Teller, and Anne Oravetz Albert, who have found a weakening of independent rabbinic authority in sixteenth-century Poland and Italy, and a hierarchy in seventeenth-century Amsterdam in which rabbis operated within the political parameters set by lay communal leaders.[53]

52. GAS 334 1052 Fol. 23a. "Que os Sabatos dispois de jantar virao parnas da quelle dia e fara meldar aparassa nas escolas donde se ensina ate ahora de minha comecando hua hora antes para que nao ſalta tempo, edispois da minha assistira nas yesibot ou argumentos, que se fizere sobre a parassa como se costuma."

53. Robert Bonfil, *Rabbis and Jewish Communities in Renaissance Italy,* trans. Jonathan Chipman (New York and Oxford: Oxford University Press, 1990); Adam Teller, "The Laicization of Early Modern Jewish Society: The Development of the Polish Communal Rabbinate in the Sixteenth Century," in *Schöpferische Momente des europäische Judentums in der frühen Neuzeit,* ed. Michael Graetz (Heidelberg: C. Winter, 2000), 333–49; and Anne Oravetz Albert, "Post-Sabbatian Politics: Reflections on Governance among the Spanish and Portuguese Jews of Amsterdam, 1665–1683" (PhD diss., University of Pennsylvania, 2008), 21–59. Bonfil identifies a decline in prestige, stemming from the over-proliferation of rabbinic ordinations during this period, as well as a decline in absolute authority, connected with the dependence of communally appointed rabbis on the lay authorities to whom they owed their position and their monopoly on teaching. Teller focuses on the changing political configuration of sixteenth-century Poland, and argues that the shift from centralized monarchical

At the same time, the particular involvement of the Portuguese Jewish community's merchants in educational activities reflects similar patterns in the seventeenth-century Netherlands. In Dutch society generally during this period, the operation and governance of schools typically shifted from the purview of ecclesiastic institutions to civil authorities.[54] So too the educational structure of the Portuguese Jewsish community in Amsterdam was firmly within the jurisdiction of the merchants who governed the community, rather than the rabbinic teachers and religious authorities who actually taught in the schools.

Part II: Education and the Bible in Seventeenth-Century Amsterdam

The *raison d'être* of the Talmud Torah educational confraternity was the maintenance of a school system for the community's children. In its fully developed form, the educational system that the Talmud Torah created was based on seven progressively more advanced classes, and was overwhelmingly oriented toward the study of Scripture. Adult education activities organized by the community's rabbis also continued to focus largely on biblical studies through to the end of the seventeenth century. As we have seen, historians such as Yosef Hayim Yerushalmi and Miriam Bodian have emphasized the wide range of Jewish literature translated into Spanish and Portuguese for the benefit of ex-conversos and their descendants. This chapter takes a closer look at what texts and genres of Jewish literature actually found their way into the curriculum of the Portuguese Jewish community, and onto the shelves of its classrooms. Descriptions of the school system in the communal record books, in book lists, and from the observations of central and east European Jewish visitors demonstrate that the community prioritized the study of Scripture, deferring the encounter with Judaism's Oral Law to the

authority to decentralized rule by nobles and towns subverted to a certain extent the authority of rabbis who had previously served in a similar capacity to royal officials. Anne Oravetz Albert shows that Rabbi Isaac Aboab da Fonseca regarded the *ḥerem* (ban) as an exclusive prerogative of the communal government in Amsterdam, in which rabbis contributed in a secondary or advisory capacity.

54. Willem Frijhoff and Marijke Spies, eds., *Dutch Culture in a European Perspective* (Assen, The Netherlands: Royal Van Gorcum; New York: Palgrave Macmillan, 2004), 1:238.

last and most advanced levels of the educational system. These pedagogical choices demonstrate both the influence of Dutch models on the structure and culture of Jewish education in Amsterdam, as well as the ongoing prioritizing of the Old Testament in converso thought.

The earliest records of the Talmud Torah society show a consistent interest in the hiring of teachers. Josef Salom was hired in April, 1619 in order to teach "all of the lessons until the Prophets." Salom was probably responsible mostly for teaching students to read and chant the Pentateuch.[55] Additionally, he may have initially been required to teach the alphabet to the youngest students, since in 1621 Yosef Yesurun was hired to take on this task and to prepare them for continuing on to Salom's class on the Pentateuch.[56] Also in 1621, Saul Levi Morteira was hired to teach Bible and Talmud. His contract specifies that he was to teach Bible "*em targum*" (in translation), which probably indicates Spanish.[57] Based on the early sources it is clear that students were taught in distinct classes, but it is difficult to tell how many different levels there were. The examination requirements instituted in 1616 do distinguish between students studying the alphabet, those studying Pentateuch, and those studying the Prophets. The fact that examinations – along with the approval of the teacher, parnassim, and the gabbai – were required in order to move through these classes indicates that these were seen as discrete levels.[58]

55. GAS 334 1051 Fol. 6a.
56. GAS 334 1051 Fol. 5b.
57. GAS 334 1051 Fol. 8b–9a. It is not entirely clear what the officials mean by *em targum*. After the unification of the Portuguese Jewish communities in 1639, there was a specific class devoted to the study of the Bible "in Ladino." GAS 334 19 Fol. 3a #22. However, from lists of the books that were employed in this classroom at the same time (GAS 334 1051 Fol. 17a) it is clear that many of the Bibles used in this class were Hebrew texts. It is unlikely that Morteira was expected to study the actual Aramaic paraphrases of the weekly Torah readings with students, given the generally low level of Hebrew (let alone Aramaic) skills in the community. Rabbis Isaac Aboab da Fonseca and Yosseph Franco Serrano much later lamented the fact that few in their community had adequate knowledge of these languages. See Isaac Aboab da Fonseca, *Parafrasis comentado sobre el Pentateuco*, "Prologo al Lector" [unpaginated]; Yosseph Franco Serrano, *Los cinco libros de la sacra Ley*, "Prohemio" [unpaginated]. It is possible that an oral translation or commentary on the verses is implied by "em targum."
58. GAS 334 1051 Fol. 2b. "O gabaj tera hum liuro de matricules de todos os talmedim

By the time of the unification of the three congregations in 1639, there was a clearly defined educational structure of seven classes.[59] It was examination and level of achievement – rather than continual attendance – that enabled students to advance to higher levels.[60] An introductory class was led at this time by Mordechai de Crasto in which young boys learned the alphabet. The second level was directed by Joseph de Faro, who taught reading and Pentateuch. Jacob Gomes continued to teach reading skills to students in the third level, and also taught them to chant passages from the Bible according to the cantillation marks. In the fourth level, Abraham Baruch (who also served as cantor in the community) taught the Pentateuch in Ladino.[61] The fifth level was taught by Salom ben Yosseph, and focused on the study of the Prophets and Rashi's commentary. Only in the sixth and seventh levels, taught by Isaac Aboab da Fonseca and Saul Levi Morteira, did students encounter the Talmud. Students in Aboab's sixth level also studied grammar.[62] At some point later in the seventeenth century, the seven classes were reduced to six.[63] The approach of dividing the Portuguese Jewish school system into sequential classes, each with their own defined curriculum, fit well with the many cultural worlds to which the community was connected: the pedagogical practices in the Iberian Peninsula that they had left, those in their new home in the United Provinces, and models in the wider Jewish world that early teachers in the community had experienced. On the one hand, the typical Jesuit lower school of the sixteenth and

q[ue] meldarem nas escolas desta S.H. cadahuno asorte em sua lisam aonde cada mes notara por sifras cada hum mostrar em seu exame para q[ue] se saiba se uaj melhorando ou se tourna atras."

59. Miriam Bodian, *Hebrews of the Portuguese Nation*, 107–9, Daniel Swetschinski, *Reluctant Cosmopolitans*, 210, Steven Nadler, *Spinoza: A Life* (Cambridge and New York: Cambridge University Press, 1999), 61–65.

60. Julia Lieberman, "Educational Institutions among the Western Sephardim in the Seventeenth Century," 14. The original statutes of the Talmud Torah educational confraternity specify that students who remained in the alphabet class for more than one year were not eligible for prizes that were awarded to outstanding students.

61. Steven Nadler, *Spinoza: A Life*, 62. Nadler describes students of this level translating the biblical text into Spanish based on Shabbetai Bass's later description of the schools.

62. GAS 334 19 Fol. 2a–2b.

63. Shabbetai Bass, *Sifte Yeshenim* (Amsterdam, 1679/1680), Fol. 8v.

seventeenth century divided its students among five classes that focused on the teaching of basic Latin syntax, grammar, and prose; Greek; rhetoric; history, and a variety of other humanistic disciplines.[64] On the other hand, children's education in the Netherlands was moving in a similar direction simultaneously, as reflected by Holland's 1625 *school-reglement* (school order), which organized Dutch Latin schools into six grades, and which exercised significant influence across the United Provinces.[65] Finally, the structuring of the multi-tiered school system in Amsterdam may reflect models encountered by the rabbis and teachers in the Portuguese Jewish community who spent time in Venice and other Italian centers – including Joseph Pardo and Saul Levi Morteira. Giulio Morosini (1612–1687), a Catholic convert from Judaism who had been born to a Sephardic family in Venice, wrote in his proselytizing tome *Via della fede* [The Way of Faith] that in Italy, Talmud Torah schools were commonly divided into discrete classes with different teachers, curricula, and educational goals. He adds that these Talmud Torah schools could be found "in any city" in Italy, and described Venice's seven-tiered school system in detail.[66]

Portuguese students in Amsterdam theoretically studied in the Talmud Torah classes between the ages of five and fourteen.[67] In early

64. Paul Grendler, *Jesuit Schools and Universities in Europe, 1548–1773* (Leiden and Boston: Brill, 2018), 6–18.
65. J. Spoelder, *Prijsboeken op de Latijnse School. Een studie naar het verschijnsel prijsuit-reiking en prijsboek op e Latijnse scholen in de Noordelijke Nederlanden, ca. 15851876.* (Amsterdam and Maarssen: Apa-Holland Universiteits Press, 2000), 76. See also Willem Frijhoff and Marijke Spies, eds. *Dutch Culture in a European Perspective.* 1:245. Julia Lieberman has also observed similarities between the educational structure of Jesuit schools and the Portuguese Jewish Talmud Torah systems. Jesuit schools, modeled on the "Modus Parisiensis," divided students into seven classes according to their knowledge. See Julia Lieberman, "Educational Institutions among the Western Sephardim in the Seventeenth Century," 7.
66. Giulio Morosini, *Via della fede mostrata agli ebrei* (Rome, 1683), 161–64. Regarding Morosini, born Samuel Nahmias, see Yaacob Dweck, *The Scandal of Kabbalah: Leon Modena, Jewish Mysticism, Early Modern Venice* (Princeton and Oxford: Princeton University Press, 2011), 181–82. See also Benjamin Ravid, "'Contra Judeos' in Seventeenth-Century Italy: Two Responses to the 'Discorso' of Simone Luzzatto by Melchiore Palontrotti and Giulio Morosini," *AJS Review* 7/8 (1982/1983): 301–51.
67. Julia Lieberman, "Childhood and Family among the Western Sephardim in the

modern Europe generally, by the age of thirteen or fourteen, young boys would begin preparations to start an apprenticeship or learn a trade, and this appears to have been the case in Amsterdam as well.[68] Yet as a result of the need to earn a living, until 1639 it was impossible for many students to continue their education into the fifth- and sixth-level classes, where Talmud was studied.[69] In fact, the founding statutes of the Ets Haim confraternity from this year lament that "many *talmidim* [students], although of great talent, were forced by the difficult [current] times to quit school in order to earn a living, just as they were beginning to collect the fruit of their labors."[70] In order to remedy this situation, between 1639 and 1652 the Ets Haim confraternity provided funding to students who reached the most advanced classes, "it being well understood that no student shall be able to receive a stipend who has not been studying Gemara for at least one year."[71]

The Portuguese Jewish school system resembles European – Iberian and Dutch non-Jewish – counterparts in at least one other respect. During the late sixteenth and seventeenth centuries, Jesuit and Dutch educational approaches sought to cultivate an intense culture of competition within their classes through the public recognition of excellence and the distribution of prizes to students who excelled in their studies. The *Ratio Studiorum* – a programmatic Jesuit pedagogical text that closely influenced Jesuit education from its composition in

Seventeenth Century," in *Sephardi Family Life in the Early Modern Diaspora*, ed. Julia Lieberman (Hanover and London: University Press of New England; Waltham, MA: Brandeis University Press, 2011), 158. See also Cristina Galasso, "Religious Space, Gender, and Power in the Sephardi Diaspora: The Return to Judaism of New Christian Men and Women in Livorno and Pisa," in *Sephardi Family Life in the Early Modern Diaspora*, 110. Galasso finds that from at least 1664, male Sephardi Jewish children attended school from the ages of six to fourteen.

68. Julia Lieberman, "Childhood and Family among the Western Sephardim," 159–60, and "Educational Institutions among the Western Sephardim in the Seventeenth Century," 18.
69. Julia Lieberman, "Educational Institutions among the Western Sephardim in the Seventeenth Century," 18.
70. Julia Lieberman, "Educational Institutions among the Western Sephardim in the Seventeenth Century," 18. See also GAS 334 1052 Fol. 1a–1b.
71. GAS 334 1052 Fol. 2a–2b. In 1652 the community expanded the eligibility requirements for stipends. See GAS 334 1052 Fol. 13b.

1599 onward – included policies on the awarding of prizes among its basic educational approaches.[72] Its chapter titled "The Laws for Prizes" specifies that "Eight awards should be offered in rhetoric: two for Latin prose, two for poetry; two for Greek prose, the same number for Greek poetry. In the humanities class and in the first grammar class, six should be offered in a like manner... Next, four awards should be offered in all the other lower classes," though the number could be adjusted higher or lower depending on the number of students in the class, and at the discretion of the instructor.[73] These outstanding students were to be identified through written examinations submitted by students using a pseudonym – to protect their anonymity, and to guarantee impartial deliberations by evaluators. Recipients were to be honored in public, before a large crowd and with lavish praise.[74] Within the Netherlands, Dutch magistrates and teachers likewise awarded prizes to outstanding students in their classes.[75] Apart from the example of a single Catholic school in Arnhem during the sixteenth century, this culture of competitive education and the distribution of books as prizes corresponds entirely with the adoption of Protestant religious reforms in Dutch cities.[76] Leiden, in 1586, was one of the earliest cities to implement ceremonies for awarding prize books, and was followed by Dordrecht and Haarlem in 1592 and 1599 respectively. Throughout the seventeenth century, a wide variety of prize books were distributed in a manner that closely corresponded to the education received in these schools.

Following the school reforms of 1625, Dutch students in the Netherlands were organized by age into six classes. The lowest level, the sixth, provided an introduction to the principles of Latin grammar and the study of basic texts, such as Mathurin Cordier's *Colloquiorum scholasticorum libri quatuor* and Erasmus's *Formulae familiaries*. In later years, students studied Cicero's *Orationes* and *Pro Milone*, Virgil's *Bucolica*

72. Cinthia Gannet and John Brereton, eds. *Traditions of Eloquence: The Jesuits and Modern Rhetorical Studies* (New York: Fordham University Press, 2016), 8.
73. Claude Pavur, S.J., ed., trans. *The Ratio Studiorum: The Official Plan for Jesuit Education* (St Louis, MO: The Institute of Jesuit Sources, 2005), 133.
74. Allen Farrell, trans. *Ratio Studiorum*, 59–61.
75. J. Spoelder, *Prijsboeken op de Latijnse School*, 731.
76. J. Spoelder, *Prijsboeken op de Latijnse School*, 79–84.

and the *Aeneid,* Ovid's *Metamorphoses,* the writings of Sallustius, and a wide range of other Latin and Greek texts.[77] Many of these classical texts, as well as works by leading Dutch scholars such as Vossius and Grotius, were given as prizes to outstanding students.[78] Award recipients were selected by a board of officials that operated at arms length from the municipal authorities, and which also controlled the promotion of students from one level to the next.[79]

Similar practices are evident in the Portuguese Jewish community, where the communal parnassim, gabbai, and rabbis awarded book prizes to outstanding students and fostered a competitive atmosphere in classes. At the very founding of the Talmud Torah educational confraternity in 1616, it was stipulated that "Prizes shall be given three times during the year to students of this holy confraternity and others who... compete well in their lessons... One [award] shall be given to each class, or more... according to the discretion of the officials. The examinations for prizes shall be secret and shall not be attended by anyone but the examiners and the parnassim and the gabbai of the holy confraternity. This is to avoid complaints and favoritism."[80] Likewise, when the officials described the schedule of examinations for students at different levels of the system, they specified that "Students of the higher classes shall be publicly examined on the first Sabbath after... Rosh Hodesh, so that they may compete with one another."[81] Whereas Dutch Latin schools tended to award editions of classical literature as prizes, Portuguese Jewish students appear to have received Spanish-language liturgical

77. J. Spoelder, *Prijsboeken op de Latijnse School,* 76–77.
78. J. Spoelder, *Prijsboeken op de Latijnse School,* 309–45.
79. J. Spoelder, *Prijsboeken op de Latijnse School,* 733.
80. GAS 334 1051 Fol. 2a–2b. "Darseam premios aos talmidim das escolas desta S.H. eaos q[ue] de outras [unclear] acompetir bom ells em suas lissoens tres veses no anno em sebuot nafesta desta S.H. serem os maiores em preto. Em simha thora nafesta de nossos dalej. Em sabat micamoha eserem os menores em preto. Darseam atodos as lissoens hum emais acada hua como ben parecer aos officiaes. Os exams de premio seram secretos enam asistiram aelles mais que os examinadores eos parnassim egabaj desta S.H. isto por euitar queixa, e affeicoens."
81. GAS 334 1051 Fol. 2b. "Os talmidim de maiores hauendo de examinaram empublico em cada Sabat, atras de primeiro de Ros hodes p[ar]a q[ue] hum e outra andem em competensia."

works. Early book lists kept by the community show a declining number of these works in the library, and specify that the missing books have been "given as prizes."[82] Thus, there appears to have been a shared atmosphere of competition and reward in the pedagogical approaches of Dutch Christians and Portuguese Jews in the seventeenth-century Netherlands.

While outstanding students may have received liturgical works as prizes, it was Scripture that received pride of place in the curriculum. Early modern visitors to the Portuguese Jewish community in Amsterdam were often struck by the prominent – and in their eyes, strikingly anomalous and atypical – place of the Bible in the educational curriculum, and the systematic approach to its study throughout the different levels of the school system. The first of these figures to remark on the study of Scripture in Portuguese Jewish Amsterdam was Shabbetai Sheftel Horowitz, the son of the famous Polish talmudist and kabbalist Isaiah Horowitz, who visited Amsterdam during the early 1640s.[83] In Amsterdam, Horowitz interacted with numerous Portuguese Jews and recorded his observations of the community and its schools in his treatise *Sefer Vave ha-Amudim* (Amsterdam, 1648):

> During my passage from Frankfurt to the Holy Community of Posen I traveled by way of the sea and passed through the Holy Community of Amsterdam, and I discovered there important people and many wise students, and I was in their houses of study, each one of which has a *meḥizah* within it. I saw that the youths study Scripture from בראשית until לעיני כל ישראל, and after this all of the twenty-four [books of Scripture], and afterward all of the *mishnayot*. And when they become older, then they begin to study Talmud, commentaries, and the Tosafot. And they mature and succeed and also bear fruit. And I exclaimed, why and for what reason is this not done in our lands? If only this custom would

82. GAS 334 1051 Fol. 13b. "Libros que mays ha sao os seguintez e os que faltao se darao de premios e hua biblia Ladina se vendeu." There is also evidence that later in the seventeenth century preaching manuals were given as prizes to advanced students in Moshe Raphael d'Aguilar's classes. See GAS 334 1052 Fol. 101/90b.
83. Miriam Bodian, *Hebrews of the Portuguese Nation*, 107–8.

> spread throughout the scattered communities of Israel! And what harm is there if [the student] fills his stomach with Scripture and Mishnah until he reaches the age of thirteen, and afterward he will begin to study the Talmud? For it is certain that in one year he will achieve the objective and several exalted degrees, a level of sharpness in Talmud study that in my opinion [in our communities] is not achieved in several years. If the leaders would gather, if the *geonim,* the leaders of our land, would gather together and implement a reform and a curriculum like this curriculum, to be a rock and foundation and an eternal law never to be broken, there is no doubt that the Divine purpose will succeed in our hands, and the hearts will be sharpened in the truth of Torah . . . and the time of redemption will be hastened.[84]

Several features of Horowitz's description deserve particular attention. First of all, he notes that the each of the "houses of study" that he visited had a dividing barrier within it to separate men and women. His finding this remarkable raises the possibility that in at least some of the community's classes, boys and girls studied together. Hypothetically, Horowitz could be referring to a synagogue *meḥizah,* but this is unlikely for two reasons. Not only does Horowitz specifically say that he visited study houses (*batei midrashot*), but the community records regularly speak about the *esnoga* (synagogue) and classrooms as if they are in separate buildings.[85] We also know that there was a society, the *Keter Sem Tob* (Crown of the Good Name) that provided an extra-curricular opportunity for young boys and girls alike to deepen their familiarity with the Bible. In 1683, Daniel Levi de Barrios wrote that there were twenty young boys and seventeen young girls who were members of this organization, and that "they study the Holy Law one hour every Sabbath . . . in order to earn an eternal reward."[86] Was it also common for boys and girls to

84. Shabbetai Sheftel Horowitz, *Vave ha-Amudim* (Amsterdam, 1648), Fol. 9r.
85. GAS 334 1052 Fol. 11b and 23a. Although not entirely conclusive, Fol. 11b describes the classrooms and the library of the community as being connected within a common structure. Fol. 23b describes how the parnas who supervises the daily classes is required to make sure that students go from their classes to the synagogue for the evening prayers, and to ensure that in the *esnoga* (synagogue) the students sit with their rabbis.
86. Daniel Levi de Barrios, *Triumpho del govierno popular,* 363. "Meditan con caridad en

study together in the Talmud Torah classes? If so, in which elements of the curriculum might girls have participated? Unfortunately, the sources do not offer ready answers to these questions, or many details beyond these references to the participation of girls in the educational system.

Additionally, we should pay attention to Horowitz's emphasis on the comprehensiveness of the biblical curriculum in the Amsterdam community. He stresses that young students studied the Pentateuch from its first verse to the last verse, and that subsequently they proceeded to master the entire biblical corpus, including the Books of the Prophets and the Writings, all of which dominated the curriculum prior to their introduction to Mishnah and Talmud.[87] Third, we should observe the degree to which Horowitz saw the Bible-centered pedagogical approach as being anomalous within the European Jewish world. The educational curriculum in the regions where he lived included much earlier and greater emphasis on the study of rabbinic Jewish literature. Nevertheless, Horowitz was deeply impressed by the Portuguese Jewish approach and exclaimed that a similar curriculum should be adopted across Ashkenaz.

Approximately two decades after Horowitz printed his description of the Portuguese Jewish school system in Amsterdam, another Ashkenazi figure, Shabbetai Bass, produced an even more systematic and detailed description of the curriculum followed in various classes. In his 1679 bibliography of Hebrew texts, *Sifte Yeshenim*, Bass includes observations of the Portuguese schools. He too was struck by the centrality of the Bible in the Portuguese Jewish curriculum. His remarks show that decades after Horowitz arrived in Amsterdam, Scripture remained the focus of the community's approach to education. Bass writes:

> Since I arrived here, the holy community of Amsterdam, I went several times to the study houses of the Sephardi community. And I saw the sons of giants, many children as small as grasshoppers

la Ley Sancta, y sonora, cada Sabado una hora, por ir a una eternidad . . . y peregrina la Academia la figura, por continua en la Escritura, por feliz enla doctrina."

87. Students encountered both Mishnah and Talmud only in the two most advanced classes. A 1642 inventory of books being used in the communal schools shows Mishnah texts only in the classrooms of advanced teachers like Saul Levi Morteira. See GAS 334 1051 Fol. 44b.

> and kids . . . and they were giants in my eyes for their considerable mastery in all of Scripture and in the wisdom of grammar and the composition of verse and poetry . . . and for speaking the Holy Tongue clearly. Up until now I had heard the voice of the holy man . . . Shabbetai Sheftel Horowitz ha-Levi in his book [*Vave ha-Amudim*] and there he opens his mouth to speak of the wonders on the subject of the educational curriculum of the Sephardi holy community.[88]

After reviewing and quoting Shabbetai Horowitz's description in full, Bass provides an even more elaborate survey of the community's schools and curriculum:

> And I will come after him and complete his words and I will expand his statements. And this is the curriculum of the holy community of the Sephardim. They built a House of the Lord, a small *Beit ha-Mikdash*, the famous synagogue. And whoever has not seen this building has not seen a beautiful building among the people of Israel. And alongside it they built six rooms for the Talmud Torah . . . and in each room there is a single instructor [*melammed*], even if there would be students in the hundreds, may they indeed multiply. In the first room the small children learn until they know how to read prayers. Then they place them in the second room, and there they learn Torah with the melody of the cantilation marks until they become experts in the Pentateuch, until לעיני כל ישראל. And then they enter the third room, and there they learn Torah until they are expert in interpreting it in their vernacular language [Spanish or Portuguese], and each week they meticulously study Rashi's commentary on the weekly pericope. And then they come to the fourth room, and there they study the Prophets and Writings according to the melody of the cantilation marks. And the child reads a verse in the Holy Tongue, and afterward interprets it in the vernacular, and all of the children listen to him, and then the second says [a verse] as well, and everyone else too. And after this [the first four classes],

88. Shabbetai Bass, *Sifte Yeshenim*. Fol. 8.

> they go to the fifth room, and the children become accustomed to read halakhah on their own until they arrive at understanding and wisdom... and there they do not speak in any other language except specifically in the Holy Tongue. Only the halakhah they interpret in the vernacular language. And they study the discipline of grammar meticulously. And each and every day they also learn one halakhah from the Gemara, and when a holiday or a Festival approaches, then all of the students study the *Shulhan Arukh* and its particulars, and the *halakhot* for Pesaḥ on Pesaḥ, and each and every holiday, until all of the children are experts in the rulings. Then they go to the sixth room, the Yeshivah of the study house of the *hakham*, the head of the rabbinic court. And there they sit in the room and study each day one halakhah with *Dikduk Rashi*[89] and Tosafot and they also perform *pilpul* (*ve-gam mepalpelim*) in the study of the rulings from the *Maimuni* and the *Tur* and the *Beth Joseph* and the other *poskim*. And within the *beit midrash* they have a special school and there they have many books, and in all the time they are in the yeshivah this room is also open and whoever wishes to study, anything he desires is lent to him. But not outside of the *beit midrash*, even if he provides a large sum of money.[90]

Shabbetai Bass's account gives a clear sense of the degree to which Bible dominated the curriculum of the Portuguese Jews. After learning to read in the first class, students in the second class mastered the Pentateuch and the cantillation notes; in the third class, they practice vernacular interpretation and the study of Rashi's commentary on the Pentateuch; in the fourth class, students practiced reading and chanting the Prophets and Writings. Only students who progressed to the fifth and sixth classes would receive systematic training in the study of Talmud and legal works. Like Horowitz, Bass was extremely impressed by the Bible-centered curriculum of the Portuguese community.

89. An abridgement of R. Elijah Mizrahi's *Dikdukei Rashi* (Venice, 1560) on the places in Rashi's commentaries where he focuses on grammatical points in the Torah. See Shabbetai Bass, *Sifte Yeshenim*, Fol. 18.
90. Shabbetai Bass, *Sifte Yeshenim*, Fol. 8.

The importance of Scripture in many levels of the educational system is evident not only from the observations of Horowitz and Bass, and from the community's own description of the tasks assigned to different teachers in 1639. In addition, from the community records we can also learn which books made their way into the classrooms. Throughout this period the community maintained extensive (though sometimes discontinuous) book lists documenting the texts being used in different classrooms and texts newly purchased for specific teachers. The data for the earliest years following the establishment of the Talmud Torah is fragmentary. However, in the inventories recorded for each year between 1621 and 1624, the community officials describe the presence of between fourteen and fifteen Bibles "which are used for instruction in the synagogue."[91] During this period, no other texts are identified as being used for instruction, although many other varieties of Jewish literature were purchased.

Records of texts that Abraham Baruch borrowed from the communal library for use in his classrooms offer the clearest picture of the central role of the Bible in the pedagogical approach of Amsterdam's Portuguese Jews. As we saw earlier, one of the most important responsibilities of communal governors in the early seventeenth century was the establishment and administration of a large communal library. This library contained texts that were important for rabbinic scholarship and the preparation of sermons, and it was also a crucial resource for the community's schools. Entries in the Talmud Torah record books from 1635 and 1638 provide lists of texts that Abraham Baruch borrowed for his students, probably in the fourth-level class he was teaching when the three congregations amalgamated in 1639. In 1635, a note was entered about "the books that are presently used in the Talmud Torah of the Beth Jacob [congregation], which the cantor Abraham Baruch returned." The community frequently lent books to its cantors and rabbis for up to a year at a time, and diligently ensured their safe return at the end of each year. Among the books that Baruch borrowed for his teaching were twelve newly bound Bibles; two old Bibles in quarto format; one Bible with the weekly pericopes and Rashi's commentary; two copies of the

91. GAS 334 1051 Fol. 13b–14a, "15 biblias por que se melda na esnoga, ebraicas."

prophetic books of the Bible printed in Frankfurt; two additional texts with the Prophets and weekly Torah readings that were printed in Venice; an old German edition of the Prophets; nine complete (but small and old) Bibles; an old German edition of the weekly Torah readings; two additional Bibles printed in Venice, plus another that was bound with Rashi's commentary; and, finally, "one complete [Bible] from here [i.e., Amsterdam] on white parchment." Later, another individual added eight more Bibles into this list, six of which contained the weekly readings from the Prophets, and were also printed in Amsterdam.[92]

Three years later, in 1638, Abraham Baruch again borrowed a large number of texts from the library, and a similar pattern is evident: there were eleven Bibles with the weekly Torah readings marked, "tables," and haftarah passages; six additional Bibles bound with one of the ancient Aramaic translations; one Bible in quarto with red binding; one Bible with the weekly readings marked and Rashi's commentary; two editions of the prophetic books; another old German edition of the Prophets, in addition to an old German edition of the weekly Torah readings; six complete copies of the entire Bible; two Bibles with the weekly Torah readings, one from Venice and the other from a German press; and two final Bibles, one printed in Venice, and the other printed in Amsterdam with tables, bound in a red cover.[93]

In 1635, Abraham Baruch borrowed no fewer than forty-three separate Bibles from the communal library. In 1638, he borrowed thirty-seven Bibles. These were probably meant to provide each individual with a text, and indicate a class size in the high thirties or low forties – likely a significant increase from the period between 1621–1624, when only fourteen to fifteen Bibles were set aside for education. In addition, combining the information contained in these book lists and Shabbetai Bass's 1679/80 description of the different classes allows us to speculate about the content and activities that were emphasized in Baruch's lessons. It appears that Abraham Baruch employed both Hebrew and Spanish Bibles in his classroom. On the one hand, it is likely that the Bibles described as having been printed in Germany generally, and Frankfurt specifically,

92. GAS 334 1051 Fol. 17a.

93. GAS 334 1051 Fol. 18a.

were in Hebrew. As Stephen Burnett has demonstrated, German presses operated by Christians and Jews dominated Hebrew printing during the sixteenth century, and it is likely that the "old" German Bibles listed in these records originated from these printing houses.[94] On the other hand, certain Bibles in these lists were in Spanish. Editions of Scripture described as having been printed in Amsterdam and including "tables" almost certainly refer to editions of the Ferrara Bible, which include chronological tables that laid out the course of Jewish history in biblical times.[95] Three decades later, Shabbetai Bass described students in the fourth class – the one being taught by Baruch at this time – as reading a verse from the Bible in Hebrew, before interpreting it or translating it in the vernacular. The use of both Hebrew and Spanish texts by Baruch's students in the 1630s suggests the possibility that they were using a similar approach.

We have more information about the texts used in Abraham Baruch's classrooms than we have about almost any other instructor. However, he was not the only teacher whose curriculum appears to have focused so heavily on the study of biblical texts. The book lists and library inventories made by the community show a variety of other instructors at different levels who taught in classrooms where the shelves were filled with Bibles. These include: Samuel Abravanel, who was responsible for the first class during the late seventeenth century; Joshua de Faro, who taught the second class later in the seventeenth century; Selomoh Salom, who taught the fifth class during the 1630s, and was actively teaching into the 1660s; and Daniel Belillos, who in the later part of the century taught the third class.[96] During this period, Moshe Raphael d'Aguilar and

94. Stephen Burnett, "Christian Hebrew Printing in the Sixteenth Century: Printers, Humanism, and the Impact of the Reformation," *Helmantica: Revista de Filología Clásica y Hebrea*, ed. Santiago García Jalón de la Lama. Vol. 51, no. 154 (January-April, 2000): 13–42. See also *idem*, "German Jewish Printing in the Reformation Era (1530–1633)," in *Jews, Judaism, and the Reformation in Sixteenth-Century Germany*, ed. Dean Phillip Bell and Stephen Burnett (Leiden and Boston: Brill, 2006), 503–27.

95. See for example the edition of the Ferrara Bible printed at Amsterdam in 1630, *Biblia en Lengua Espanola, Traduzida palabra por palabra de la verdad Hebrayca por muy excelentes letrados*, EH 15 A 42, and the discussion of these volumes in Harm den Boer, "La Biblia de Ferrara y otras traducciones españolas de la Biblia," 251–52, 257.

96. Kenneth Scholberg, "Miguel de Barrios and the Amsterdam Sephardic Community," *The Jewish Quarterly Review* 53, no. 2 (October, 1962): 129.

Isaac Aboab da Fonseca provided instruction in the two most advanced classes. These records list the specific teacher and class in which newly acquired texts were intended to be used.

The records for the period between the 1640s and 1680 reveal a striking dichotomy regarding the types of texts that were assigned to teachers in the first four classes, and those used by Saul Levi Morteira, Menasseh ben Israel, Moshe Raphael d'Aguilar, and Isaac Aboab da Fonseca in the advanced classrooms. During these years Joshua de Faro regularly received allotments of Pentateuchs, Bibles, and books of Psalms – twenty newly bound books of psalms in 1660, four Pentateuchs in 1668, five Bibles and twelve prayer books in 1669, four additional Pentateuchs in 1670 and three more in 1671, along with an unspecified number of books of Psalms in 1673 and eight further Bibles in 1678. Selomoh Salom was given a number of Pentateuchs and introductory alphabet primers during the 1660s; Daniel Belillos received two shipments of Bibles during the 1670s; Samuel Abravanel received mostly alphabet primers during this period, but also received a number of Bibles for his classroom in 1676; and Jacob Judah Leon received numerous editions of the Bible with Rashi's commentary in 1665 and 1668.

During the same period of time, the literary diet of the advanced classrooms was far more diverse and omnivorous. A survey of the "cabinets" in Saul Levi Morteira's classroom from 1642 revealed the presence of a truly diverse library used for educating elite students. Peering inside the cabinet doors, communal officials saw the complete volume of Joseph Karo's *Beit Yosef* and several editions of the *Shulhan Arukh,* along with a number of Rabbinic Bibles, books of Psalms, a complete set of Abraham ben Mordecai Jaffe's *Levushim,* and an array of Talmud tractates that cut across the corpus of rabbinic literature: Berakhot, Kil'ayim, Shabbat, Eruvin, Pesaḥim, Sukkah, Ta'anit, Megillah, Ḥagigah, Mo'ed Qatan, Bava Qamma, Sanhedrin, Zevaḥim, Menaḥot, Ḥullin, Bekhorot, Teharot, Niddah, Yevamot, Nedarim, and Gittin. In Menasseh ben Israel's classroom, in addition to a complete set of the *Levushim* there were four volumes of the tractate Berakhot, along with volumes of Betzah, Sanhedrin, Shev'uot, Megillah, Ta'anit, Rosh HaShanah, Yoma, Mo'ed Qatan, Pesaḥim, Sukkah, Ḥagigah, Nedarim, Nazir, and Sotah. Isaac Aboab's classroom was inventoried at the same time as those of his colleagues, and a similar pattern emerges. Officials of the community recorded that he was using the following books to teach his advanced students: complete sets of the *Beit Yosef* printed at Venice and Krakow; the *Levush*; a complete *Shulḥan Arukh*; and a wide array of Talmud tractates including Yevamot, Gittin, Nedarim, Nazir, Qiddushin, Sotah, Niddah, Teharot, Bava Batra, Pesaḥim, Ḥagigah, Ḥullin, Zevaḥim, Bava Metz'ia, Shevu'ot, Qodashim, Ketubbot, Eruvin, Pesaḥim, and Shabbat.[97] Later, in the 1660s and 1670s, teachers of the advanced classes, including Aguilar and Aboab, regularly received new volumes of Talmud and the *Shulhan Arukh*, along with Bibles with Rashi's commentary.[98] Additionally, Aguilar was given dozens of grammatical textbooks, books of Psalms, manuals for the composition and delivery of sermons, and a biblical concordance.[99] The near homogeneity of the books purchased for and used in the classrooms of Abraham Baruch, Joshua Faro, Jacob Judah Leon, Daniel Belillos, and Samuel Abravanel stands in stark contrast to the dynamic varieties of books regularly purchased by the same communal officials for instructors of the most advanced religious academies. During the middle and late decades of the seventeenth century there were numerous teachers providing a biblically-oriented education to children in a variety of levels within the Talmud Torah school system, while only the most advanced students would come into contact with Judaism's legal texts.[100]

97. GAS 334 1052 Fol. 19 and Fol. 44a–44b.
98. GAS 334 1052 Fol. 103/92–104/93; Fol. 108/97; Fol. 115/104;
99. GAS 334 1052 Fol. 101/90; Fol. 104/93; Fol. 106/95; Fol. 109/98; Fol. 111/100; Fol. 113/102; Fol. 115/104.
100. For a more detailed study of the purchase and use of books for educational purposes in the Amsterdam community, see (for the seventeenth century) Benjamin Fisher, "From Boxes and Cabinets to the Bibliotheca: Building the Jewish Library of the Ex-Conversos in Amsterdam, 1620–1665," *European Journal of Jewish Studies* 13 (2019): 43–76; and (for the eighteenth century) David Sclar, "Books in the Ets Haim Yeshivah: Acquisition, Publishing, and a Community of Scholarship in Eighteenth-Century Amsterdam," *Jewish History* 30 (2016): 207–32. Sclar observes in his study that during the mid-eighteenth century, administrators of the Ets Haim, under the leadership of co-chief rabbis David Israel Athias and Isaac Hayim Abendana de Britto, made a conscious effort to collect "cutting edge," recently published rabbinic scholarship, but focused their teaching on halakhic texts with "practical" application – the first part of the *Shulḥan Arukh* (Oraḥ Ḥayyim which deals with matters of ritual and daily life; and Talmud tractates dominated by volumes from *Seder Mo'ed* related to Jewish

Horowitz and Bass had good reason to be surprised by the Portuguese Jewish pedagogical approach and school system that they discovered in Amsterdam. In light of the typical approaches to education in central and eastern Europe during the seventeenth century and earlier, the Portuguese community's practices would have seemed unfamiliar in at least two respects. Institutionally, the six-tiered communally supported school system taught by highly trained rabbis, and open free of charge to all, differed greatly from the approach to children's education in central and eastern Europe. In these regions, prior to the nineteenth century, the basic framework for early Jewish education was the *ḥeder*, a private one-teacher school in which a single *melammed* (teacher) was hired by a parent or group of parents in order to teach one or more children. Classes took place in the home of the teacher, or in rooms rented specifically for this purpose.[101] Neither in medieval Ashkenaz nor in modern eastern Europe did the community intervene in educational matters or organize a systematic network of schools.[102]

The biblically-oriented curriculum taught to students was even more unusual from the perspective of pedagogical practices traditionally used in central and eastern Europe, and it was these features of the Portuguese Jewish schools that particularly drew Horowitz and Bass's attention.

rituals. Study of the seventeenth-century library catalogues and book collecting practices reveals that the curriculum taught in the elite, advanced classrooms was substantially more varied and included materials from a much broader spectrum of talmudic literature.

101. Ephraim Kanarfogel, *Jewish Education and Society in the High Middle Ages* (Detroit, MI: Wayne State University Press, 1992), 19–24; Shaul Stampfer, "Heder Study, Torah, and Social Stratification," in *Families, Rabbis, and Education: Traditional Jewish Society in Nineteenth-Century Eastern Europe*, ed. Shaul Stampfer (Oxford: Littman Library of Jewish Civilization, 2010), 149.

102. Ephraim Kanarfogel, *Jewish Education and Society in the High Middle Ages*, 24–25; Shaul Stampfer, "Heder Study, Torah, and Social Stratefication," 149. However, see Jacob Katz, *Tradition and Crisis: Jewish Society at the End of the Middle Ages* (New York: Syracuse University Press, 1961), 160–61. Katz notes that some communities did appoint functionaries or create *ḥevrot Talmud Torah* (Talmud Torah Societies) whose function it was to supervise teachers, and to ensure that the poor had access to educational opportunities. Katz also notes that communities typically did not exercise any authority over the selection of teachers or the establishment of new schools.

While Bible appears to have formed a significant component of the educational curriculum under the Ashkenazi Pietists, and expertise in biblical texts is common in many areas of Tosafist literature, it appears that the place of the Bible in the educational curriculum for children in Ashkenaz receded in the period following the Crusades.[103] In the post-Crusade period through the seventeenth century, to the extent that Bible appears to have been taught in Ashkenazi *ḥeders,* it was seen as a preparatory subject leading as quickly as possible to the study of Talmud. According to Rabbi Isaac Or Zarua', a teacher who taught the weekly Torah reading with Rashi's commentary or the Aramaic paraphrases was known as a "teacher of infants" (*melammed tinoqot*), indicating the age and level of students studying Bible. In general within Tosafist society, the early phase of childhood education was intended to introduce students to Scripture, and begin the development of basic literacy skills. Bible was far from center stage in the educational curriculum as a whole.[104] As Chava Turniansky has shown, at the level of children's education Bible study in early modern Ashkenaz was also limited to the Pentateuch, which was taught according to the liturgical cycle of the Jewish calendar. Teachers taught elements of the weekly Torah portion, but were normally unable to thoroughly analyse the text before it was necessary to proceed to the following week's pericope.[105] Because of this emphasis on the reading and chanting skills necessary to participate in synagogue services, in terms of biblical study the curriculum emphasized the weekly readings from the Pentateuch and Prophets (*Haftarot*).[106] In

103. Ephraim Kanarfogel, *Jewish Education and Society in the High Middle Ages,* 30–31, 80, 89–90. Kanarfogel emphasizes the gravitas with which pre-Crusade German Jewish rabbinic scholars regarded the study of Scripture. Bible was used as a primary resource in deciding legal questions, and was seen as a text of central importance at the highest level of Jewish thought. In the post-Crusade period, Ashkenazi Pietists lamented and protested the erosion of Bible in the scholarship and curriculum of the Tosafists. The Pietist critique of Tosafist religious culture emphasized the need to prioritize the study of Scripture by advanced students as well as the general population, and to teach Bible more consistently at the elementary level as well.

104. Kanarfogel, *Jewish Education and Society in the High Middle Ages,* 31.

105. Chava Turniansky, "La pedagogia dell'insegnamento della Bibbia nell'Europa orientale," in *La lettura ebraica delle scritture,* ed. Sergio Sierra (Bologna: Edizioni Dehoniane Bologna, 1995), 330–31.

106. Chava Turniansky, "La pedagogia dell'insegnamento della Bibbia nell'Europa orientale," 346.

the seventeenth century, as before, the educational system as a whole did not prioritize the study of Scripture, but rather viewed this phase of study as a brief way-station, propaedeutic to the main event: Mishnah and Talmud.[107] The thorough mastery of Scripture acquired by students in the Talmud Torah classes would have appeared highly anomalous to Horowitz and Bass.

Engagement with the Bible in children's education was more prominent in certain early modern Italian contexts than in the east European worlds that Bass and Horowitz knew so well. Giulio Morosini's *Via della fede* provides a synopsis of the curriculum followed by young Jewish children in Italian – and especially Venetian – schools, and the diverse Jewish texts and traditions that were emphasized. After an initial class where young children began to learn basic writing and reading skills, they moved "to the second class, where the reading and interpretation of the Pentateuch is taught," as well as chanting according to the cantillation notes of the biblical text.[108] In the third class, students begin their study of Prophets, reading and interpreting limited parts of these texts – "they do not hurry to finish these texts, because the time does not permit, but they only have the goal to make a good explanation or interpretation of one part."[109] Notwithstanding the attention to Scripture that small children received in the Italian Talmud Torah schools that Morosini describes, the curriculum quickly takes a turn that would have been quite foreign to Amsterdam's teachers and students. In the fourth classroom, intermediate students younger than ten years old added serious engagement with rabbinic and halakhic texts to their repertoire – the *Shulhan Arukh* of Joseph Karo, Jacob ben Asher's *Turim*, Maimonides' *Mishneh Torah*, Isaac Aboab's *Menorat ha-Ma'or*, and "other rabbinic books that the teacher deems appropriate to explain."[110] In the fifth class that Morosini describes, Jewish students in Italy, at approximately the age of ten, would begin their direct study of the Mishnah and the Talmud, which in the eyes of the convert was "overflowing with perverse doctrines." These texts are pursued in the sixth and seventh classrooms

107. Chava Turniansky, "La pedagogia dell'insegnamento della Bibbia nell'Europa orientale," 346.
108. Morosini, *Via della fede*, 161.
109. Morosini, *Via della fede*, 162.
110. Morosini, *Via della fede*, 163.

as well, stretching the study of rabbinic law from the intermediate stages of the educational process through the apex in order to inculcate a deep and penetrating understanding of Jewish law and practice in the minds of the students – who typically finish their education around the age of fifteen.[111]

The printed biblical culture of Amsterdam's adult Portuguese Jews would have appeared as foreign to Bass and Horowitz as the educational curriculum. As Harm den Boer has demonstrated, throughout the seventeenth century Portuguese Jewish scholars and printers produced a constant stream of literal translations of the Bible or of specific biblical texts. They constantly debated the best approaches for translating Hebrew into Spanish, and wrestled with the popular 1553 Ferrara Bible, which served as the basic text for many members of the community and the model for numerous later editions.[112] Leading rabbis, as we have seen, produced a wide range of biblical commentaries and paraphrases of Scripture. The Portuguese Jewish community supported a voracious market of readers interested in biblical literature.

In contrast, translations of the Bible into Yiddish were exceedingly rare in the sixteenth and seventeenth centuries. There was no appreciable market for Bible translations, and despite the fact that Hebrew was not systematically taught or understood by many members of these Jewish communities, no translation of Scripture from Hebrew into Yiddish was produced between 1610 and 1679.[113] Although two translations of the Bible into Yiddish were published in Amsterdam in 1678 and 1679, both were commercial failures and neither was reprinted.[114] For

111. Morosini, *Via della fede*, 163.
112. Harm den Boer "La Biblia de Ferrara y otras traducciones españolas de la Biblia," 251–67. See also Harm den Boer, *La literatura sefardi de Amsterdam* (Alcala: Instituto Internacional de Estudios Sefardíes y Andalusíes, Universidad de Alcalá, 1995), 20, 39–40. Portuguese Jewish writers regularly criticized the translation principles and approaches adopted by the editors of the Ferrara Bible of 1553, as well as those used by their colleagues in the Netherlands. See the introductory material in Jacob Judah Leon, *Kadosh Hillulim. Las Alabanças de Santidad* (Amsterdam, 1671), and the introduction to Yosseph Franco Serrano, *Los cinco libros de la sacra Ley*.
113. Chava Turniansky, "La pedagogia dell'insegnamento della Bibbia nell'Europa orientale," 331–36.
114. Marion Aptroot, "Yiddish Bibles in Amsterdam," in *The Bible in/and Yiddish*, ed. Shlomo Berger (Amsterdam: Menasseh Ben Israel Institute, 2007), 42–60.

many adult Jews in the regions where Horowitz and Bass were raised and educated, familiarity with the Bible was mediated through works such as the *Tsene-rene,* an early seventeenth-century Yiddish adaptation, paraphrase, and homiletic commentary on the Pentateuch, the Five Scrolls, and the weekly readings from the Prophets.[115] When Horowitz and Bass traveled to Amsterdam, they encountered students studying the Bible comprehensively, from the Pentateuch to the Books of the Prophets to the Writings, and they witnessed a community of adult readers that demanded vast numbers of systematic Bible translations. Furthermore, they had shifted from a cultural world that prioritized talmudic scholarship to one in which leading authorities like Menasseh ben Israel, Saul Levi Morteira, Jacob Judah Leon, and Isaac Aboab da Fonseca demonstrated their erudition by composing sophisticated works of biblical scholarship. Little wonder, then, that the biblical culture of seventeenth-century Amsterdam and its educational curriculum seemed highly unique to the eyes of Ashkenazi outsiders.

Part III: Adult Education in Early Modern Amsterdam: The Bible Beyond the Schools

In his ethical treatise *Sefer ha-zikhronot* (ca. 1650), the Italian rabbi Samuel Aboab remarked on the challenges of integrating converso New Christians into the Jewish community of Venice, the variety of bridges that needed to be crossed by the prospective neophyte, and the types of institutions that practicing Jews could establish to facilitate this process of transformation:

> And how much more so with our brothers the Children of Israel who come from the lands of the dispersion, who have neither known nor seen the path on which any person who is called by the name of Israel should walk! For these above all require many teachers and exhorters who shall set the truth before them and

115. Marion Aptroot, "Yiddish Bibles in Amsterdam," 44; Chava Turniansky, "La pedagogia dell'insegnamento della Bibbia nell'Europa orientale," 338–39. Following the success of the *Tsene-rene,* its author Yankev ben Yitskhok produced a similar composition on the rest of the books of the Bible, the *Maggid,* which was printed in five editions between 1623 and the end of the seventeenth century.

> teach them the road whereon to tread and the deed to be done... For to tell the truth, there should be in each and every city in Israel a special brotherhood for this purpose, and just as there are brotherhoods for every other holy task, so there should be none lacking for this. And this one is really the cornerstone... And why should there not be a holy brotherhood of scholars to aid in redeeming the souls of their brethren whom the Holy One has drawn up from slavery to freedom, and from anguish to joy?[116]

The need for confraternities led by prominent scholars in the community was essential, in Aboab's view, to introduce New Jews to the principles of Judaism and to God's commandments, including dietary restrictions and the observance of the Sabbath and festivals. Nevertheless, Yosef Hayim Yerushalmi observes that it is not clear whether such an institution was ever established in Venice.[117] In Amsterdam, the case is very different.

Throughout Amsterdam there were numerous confraternities that performed important social and religious services: they provided funds for widows, the sick, the poor, and orphans, they administered the school system and maintained the cemetery, and they prepared the dead for burial. These societies also organized regular meetings for the study of Jewish theological and religious texts, and often focused especially on the Bible. Many New Christian immigrants to Amsterdam arrived as adults, and these societies' educational activities played a key role in their integration into the Jewish community. Study of these confraternities and societies reveals that the biblical orientation of the Portuguese Jewish curriculum was not limited to the confines of the Talmud Torah classrooms. Confraternities were familiar features of the Iberian landscape, and Amsterdam's ex-conversos were certainly familiar with religious and literary societies established in Spain during this period.[118] There may also have been a conscious desire to emulate the societies for religious

116. Yosef Hayim Yerushalmi, *From Spanish Court to Italian Ghetto*, 198–99. See Samuel Aboab, *Sefer ha-zikhronot* (Jerusalem: Ahavat Shalom, 2001), 158. From 1637–1650, Aboab lived in Verona and was a significant rabbi in northern Italy. In 1650 he became the rabbi of the Ponentine Jewish community of Venice and developed a close relationship with Isaac Cardoso.

117. Yosef Hayim Yerushalmi, *From Spanish Court to Italian Ghetto*, 200.

118. Julia Lieberman, "Academias Literarias y de Estudios Religiosos en Amsterdam en el

study founded in Safed by Spanish exiles, at least one of which (*Ba'ale Tesubah*) bears a very similar name to an Amsterdam confraternity.[119]

One of the major sources for studying these confraternities is Daniel Levi de Barrios's *Triumpho del govierno popular* [Triumph of Popular Government; Amsterdam, 1683], which provides a rich description of the institutions' founders, important members, and the activities in which the societies engaged. De Barrios was intimately familiar with the operations of many confraternities, and became a member of the *Gemilut Hasadim* (Society for the Performance of Charitable Acts) in 1677.[120] Two of the most active confraternities in both the educational and charitable spheres were the *Gemilut Hasadim* and the *Honen Dalim*.[121] The *Gemilut Hasadim* was founded in 1639 under the direction of Mosseh Belmonte. The society chose its administrators and board members independently until Belmonte's death in 1648, at which point the communal *Mahamad* invoked its authority to intervene in the affairs of the confraternity. Early in the 1670s, Rabbi Selomoh de Oliveira was appointed the confraternity's spiritual director and instructor. According to de Barrios, the *Gemilut Hasadim* fulfilled two functions, one educational, and the other its responsibilities for burying the dead.[122] Describing the educational activities specifically, de Barrios writes that "In the first four years, it was ordained that the Pentateuch would be discussed... In the next four successive [years], the Sacred History of the supreme poets [i.e., the prophets] was discussed." The ninth year, according to de Barrios, focused on "rabbinic teachings."[123]

Siglo XVII," *Los Judaizantes en Europa y la Literatura Castellana del Siglo de Oro*, ed. Fernando Díaz Esteban (Madrid: Letrúmbo S.L., 1994), 248–51.

119. Julia Lieberman, "Academias Literarias y de Estudios Religiosos en Amsterdam en el Siglo XVII," 251; Gershom Scholem, *Sabbatai Sevi: The Mystical Messiah, 1626–1627* (Princeton, NJ: Princeton University Press, 1973), 518–45.

120. Selomoh de Oliveira, *Sefer Har ha-zeitim* (Amsterdam, 1673–1698), 2:227.

121. Regarding the *Honen Dalim* confraternity, see Julia Lieberman, " 'Jonen Dalim,' Auto Alegórico de Miguel (Daniel Leví) de Barrios," in *From Iberia to Diaspora: Studies in Sephardic History and Culture*, ed. Yedida K. Stillman and Norman Stillman (Leiden and Boston: Brill, 1999), 300–315.

122. Daniel Levi de Barrios, *Triumpho del govierno popular*, 205. See also Kenneth Scholberg, "Miguel de Barrios and the Amsterdam Sephardic Community," 133–34.

123. Daniel Levi de Barrios, *Triumpho del govierno popular*, 220.

This combination of educational and charitable activities is also evident in the *Honen Dalim* confraternity. The *Honen Dalim* was founded in 1667 by a faction of dissatisfied members of the *Temime Dareh* (*Los perfectos de Carrera*; The Perfect of the Way), a mutual aid society established two years earlier to provide medical services to sick members of the confraternity, as well as burial services and rites.[124] The new *Honen Dalim* confraternity likewise provided assistance to members in distress, and distributed bread each week to their widows. The spiritual leader of the confraternity was enjoined to offer prayers for the deceased in the month and year after their passing. The religious and pedagogic needs of the confraternity were first administered by the *Haham* Josiahu Pardo. However, Pardo left Amsterdam in 1674 to become rabbi of Willemstad in Curaçao, and Selomoh de Oliveira assumed responsibilities for religious instruction and guidance of the society.[125] Like the *Gemilut Hasadim*, the *Honen Dalim* also incorporated frequent educational meetings into its regular activities. According to de Barrios, "On the first day [Sunday], they meditate upon some faithful commentator upon the Bible with the opinion that occurs to the reader, and the difficulties that he reconciles."[126] Thus, according to Daniel Levi de Barrios, confraternities established to provide essential, charitable services such as provisioning the poor and caring for the deceased also served vital educational roles in the community. As de Barrios testifies, under Oliveira's guidance and supervision, over the course of three decades the membership of these societies received a thorough and systematic grounding in texts from throughout the biblical corpus, though admittedly very little (and belated) instruction in rabbinics.

These descriptions of the *Gemilut Hasadim* and *Honen Dalim* confraternities give the impression that their educational activities focused predominantly on biblical studies. The depth of biblical engagement

124. Daniel Levi de Barrios, *Triumpho del govierno popular*, 265–66., and Kenneth Scholberg, "Miguel de Barrios and the Amsterdam Sephardic Community," 135–36.

125. Daniel Levi de Barrios, *Triumpho del govierno popular*, 265–66, and Kenneth Scholberg, "Miguel de Barrios and the Amsterdam Sephardic Community," 135–36.

126. Daniel Levi de Barrios, *Triumpho del govierno popular*, 265–66. "En el dia primeiro se discurre sobre algun fiel Comento de la Biblia: con el concepto que al Letor ocurre, y las dificultades que concilia."

within these communities is reinforced by a number of different types of sources, including the burial society's statutes themselves. The very first ordinance of the confraternity in 1660 – before any mention is made of its ostensible charitable purpose – emphasized that "each day during the week a Torah portion, Prophets, and Psalms will be taught (*semeldara*)... and on the Sabbath [there should be] debates about the weekly Torah portion – something that should be avoided as much as possible during the week."[127] Inventories of the *Gemilut Hasadim* library reveal that the society was more than capable of supporting this type of study among its membership. A book list from 1668 reveals the presence on its shelves of: two large format editions of the *Mikra Gedolah* printed by Johannes Buxtorf in Basel; four volumes of the Hebrew Bible with the Aramaic translation of the Bible and Rashi printed in Venice; fourteen Hebrew liturgical Bibles with Torah; eleven Bibles produced by Menasseh ben Israel in Amsterdam; and an eclectic assortment of other Bibles.[128] This would almost certainly have been sufficient to supply Bibles to each of the eleven members who attended Bible study sessions in the two confraternities in 1673–1674, when the Bible study sessions were first organized. In this fashion, under Oliveira's guidance and supervision members of the confraternities – including prominent figures like Daniel Levi de Barrios himself, and future leading rabbis such as David Nunes de Torres – regularly met to study, discuss, and debate Scripture.[129]

The most detailed documentation about the Jewish approach to Bible study in these societies that we possess comes from the notes that

127. GAS 334 1191 Fol. 3. On the significance of "meldar" a Judeo-Spanish word likely of Greek origin that pertains to activities related to the study of religious texts, contemplation, and prayer, see David M. Bunis, "Judezmo: The Jewish Language of the Ottoman Sephardim," *European Judaism: A Journal for the New Europe*, 44, no. 1 (Spring 2011): 22–35.

128. GAS 334 1191 Fol. 7

129. Lists of the membership in the *Honen Dalim* and *Gemilut Hasadim* confraternities are preserved in Oliveira's notes on the Bible study meetings, *Sefer har ha-zetim* (mss., 3 vol.) EH 47B 12–14. In 1673–1674, when Selomoh de Oliveira took leadership of both confraternities, there were eleven participants between the two groups. The membership rolls list additional individuals who joined in subsequent years, but not whether any existing members left the organizations or not. It is thus difficult to get an accurate sense of total membership at any given point.

Selomoh de Oliveira made regarding the educational meetings that took place at both confraternities. Oliveira served as the spiritual guide for both societies for a period of twenty-five years, between 1674 and 1698. He documented the topics and texts discussed at these sessions in his *Sefer har ha-zeitim* [Book of the Mount of Olives], a collection of the "questions and doubts and their resolutions and solutions [discussed] in the academy of the *Gemilut Hasadim* and also [those] of the *Honen Dalim* upon the Torah and on the Prophets and the Writings from one Shabbat to the other, and on the occasion of Holy days."[130] The importance of biblical study in the curriculum of Oliveira's societies is evident from the outset. On the title page of his collected notes, Oliveira gives a succinct breakdown of the time spent studying different Jewish texts: "And this is the performance of the work [*ma'ase ha-melaha*]: four years on the five books of the Torah; four years on the early prophets; one year on the teachings of the sages; four years on the later prophets; four years on the Writings and the Five Scrolls."[131] This confirms what de Barrios wrote about the confraternities, and underscores the dominant place of the Bible in the curriculum of their educational activities. The biblical orientation is also evident in the summary of Oliveira's introductory remarks that he delivered at the *Gemilut Hasadim* confraternity shortly after taking responsibility for its educational and spiritual activities. He writes that,

> First, the matter of the purpose of our gathering that we have agreed upon: to propose a question or proposition on every Sabbath of rest and to expound upon it, each according to his ability after studying. And in this manner, each discourse will be explored thoroughly in the five books of the Torah (and after this on the remaining of the twenty-four books [of Scripture]).[132]

130. Selomoh de Oliveira, *Sefer har ha-zeitim*, vol. 1 [title page and introduction; unpaginated] (Amsterdam, 1673–1698). Mss EH 97B 12–14.
131. Selomoh de Oliveira, *Sefer har ha-zeitim*, vol. 1 [title page and introduction; unpaginated].
132. Selomoh de Oliveira, *Sefer har ha-zeitim*, vol. 1 [title page and introduction; unpaginated].

Oliveira offered a prayer for the success of this curriculum and the meetings, and then told the members that "The first exploration on this Sabbath in order is *Ki Tetzei la-milḥamah* [When you take the field against your enemies], and we shall go to the battle for the Torah."[133] Oliveira also records that he systematically and comprehensively taught all canonical books of Jewish Scripture: "Beginning in the year 5434 [1674] with *parashat* [*Ki*] *Tetzei* until this year 5451 [1691] and *parashat Shoftim*, with which we completed all of the twenty-four Holy Books . . . and this was in the *Gemilut Hasadim* yeshivah, and there were in seventeen years 1,390 questions, including those of the *Honen Dalim*." Direct study of Scripture was not the only focus of Oliveira's teachings. Oliveira writes that "there are also included in them [the questions] the interpretation and exploration of the teachings of the rabbis." Talmudic and midrashic exegesis was sometimes used to understand biblical verses, and occasionally Oliveira attempted to study rabbinic literature systematically with the members of his confraternities. He also kept notes on their study of *Pirkei Avot*, the Passover Haggadah, and the prayerbook. Nevertheless, Oliveira's description of the amount of time spent studying Bible and rabbinic literature illustrates the centrality of the Bible in the educational activities of the *Gemilut Hasadim* and *Honen Dalim* societies.[134]

The focus on biblical studies at the *Gemilut Hasadim* and *Honen Dalim* confraternities was typical for other charitable societies, including the *Maskil el Dal*. The original "Enlightener of the Poor" society was founded in 1673 by its spiritual director, Rabbi Daniel Bellilos.[135] The confraternity provided needy members with medicine and food in the event of illness, and made arrangements for its members' funerals.

133. Selomoh de Oliveira, *Sefer har ha-zeitim*, vol. 1 [title page and introduction; unpaginated].
134. Selomoh de Oliveira, *Sefer har ha-zeitim*, vol. 1 [title page and introduction; unpaginated].
135. Daniel Levi de Barrios, *Triumpho del govierno popular*, 282–84. See also Kenneth Scholberg's discussion in "Miguel Levi de Barrios and the Amsterdam Sephardic Community," 136–38. The original *Maskil el Dal* society split into two separate factions for unspecified reasons in 1681. De Barrios says that he tried to reconcile the parties but was unsuccessful.

Members of the confraternity would accompany the coffin to its resting place, and the head of the confraternity, Daniel Belillos, would lead services. The treasurer would also name ten men to recite prayers on behalf of the deceased. In addition to caring for its own indigent members, some of the funds collected from members were used to support destitute Jewish refugees from Poland-Lithuania who arrived in significant numbers during the middle and late decades of the seventeenth century.[136] According to de Barrios, the confraternity was comprised of thirty members initially, and grew to include more than 275, including 125 men and 150 women.[137] In addition to the charitable work that many of these supported and performed, confraternity members also had the opportunity to sharpen their understanding of biblical texts: de Barrios writes that Portuguese Jews should "applaud and praise the political and charitable governors, the noble guardians of the sick," as well as "the studious who meditate upon the Sacred Letters and respond to the propositions."[138] De Barrios also leaves a tantalizing but cryptic clue as to the specific texts studied in the confraternity. He writes that the confraternity pays the salary of the rabbi and director, "the *Preceptor* who teaches the Holy Law on pages from the *impressa planta*," possibly alluding to the Plantin printing press.[139] In addition to the famous Antwerp polyglot Bible, during the last three decades of the sixteenth century Christophe Plantin printed numerous complete

136. Kenneth Scholberg, "Miguel Levi de Barrios and the Amsterdam Sephardic Community," 138. Regarding the overall relationship between the Portuguese Jews and Ashkenazi refugees and immigrants, see Yosef Kaplan, "Amsterdam and the Ashkenazi Migration in the Seventeenth Century," in *An Alternative Path to Modernity: The Sephardi Diaspora in Western Europe*, ed. Yosef Kaplan (Leiden and Boston: Brill, 2000), 78–107.

137. Daniel Levi de Barrios, *Triumpho del govierno popular*, 287. See also Kenneth Scholberg, "Miguel Levi de Barrios and the Amsterdam Sephardic Community," 137. Scholberg emphasizes that Barrios lists as members relatives of his who had never lived in Amsterdam, and that the list probably reflects the number of people for whom memorial prayers were recited regularly.

138. Daniel Levi de Barrios, *Triumpho del govierno popular*, 291. "Aplaude y bendice al Govierno Politico y Caritativo, a los nobles Curadores de sus enfermos, y a los estudiosos que meditan en las sacras letras y responden a las Proposiciones."

139. Daniel Levi de Barrios, *Triumpho del govierno popular*, 284–85. "Senala tres salarios, el primeiro al Ros, o Preceptor que a la Ley santa ensena en hojas de la impressa planta."

Hebrew Bibles, with and without vowels, as well as individual editions of the Pentateuch, Psalms, and Prophets in Hebrew.[140] The evidence does not enable identification of the specific version of the Plantin Bible that might have been read in this confraternity, but it is intriguing that Daniel Belillos appears to have preferred biblical texts from this famous printing house to Spanish, Portuguese, and Hebrew Bibles printed by members of the Jewish community in Amsterdam. We know that in other contexts, some Portuguese Jewish readers of the Bible turned to Christian editions of the Old Testament when they were unsatisfied with the difficult language and strange linguistic features of the Ferrara Bible, and it may be the case that a similar dissatisfaction was present among members of this confraternity as well.[141]

Confraternities in Amsterdam also provided opportunities for children, as well as adults, to supplement their biblical education. The *Abi Yetomim* ("Father of Orphans") society, for instance, was founded in 1643. The original members apparently broke apart from the *Gemilut Hasadim* confraternity for burial of the dead, and established a separate society.[142] According to de Barrios's description, "This charitable confraternity supports the orphan for three years with such skill that it gives him the Law, through which he lives, and each year it gives him clothes . . . and if he falls ill, it will request a compassionate cure, and at the end he leaves with the trade that he wishes, and if he desires he may receive another three years of education."[143] Members of the *Abi Yetomim* society viewed

140. Leon Voet, *The Plantin Press (1555–1589): A Bibliography of the Works Printed and Published by Christopher Plantin at Antwerp and Leiden*, 6 vols. (Amsterdam: Van Hoeve, 1980), 323ff. See also Leon Voet, *The Golden Compasses: A History and Evaluation of the Printing and Publishing Activities of the Officina Plantiana at Antwerp*, 2 vols. (Amsterdam: Vangendt, 1969–1972). See also Marvin Heller, *The Sixteenth Century Hebrew Book: An Abridged Thesaurus* (Boston and Leiden: Brill, 2004), xxxiii. Plantin printed the *Biblia Hebraica* (1566) in multiple formats.

141. Yaacob Yehudah Leon, *Kadosh Hallulim: Las Alabanças de Santidad*, "Al Pio Lector." See also the discussions in Harm den Boer, *La literatura sefardi de Amsterdam*, 39–40.

142. Daniel Levi de Barrios, *Triumpho del govierno popular*, 186–87.

143. Daniel Levi de Barrios, *Triumpho del govierno popular*, 183. "Sustenta esta Hermandad caritativa, al Huerfano tres anos con tal arte, que le da Ley, porque con ella viva, y cada ano un vestido le reparte, mantienele, y si enferma; compasiva curarlo solicita, y al fin parte con oficio que elige, y si se queda, otros tres anos de doctrina hereda."

Bible study as being especially important for the children: "the orphans who are fed at the breasts of the Sacred Confraternity with the milk... of the Mosaic Law" are raised in order to possess deep knowledge of the teachings of Sacred Letters.[144]

As much as Portuguese Jews – children and adults alike – were immersed in the study of Scripture in schools and confraternities, perhaps no setting provided more regular contact with the Bible and its interpretation than the weekly sermons heard in synagogue. Members of the Portuguese Jewish community had an apparently voracious appetite for preaching. Its rabbis gave sermons regularly on Sabbaths as a matter of course, and on special occasions such as important weddings and funerals, anniversaries commemorating the establishment of communal institutions, and the arrival of visiting dignitaries. Menasseh ben Israel is said to have delivered 450 sermons during a twenty-five-year period of his career, although these have been lost to posterity. Saul Levi Morteira gave weekly sermons in Amsterdam over the course of his four-decade career as one of the most prominent rabbis in the community, between his arrival in 1616 and his death in 1660. Over five hundred of Morteira's sermons survive in manuscript format, although his contemporaries allude to a manuscript collection of well over one thousand manuscript sermons already in 1645. Morteira's reputation as a superior preacher was well established by this point, and was underscored by the decision of Moses ben Benjamin Belmonte and Benjamin ben Jacob Dias Fatto to publish a collection of fifty Morteira sermons under the title of *Givat Sha'ul* (Amsterdam, 1645).[145] The esteem in which Morteira was held by the community – as a rabbi, scholar, and preacher – is perhaps best exemplified by the place that this collection of Morteira's sermons found in the community's library. Over the course of Morteira's lifetime, the community amassed a collection of several hundred books for the use of students, scholars, and educated members of the community. This

144. Daniel Levi de Barrios, *Triumpho del govierno popular*, 187. "...los Huerfanos que a los pechos de la Sacra Hermandad alimentandose con el laeteo licor de la Ley Mosayca se criaron con elegencia para los Sermones, y con el Divino Temor para la inteligencia, y ensenanca de las Sagradas letras."

145. Marc Saperstein, *Jewish Preaching, 1200–1800: An Anthology* (New Haven, CT: Yale University Press, 1989), 6.

collection was ultimately housed in a dedicated building, with communally appointed caretakers who employed a double-ledger accounting system to keep track of circulation. The library contained a thorough – if not comprehensive – catalogue of the most famous and enduring classics of rabbinic and medieval Jewish literature. Intriguingly, however, the considerable scholarly and literary products of Amsterdam's own rabbis are almost entirely absent from this collection. *Givat Sha'ul*, however, appears in an inventory of the Portuguese Jewish community's library entered into the communal record books in 1665. It is one of only *two* books by Amsterdam's religious scholars that I have positively identified.[146] Morteira, and his sermons, clearly mattered to the members of this community.

Sermons were a powerful and dynamic platform for Morteira, as one of the leading religious figures in the Portuguese Jewish community. They were an essential tool for educating his congregants, especially those who arrived in Amsterdam as adults and had not been educated in Judaism as children. In his sermons Morteira could shape their understanding of key Jewish concepts, beliefs, and practices; he could address contentious intellectual and religious issues in the community; and he could guide their understanding of the past, present, and future. Occasionally, they provided a platform for rebuke and chastisement. Overall, sermons were a vital tool for helping his congregants navigate the dangerous, and intellectually complicated, shift from Catholic life in Spain and Portugal to Jewish life in the northern Low Countries. A critical component of this geographic and religious reorientation was learning to think about the Bible in new ways, and from a very different perspective.

Looking closely at Morteira's sermon "Do Not Add to His Words" – delivered in Amsterdam around 1630 – illustrates how sermons provided Morteira with an ideal platform for helping his congregants transition from a Christian to a Jewish view of Scripture – and the centrality of the Hebrew Bible in their new identity as Jews.[147]

146. GAS 334 1051 Fol. 43b. Benjamin Fisher, "From Boxes and Cabinets to the Bibliotheca," 43–76.

147. Saperstein, *Exile in Amsterdam*, 408–29.

Morteira's sermon addressed two key verses that had great significance in the ex-converso mentalité: "You must not add to what I command you or take away from it, but keep the commandments of the Lord your God that I enjoin upon you (Deut 4:2)"; and the repetition of this injunction in Deuteronomy 13:1: "All that I command you, that you shall be careful to observe; you must not add to it or take away from it." Morteira addresses two questions – differing in importance – connected with these two verses. First, he considers the order in which the commandments are given in both verses – why the instruction not to add is given prior to the instruction not to take away. Morteira sees the solution to this question as being relatively straightforward, and so dispenses with it quickly: additions to and tampering with the Bible would eventually lead to a blurring of distinctions between those sections that were "original," and those that had been created later, creating a situation where ultimately the entirety of the Bible is regarded as belonging to the latter category of man-made law. The act of adding to the law thus implicitly leads to its diminution.[148] Yet if this were the endpoint that Morteira envisioned for his sermon, the congregants would not have had to sit still for very long. Morteira had larger goals in mind when he delivered these remarks: proving the superior status of Judaism versus Christianity.

"What greater comfort and joy can there be for a seafarer," Morteira declared, "than to know that his ship is strong and will not break, and that the captain is beyond compare in expertise. The same is true for us in knowing that the Torah, the lamp for our feet and the light for our path, is eternal and perfect, leaving nothing to be added to it or taken away, knowing also that all that the gentiles have concocted is external to it." Morteira's deeper goal on this occasion was to confront the way in which many people – Christians – allegedly *did* add to the text and legal content of Scripture, in flagrant ways from his perspective. Many ex-conversos among Morteira's audience had been raised in a culture that – from the Jewish perspective – was predicated on this type of manipulation of Scripture. Acculturating to a Jewish perspective on the Bible required that this question be dealt with directly. Drawing

148. Saperstein, *Exile in Amsterdam*, 408–13.

on an unnamed Christian text – possibly, though not definitively, by the French preacher Jean Pierre Camus – Morteira attacks several core theological values of Catholicism.[149] He assails "four things [that] were changed when their [Christian] Messiah came." Specifically, Morteira inveighs against the Christian antipathy toward wealth and valorization of poverty, the priorization of chastity and "childlessness" in Christianity, and an overzealous desire for martyrdom that he saw as a characteristic of Christian society and belief. Morteira also targets what he sees as a blanket prohibition against hatred of others within Christianity: "You have heard that it was said, 'Love your neighbor and hate your enemy.' But I tell you, love your enemies and pray for those who persecute you." (Matthew 5: 43–44). In Morteira's thought it is entirely appropriate to vent hatred at the enemies of God.[150] These "ideals newly introduced" – in Morteira's view – were not just erroneous theological positions but deliberate, harmful additions to the Bible – God's Word – that were "external to it," and therefore detracting from it, threatening the integrity of the whole.[151] Morteira also saw some of these perspectives as simply impractical. Carried to its logical end, for example, the fetish for poverty will lead to the breakdown of organized society as all eschew their money and possessions. A wide adoption of celibacy would lead to a genealogical death spiral; and the extreme humility described in Matthew will lead quickly to defeat by one's enemies. Lust for martyrdom will lead to a religious community of corpses. These, Morteira argues, are not beliefs that can be practical – they are truly impossible. Furthermore, unlike the "crown of Torah" – the observance of Judaism, which Morteira sees as being "accessible to all who will take of it – " these commandments can only apply to or be fulfilled by a tiny minority of the Christian population. Because these interpretations cannot apply to all individuals

149. Saperstein, *Exile in Amsterdam*, 409.
150. Saperstein, *Exile in Amsterdam*, 422. Morteira's hostility toward Christianity, as expressed in this relatively early sermon, is typical of the rabbi's early negative perspective. Later in life, he adopted a much more nuanced and often conciliatory posture toward Christian beliefs and interpretations – as seen in this passage about hatred of others. The changing perspective on Christianity is explored in depth below, in Chapter 4.
151. Saperstein, *Exile in Amsterdam*, 426.

they cannot – according to Morteira – be the foundation of anything universal or anything resembling spiritual perfection.[152]

Returning to the original verses that prompted the sermon in the first place: "*you must not add to it or take away from it* (Deut 13:1), Morteira draws attention to the fact that the commandment is given in the first person singular, "you." This indicates both that the individual is obliged to observe the entire set of commandments that have been given, and also that this body of laws is sufficient for every person to attain perfection. There is no need to add new laws or rescind existing ones – much less to suggest that "there are some other commandments and character traits that are on a higher level than those that God commanded." The solution that Morteira offers his congregants is a Jewish Bible as a replacement for the Christian Bible, a Jewish Bible that is perfect, and "cannot be diminished or supplanted."[153]

Sermons took place in additional settings as well, beyond the environment of Sabbath addresses. The statutes created to govern the community in 1639 shed light on this. Paragraph #22 of the statutes describes the responsibilities of different rabbis in the community, and stipulates that Isaac Aboab da Fonseca was responsible for providing grammar and introductory Talmud lessons to children, as well as for giving sermons "at night" in the religious academy.[154] Daniel Levi de Barrios's description of Aboab's contributions to the community clarifies the nature of these "*derasiot*." After describing Aboab's arrival in the community as a child after fleeing Portugal with his family, de Barrios writes that "he preached upon the Prophet Isaiah on winter nights to the great praise of the three Israelite congregations in Amsterdam."[155] The fact that de Barrios speaks about the three separate congregations at this time indicates that Aboab was providing winter sermons well before the unification of the community, and the statutes of 1639 indicate that these activities went on

152. Saperstein, *Exile in Amsterdam*, 423–24.
153. Saperstein, *Exile in Amsterdam*, 428–29.
154. GAS 334 1052 Fol. 23a. "Meldasse emsima no corpo da esnoga, despois de arbit e daras q[ue] se custuma fazer no ynverno."
155. Daniel Levi de Barrios, *Triumpho del govierno popular*, 80–81. "Y p[r]edico en las noches de invierno sobre el Profeta Esaias con general aplauso de las tres congregaciones Israeliticas de Amsterdam."

afterward as well. Throughout the seventeenth century, the Portuguese Jewish community's officials went out of their way to organize sermons on biblical topics at different times throughout the year as an edifying form of leisure and diversion.

The maintenance of the "winter lecture series" played an important role in both adult education and in the training of advanced students to become preachers. Members of the community benefited from the edifying sermons that they heard, many of which were given by students supported by communal resources; and the students themselves received valuable training in the composition and delivery of public presentations. The practice of delivering winter sermons continued during the 1640s and the 1650s, and are mentioned obliquely in a 1642 entry to the communal record books describing the decision to create a communal yeshivah. The text states that the academy will be located in the classroom used by Rabbi Joseph de Faro for his lower-level class of students, and that the religious school will offer lessons "upstairs in the body of the synagogue, after the evening prayers and the sermon that is customarily given in the winter."[156] Two leading rabbis in particular appear to have been involved in organizing the lecture series on biblical texts and themes, both in the winter and at other times during the year: Saul Levi Morteira and Moshe Raphael d'Aguilar. A 1653 entry in the communal record books describes a meeting during which the governors of the Talmud Torah gave instructions for the organization of these educational activities: "On the 20th of Heshvan the *senores* of the *Mahamad* assembled together with the parnassim of the T[almud] T[orah],

> discoursing upon how to train the *ba'alei Torah* [Torah students] in the academy of the *senor H[akham]* Saul Levi Morteira. It appeared appropriate to them to begin with the sermons that they are accustomed to deliver [lit. say] on winter nights in this holy congregation, which was approved by everyone unanimously."[157]

156. GAS 334 1052 Fol. 23a. "Meldasse emsima no corpo da esnoga, despois de arbit e daras q[ue] se custuma fazer no ynverno."
157. GAS 334 1052 Fol. 15b. "Em 20 de Hesuan se juntaraõ os senores do mahamad com os parnassim de T:T discursando sobre que para exercitar os baale thora do midras

The communal governors also laid out specific requirements for the schedule of these sermons:

> They agreed to pass this ordinance . . . through which they resolved that all of the individuals who . . . enjoy the apportionment of the stipend must give their sermon on the night that is his turn. And if for a satisfactory reason one of them is absent on his scheduled night, he who is next in order must go in his place. And he who wishes to be exempted from this virtuous exercise that results so much in his betterment, shall be excluded from the [stipend] apportionment.[158]

Although sermons fulfilled an important leisure function during Amsterdam's long winter nights, the communal governors also organized public lectures during other parts of the year. More than a decade after asking Morteira to assign his students the task of giving sermons on winter nights, communal officials approached Moshe Raphael d'Aguilar with a similar request. In Aguilar's miscellanious collection of manuscripts, he writes that

> In the year 5425 [1665] the *senores* parnassim of the T[almud] T[orah] ordered that my students practice deciding in public a question or difficulty of the weekly Torah reading on Sabbath afternoons of the summer, in the form of a debate, and this followed in the following manner. On the *Parashah* of *Shelaḥ Lekha*, which is the third [*sic*] of Numbers, three students began, and the first spoke in the following manner.[159]

dosenor H: Saul Leuj morteira. Lhes parecia conuiniente empiesalos nos darasiot que se custumaõ dizer as noites de jnverno neste K:K o qual aprouado por todos unanimamente."

158. GAS 334 1052 Fol. 15b. "Acordarao fazer este termo . . . resoluerаõ q[ue] todos os sujeitos que forem admitidos a este exercicio eque gozaõ da repartisaõ da espaca ajaõ de fazer seo daras anoite que lhe tocca por giro, e se por causa sufesiente algun delles faltare a este acto, sua ves, aja de seguir em seu lugar oque lhe segue por seu turno. Eo que se quiser eximir de taõ virtuoso exercicio e que redunda tanto em seo melhoramente se va excluido de repartisaõ."

159. This comment appears alongside numerous examples of the sermons that Aguilar's students gave during the summer months of 1665. See EH (Ets Haim) 48 A 11. "No ano

This custom of organizing a regular series of sermons by advanced students is emphasized in the communal record books, by Morteira in the 1650s, and by Daniel Levi de Barrios in the early 1680s. However, from the remarks of one of Aguilar's students, it appears as though the custom fell into disuse at some point between 1653, when Morteira organized the sermons, and 1665, when the officials approached Aguilar and his class. The anonymous student who presented the first sermon of this year remarked that

> After several years that this exercise was absent from this Sacred Place, it appeared good to the *Senores* parnassim of the T[almud] T[orah], with the permission of the officials of the *Mahamad* and the approval of the *senhor Hakham* [Aguilar] to return it and instate [it]: and thus, we having been selected [*havendonos tocado*] to begin this first turn, we give an introduction [*exordio*], hoping that the holy congregation will be very grateful to see the splendour and to gather here the fruit of this, their *ets haim*, the tree of life, from the Law that is taught in the *midrash* of the *senor*, my *h[akham]* [Moshe Raphael d'Aguilar].[160]

One last, salient point about preaching in the Portuguese Jewish community deserves to be emphasized: its members *enjoyed* listening to sermons. They were seen as religiously and culturally edifying, and pedagogically important, but they appear above all to have been an

5425 ordenarao os Senores Parnassim de T.T. que os meus discipulos se exercitasem nas tardes de Sabat do verao en dicidir en publico hua questao ou dificuldade da Parasa en forma de coloquio e seguio o dito anno na forma seguinte . . . Na Parasa Selah Leha que he a terceira de Numeros comesarao tres discipulos, e falou o primeyro na forma seguinte a saber." These documents are preserved in a collection of diverse texts, which include Aguilar's *Tratado da immortalidade da alma* and his *Tratado de la retórica divide en ocho libros que cology de los megores autores griegos y latinos*. Aguilar's comment appears in Fol. 437, and the sermons continue through Fol. 481.

160. EH 48 A 11. "Despois de alguns anos que faltou este exercicio neste Lugar Sagrado pareceo bem aos Senores Parnassim de T.T. con licensia dos Senores do Mahamad e aprouacao do Senhor H. tornalo a introdusir: e assi havendonos tocado anos o comencar este primeyro giro daremos exordio, esperando sera muy grato do Santo K over luzimento, e colher aqui o fruto deste seu ets haim [Hebrew] aruore de vidas da Ley que se ensina no medras do senor meu H."

activity that was a source of diversion and pleasure that one could look forward to; a way of filling time that might otherwise be unprofitably wasted. The demand for preaching in Amsterdam was such that lay and rabbinic figures sought further opportunities and occasions for sermons *beyond* the already considerable preaching the community's rabbis performed regularly on Sabbaths. These sermons constitute an additional, important context in which Amsterdam's Jews encountered and engaged with Scripture, and became New Jews.

Conclusion

The Bible-centered educational culture of Amsterdam's Portuguese Jewish community was highly unusual in the world of early modern Judaism. The cultural and political ramifications that this approach to Jewish education could have can be seen through the lens of a traditionally trained rabbinic scholar whose values were widely shared across the Jewish world. Rabbi Jacob Sasportas (1610–1698) was born in Oran, Morocco in 1610 to a prominent family of diplomats, government administrators, and scholars. Distantly descended from the famous medieval rabbi Moses Naḥmanides, the family moved from Spain to Morocco in the late fourteenth century. Sasportas has been described as an unimpeachably traditional rabbi who regarded the rabbinate, rabbinic literature, and Jewish law as the central and all-encompassing focus of Jewish life, belief, and behavior. Sasportas distinguished himself in religious studies as a child, apparently becoming a member of the rabbinical court at Tlemcen at the age of eighteen, and the chief judge of this court only five years later. Forced abroad by financial scandals and judicial problems, Sasportas led a distinguished – but quintessentially itinerant – life that would take him across the Mediterranean and European worlds. These travels led him to spend significant time living and working in important centers of ex-converso life across southern and western Europe: he lived in Amsterdam beween 1650/51–1659, London in 1664–1665, Hamburg from 1665–1673, Amsterdam again between 1673–1678, and Livorno from 1678–1680, before returning to Amsterdam yet again, where he would remain until his death in 1693.[161]

161. Matt Goldish, "Hakham Jacob Sasportas and the Former Conversos," *Studia Rosenthaliana* 44 (2012): 149–72.

Sasportas was thus perhaps uniquely positioned to comment upon the religious culture of the ex-conversos as a group. And, his perspective was critical: he believed that the ex-conversos had a "halakhic problem," a flippant, selective, and lackadaisical attitude toward the rigorous and all-encompassing observance of Jewish religious law. "Sasportas' world," as Matt Goldish has observed, "was one in which the Talmud and its teachers were venerated."[162] Many in the ex-converso communities that Sasportas encountered had been raised as Christians with – at best – only hazy ideas about the Talmud and rabbinic law, and with a deeply engrained and well-developed antipathy toward ecclesiastic authorities. At numerous junctures in his travels, Sasportas found himself in conflict with ex-converso communities and individuals who, in his estimation, did not take the observance of Jewish religious law and its rabbinic interpreters with sufficient gravitas. From London, to Livorno, to Hamburg and Amsterdam, Sasportas repeatedly clashed with ex-converso communities whose attitudes toward the Talmud and rabbinic authority differed starkly from his own. In Livorno, Sasportas encountered a community where the lay leaders utterly disregarded the relevance of Jewish religious law in the economic sphere, confining rabbinic authority to cases of personal and family matters, and he met many ex-conversos who disregarded the laws of the Sabbath in the service of their business dealings. Of these individuals, Sasportas remarked that, "It might almost be said of them that they know their Master and rebel against him intentionally." When the crisis over the messianic movement of Shabbetai Zevi erupted in 1665, leading many of Zevi's followers to violate and abandon core elements of Jewish law, Sasportas saw the entire movement as part of a rebellion against Jewish law, and singled out a number of prominent Amsterdam ex-conversos for severe criticism.[163]

Modern historians, too, have long observed that Amsterdam's ex-conversos had a problem with halakhah. There was a tremendous degree of laxity with respect to Jewish observance and law within the Portuguese Jewish community, far more, apparently, than in traditional Jewish communities across Europe at this time. Amsterdam has long been

162. Matt Goldish, "Hakham Jacob Sasportas and the Former Conversos," 162.
163. Matt Goldish, "Hakham Jacob Sasportas and the Former Conversos," 160–64.

recognized as a hotbed of heterodox thinking, and for being the petri dish that allowed Uriel da Costa, Juan de Prado, and Spinoza to become some of the most famous Jewish heretics of the early modern period. But the problem extended well beyond these extreme manifestations. It encompassed a much wider swath of the Portuguese of the *nacão* who lived deliberately on the margins of the community, with no desire to affiliate strongly with the city's Jewish infrastructure. In fact, the ex-converso problem with halakhah colored the very nature of the "rabbinic Judaism" practiced by the Spanish and Portuguese Jews in Amsterdam, giving it a highly unique hue. Outwardly, the Portuguese Jewish community appeared very much aligned with the broader Jewish world of the time period with regard to religious observance. They accepted the framework of rabbinic Judaism and openly embraced the "faith of the sages," and the *Mahamad* recognized rabbinic authority in all explicitly religious matters. But beneath the surface, major differences lurked.

In Amsterdam, religious law was often neglected. Among the merchants who governed the community there was no appetite for enforcing the strictures of Jewish law over economic activities, and there are virtually no religious regulations on economic practices in the communal ordinances of the period. Strict religious observance was increasingly limited to the Sabbath, holidays, and synagogue. Unlike Jews in many other communities, it was common in Amsterdam to regard Judaism as a religion, but not an all-encompassing way of life. The ex-converso practice of Judaism in Amsterdam, and in other centers, was thus dramatically different from that found in traditional centers across the Jewish world.[164]

The educational practices of Amsterdam's Portuguese Jewish community may have helped foster and perpetuate the problem of halakhic laxity and disregard for the all-encompassing authority of Jewish law and its interpreters. As we have seen in this chapter, the Portuguese Jews created an educational system that centered the Bible to a degree that was without parallel in the Jewish world. For many adults, the Bible remained a central motif of cultural life and study in confraternity

164. Yosef Kaplan, "Bom Judesmo: The Western Sephardi Diaspora," in *Cultures of the Jews: A New History*, ed. David Biale (New York: Schocken Books, 2002), 644–58.

settings. The reticence of some ex-conversos to accept rabbinic authority and to live their lives according to rabbinic law was not only rooted in the experience of living in Catholic Spain and Portugal, and in the biblical mentalité of the conversos; in addition, it was reinforced and – crucially – also perpetuated by an educational system that relegated the formal study of the Talmud and core halakhic texts to an advanced stage of the school system that many students would never reach. While it perhaps makes sense that the early ex-conversos focused particularly on the Bible as the embodiment of Judaism, there is no reason – in theory – why this had to be the default perspective for successive generations, and for members of the community who never knew life in Spain and Portugal. An educational emphasis on Jewish law was theoretically an option for the community, but it was one that the leaders and educators by and large did not take.

The consequences of these educational decisions can be appreciated by reflecting on Jewish approaches to education from a far different time and place. Although Shaul Stampfer's study of Jewish education, social stratification, and authority focuses on Jewish society in eastern Europe in the nineteenth century, his sociological and social historical insights are revealing, and may help us understand the problem of halakhic laxity in Amsterdam in new ways.[165] As Stampfer has observed, "schools have many functions beyond the transmission of knowledge and training in skills." Education also played an integral role in the construction of socio-political hierarchies based on knowledge and expertise, positioning those who excelled in these fields at the top of the mountain. The authority of rabbis was based on their acknowledged expertise in a field of legal and traditional knowledge that others lacked, but – crucially – *respected*, in part because of their partial, if unsuccessful experience with the same curriculum. "Failure in Talmud study," Stampfer concludes, "could ultimately contribute to rabbinic authority."[166] In Amsterdam,

165. Shaul Stampfer, "Heder Study, Knowledge of Torah, and the Maintenance of Social Stratification," in *Families, Rabbis, and Education: Traditional Jewish Society in Nineteenth-Century Europe*, ed. Shaul Stampfer (Oxford: The Littman Library of Jewish Civilization, 2010), 145–66.

166. Shaul Stampfer, "Heder Study, Knowledge of Torah, and the Maintenance of Social Stratification," 164.

many students never began to study Talmud and halakhah formally, and thus could not develop this type of appreciation, and especially respect, for the authority of those who mastered this knowledge. It may be that the disjuncture between the curriculum of the advanced academies, and that of the lower levels of the Talmud Torah, was in part responsible for the disregard for halakhic strictures that rabbis like Sasportas sensed, and encountered, in the communities of the Western Sephardi diaspora.

TWO

Centering the Bible in Jewish Theology: Salvation and Scripture

IF A SEVENTEENTH-CENTURY READER PERSEVERED THROUGH THE long and difficult biblical contradictions that Menasseh ben Israel examines in the first volume of his *Conciliador* (Amsterdam, 1632), he or she would encounter a fascinating discussion about the vital role of the Bible in Jewish and Christian theology. In Question 125, Menasseh examines the perfection of the Law of Moses from a number of philosophical and theological perspectives. One of these is the perfect manner in which the Law was given to the Israelites. The conditions under which the Israelites received the Law had to be perfect, because it is through the Bible and its doctrines that they were to achieve salvation. Menasseh elaborates on his understanding of who is able to secure their salvation through reflection on the Bible. It is not only Jews who achieve salvation, but Christians as well. He emphasizes that just as Scripture was revealed in the desert, "a location common to all," so too the Bible is the shared patrimony of "all those who desire to be saved by it, even though at first it was given only to Israel."[1] In this remarkable passage, Menasseh appears to locate

1. Menasseh ben Israel, *Conciliador, sive De convenientia locorum S. Scripturae, quae pugnare inter se videntur... Esto es, Conciliador o de la conveniencia de los Lugares de la S. Escriptura, que repugnantes entre si parecen* (Frankfurt, 1632) 1:285. "[E]l tiempo fue idoneo. Pues assi mismo lo fue el lugar, y esto por aver sido enel desierto lugar general á todos, en lo qual se significó ser la Ley comua per todos los que en ella salvar se quisieren, aun que de primera intencion solamente fue dada a Israel." Menasseh

Jews and Christians as part of a single spiritual community that finds in Scripture the necessary doctrines and truths required for salvation.[2]

What is it that led Menasseh to articulate such an intriguing understanding of how Jews and Christians alike attain salvation, and the Bible's role in these efforts? On the one hand, the term *yeshuah*, which signifies salvation, appears several times in the Bible, particularly in the Book of Isaiah. Menasseh would certainly have come upon it through his meticulous reading of Scripture.[3] On the other hand, salvation as a theological concept never attained the same traction in rabbinic and medieval Judaism as it did in Christian religious thought. Thus, Menasseh's emphasis on the role of the Bible in the salvation of Jews and Christians is unusual, and raises questions about the lingering resonance of Christian theology in the perspectives of Amsterdam's ex-conversos. This chapter argues that Menasseh's preoccupation with the pivotal role of the Bible in achieving salvation is part of a broader phenomenon in the Portuguese Jewish community. When Amsterdam's ex-conversos moved from the world of Iberian Catholicism to Amsterdam's Jewish community, they arrived with a characteristically Christian concern about personal salvation that colored their theological perspectives as Jews, and their approaches to reading the Bible.

Part I of this chapter shows that although members of this community would have been familiar with a wide variety of rabbinic and medieval Jewish texts discussing the world to come and eternal reward

frequently emphasized salvation for the just, both Jewish and Christian, in his published works. See Menasseh ben Israel, *The Hope of Israel*, ed. Henry Méchoulan and Gérard Nahon, trans. Richenda George (Oxford: Oxford University Press, 1987), 32–45.

2. See Sina Rauschenbach, "Mediating Jewish Knowledge: Menasseh ben Israel and the Christian *Respublica literraria*," *The Jewish Quarterly Review*, vol. 102, no. 4 (Fall 2012): 568. Rauschenbach frames this passage as Menasseh's first "plea" for Jewish-Christian collaboration in Bible study. Henry Méchoulan and Gérard Nahon have also observed that Menasseh emphasized the universality of salvation in many of his other works, including *De la resurreccion de los muertos* (On the Resurrection of the Dead; Amsterdam, 1636) and his commentary on the Book of Daniel, *Piedra Gloriosa* (Glorious Stone; Amsterdam, 1655). See Menasseh ben Israel, *The Hope of Israel*, 34, 42.
3. For appearances of the term in the Bible, see Isaiah 26:1, 49:8, 52:7, 59:17, 60:18; Psalm 119:155.

and punishment, the particular concern for salvation is rooted in converso experiences as Christians in Spain and Portugal, and ex-converso experiences as Jews in the Netherlands. The belief that it was specifically the Bible that provided crucial doctrines and laws required for salvation was prominent in New Christian religious perspectives, and was also emphasized by Reformed Protestants in northwest Europe, who frequently made this belief the center of their theological perspectives and argued passionately for the doctrine in their disputes with Catholics. In an environment where emphasis on the centrality of the Bible's doctrines for salvation was commonplace among Christian theologians, Jews too developed theological perspectives about salvation centered on the Hebrew Bible. Not all Portuguese Jews (and European Christians) accepted this view, however. Part II and Part III show how leading rabbis responded to two very different challenges that threatened to subvert their commitment to the Bible as the foundation of efforts to secure their salvation. The first challenge was presented by heterodox ex-conversos like Uriel da Costa, who denied that the Bible taught any doctrines whatsoever regarding salvation or post-mortem reward and punishment.

The second challenge came from Protestant Christians who denied that the Hebrew Bible's laws and commandments had any connection to salvation. It was frequently argued that it was faith in the Word of God (rather than active observance of biblical laws and commandments), that led individuals to justification, and ultimately to eternal reward.[4] Although there are many differences and subtle nuances among the various Protestant confessional movements, in general it was agreed that through faith in Christ an individual receives divine grace and may be justified – recognized as righteous – even though he or she remains a fallible sinner. For all Protestant confessions, justification was a stepping-stone to salvation – the attainment of eternal life after death. Luther and Calvin denied that good works and biblical laws played any role in achieving salvation, based on their interpretation of Pauline teachings such as Galatians 2:16 and 3:10, although certain later Reformed

4. Donald McKim, ed. *The Westminster Handbook to Reformed Theology* (London and Leiden: Westminster John Knox Press, 2001), 200–201.

theologians argued that human agency played a limited, cooperative role in these processes.[5] Jews, in contrast, insisted that performance of the Bible's commandments was crucial to their justification – a concept borrowed from Christian theology – and their subsequent salvation. As a whole, this chapter shows how the New Christian background and the ex-converso present made the relationship between Bible and salvation a key concept in the Portuguese Jewish community, and how their understanding of key theological terms such as salvation, justification, faith, and law were influenced by the Protestant environment in which they constructed their Jewish society.

Part 1: The Christian and Converso Prologue to Jewish Perspectives on Scripture

Menasseh ben Israel was not by any means the only member of his community to affirm a strong belief in the relationship between the Bible and salvation. Menasseh's Jewish contemporaries from within the ex-converso community likewise presented salvation and the study of Scripture as being intimately linked. The idea is present in some of the earliest literature generated by (and for) the ex-conversos, including Rabbi Isaac Athias's *Fortificaccion de la ley de Moseh* [Strenthening of the Law of Moses] – a translation of the sixteenth-century Lithuanian Karaite Isaac Troki's *Sefer Hizzuk Emunah* [Strengthening of the Faith], copied in Amsterdam in 1624. The very shift in the title from Troki's original to the Spanish adaptation is tantalizingly telling, accentuating as it does the primacy of Scripture in the religious perspective of the ex-conversos. In the *Fortificaccion*'s prefatory synopsis, Athias describes

5. Donald McKim, ed. *The Westminster Handbook to Reformed Theology*, 97–99, 127–29. For a survey of the diverse Protestant doctrines of salvation, faith, good works, and justification, see Berndt Hamm, "What Was the Reformation Doctrine of Justification?," in *The German Reformation: The Essential Readings*, ed. C. Scott Dixon (Oxford: Blackwell Publishers, 1999), 56–90. See also Alister McGrath, *Iustitia Dei: A History of the Christian Doctrine of Justification*, 3rd edition (Cambridge: Cambridge University Press, 2005). Jacob Arminius and his theological successors (such as the Remonstrants) advocated for a more moderate understanding of these doctrines. See Th. Marius van Leeuwen, Keith D. Stanglin, and Marijke Tolsma, eds. *Arminius, Arminianism, and Europe*, x–xx.

his defense of the Hebrew Bible and his critique of the New Testament as "announcing" to the ex-conversos (the *'aflictos coraçones de la caza de Ysrael captiua'*) the "eternally hoped for salvation."[6] Much later, in his description of the *Keter Sem Tob* (Crown of the Good Name) society for young Portuguese Jewish boys and girls, Daniel Levi de Barrios described the biblically-oriented curriculum that the young children studied, and also linked this focus to the children's future spiritual salvation. The *Academia* teaches its young participants "to continue in Scripture, happy in the doctrine."[7] He emphasizes that the young members of the *Keter Sem Tob* society "study the Holy Law one hour every Sabbath with charity... in order to go to an eternity," and to leave the path of ruin for the "path of salvation." Intriguingly, de Barrios describes the *Keter Sem Tob* confraternity as a place where young boys and girls studied together, twenty *hermanos* with seventeen *hermanas*.[8] The Bible-centered curriculum taught to these Portuguese Jewish children by the confraternity administrators Joseph Senior Coronel, Mosseh Sasportas, and Abraham Orobio de Castro was viewed as especially significant because rigorous study of the Hebrew Bible was necessary for their future salvation.

Casual, nonchalant statements such as these about the link between Scripture and salvation recur frequently in the introductions that Menasseh ben Israel wrote to the Bibles he edited and his biblical commentaries. In the Portuguese introduction to his volume of the Pentateuch with readings from the Prophets, *Humas de Parasioth y Aftharoth* (Amsterdam, 1627), Menasseh explains the spiritual utility of regularly reading from Scripture to his readers:

> During the day and the night you shall not have any other occupation than divine meditation': because in this (according to the wise interpretation) the path to salvation is found, and the life of the spirit; and thus, throughout history many virtuous men were accustomed to this: and Rabbi Shimon bar Yohay... spent his entire life in contemplation. However, since on account of

6. Isaac Athias, *Fortificaccion de la ley de Moseh*, Ms. EH 48 C6 (unpaginated).
7. Daniel Levi de Barrios, *Triumpho del govierno popular*, 359–63.
8. Daniel Levi de Barrios, *Triumpho del govierno popular*, 361–62, 364.

> the captivity and persecutions of Israel it was impossible to follow this strictly, the sages ordained and diffused the custom throughout all of Israel to read the law three days each week in the prayer house.[9]

Menasseh writes that the "advantage I wished to show you [the reader]," of this book, of assiduously reading Scriptures each week, was eternal salvation.[10] Menasseh returns to the theme of Scripture and salvation in the introduction to his magisterial compendium of conflicting biblical verses, the *Conciliador.* In the preface to Volume 1, printed in 1632, Menasseh insists that

> It is a civil right established by the ancient sages, that in all contracts the vendor must proclaim all of the details about the item being sold, in such a way that the purchaser is not unaware of anything that the seller knows: because otherwise, abhorring the utility of honesty, the sale and the contract will be invalid... Presuming this, (dear reader) it appears to me good and even necessary, in this preface, to declare to you in detail that which this labour and work of mine contains; so that in the event that you will think to buy it beneficially, you will employ it well to your enjoyment and salvation.[11]

9. Menasseh ben Israel, *Humas de Parasioth y Aftharoth* (Amsterdam, 1627), "Prologo ao lector" [unpaginated]. "Aquelle Rey perfeito, que na terra achou el Dio a seu coracam conforme, publica muytas vezes, nã [sic, não/nem] ter de dia, ne[m] de noite outro exercisio, que a meditacam diuina: porque nella (segundo o sabio entendia) achaua o caminho de saluacam, e vida espiritual; e assi seguindo o tempo, muitos virtuozos usaram o mesmo: e Rebi Simon ben Yohay, como diuino, passou a vida toda contemplando. Mas como por cauza do catiueiro, e persegiçoens de Israel, era imposiuel seguir isto avante, ordenaram os sabios, & se espalhou o costume em todo Israel, na caza de oraçcam, lerem tres dias na semana ley." The biblical verse that Menasseh quotes closely resembles Joshua 1:8: "Let not this Book of the Teaching cease from your lips, but recite it day and night, so that you may observe faithfully all that is written in it."
10. Menasseh ben Israel, *Humas de Parasioth y Aftharoth*, "achaua o caminho da saluacam." Prologo ao lector (unpaginated).
11. Menasseh ben Israel, *Conciliador*, vol. 1 "Al lector" [unpaginated]. "Derecho civil establecido es de los antigos sabios, que en todas contrataciones, el vendedor deue dezir todas las particularidades dela cosa que vende, de tal manera que el comprador ninguna cosa ignore, la qual sepa el vededor: por que de otra manera, repugnando la

Similar connections between Scripture and salvation are found in the *Maḥzor* (High Holiday prayer book) volume edited by David Pardo and Salom ben Yosseph in 1630, and printed by Menasseh ben Israel. David Pardo was a rabbi and founding member of the *Honen Dalim* confraternity for poor relief, and later became a cantor in the Portuguese Jewish community in London. Salom ben Yosseph was the son of one of Amsterdam's earliest rabbis, Josef Salom, who emigrated from Venice and was hired in April 1619. Salom became a significant rabbi in the community in his own right.[12] Pardo and Yosseph financed the publication of this prayer book for Rosh Hashanah and Yom Kippur, and penned a dedicatory address to the "very magnificent [rabbi] señor Selomoh Abas." As is common in these compositions, Pardo and Yosseph offer obsequious praise for the piety of señor Selomoh Abas, "which all men wish to achieve," and his assiduous observance of the Law, "the source and deliverer of life and salvation."[13]

In the literature produced by Portuguese Jews in Amsterdam, it was common to assert that the Hebrew Bible was the foundational text for Jewish efforts to achieve salvation, that all doctrines and truths required for salvation were contained within Scripture, and that personal salvation depended on performance of the Bible's precepts. There is a specific historical importance in the understated, casual manner in which Daniel Levi de Barrios, Menasseh ben Israel, Saul Levi Morteira, and other members of the community draw a link between the Bible and salvation. Writers deployed this notion nonchalantly in their compositions and biblical commentaries because they assumed it would be accepted without challenge by their readers, and because it was basic to the ideas they discussed at greater length. The connection between salvation and

utilidad á la honestidad, la vendida y contrato seria nulo, y no tendria algun vigor y fuerca. Prosupuesto lo dicho (lector afficionado) me parecio descente y aun forçoso, en esta Praefacion declararte con particulardad, lo que contiene este lavor y trabajo mio; porque si a caso te pareciere la compra provechosa, podras emplear mas á tu salvo, y gusto."

12. David Pardo and Salom ben Yosseph, eds. *Mahzor. Orden de Ros Asanah y Kipur* (Amsterdam, 1630). See Daniel Levi de Barrios, *Triumpho del govierno popular*, 69 and 144; and GAS 334 1051 Fol. 6a.

13. David Pardo and Salom ben Yosseph, eds. *Mahzor. Orden de Ros Asanah y Kipur* [Dedicatory Address; unpaginated].

Bible study was not a topic that was contested or controversial among Portuguese Jews, and was frequently articulated in a way that suggests this was received wisdom or common knowledge within the community. The regularity of these claims provides a valuable window into the religious mentalité of the Portuguese Jewish community, offering a glimpse at ideas that were atypical in the broader Jewish world, but which they took for granted. How do we understand the great emphasis given to the link between Scripture and salvation by many members of the Portuguese Jewish community? On what traditions and ideas might they have been drawing? By what communities, past and present, might they have been influenced? There were certainly precedents in the Jewish past for linking Scripture and salvation. Few of these were more forceful than Profet Duran's effort in *Sefer Ma'aseh Efod*, where he passionately defends the critical role of physical observance of the Bible's commandments and intellectual or theoretical meditation upon them as crucial religious acts that are intimately tied to an individual Jew's salvation.

As Maud Kozodoy has shown, the fourteenth-century converso physician, scholar, and polemicist Profet Duran represents a stridently Bible-centric stratum of medieval Jewish thought. The introduction to *Sefer Ma'aseh Efod* is replete with Duran's emphatic insistence upon the crucial role of the Bible in the journey of a Jewish individual to attain their "ultimate, eternal happiness, immeasurably greater and more elevated than any [happiness] in this our life." To attain the wonders of the eternal reward, Duran affirms, "The way to attain it, leading to it, is to keep the divine Torah and to perform the commandments."[14] Performing the commandments was important to Duran, since through the performance of the Bible's injunctions and strictures an individual's earthly welfare was assured. More important, though, was the *keeping* of the commandments, by which Duran understood a deep, meditative, intellectual engagement with the text: a "constant occupation with it [the Bible] and keeping it in the heart and the contemplation of it and keeping its presence in the memory and not turning one's thought from

14. Profet Duran, *Ma'aseh Efod* (Vienna, 1865) 1, and Maud Kozodoy, *The Secret Faith of Maestre Honoratus: Profayt Duran and Jewish Identity in Late Medieval Iberia* (Philadelphia: University of Pennsylvania Press, 2015), 163.

it toward any other thing during the time one is occupied with it, all this directs a man straight to the ultimate eternal felicity."[15]

Alongside these Bible-centric perspectives on Jewish efforts to attain eternal reward, Duran is careful to couch his emphasis on Bible study within a Jewish devotional framework that incorporates a variety of other disciplines, or "wisdoms." In general terms, he is supportive of the idealized framework drawn from rabbinic literature in which the scholar's day is divided into equal thirds of Bible, Mishnah, and Talmud study. Duran insists that the study of Talmud also has significant religious and spiritual value for Jews: "for it is in this way that the opaque laws of the Torah may be determined... which are incumbent upon Israel to know in order to understand how to act."[16] Yet as he surveyed the intellectual and religious landscape of Jewish society in the late fourteenth century, he saw a culture of Talmud study that he believed had gone too far – that had begun to marginalize vital disciplines and "wisdoms" that were essential to Judaism and the effort to attain salvation. Some Talmud experts – he writes – claim that it is *only* through Talmud study that an individual attains the ultimate, eternal reward.[17] He also discerned a condescending attitude particularly with respect to the Bible and its relationship to the Talmud: "some proponents of this perspective reason because of this that all who exert themselves and investigate other disciplines apart from it... toil for nothing."[18] Duran had serious reservations about what he saw as an inflated understanding of the importance of Talmud study. Talmud contained a great many matters that evidently had no bearing on the question of a person's eternal reward, and inconclusively resolved debates found throughout the Talmud could not guide an individual. Furthermore, Duran insists that the Talmud could not have been a factor in the salvation of Jews during the four centuries between the destruction of the Temple and the composition of the text. At a minimum, other factors must be involved. Duran believed that the most important, by far, was the Bible – which was the

15. Duran, *Ma'aseh Efod*, 10; Kozodoy, *Secret Faith*, 175.
16. Profet Duran, *Ma'aseh Efod*, 15.
17. Profet Duran, *Ma'aseh Efod*, 4.
18. Profet Duran, *Ma'aseh Efod*, 5.

object of serious neglect. As Talya Fishman observes, Duran attributed a severely diminished interest in Bible study to the Talmud's curricular ascent in Europe generally, and in Spain in particular: "And that which has led people to laziness regarding engagement with Scriptures is the investigation of the wisdom of the Babylonian Talmud, which is deep and wide – and people's inadequacy in grasping it, given its depth and difficulty. They terminate their days in its pursuit and have totally abandoned Scripture, throwing it behind their backs."[19]

There was certainly, then, a precedent for thinking about – and emphasizing – the crucial role of the Bible in the Jewish effort to attain salvation, in medieval Spain and among the conversos. Yet we should also be cautious about extrapolating too far from this medieval tradition and assuming the degree to which it may have resonated in the seventeenth century. First of all, the Amsterdam ex-conversos were separated from the tradition of medieval Jewish thought by many generations of life as Christians in Spain and Portugal, and were not raised in a culture emphasizing either Duran's perspectives on Bible and eternal reward, or those of the talmudists he criticises. Second, the specific influence of *Sefer Ma'aseh Efod* and its perspectives should not necessarily be taken for granted. The text of *Sefer Ma'aseh Efod* was never present in the communal library surveyed in the preceding chapter. At no point during the period between the early 1620s and the mid-1660s can the text be found on the shelves of this impressive collection; nor does it appear on the shelves of the intermediate or advanced classrooms, which were inventoried frequently during this same period of time. Thus, it is not clear that this type of perspective was "on the radar screen" of the Portuguese Jewish community in Amsterdam and its religious leadership. Finally, as Talya Fishman has argued, even in his own time Profet Duran's emphasis on the Bible as the focal point of Jewish efforts to earn an eternal reward were atypical. He represented a dissenting voice objecting to the growing primacy of Talmud study that he observed to be ascendant wherever he looked in his society. Duran, in arguing that it was Bible study that paved

19. Talya Fishman, *Becoming People of the Talmud: Oral Torah as Written Tradition in Medieval Jewish Cultures.* Jewish Culture and Contexts (Philadelphia: University of Pennsylvania Press, 2011), 159.

the way to salvation, was not broadly representative of his times or their outlook.[20] In Amsterdam, the Bible was central to Jewish education and religious culture in a way that it was generally not for most individuals in the world that Profet Duran inhabited.

The concern of Portuguese Jews for their salvation, and the crucial role of the Bible in their efforts, likely reflects additional origins. There were at least two such stimuli: the environment of Iberian Catholic theology, within which many members of the community were raised and educated, and the milieu of the Protestant Reformation and Calvinist society in the Netherlands, in which these ex-converos constructed their community and religious institutions from scratch. Historians have long observed the particular fixation of conversos and crypto-Jews with their personal salvation, and have shown that the Iberian context in which they lived provides a crucial backdrop to this preoccupation.[21] As Carlos Eire has demonstrated, during this period in general, and especially after the 1530s, members of diverse social strata in Spain thought intently and incessantly about death and how to assure their salvation.[22] A vast literature of *Ars moriendi* (the art of dying) counselled Spaniards on the best way to achieve this goal. Late sixteenth-century examples of these works emphasized the vital role played by the free will of the individual Christian, the intercessory role of saints, and the power of the sacraments. Baptism, penance, confession, orders, last rites, and above all the Eucharist were essential for securing one's salvation.[23] Wealthy individuals arranged for large numbers of masses to be performed in

20. Talya Fishman, *Becoming People of the Talmud*, 157–59.
21. Miriam Bodian, *Hebrews of the Portuguese Nation*, 97–101. Bodian stresses the absorption of Catholic preoccupations with salvation from the Iberian milieu, and illustrates the impact of these perspectives on the unique ex-converso understanding of circumcision that developed, and which differed starkly from traditional Jewish formulations. Conversos who joined the Jewish community of seventeenth-century Amsterdam regarded circumcision as a rite with direct salvific significance akin to a Christian sacrament, a "mysterious sacrifice" in the words of the ex-converso scholar Isaac Cardoso – a ceremony that redeemed an individual from Adam's original sin, and without which a Jew could not be saved.
22. Carlos M.N. Eire, *From Madrid to Purgatory: The Art and Craft of Dying in Sixteenth-Century Spain* (Cambridge: Cambridge University Press, 1995), 26.
23. Carlos M.N. Eire, *From Madrid to Purgatory*, 30–31, 81–82, 170.

their honor in order to shorten the path through purgatory, while many less well-to-do members of society desperately tried to collect money in order to purchase similar services, and to expedite their time in purgatory as much as possible.[24]

In an environment in which the question of the afterlife, hell, salvation, and purgatory loomed so ubiquitously at the forefront of Spanish religious culture, it is little wonder that salvation became a topic of great concern to conversos.[25] Influenced by the broader religious culture and its preoccupation with salvation, conversos frequently repackaged these beliefs with a Jewish inflection. Not unlike Uriel da Costa's initial beliefs as a young adult in Portugal, they emphasized a conviction that it was the Law of Moses, rather than the New Testament, that illuminated the true path to salvation. In the seventeenth century, heterodox Judaizers emphasized the importance of reading the Old Testament (even sometimes in Hebrew) for their salvation. For instance, Lope de Vara, arrested in 1639 and burned as a heretic in 1644, underwent an especially profound transformation in his prison cell. At the time of his initial arrest, he expressed heterodox, but not especially innovative or extreme ideas: a moderate degree of anticlericalism, as well as curiosity about the relative merits of Christianity, Islam, and Judaism, and their Holy Scriptures.[26] However, the experience of his trial radicalized his perspectives, and after six months of questioning, Lope de Vara dramatically circumcised himself with a chicken bone in his Inquisition cell and asserted the firm conviction that his personal salvation depended entirely on his commitment to the Law of Moses, the "*pentateuco torat adonay*."[27]

Undoubtedly, the ex-converso preoccupation with personal salvation owes a large debt to the prominence of this concern in the Iberian Peninsula. However, while crypto-Jews like Lope de Vara and the ex-conversos in Amsterdam were fixated on the role of the Bible in their quest for eternal reward, early modern Spanish Catholicism focused

24. Carlos Eire, *From Madrid to Purgatory*, 170–231.
25. Miriam Bodian, *Dying in the Law of Moses*, xiii. Bodian notes the role played by Spanish *Ars moriendi* literature for conversos to the need to die well.
26. Miriam Bodian, *Dying in the Law of Moses*, 159–60, 169–70.
27. Miriam Bodian, *Dying in the Law of Moses*, 153–67.

on an eclectic range of additional devotional and sacramental avenues. How should this discrepancy be understood? Miriam Bodian provides an intriguing answer in her analysis of Lope de Vara's confrontation with the Inquisition. Conversos and crypto-Jews were shaped not only by Catholic soteriology, but by Protestant biblicism and critiques of Catholicism as well. During his interrogations, Lope de Vera expressed a number of ideas that recall the theological positions of radical Protestant movements, such as the adamant rejection of the Trinity, the Incarnation, and the real presence of God in the consecrated Host. Furthermore, he dissociated himself from Catholic beliefs about the mediating role played by saints, and the miracles supposedly attributed to "images" and men.[28] In the course of his trial, Lope testified that he read a wide range of forbidden works, including Erasmus's *Annotations upon the New Testament* as well as unspecified texts by Ibn Ezra and the Calvinist theologian Johannes Drusius.

Bodian emphasizes that Protestant texts and ideas circulated in the Iberian Peninsula to a greater degree than is often assumed. Early in the Reformation, Lutheran books translated into Spanish were imported clandestinely into Spain.[29] During the later sixteenth century, the Iberian Protestant religious exile Cipriano de Valera, living in London, composed Spanish-language polemical works against the papacy and the Catholic Mass, as well as translations of key Protestant theological texts, including an edition of the Old and New Testaments and the fifth (and definitive) edition of Calvin's *Institutes of the Christian Religion*. These works were designed to be smuggled into Spain and read by a Catholic audience.[30] Furthermore, Spain's commercial exchanges with the Netherlands provided an official channel for the entry of Dutch Christians into Spain during the Twelve Years Truce (1609–1621) and after the Treaty of Munster (1648) that facilitated contact with Dutch Protestants.[31] Appreciating the circulation of Protestant ideas, individ-

28. Miriam Bodian, *Dying in the Law of Moses*, 159–60. Regarding Lope de Vera's self-circumcision, see pp. 169–70.
29. Miriam Bodian, *Dying in the Law of Moses*, 24.
30. A. Gordon Kinder, "Religious Literature as an Offensive Weapon: Cipriano de Valera's Part in England's War with Spain," *Sixteenth Century Journal* 16, no. 2 (1988): 223–35.
31. Jonathan Israel, "Spain and the Dutch Sephardim, 1609–1660," 1–61.

uals, and texts in Spain during the sixteenth and seventeenth centuries informs our understanding of the literal biblicist, anti-clerical, and anti-Trinitarian ideas expressed by crypto-Jews, and their willingness to "die in the Law of Moses."

In addition to the converso and Iberian background of Amsterdam's ex-conversos, the environment of Protestant theology is important for understanding the religious perspectives that emerged in this community and their repeated emphasis on the connection between the Bible and salvation. During the late sixteenth and seventeenth centuries, Reformed scholars produced some of the most extensive doctrines of Scripture ever written, and positioned the Bible at the center of their theological outlooks. Frequently, they made connections between the properties of Scripture and the Bible's salvific function. John Calvin, in his commentary on Ephesians 3:4, stresses that Scripture is a "complete and sufficient rule," and that no other sources of authority are required for achieving salvation. In Calvin's view, no unwritten traditions observed by Roman Catholics play any role in the achievement of salvation. Nor is it problematic that certain texts written by Paul may have been lost. Even if this were so, Calvin insists that "Those which the Lord foresaw to be necessary for His Church He consecrated by His providence for everlasting remembrance. Let us know then, that what is left is enough for us, and that its smallness is not accidental; but that the body of Scripture, which is in our possession, has been controlled by the wonderful counsel of God."[32]

Referring to Psalm 19, "The Scripture is perfect," the English theologian Edward Leigh (1602–1671) emphasized that "as many [books] as were useful to our salvation . . . have been kept inviolable in the Church,"[33] and later affirms that "the holy Scripture doth sufficiently containe and deliver all Doctrines which are necessary for us to eternall salvation, both in respect of Faith and good works."[34] Leigh's commitment to the self-sufficiency of Scripture's contents for salvation even led him

32. T.H.L. Parker, ed. *Calvin's Commentaries: The Epistles of Paul the Apostle to the Galatians, Ephesians, Philippians, and Colossians* (Grand Rapids, MI: Eerdmans, 1965), 159.

33. Edward Leigh, *A Treatise of Divinity Consisting of Three Bookes* (London, 1646), 138.

34. Edward Leigh, *A Treatise of Divinity*, 141.

to remarkable conclusions about the intrinsic properties of the Old Testament and the salvation of Jews. He believed that: "The Covenant of grace which God made with man is an everlasting Covenant, therein the Lord hath revealed himself to be one and unchangeable... and that as well toward the gentiles as toward the Jewes, so hee would justifie both the circumcision and the uncircumcision, the Jew and the gentile by one way of Religion." Furthermore, in earlier times, "The Church of the Jewes in the severall Ages thereof was sufficiently taught, and instructed in all things necessary to salvation by the writings of Moses and the Prophets."[35] Leigh thus links Scripture to salvation in both Jewish and Christian terms.

Part of the reason for the intensity and frequency of these claims about the necessity of Scripture for salvation in Protestant theology was the ongoing polemic with Roman Catholicism. Protestant religious scholars were acutely sensitive to claims made by Roman Catholics that ambiguous or obscure passages in Scripture posed a challenge to the *sola scriptura* foundation of their theology, and that the Bible was not the exclusive resource required for resolving theological controversies.[36] Roman Catholic assertions about the fallibility of Scripture were thus an important reference point for Protestant polemicists arguing for a *sola scriptura* perspective. The Puritan clergyman and Cambridge theologian William Perkins (1558–1602) writes that "Papists teach, that beside the written word, there be certain unwritten traditions, which must be

35. Edward Leigh, *A Treatise of Divinity*, 141–46.
36. This is one reason why the seventeenth-century controversy over the antiquity of the vowel points loomed so large in Catholic and Protestant disputes. This debate brought into focus potential tensions in the central Protestant claim that the Bible was a self-sufficient interpreter of itself. A Bible whose vowel points were ancient features of the text, or that were at least transmitted orally from ancient times, aligned much better with Protestant *sola Scriptura* perspectives. Alternatively, if the vowel points were a late accretion, and therefore inauthentic as part of divine revelation, then Catholic arguments for the importance of church interpretation and councils were harder to dismiss. Regarding these disputes, see Stephen G. Burnett, *From Christian Hebraism to Jewish Studies: Johannes Buxtorf (1564–1629) and Hebrew Learning in the Seventeenth Century* (Leiden: Brill, 1996), 203–39; Richard Muller, *After Calvin: Studies in the Development of a Theological Tradition* (New York: Oxford University Press, 2003), 146–55.

beleeued as profitable and necessarie to saluation. And these they say are twofold; Apostolicall, namely such as were deliuered by the Apostles and not written; and Ecclesiasticall, which the Church decreeth as occasion is offered. We holde that the Scriptures are most perfect, containing in them all doctrines needfull to salvation."[37] As John Cameron (1579?–1625) observes, Catholic polemicists assert that "the Scripture is defectiue, and imperfect, and therefore cannot be extended, nor applied to the decision of our controversies."[38] Some Catholic scholars, Perkins knew, argued that Scripture was imperfect based on the fact that "some bookes of the canon of the scripture are lost, as the *booke of the warres of God*. Num 21. 14. *The booke of the just*. Iosua. 10. 13. the bookes of Cronicles of the kings of Israel and Iuda. 1. King. 14. 19. the books of certain prophets, Nathan, Gad, Iddo, Ahiah, and Semiah."[39] Nevertheless, Perkins insists that "Though it be granted that some bookes of Canonicall scripture be lost: yet the scripture still remains sufficient because the matter of those bookes (so farforth as it was necessary to salvation) is contained in these bookes of scripture that are now extant."[40] Likewise, John Cameron responds to the charges of Scripture's imperfection by emphasizing that this incompleteness has no bearing on those doctrines central to salvation, such as the Trinity, incarnation, redemption, and faith in Jesus Christ, among several others. "These points and those that depend on them are without doubt retained in the Scripture."[41]

These sentiments and beliefs of Reformed Protestants mirror Menasseh ben Israel's convictions. In his encyclopaedic reconciliation of contradictory verses in the Hebrew Bible, the *Conciliador* [Reconciler], Menasseh sought to demonstrate that obscurities and inconsistencies in Scripture did not subvert the overall authority of the text, and, above all, that they in no way infringed upon the biblical doctrines necessary for

37. William Perkins, *A reformed Catholike: or, A declaration shewing how neere we may come to the present Church of Rome in sundrie points of religion* (London, 1597), 137.
38. John Cameron, *A tract of the soueraigne iudge of controuersies in matters of religion* (Oxford, 1628), 13.
39. William Perkins, *A reformed Catholike*, 145–46.
40. William Perkins, *A reformed Catholike*, 146.
41. John Cameron, *A tract of the soueraigne iudge of controuersies in matters of religion*, 17. See also Richard Muller, *Post-Reformation Reformed Dogmatics*, 2:314.

salvation. In the introduction to the second volume (published in 1641), he poses the question: "What if someone asks why God did not speak more clearly? And what good does it serve to confuse the wisdom with ambiguities and doubtful words?"[42] These types of ambiguities in the text are ubiquitous, for a number of reasons that Menasseh attempted to define: there are instances where Scripture must be read metaphorically as opposed to literally; there are uncertainties regarding various elements of the Bible's vocabulary; and there is a general absence of sufficient historical and doctrinal information.[43] Yet Menasseh also insists that "God wished there to be many obscurities in sacred Scripture, in order that many opinions would result from these, and none of them contrary to the faith."[44] Crucially, he stresses that whatever ambiguity or lack of clarity may be found in Scripture, "it is necessary to warn that this 'obscurity' we speak about is not found in any matter upon which the health and salvation of man depends: because in such matters God speaks clearly and most simply."[45] Alongside Reformed theologians such as Edward Leigh, John Cameron, William Perkins, and Matthew Poole, Menasseh ben Israel recognized the pervasiveness of ambiguity and inconsistency in the Bible, while at the same time asserting that all essential doctrines and teachings required for salvation remained free from any uncertainty.

In Volume 1 of the *Conciliador,* Menasseh uses apparent ambiguities in narratives about the giving of the Law at Sinai to further explain the Jewish perspective on the link between salvation and Scripture. On the one hand, Exodus 34:1 states "I shall carve for you two stone tablets like

42. Menasseh ben Israel, *Conciliador,* vol. 2, "al Lector" [unpaginated]. "Preguntará ya puede ser alguno, leyendo tan varias y difficultosas questions, que es la causa, por que Dios no habló con los hombres claramente? Y de que servia confundir el ingenio con amphibologias, y palabras dudosas?"
43. Menasseh ben Israel, *Conciliador,* vol. 1, "al Lector" [unpaginated].
44. Menasseh ben Israel, *Conciliador,* vol. 2, "al Lector" [unpaginated]. "Quiso Dios vuiesse muchas escuridades en la sagrada Escritura, para que dellas resultassen muchos pareceres, y ninguno contrario a la fe."
45. Menasseh ben Israel, *Conciliador,* vol. 2, "al Lector," [unpaginated]. "Empero es de advertir que esta obscuridad que dezimos, no se halla en alguna cosa en que consiste la salud y salvacion del hombre: porque en semejantes cosas hablo Dios muy clara y cenzillamente."

the first ones, and inscribe upon the tablets the words that are on the first tablets," indicating that God would personally engrave the stones on which the Ten Commandments would be inscribed. Likewise, in Deuteronomy 10:2 God clearly says, "I will inscribe on the tablets the commandments that were on the first tablets that you smashed, and you shall deposit them in the ark," and Deuteronomy 10:4 states that "The Lord inscribed on the tablets the same text as on the first." At the same time, despite numerous verses in which God is the central agent in the inscription of the Ten Commandments, Exodus 34:27 holds that: "The Lord said to Moses: write down these commandments, for in accordance with them I make a covenant with you and with Israel." Furthermore, Exodus 34:28 specifies that "Moses wrote down on the tablets the terms of the covenant, the Ten Commandments." The question was thus whether the commandments were written directly by God, or the potentially fallible hand of a human being – Moses. Ultimately, Menasseh insists that the verses indicating that Moses engraved the Decalogue must be reinterpreted in some other fashion, because teachings so vitally important to an individual's salvation *must* necessarily have been written by God: "It is an opinion received from both the ancients as well as modern authorities, that the first and second tablets were written by the hand of the blessed Lord, as is most clearly held by the first verses presented; and the reason for this appears to be given: because it is necessary to believe that the Law that God gave to humans in a manner appropriate *in order to save them* should have in it nothing that was implemented by the hands of humans" [my emphasis].[46] Furthermore, Menasseh stresses that in light of the fact that "the ten commandments are the essence of the entire law, and within them all 613 precepts are contained, as R. Bahya [Ben Asher] demonstrates in *Kad ha-kemaḥ* [Vessel of Flour][47] . . . it is certain that they must have been written by God.[48]

46. Menasseh ben Israel, *Conciliador*, 1:245. "Es opinio[n] recebida ansi de antigos, como modernos authores que las primeras y segundas tablas fueron por mano del Dio bendito escritas, como clarissimamente consta de los primeros versos alegados; y la razon parece está dictando: porque es de creer, que la Ley que el S[e]ñor daua por medio conuenie[n]te para los humanos se salvaren, no avia de aver en ella cosa q[ue] por manos humanos fuesse hecha."
47. Bahya ben Asher, *Kad ha-kemaḥ* (Jerusalem and New York: Mishor, 2006), 496.
48. Menasseh ben Israel, *Conciliador*, 1:245. Menasseh is referring to the pericope of

Menasseh ben Israel, Saul Levi Morteira, and other figures central to the leadership of the Portuguese Jewish community in Amsterdam, like their Protestant counterparts, made a deep and concerted effort to acknowledge the importance of and connection between salvation and Scripture, and articulated a Jewish pathway to its achievement. The overwhelming centrality of debates about salvation in the Christian world of the seventeenth century motivated Portuguese Jews to turn their attention to similar issues in their thought about Judaism, and to reinscribe elements of these ideas in a Jewish idiom that stressed the study and practice of the Hebrew Bible's commandments, rather than the teachings of the New Testament.

Part II: Scripture and Salvation: The Connection Under Assault

One reason why Menasseh was especially concerned to articulate and defend the link between Scripture and salvation was the challenge posed by heterodox members of the community such as Uriel da Costa. Gabriel da Costa arrived in Amsterdam from Oporto in 1615, joined the Jewish community, took Uriel as his new name, and soon after traveled to Hamburg in order to establish a commercial outpost on behalf of his family. From the beginning, Uriel's experiences in organized Jewish communities were defined by tumultuous confrontation. Very soon after arriving in Amsterdam, undergoing circumcision, and joining the Jewish community, he discovered that instead of a Jewish community living strictly and exclusively according to the laws and guidelines of the Bible, in Amsterdam he had joined a community of Jews who lived according to the laws and interpretations of rabbinic Judaism and its authorities.[49] This dissonance motivated Uriel to compose a catalogue

Mishpatim, which lists laws concerning slavery, cities of shelter, kidnapping, and interpersonal quarrels, among much else.

49. Uriel da Costa, *Exemplar Humanae Vitae*, 557. In Uriel da Costa's retrospective formulation of his transition from Roman Catholicism to Judaism, composed near the end of his life in Amsterdam, he asserts that he was drawn to Judaism by contradictions between the New Testament and the Old Testament, and by the persuasiveness of the Hebrew Bible's doctrines and truths. Consequently, he desired to become a convert to the "Law of Moses." Regarding the composition of the *Exemplar humanae vitae*

of what he saw as the most striking discrepancies between Judaism's Written and Oral Laws, leading to his excommunication from the Jewish community of Hamburg, as well as that of Venice (*in absentia*). Da Costa's specific contentions focused on rabbinic Jewish practices of circumcision, the design and use of phylacteries and the mezuzahs, the custom of celebrating Jewish festivals on consecutive days outside of the land of Israel, and the "hedges" constructed by rabbis to protect certain laws. Although the rabbis frequently commuted bodily punishment of the guilty party to a financial penalty, da Costa insisted that "he who kills a man or maims a man, so too will be done unto him; fracture for fracture, eye for an eye, tooth for a tooth, etc."[50] The composition triggered a vigorous public debate that involved rabbinic figures in Venice, Hamburg, and Amsterdam.[51] According to his autobiographical reflections, during the period of his excommunication da Costa composed a sophisticated treatise elaborating on his views, adding a crucial new argument: "I entirely agree with the opinion of those who confine the rewards and punishments proposed in the Old Testament to this life only, and seem to be little concerned about a future state, or the immortality of the soul."[52] Denying that the Old Testament taught anything connected with eternal life or punishment, the immortality of the soul, or any other type of "future state" brought Uriel da Costa into conflict with a core, and very dearly held, belief of Menasseh ben Israel and the broader community: the connection between the biblical commandments and personal salvation.

toward the end of Uriel da Costa's life, see Uriel da Costa, *Examination of Pharisaic Traditions*, 22–23.

50. Uriel da Costa *Examination of Pharisaic Traditions*, 13. Cf. Leviticus 24:17–22.

51. Uriel da Costa, *Examination of Pharisaic Traditions*, 9–13, 24–28. Regarding the original 1616 arguments, see Uriel da Costa, *Propostas contra a tradiçao*, in *Die schriften des Uriel da Costa*, ed. C. Gebhardt (Amsterdam, 1922). See also Rabbi Leon Modena's response, *Magen Vi-Tzina*, which was published by Abraham Geiger in 1856 in *Leon da Modena, Rabbiner zu Venedig (1571–1648), Und seine Stellung zur Kabbalah, zum Thalmud und zum Christenthume* (Breslau, 1856). Regarding the inter-communal and international dimensions of the first Uriel da Costa controversy, see Talya Fishman, *Shaking the Pillars of Exile: Voice of a Fool, an Early Modern Jewish Critique of Rabbinic Culture* (Stanford, CA: Stanford University Press, 1997), 49–52.

52. Uriel da Costa, *Exemplar humanae vitae*, 558.

In the complete edition of his *Examination of Pharisaic Traditions,* Uriel da Costa sought to systematically dismantle the basis for Jewish belief in the immortality of the soul by subverting the ostensible biblical foundations of this key doctrine. The opening chapter of the second part of the treatise provides a broad overview of his arguments and methodology. The basic question, as Uriel frames it, was "whether the soul is mortal or immortal." His answer to this rhetorical question, which appears to be based on an extremely literal interpretation of Leviticus 17:10–14, is that:

> What we would call the human soul is that vital spirit which animates the individual, and which is contained in the blood. Human beings live, work and move by that spirit, which lasts them until nature or violent means extinguish it. There is no difference between the soul of an animal and the soul of a human being other than that man's soul is rational and the beast's is devoid of reason. As for the rest, as far as being born, living, and dying is concerned, man and beast are exactly the same, as Selomo put it [cf. Eccl 3:19], and man has no preeminence over a beast as regards permanence, for all is vanity. Just as the soul of an animal is contained in its life-blood, as the Law tells us, so too is the human soul, which is vital spirit, also in the blood... To the question as to whether the soul of a human being is mortal or immortal we reply that, from the preceding, it seems evident that it must be mortal if it is contained in the blood, as we have already ascertained. It is in fact the vital spirit which dies and is extinguished before the human being can expire.[53]

53. Uriel da Costa, *Examination of Pharisaic Traditions*, 311–13. To the best of my knowledge, historians who have studied Uriel da Costa's writings have not connected his denial of the immortality of the soul and post-mortem reward and punishment with the extremely literal approach to biblical exegesis that is typical of his writings. Yet, the language of Leviticus 17:10–14 clearly forbids the Israelites from consuming blood, in which the *nefesh* resides (see esp. Lev 17:11). Likewise, the second part of his argument – that there is no difference between the soul of men and the soul of animals – may be rooted in Leviticus 17:13–14, which likewise forbids the consuming of blood from slaughtered animals, because the "*nefesh*" of the animal resides in its blood.

The publication of da Costa's book in 1623 initiated a prolonged communal dispute regarding the topic of the immortality of the soul. As da Costa recalls in the *Exemplar humanae vitae,*

> No sooner had [my book] appeared in print than the senators and rulers of the Jews agreed to [inform] against me before the public magistrate, setting forth that I had published a book to disprove the immortality of the soul, and with a view to subvert not only the Jewish but also the Christian religion. Upon this information I was apprehended and sent to prison, whence, after a confinement of eight or ten days, I was discharged upon giving security. For I was fined by the magistrate in the penalty of three hundred florins, beside the forfeiture of my books lately published.[54]

Nearly the entire print run of the *Examination of Pharisaic Traditions* was publicly burned, and Uriel da Costa left Amsterdam in voluntary exile, moving to Utrecht.[55] The controversy over Uriel da Costa and his treatise reverberated within the Portuguese Jewish community long after the initial reaction against the *Examination of Pharisaic Traditions.* Discussion and dispute about the immortality of the soul remained a matter of acute importance for rabbis in the community, as well as for members of the congregations that they served.[56]

Menasseh was extraordinarily sensitive to Uriel da Costa's arguments because they threatened to subvert the biblical foundation of key Jewish doctrines: the immortality of the soul and post-mortem reward and punishment, as well as his belief in salvation, a core doctrine that Menasseh locates in the Hebrew Bible, and without which there can be neither salvation nor eternal reward and punishment. Therefore, Uriel's challenge struck at the heart of some of Menasseh's

54. Uriel da Costa, *Examination of Pharisaic Traditions,* 17.
55. Uriel da Costa, *Examination of Pharisaic Traditions,* 17.
56. Regarding the wider resonance of Uriel da Costa's arguments and rabbinic efforts to refute them, see Marc Saperstein, "Saul Levi Morteira's Treatise on the Immortality of the Soul," *Studia Rosenthaliana* 25, no. 2 (1991): 140–41. From remarks preserved in manuscripts of Morteira's sermons, it appears that he spoke publicly about the importance of specifically proving the immortality of the soul, the very point that da Costa contested.

most important commitments. Four years after completing the first volume of the *Conciliador*, Menasseh produced a detailed response to Uriel da Costa in his *De la resurreccion de los muertos* (Amsterdam, 1636). Menasseh expressed deep anxiety about "the nefarious wickedness of the Sadducees, degenerate in everything, and how today in this wretched century some, persuading themselves about the mortality of the souls, give free reign" to their "lascivious appetites."[57] He therefore dedicated several chapters of this text to presenting and systematically refuting "the arguments of the Sadducees and Atheists regarding the immortality of the soul and the resurrection of the dead."[58]

Before attempting to dismantle these unorthodox doctrines, Menasseh offers a reasonably balanced presentation of the positions held by "Sadducees" and "Atheists" in his community, the logic of their arguments, and the proof texts that they cite in support of their beliefs. Using language that unmistakably recalls Uriel da Costa's arguments,

57. Menasseh ben Israel, *De la resurreccion de los muertos, libros III. En los quales contra los Zaduceos, se prueva la immortalidad del Alma, y resurreccion de los muertos* (Amsterdam, 1636), Epistola Dedicatoria [unpaginated]. "Considerando pues la nefaria maldad de los Zaduceos en todo depravados, y como oy en este miserable siglo se van algunos persuadiendo a la mortalidad de las almas, para mas a rienda suelta, se dexaren llevar de sus lassivos apetitos, me determine à escrevir este libro."

58. Menasseh ben Israel, *De la resurreccion de los muertos*, 25–70. Terms such as "atheist" were very highly charged in the seventeenth century, and it is not entirely clear what Menasseh ben Israel means by his use of this term. One very likely possibility is that he refers to people who reject the authority of rabbis and the laws of rabbinic Judaism, as Uriel da Costa most certainly did. Menasseh's colleague, Saul Levi Morteira, inveighs against "libertines" who reject both the Old and the New Testaments and thus all systems of Jewish or Christian law. See Morteira's *Tratado da verdade da lei de Moisés*, Fol. 3. He insists that denying the Law of Moses in particular "causes the house to crumble," because the Old Testament is the foundation of the New Testament without which the Gospels cannot stand: "And denying the Law of Moses is nothing less than confessing oneself a libertine, without Law or divine precepts, since these have no other origin." Alternatively, the term atheist served in this period as a catch-all phrase that was used to describe all doctrines that were perceived to be heretical or potentially heretical. See especially Alan Kors, *Atheism in France, 1650–1729: The Orthodox Sources of Disbelief* (Princeton, NJ: Princeton University Press, 1990); and Martin Mulsow and Jan Rohls, eds. *Socinianism and Arminianism: Antitrinitarians, Calvinists, and Cultural Exchange in Seventeenth-Century Europe* (Leiden and Boston: Brill, 2005), 243.

Menasseh writes that these individuals hold that "the soul is the spirit of life through which [one] lives, which is blood, and with this it lives and performs its actions, and there is no difference between the soul of man and that of the beast." In death, "all is equal." Second, some members of the Portuguese Jewish community believed that: "It is not held in the Law that man's soul is immortal, and it is completely impossible that no mention would be made of this, it being such an important matter."

One argument of the "Atheists" and "Sadducees" concerned Menasseh above all others: "In the third proposition," he writes, "the Sadducees and some atheists say that in the promises of the Law there are no spiritual rewards to be found, but all of them [are] temporal, and it is necessary to believe that if there were to be some reward or punishment in the other life, it would be described in the Law."[59] Menasseh rejects this proposition vehemently, but confesses – acknowledging the argument of his adversary – that "this does not stop the doubt, seeing that in the Law... this is not treated with particular clarity."[60] It was a matter of great importance for Menasseh to demonstrate that the doctrines of divine reward and punishment and the immortality of the soul *were* in fact firmly embedded within the pages of Scripture, that the Bible contained all essential doctrines related to salvation. Although Menasseh emphasizes a number of classical and contemporary writers who have discussed this topic, his main line of defense is a prolonged recitation of dozens of biblical verses from throughout the canon of Scripture that, in his view, prove the immortality of the soul and the existence of the "other world." Menasseh devotes whole chapters to identifying these proof texts in the books of the Pentateuch, Prophets, and Writings. Although these passages are not necessarily more convincing than the

59. Menasseh ben Israel, *De la resurreccion de los muertos*, 25–26.

60. Menasseh ben Israel, *De la resurreccion de los muertos*, 50–51. "En la tercera proposicion, dizen los Zaduceos, y algunos Atheystas, no se halla en las promessas de la Ley, espirituales bienes, mas todas temporales, y es de creer, que si aviesse algun premio, o pena en la otra vida, se avia de expecificar en la Ley. A esto dezimos, que aun que es verdad, que segun avemos demostrado, assaz bastantemente se prueva por la Ley la immortalidad de las almas, y el premio o pena que tienen, segun sus meri[t]os os demeritos, no dexa de ser duda, ver que en la Ley (como bien observado está del excelente en dignidad, y immense erudicion el señor Hugo Grosios,) especialmente con claridad no se trate desto; empero a esto se pueden dar varias razones."

arguments of the "Sadducees" and "Atheists" that Menasseh had already presented, they are certainly more numerous. Menasseh hoped to defeat his skeptical adversaries by virtue of the overwhelming quantity of his evidence, rather than by outmanoeuvring his opponents logically or theologically.

Menasseh lingers particularly extensively upon proofs of the immortality of the soul in Ecclesiastes and Psalms, books of Scripture that provided some of the most extensive arguments used by the "Atheists" and "Sadducees." Menasseh reflects on Ecclesiastes 4:1–2, "A good name is better than a good oil, and the day of the death more than the day of the birth, it is better to go to the house of mourning than to go to the house of feasting." "If the death of the body ended everything," Menasseh observes, "then certainly it would be better to live and still to delight and have delights, since this is the position of the Atheists, to eat and drink since tomorrow we shall die. However, the wise man [Solomon] understands differently."[61] Menasseh also emphasizes Ecclesiastes 11:9, "O youth, enjoy yourself while you are young! Let your heart lead you to enjoyment in the days of your youth. Follow the desires of your heart and the glances of your eyes, and know well that God will call you to account for all such things." "This is as if to say," Menasseh writes, "you can indeed act according to your wishes, you have complete freedom in everything, however be warned that there is a day of judgement in which everything is accounted, which is after death." Regarding Ecclesiastes 12:7, "And the dust returns to the ground as it was, and the soul returns to God who gave it," Menasseh concludes that "in this verse there can be given no way out that contradicts the truth we are trying to prove."[62]

Finally, Menasseh turns his attention to "the true interpretation of those verses from the Psalms [and other passages involving David] that the Atheists and Sadducees can put forward in favor of their wicked sect, which we have already cited." Whereas these skeptics deny that there is any doctrine rooted in the Bible that teaches the immortality of the

61. Menasseh ben Israel, *De la resurreccion de los muertos*, 48. "Si muerto el cuerpo, todo acaba, por cierto mejor seria vivir y aun con delicias y deleites, pues es sentencia delos Atheystas, comer y beber, que manaña moriremos: pero el sabio otra cosa entiende."

62. Menasseh ben Israel, *De la resurreccion de los muertos*, 49. "En cuyo verso no se puede dar alguna salida que contradiga esta verdad que provamos."

soul or divine reward and punishment, Menasseh fervently insists that "There is no doubt David speaks about the immortality of the soul clearly and distinctly, not in one but in many places that we have cited; therefore, according to this, the verses that appear to contradict this, require another interpretation."[63] He writes that, "First of all, they put forward the text of Samuel, where David speaks regarding the child who had died, [which] says "Can I bring him back again? I shall go to him, but he will never come back to me." (2 Sam 12:23). "To this I respond," Menasseh writes, "that not only can the mortality of the soul not be deduced from this verse, but that... the contrary can be deduced, that after death there is existence and being... Because here David says that after death [there is] movement, and the son is and exists, and thus he [David] says, 'I shall go to him," which could certainly not possibly be reconciled if everything were finished with death."[64] To clinch his argument, Menasseh writes that "they cite further in their favor the verse of the sixth Psalm [v. 6] where it says, "'For in death there is no memory of you; who shall praise you from the grave,' which certainly does not persuade [one] to something absurd, because David asks for the salvation of the soul in the previous verse, 'O Lord, turn, rescue my soul, save me through your mercy."[65] In this manner, Menasseh responded vigorously to Uriel da Costa's arguments that the immortality of the soul and post-mortem reward and punishment were not taught in Scripture. Menasseh believed that the weight of the verses he could cite showed beyond any doubt that these important (and traditional) Jewish doctrines *were* rooted in the Bible, and that the central importance of salvation – which he absorbed from

63. Menasseh ben Israel, *De la resurreccion de los muertos*, 56. "Viniendo pues a la verdadera explicacion de los versos que del Psalmista pueden los Atheystas y Zaduceos alegar en favor de su malvada secta que atras citamos, diremos lo siguiente. No ay duda que clara y distintamente habla David de la immortalidad del alma, no en uno mas en muchos lugares, que avemos referido; luego segun esto los versos que parece contradizen esto, otra explicacion requieren."
64. Menasseh ben Israel, *De la resurreccion de los muertos*, 56–57.
65. Menasseh ben Israel, *De la resurreccion de los muertos*, 57. "Citan mas en su favor, el verso del Psalmo sexton donde dize, *que no en la muerte tu memoria, enel infierno quien loara a ti?* el qual ciertamente no persuade a semejante absurdo. David pide enel verso precedente la salvacion del alma, *Torna .A. escapa mi alma salvame port u misericordia.*"

the Christian world – was likewise taught in Scripture. Thus, Menasseh believed he could safeguard the biblical foundations of beliefs that were important to him, and to many of his coreligionists in Amsterdam.

Part III: Saul Levi Morteira and Jewish Salvation: Between the New Testament and the Hebrew Bible

Within the Portuguese Jewish community, discussion of the link between salvation and Scripture took place on the terrain of the New Testament as much as it did within the Hebrew Bible. In a sermon on Exodus 10:16 that he delivered in 1640, Rabbi Saul Levi Morteira spoke to his congregants about how Christians believe they achieve salvation through faith alone, to the complete exclusion of good works and biblical precepts. For many Protestant Christians in the United Provinces of Morteira's time, Scripture was important because it taught the faith required for salvation.[66] Biblical laws and precepts, however, were another story, and did not factor into the equation of eternal reward. Morteira's ultimate aim was of course to refute these beliefs. First, however, he gave a surprisingly accurate sketch of these Christian doctrines, which are based in part on Paul's Epistle to the Galatians 3:10, "For all who rely on the works of the law are under a curse; for it is written (Deut 27:26) 'A curse upon the person who does not fulfill this law by doing all that it prescribes.'" Morteira told his listeners that according to Christians, the laws of the Old Testament are impossible to observe for two reasons: first, every individual bound by the "curse" of the law must fulfill each and every precept flawlessly, and since this is impossible, sin is inevitable; and second, because there is no repentance possible for this sin, therefore eternal punishment is also assured.[67]

It was important for Morteira to address the topic of what Christians believe about salvation for two reasons. First, since Morteira delivered this sermon before a community of ex-conversos and their descendants, it is likely that he was *reminding* them about Christian doctrines of salvation, rather than introducing these beliefs to them for the first

66. Donald McKim, ed. *The Westminster Handbook to Reformed Theology*, 200–201.
67. Marc Saperstein, "Christianity, Christians, and 'New Christians' in the Sermons of Saul Levi Morteira," *Hebrew Union College Annual* 70–71 (1999–2000): 339–43.

time. Morteira knew that the question about personal salvation was an ongoing concern for many members of the community, as it had been for them as New Christians in the Iberian Peninsula. The Catholic preoccupation with eternal salvation was part of the baggage that ex-conversos brought with them to the banks of the Amstel. Second, Morteira wished to teach his congregants the *correct* way to achieve salvation, which – contrary to the Pauline critique – was rooted firmly in the observance of biblical law.[68]

Morteira had been contemplating Christian and Jewish approaches to attaining salvation for some time. The sermon described above is in fact based on a longer discussion of Paul's Epistle to Galatians in Morteira's *Preguntas que hizo un clerigo de Ruan* [Questions posed by a priest from Rouen], which was written around 1631.[69] The *Preguntas* is a polemical anti-Christian treatise in which Morteira scrutinizes the books of the New Testament comprehensively, and responds to a series of theological challenges presented by Diego de Cisneros, a Portuguese Christian priest. The final section of this chapter examines Morteira's discussions of the link between Bible and Jewish salvation in the *Preguntas*. Although a very different genre of literature from those examined above, which are mostly Jewish exegetical and theological works, Morteira's religious polemic nevertheless offers a fascinating window into his perceptions of Jewish efforts to attain salvation.

Morteira saw Galatians 2:11–17 as being particularly crucial for understanding Jewish and Christian doctrines of salvation, and the specific role of the Bible:

> When Cephas [Peter] came to Antioch, I [Paul] opposed him to his face, because he stood condemned. For before certain men came from James, he used to eat with the gentiles. But when they arrived, he began to draw back and separate himself from the gentiles because he was afraid of those who belonged to the circumcision group. The other Jews joined him in his hypocrisy,

68. Marc Saperstein, "Christianity, Christians, and "New Christians" in the Sermons of Saul Levi Morteira," 344–45.
69. Saul Levi Morteira, *Preguntas que hizo un clerigo de Ruan* (Amsterdam, ca. 1631). MS EH 48 D 38.

> so that by their hypocrisy even Barnabas was led astray. When I saw that they were not acting in line with the truth of the gospel, I said to Cephas in front of them all, "You are a Jew, yet you live like a gentile and not like a Jew. How is it, then, that you force gentiles to follow Jewish customs? We who are Jews by birth and not sinful gentiles know that a person is not justified by the works of the law, but by faith in Jesus Christ. So we, too, have put our faith in Jesus Christ that we may be justified by faith in Christ and not by the works of the Law, because by the works of the law no one will be justified. But if, in seeking to be justified in Christ, we Jews find ourselves also among the sinners, doesn't that mean that Christ promotes sin? Absolutely not!

This forceful exchange between the Apostles Paul and Peter has become known as the "Incident at Antioch," which is believed to have taken place in the late 40s of the first century.[70] As James Dunn observes, this narrative describes practices of table-fellowship between Jews and gentiles in Antioch that probably followed some basic dietary laws of the Torah, but which disregarded more rigorous precepts that were emphasized by diverse Jewish religious authorities at this time. Table-fellowship during the period of late Second Temple Judaism was a sensitive act with deep religious implications. Within an environment in which numerous Jewish movements proliferated, strict laws were developed in order to regulate the table-fellowship of Jews in diverse states of purity, as well as the sharing of meals between Jews, gentiles, converts to Judaism, Judaizers, and resident aliens.[71] Peter, having already experienced his heavenly vision rescinding the Jewish prohibition against impure foods (Acts 10:9) would have had little difficulty engaging in table-fellowship with gentiles. However, the more conservative representatives of James were taken aback at what they viewed as the minimalist observance of Jewish dietary laws, and demanded a far more attentive approach. Peter

70. James Dunn, "The Incident at Antioch (Gal. 2:11–18)," *Journal for the Study of the New Testament* 18 (1983): 4. See also James Dunn, *Jesus, Paul, and the Law: Studies in Mark and Galatians*, Chapter 7: The New Perspective on Paul (Louisville, KY: Westminster/John Knox Press, 1990), 184–214.
71. James Dunn, "The Incident at Antioch," 12–25.

concedes the authority of the "men from James," and withdraws from table-fellowship with gentile believers. At this stage, Paul confronts Peter. Paul rejects the characterization of the table-fellowship between Peter and the gentile believers at Antioch as being at all sinful in the first place, on the grounds that "man is justified not by works of law but through faith in Jesus Christ" (Gal. 2:16).[72]

The Incident at Antioch provides the foundation for Calvin to articulate central Protestant beliefs about the relationship between justification, faith, and good works, which as the following quote demonstrates, were inextricably linked to the attainment of salvation. Commenting on Paul's statement, "We being Jews by nature, and not gentile sinners, knowing that a man is not justified by the works of the law, but only through the faith of Jesus Christ, even we have believed in Jesus Christ," Calvin insists that:

> The law holds all men under its curse. From the law, therefore, it is useless to seek a blessing. He [Paul] calls them *of the works of the law* [those] who put their trust for salvation in those works... Now we know that the controversy here relates to the cause of righteousness. All who wish to be justified by the works of the law are declared to be liable to the curse... The sentence of the law is that all who have transgressed any part of the law are accursed. Let us now see if there is any man living who satisfies the law. It is certain that none has been or ever can be found. Every individual is here condemned.[73]

In this succinct commentary, Calvin expresses some of his most significant beliefs about how an individual achieves salvation. Through faith alone and trust in God, rather than through the performance of good works prescribed in the Law (Scripture), an individual may receive God's grace and be recognized as "righteous," a crucial precondition for attaining the eternal reward, salvation.[74] The centrality of justification

72. James Dunn, "The Incident at Antioch," 35–36.
73. Parker, T.H.L., ed. *Calvin's Commentaries: The Epistles of Paul the Apostle to the Galatians, Ephesians, Philippians, and Colossians*, 37.
74. Donald McKim, ed. *The Westminster Handbook to Reformed Theology*, 127–28. See

through faith alone in the process of attaining salvation remained a prominent feature of later Reformed orthodox theology from the late sixteenth century into the seventeenth century. The Leiden Synopsis of 1625 followed Luther and Calvin in identifying the doctrine as a crucial spiritual stage in which God declares an individual righteous based entirely on their faith, rather than on the merit of good works.[75]

Later in the seventeenth century, in *A commentarie upon all the epistles of the apostle Saint Paul* (London, 1631), the English theologian John Mayer (1583–1664) also commented upon the passage, "We who are Jews by birth and not sinful gentiles know that a person is not justified by the works of the law, but by faith in Jesus Christ." Mayer explains the reasons for Paul's rebuke of Peter. Although Peter had already "forsaken the Law, as unable to justifie and save them, and sought justification by the grace of God alone in Christ," after the coming of "certain men from James," Peter withdrew from his practices of table-fellowship with the gentiles until the gentiles adopted Jewish dietary laws more rigorously. According to Mayer, "by handling the matter so, as that it should seeme that he which keepeth not the Law of ceremonies, shall still be counted unclean, they themselves became unclean and sinfull, seeing they did not generally observe these ceremonies." Christ, Mayer insists, "set forth justification by faith without these things being an occasion to them."[76]

Morteira, like diverse Christian theologians, was also intensely interested in Paul's statement in Galatians 2:16, which he quotes in the *Preguntas*: "Know that a person is not justified by the works of the law, but by faith in Jesus Christ. So we, too, have put our faith in Jesus Christ that we may be justified by faith in Christ and not by the works of the law, because by the works of the law no one will be justified." However, Morteira forcefully rejects Calvin's reading of Galatians and Paul's statements about justification and salvation without the Law. He could not accept a doctrine of salvation that discounted any role for the laws and precepts of the Hebrew Bible. Against this position, he repeatedly insists

also Berndt Hamm, "What Was the Reformation Doctrine of Justification?," in *The German Reformation: The Essential Readings*, 77.

75. Donald McKim, ed. *The Westminster Handbook to Reformed Theology*, 128.

76. John Mayer (1583–1664), *A commentarie upon all the epistles of the apostle Saint Paul* (London, 1631), 322.

that the Bible's laws are *directly* relevant to justification and salvation, and that indeed this is the primary purpose of Scripture's precepts:

> Because by the works of the Law, no flesh shall be saved, Paul to Galatians, Chapter 2:16: I ask, it can only be the intention of this man to produce in this one blasphemy or another: either he suggests that there is a fault within the Law itself, not possessing in itself sufficient virtue in order to justify its adherents, or that the deficiency comes from men, who because of their inherent weakness are not able to carry out the commandments of the Law, through which they are justified, if it could possibly be observed. Now, examining both these tensions, we see that they are totally repugnant to the truth.

In fact, Morteira finds a litany of biblical proof texts to support his view, including Psalm 19:8, "The teaching of the Lord is perfect, renewing the soul." As we have already seen, this verse was a *locus classicus* for Reformed discussions of the Bible's salvific properties. In his comments on this verse, Morteira asks: "How can the Prophet of God call the Law perfect if it lacks the greatest perfection, which is justification?" Furthermore, Morteira emphasizes that the end of Psalm 19 describes this perfection as "renewing the soul to appreciate God... whose glory cannot be enjoyed without being justified."[77] It is worth pausing here

77. Saul Levi Morteira, *Preguntas que hizo un clerigo de Ruan*, Fol. 157–58 "Por quanto por las obras de la Ley, ninguna carne sera justificada, Pab: ad Gal: Cap: 2:16: Pregunto no puede dexar de ser la intencion deste hombre en esta blasphemia, una de doz o que entienda que la falta procede de la misma Ley, por no tener en sy [sic, su] virtud bastante para justificar sus observantes, o que la falta procede de los hombres que por cauza de la flaqueza de su material no pueden cumplir las obras de la Ley, la qual tiene virtud de justificar, si fuera possible, ser observada, ora examinando qual quiera destas tenciones, veremos que repugnan totalmente la verdad. Y comensando de la primera hallaremos ser refutada de muchas partes de la Sagrada Escriptura. Y por escuzar prolixidades entre su multitude, tomaremos dos otros lugares solamente, y sea el primero el verço que dize Deut: Cap: 4:8: y que gente ay grande que tenga estatuos, y derechos justos, como es toda esta Ley que yo dan delante vosotros. Ya queda de aqui daro que la Ley tiene virtud de justificar: pues sus decretos y estatuos se llaman justos los decretos Divinos. Si carecieran de su propiedad esencial que es justificaren quanto mas que es coza agena de toda razon, que no es como la Ley natural fuesse justificado, pues se llamo justo, y que los observantes de la Divina Ley dize

to consider the remarkable fact that Morteira offers a portrait of how Jews attain personal salvation using a contentiously debated Christian proof text from Galatians, and drawing upon a theological concept – "justification" – taken straight from the world of Christian theological discourse, and utterly foreign to medieval and early modern Jewish thought about eternal reward.

Continuing, Morteira brazenly explains that many Christians have serially misunderstood the key passages from Galatians, and reinterprets the verses for Jews and Christians alike. First, Morteira alleges that Christian theologians who deny any role for the Bible's commandments in achieving salvation have thrown the baby out with the bathwater through an inaccurate reading of Galatians 3:10, "All those who rely on the works of the Law are under a curse, as it is written [Deut. 27:26], 'Cursed is everyone who does not continue to do everything written in the Book of the Law.'" In fact, Morteira insists, it is not biblical precepts in general that bring a curse upon an individual, but rather only the violation of a limited set of laws specified directly above, in Deuteronomy 15–25: the commandments to not worship idols, dishonor the father and mother, move the neighbor's boundary stone, lead the blind astray, withhold justice from the weak, sleep with the father's wife, have sexual relations with animals, or with one's sister or mother-in-law:

no merescan gozar este titulo; Fuera desto dize la Sagrada Escriptura Deut: 32:43: y dixo a ellos Mosseh, poned vuestro coracon a todas las cozas que yo os protesto, y par alas encomendeys avuestros hijos para guarder y hazer atodos las palabras desta Ley, por que no es cosa vana ella devos. He aqui expresamente donde dize que no era observancia de la Ley sino atoda la perfeccion que el hombre puede aspirer, por su medio se alcanca, tanto los bienes corporals como sprituales [sic], por que si la Ley no fuera bastante para hazer adquerir qual quiera destes bienes fuera vano para aquel intent, y quien la dio da testimonio della que no es coza vana, ni carece de coza alguna, fuera desto dize David la Ley del Señor es perfecta que buelve el alma, o en otro sentido, que aquieta el alma, como pudiera llamar el Propheta de Dios a la Ley perfecta, si careciera de la mayor perfeccion que es la justificacion, mas antes en el fin del verço declara los quilates desta perfeccion, diziendo q[ue] buelve el alma agozar de Dios que la dio, cuya Gloria no podia gozar sin ser justificada, pues tambien con otro sentido, que dize que haze a quieter el alma, no prueva menos esta verdad por que quietud podia dar la Ley alas almas, dexandolas anciosas y faltas del mayor bien que desean que es el justificarse."

> [For if] it is to be understood that adherents to the Law are under a curse, hear the sayings that come out of [their] mouth... they say nothing less than this, that it shall be licit to worship idols, to dishonor the father and mother, to take in the boundary marker of a neighbor, to cause the blind to err on the path, to reject justice for the stranger, the orphan, and the widow, to marry the wife of the father, to lie with animals, the mother-in-law, and with sisters, to wound a neighbor in the shelter, [and] taking a bribe to murder the innocent. Is it beneath these enormities, the curse that we are dealing with?

"My soul does not go with their mystery," Morteira caustically remarks, because, in his view, a theology that excludes commandments such as these cannot possibly lead to justification and salvation. To clinch his argument, Morteira quotes James 2:14, "My brothers, what advantage is there if some say that they have faith, but they do not have good works? Is faith able to save?"[78] Again, Morteira emphasizes the link between performance of the Bible's commandments, justification, and salvation.

Concluding this discussion, Morteira offers what he sees as the correct exegetical reading of Paul, which permits justification and salvation through a Jewish perspective combining faith and rigorous adherence to the laws and precepts given in Scripture:

> When Paul says that nobody shall be justified through the works of the Law, he means to say that without their being accompanied by faith. In this manner we shall be in agreement easily: for

78. Saul Levi Morteira, *Preguntas*, 160. "Pero como vido la flaqueza de sus pruevas, falcefico como acostumbran, y de qual quiera modo quiero preguntar qual sea su intencion en estas palabras, para q[ue] si el entendiere que los professors de la Ley estan debajo de la maldicion, oigan sus oydos lo que sacan por la boca... pues no dizen menos con esso que ser licito ydolatrar deshonrar padre y madre, estrechar el termino de su compañero, hazer errar el ciego en el camino, a[b]orcer el juizio del peregrine huerfanos ybiudas, yazer con la mugger del padre, con quatropea, suegra, y con hermana, herir al compañero en lo encubierto, tomar cohecho para matar ynocentes, que sobre estas ynormidades son las maldiciones de que tratamos, y dizen que solo con creer la venida de aquel hombre queda libre de todo escrupulo, en su secreto no venga mi alma, quanto mas que dize Diego, Epist: Cap:2:14: hermanos mios, que aprovecha si algunos dizen, que tienen fee, y no tienen las obras. Podra la fee salvar?"

> neither good works without faith, nor faith without good works, can save. However, this faith is that which God teaches in his Law: his Essence, his most pure Unity, his Providence, his reward and punishment, his prophecy, and others like these. And whoever performs the works of the Law without believing these articles, and others like them, will surely not be justified... in such a way that Paul concludes well in the end of the same chapter, where he says: "If the Law was righteousness, then Christ [would not have] died for the rest of us." [Gal. 2:21] [This shows that] neither faith alone without good works of the Law justifies, because such a faith is not real. Given that God commanded we do this, if we do not do it we do not believe, we do not have faith. Thus, they themselves confess this proposition, as is seen in the Epistle of James (2:26): and in particular in the verse at the end, which says that because the body without the spirit is dead, so too faith without works is dead.[79]

Some of Morteira's statements about the ongoing validity of the commandments have precedents in earlier Jewish writings about the New Testament. We have already seen that Profet Duran saw Bible study and the observance of the commandments as crucial for an individual

79. Saul Levi Morteira, *Preguntas*, 159–60. "Concluyse de lo dicho, que ni por falta de la Ley ni dificultad de su observançia se pueden confirmer las calumnias que aqui se le ponen, y sino bastare lo ya dicho en esta material por daren otra declaracion alas palabras argumentadas, y q[ue] lo que Pablo dixo que par alas obras de la Ley ninguna carne sera justificada, quizo entender por las obras de la Ley solamente sin seren acompañadas con la fee, en esto acordaremos facilmente: por que ni obras sin fee, ni fee sin obras, pueden salvar, pero esta fee, es aquella que Dios enseño en su Ley, su Essencia, su Unidad purissima, su Providençia, se ha premio, y pena, su prophecia, y sus semejantes, y quien hiziere las obras de la Ley, no creyendo estes articulos, y otros como estos, cierto que no sera justificado, y assi sin introduzir fee nueva, no declarada en la Santissima Ley con sus obras, y fee; de modo que bien ha concluydo Pablo en el fin del mismo Cap: quando dize, por que, si por la Ley fuesse la justicia luego xpo por demas seria muerto, ni la fee sola sin las obras de la Ley se justificava, por que la tal fee no es realmente, siendo que Dios mando que hiziesse el, no las hizo, luego no cree, y no creyendo no tiene fee, quanto mas que ellos mismos confiesan esta propoçiçion como se vee en la Epistola de Diego Cap:2:26: y en particular en el verço con acaba, que dize, por que como el cuerpo sin espirito esta muerto, assy tambien la fee sin obras es muerta."

to attain eternal life, and that many conversos and crypto-Jews saw the Law of Moses as being vital for their salvation. In addition, assertions that Jesus had no intention of abrogating the Law, and that in fact he and his followers were assiduous in observing the Torah, are commonplace in Jewish readings of the New Testament between the fifteenth and seventeenth centuries. Profet Duran, Shimon ben Zemaḥ Duran, and Leon Modena all emphasize the famous passage of Matthew 5 in which Jesus states, "Do not think that I have come to abrogate the Torah and the Prophets. I did not come to annul them but rather to fulfill them. And indeed I say to any who would annul one of the commandments or would teach this to the people, he has a very small share in heaven."[80] Shimon ben Zemaḥ Duran and Profet Duran cite examples showing that Jesus's followers continued to observe the commandments even after his death, and that Jesus taught that his followers should obey the instructions of the Pharisees.[81] Profet Duran specifically comments on Paul's statement on justification through faith in Galatians 3. He insists that while this may be true for Christians, Paul also teaches in Galatians 3 that anyone who is circumcised is obliged to observe the Law in its entirety. Thus, Jews can and should observe the biblical precepts in perpetuity.[82]

However, the depth and extended length of Morteira's engagement with Galatians, his efforts to offer a Jewish interpretation of the text that would be edifying to both Jews and Christians, his creative use of other Christian sources, and – crucially – his internalization of key Christian theological terms, such as justification, mark Morteira's commentary as a highly atypical example of Jewish engagement with Christian Scriptures. Morteira is clearly reacting quite strongly against a view of salvation based on faith alone that was especially prominent in the theological writings of Luther and Calvin. Morteira's specific focus on

80. Frank Talmage, ed. *The Polemical Writings of Profiat Duran: The Reproach of the Gentiles and "Be not like unto thy fathers"* (Jerusalem: Mercaz Dinur, 1981), 24; Shimon ben Zemaḥ Duran, *Keshet u-magen* (Jerusalem: Makor, 1969), Fol. 2b, 3a, 9b; Leon Modena, *Magen va-ḥerev*, ed. Shlomo Simonsohn (Jerusalem, 1960), 44.

81. Frank Talmage, ed. *The Polemical Writings of Profiat Duran*, 25–26; Shimon ben Zemaḥ Duran, *Keshet u-magen*, 3a.

82. Frank Talmage, ed. *The Polemical Writings of Profiat Duran*, 27, 29.

Galatians is far more extensive than were earlier Jewish commentaries on the New Testament, reflecting the centrality of these passages in Protestant theology during the Reformation. Second, Morteira's view of how Jews achieve salvation shows that he internalized certain theological doctrines from his Christian environment, particularly the emphasis on justification as a precondition for salvation. Morteira's repeated emphasis that Jewish salvation depends upon first being justified through the performance of God's commandments laid out in the Bible shows how a quintessentially traditional Jewish idea was repackaged in language heavily influenced by Christian theology.

Third, it is worth asking whether Morteira's rereading of Paul, stressing that Paul should be seen as advocating a symbiotic relationship between faith and biblical precepts, can be located with any precision within the sixteenth or early seventeenth-century Christian discussions about the relationship between these contentious doctrines. There are strong parallels between Morteira's understanding of Paul and the perspectives of some early Reformed theologians such as Martin Bucer (1491–1551). Whereas Luther viewed Old Testament law essentially as a "bad thing which is now abolished," Bucer and Zwingli regarded these laws more positively as "a good thing now fulfilled."[83] Departing from Luther's strict exclusion of good works of the law from having any role in attaining salvation, Bucer developed a doctrine of double justification in which good works of the law play an important role. While in the "first justification," human sins are forgiven on the basis of faith alone, Bucer stressed that a secondary justification took place on the basis of good works on the part of the believer.[84] In order to reinforce his position, Bucer cited the Epistle of James, which taught that a combination of devout faith and good works was required to achieve salvation, which Luther famously dismissed as an epistle of "straw."[85] It is probably not a coincidence that Morteira went to the same textual well in order to support his own argument for the combination of faith and the performance

83. Alister McGrath, *Iustitia Dei: A History of the Christian Doctrine of Justification*, 249.
84. Alister McGrath, *Iustitia Dei: A History of the Christian Doctrine of Justification*, 252.
85. Alister McGrath, *Iustitia Dei: A History of the Christian Doctrine of Justification*, 249–52; Richard Muller, *Post-Reformation Reformed Dogmatics* 2:67, 374.

of biblical precepts being necessary for attaining salvation, James 2:14: "My brothers, what advantage is there if some say that they have faith, but they do not have good works? Is faith able to save?"[86]

Within the seventeenth century specifically, moderate or liberal Protestant movements likewise made human free will more relevant in the attainment of salvation than did orthodox Calvinists. Arminians, and later on Remonstrants, were among the most prominent of these groups in the Netherlands. Jacobus Arminius (1559/1560–1609), born in Oudewater, a small town in Holland, was trained first in Utrecht and Marburg, and then – with the support of a grant from the Amsterdam merchants guild – in Geneva (1582–1587), where he studied under the French Protestant theologian Theodor Beza (1519–1605). He later studied at Basel and Padua, before returning to Amsterdam to serve as a pastor in 1588.[87] After his appointment as professor at Leiden in 1603, Arminius began to articulate theological doctrines on predestination that differed from those of orthodox Calvinists. Instead of a strict doctrine of double predestination of the saved and the reprobate, Arminius insisted that salvation required a cooperative effort between Christ and the believer in which human free will played a definite role. Christ could offer his grace, but individual Christians were required to repent and believe with full faith in order to achieve salvation.[88] Arminius's doctrines were espoused by Remonstrant theologians following his death in 1609, and were institutionalized later in the century through the establishment of the Brotherhood of Remonstrant Ministers.[89]

Morteira grew up and spent his life in geographical settings where it was increasingly common to adopt perspectives on salvation that differed significantly from the models established by Luther and Calvin. Catholic theologians at Trent, and earlier, stressed the ongoing impor-

86. Saul Levi Morteira, *Preguntas*, 160. "Dize Diego, Epist: Cap:2:14: hermanos mios, que aprovecha si algunos dizen, que tienen fee, y no tienen las obras. Podra la fee salvar?"
87. Th. Marius van Leeuwen, Keith D. Stanglin, and Marijke Tolsma, eds. *Arminius, Arminianism, and Europe*, x–xi.
88. Th. Marius van Leeuwen, Keith D. Stanglin, and Marijke Tolsma, eds. *Arminius, Arminianism, and Europe*, xiii–xiv, xix.
89. Th. Marius van Leeuwen, Keith D. Stanglin, and Marijke Tolsma, eds. *Arminius, Arminianism, and Europe*, xvi–xvii.

tance of faith and good works for achieving salvation, as did Reformed theologians such as Bucer, and moderate Calvinists such as the Arminians and Remonstrants. In combination with medieval Jewish sources that Morteira surely knew, these figures collectively help us to better understand how Morteira formulated his positions on Jewish justification and salvation in a seventeenth-century community of ex-conversos and their descendants.

* * *

Conclusion

For many members of the Portuguese Jewish community, the connection between Scripture and salvation was an important theological concept at the front of their minds and on the tips of their tongues. Leading rabbis and prominent members of the community frequently articulated this idea as a basic foundation of how they thought about the Bible, and as supporting the importance of studying and practicing the commandments of Scripture. The link between salvation and the Bible was important to members of the community for diverse reasons, and appeared in a wide range of Jewish texts. It appears in Isaac Athias's *Fortificaccion de la ley de Moseh*, and in Daniel Levi de Barrios's discussions of Bible study in Portuguese Jewish confraternities. The link between Scripture and salvation is emphasized in the introduction to Menasseh ben Israel's *Humas de Parasioth y Aftharoth* (Amsterdam, 1627) and his *Conciliador* (Amsterdam, 1632), and in the prayer book edited by David Pardo and Salom ben Yosseph (Amsterdam, 1630). The link between Scripture and salvation is also strongly emphasized in Menasseh ben Israel's attack on Uriel da Costa, and it appears again, more elaborately, in Saul Levi Morteira's polemical writings, in which he refutes Luther and Calvin's perspectives on the relationship between good works of the law and faith, and proposes a rereading of Paul that emphasizes a combination of faith and the performance of biblical commandments.

While there are a number of similar concepts and doctrines native to rabbinic and medieval Jewish theology, such as the world to come, immortality of the soul, and reward and punishment, Jewish discussions about salvation were also informed by ideas Jews had absorbed as New Christians living as Catholics in Spain and Portugal. After joining the

Jewish community in Amsterdam, these Christian beliefs about salvation were reformulated in a Jewish idiom emphasizing the priority of the Hebrew Bible, and the centrality of biblical commandments rather than faith or sacraments.

The centrality of the Bible for leading Portuguese Jews had important consequences for the social and cultural development of the community. As we saw in the previous chapter, the systematic study of Scripture was a defining characteristic of the curriculum at most levels of the educational system in Amsterdam. The shape of this curriculum should be understood, at least in part, as being formed by leading rabbis who internalized the ethos of a Christian religious culture preoccupied with salvation, and a converso culture that connected salvation with the Old Testament. Many of the rabbis who taught in the Talmud Torah saw a strong connection between the performance of biblical commandments and the achievement of salvation, and brought these perspectives into their classrooms. In Chapter 3, we shall see how the assumed connection between Scripture and salvation in part motivated Menasseh ben Israel to reconcile every contradiction that he could identify in the Bible. For Menasseh ben Israel, a Bible that was to play a central role in Jewish efforts to achieve salvation, and serve as the foundation for the theological and moral ordering of society, could not contain serious, unresolvable contradictions.

THREE

"One of the Greatest Problems That There Is in Scripture": Menasseh ben Israel, Mathematics, and the Authority of the Bible

"IT IS ASTOUNDING," SPINOZA WRITES, "HOW READILY ALL THE commentators have embraced the notion that the prophets knew everything that human understanding can attain. Even though certain passages of the Bible tell us in the plainest terms that there were some things the prophets did not know."[1] In one breath, Spinoza expressed many of the devastatingly subversive ideas that he held about Scripture: the notion that the knowledge contained in the Bible is limited; the possibility that there could be serious error in God's Word; the frightening notion that prophetic knowledge in general was unreliable; and the possibility that generations of interpreters had traveled blindly down paths to nowhere. Scholars have long identified the seventeenth century as a period of social, political, and religious upheaval that left permanent scars on the sanctity and authority of the Bible. For the early twentieth-century French historian Paul Hazard, "it was not to be expected that the Bible would escape the onslaught" of the "War Against Tradition" that took place during the

1. Benedict Spinoza, *Theological-Political Treatise*, ed. Jonathan Israel and trans. *idem* and Michael Silverthorne (Cambridge: Cambridge University Press, 2007), 33.

later decades of this century, as it was "the symbol" of an "Authority" that he viewed as being in precipitous decline.[2] Anthony Grafton and other scholars have described this period as witnessing a veritable "exegetical revolution" in which philological scholarship, historical studies, the practice of chronology, and other disciplines chipped away at the veneer covering the Bible's authority.[3] Amos Funkenstein insisted that the seventeenth century witnessed a theological revolution that produced what he called a "secular theology" based on the new science and a mathematical worldview, and historians have described a broader "mathematization" of knowledge that took place during this period. Sixteenth- and seventeenth-century luminaries including Galileo, Descartes, Spinoza, and others increasingly sought to understand the world around them – and the Bible – in the "language of mathematics."[4]

Late seventeenth-century readers of Spinoza's *Theological-Political Treatise* would have quickly encountered the use of mathematical and natural philosophical arguments to subvert the authority of Scripture and the claims of its traditional interpreters. Offering one of the most powerful examples he could summon at this time, Spinoza invoked the famous passages in Joshua 10:12–13: "On the day when the Lord gave the Amorites over to the Israelites, Joshua spoke to the Lord; and he said in the sight of Israel, 'Sun, stand still at Gibeon, and Moon, in the valley of Aijalon.' And the sun stood still, and the moon stopped, until the nation took vengeance on their enemies." For many, this famous passage evoked a miracle. "But why," Spinoza asks, "are we obliged to believe the word of a soldier in astronomical matters?" And yet most of Spinoza's contemporaries took it for granted that Joshua was correct. Even those who – according to Spinoza – "have learnt to philosophize more accurately and recognize that the earth moves and the sun is at rest" insist on making "great efforts to derive this from the passage, even

2. Paul Hazard, *The Crisis of the European Mind: 1680–1715* (New York: NYRB Classics, 2013), 180–98.
3. Anthony Grafton, *Defenders of the Text: The Traditions of Scholarship in an Age of Science, 1450–1800* (Cambridge, MA and London, England: Harvard University Press, 1991), 205.
4. Amos Funkenstein, *Theology and the Scientific Imagination from the Middle Ages to the Seventeenth Century* (Princeton, NJ: Princeton University Press, 2007), 3–22.

though it will obviously not permit this reading." Spinoza, for his part, totally eschewed reconciling Scripture with the findings of natural philosophy: "I prefer to say frankly," he explains, "that Joshua was ignorant of the true cause of that longer-lasting light." In reality, Spinoza wrote, "They had no idea that as a result of the large amount of ice which was in the air there at the time [see Joshua 10:11] . . . there was a greater refraction than normal, or something of the kind."[5]

As Steven Nadler and Jonathan Israel have emphasized, Spinoza's rejection of miracles was one of the most scandalous and enraging claims delivered in his *Theological-Political Treatise*.[6] Two salient aspects of Spinoza's arguments about Joshua's miracle deserve emphasis. First, we should note the contrast between prophetic knowledge and natural knowledge. Spinoza's remarks on Joshua 10:12 were part of a larger effort to circumscribe the authority of the Bible, illuminating categories of knowledge where the Bible's information abounded in error and uncertainty. More bluntly, Spinoza later writes that "those who look in the books of the prophets for wisdom and knowledge of natural . . . things are completely on the wrong track"; prophecy is in fact categorically inferior to natural knowledge, since knowledge of nature "needs no confirmation from God." Second, we should note the importance of specifically mathematical knowledge in Spinoza's reading. The entire problem with Joshua 10:12 that he (and many others) perceived was that it conflicted with the mathematical models of Copernicus and Galileo that supported a heliocentric model of the universe. Spinoza generally viewed the Bible as rife with mathematical deficiencies that completely undermine the text. And the mathematical problems of Scripture were not limited to the heavens. Spinoza also identified them closer to home: the dimensions of Solomon's Temple and the molten sea constructed

5. Jonathan Israel, ed. *Theological-Political Treatise*, 33–34. For a detailed survey of Spinoza's general rejection of the Bible's miraculous narratives and the radical nature of his critique, see Steven Nadler, *A Book Forged in Hell: Spinoza's Scandalous Treatise and the Birth of the Secular Age* (Princeton, NJ: Princeton University Press, 2011), 76–104.
6. Steven Nadler, *A Book Forged in Hell*, 76; Jonathan Israel, *Radical Enlightenment: Philosophy and the Making of Modernity 1650–1750* (Oxford: Oxford University Press, 2001), 218.

by Hiram: "Solomon, not being a mathematician, did not know the true ratio between the circumference of a circle and its diameter, and supposed like other craftsmen that it was 3 to 1" (1 Kings 7:23). Third, and finally, we should note that Spinoza views mathematically verifiable information as providing a higher and more reliable degree of certainty than prophecy: "the certainty the prophets derived from signs was not mathematical certainty... but only moral certainty, and the signs were given for nothing other than to convince the prophet..."[7]

Menasseh ben Israel, a rabbi in the Portuguese Jewish community and a contemporary of Spinoza, was deeply concerned about the implications of the mathematical and scientific contradictions in the Bible that Spinoza and his contemporaries highlighted. In response, he produced the most monumental effort to resolve these inconsistencies ever written by a pre-modern Jew. Historians have explained many of Spinoza's ideas, and his attack on the Bible and traditional religious authority, by pointing to his contacts with radical Christian movements in the Netherlands – Socinians, Quakers, libertines, and others condemned as "heretics" by their contemporaries in the Christian world. However, Spinoza has rarely been studied as a reader of the Bible whose methods of biblical scholarship were shaped by the culture of biblical studies within the Jewish community in which he was born and raised, and where Menasseh served as a prominent rabbi. The central problem that this chapter explores, and the question that it asks, is how our image of Spinoza – and our understanding of Amsterdam's broader Portuguese Jewish community as a whole – would look different if we try to connect these two figures, exploring how the culture of biblical studies in the ex-converso community might have helped shape the concerns, interests, and conclusions that Spinoza drew in the *Theological-Political Treatise*. I hope to show that Spinoza emerged out of a community where there was already an awareness of – and a deep anxiety about – the mathematization of knowledge and its implications for the authority of the Bible. What we see as being "orthodoxy" and "heterodoxy" in this community may in fact be closely related phenomena engaged with a common set of concerns, but arriving at very different answers.

7. Jonathan Israel, ed. *Theological-Political Treatise*, 30.

Menasseh ben Israel's Project – an Introduction

Along with famous heterodox figures like Uriel da Costa and Spinoza, Menasseh ben Israel is one of the most extensively studied members of the seventeenth-century Portuguese Jewish community in Amsterdam. Sina Rauschenbach has thoroughly explored Menasseh's role as an intermediary between medieval Jewish knowledge and the seventeenth-century world of Christian Hebraist scholarship, through a study of his Latin and vernacular writings.[8] Scholars have explored Menasseh's contributions to northwest European and Portuguese messianic movements,[9] and his approaches to reading sixteenth-century Spanish literature.[10] His Hebrew treatise defending the reality of occult and demonological phenomena, *Nishmat Ḥayyim*, has been studied in detail,[11] as have his broader perspectives on kabbalah.[12] A vast literature has traced Menasseh's contacts with radical Christians in the Netherlands and northwest Europe,[13] and his efforts to secure settlement rights for Jews in England.[14] Menasseh has been the subject of four extensive

8. Sina Rauschenbach, "Mediating Jewish Knowledge: Menasseh ben Israel and the Christian Respublica litteraria," *The Jewish Quarterly Review*, vol. 102, no. 4 (Fall 2012): 561–88.
9. See Antonio Jose Saraiva, "Antonio Vieira, Menasseh ben Israel, et le cinquième empire," *Studia Rosenthaliana* 6 (1972): 25–57, and Menasseh ben Israel, *The Hope of Israel*.
10. H. Mechoulan, "Menasseh ben Israel: lecteur du docteur Juan Huarte de San Juan dans 'De la fragilidad humana' et 'Esperanza de Israel.'" *Revue des études juives* 163, no. 3–4 (2004): 463–74.
11. J.H. Chajes, *Between Worlds: Dybbuks, Exorcists, and Early Modern Judaism*, 119–33.
12. Joseph Dan, "Menasseh ben Israel: Attitude Towards the Zohar and Lurianic Kabbalah," in *Menasseh ben Israel and His World*, ed. Yosef Kaplan, Henry Méchoulan, and Richard Popkin (Leiden and New York: Brill, 1989), 199–206, and Moshe Idel, "Kabbalah, Platonism and Prisca Theologia: The Case of R. Menasseh ben Israel," in *Menasseh ben Israel and His World*, 207–19.
13. David Katz, "Menasseh ben Israel's Christian Connection: Henry Jessey and the Jews," in *Menasseh ben Israel and His World*, 117–38. Ernestine G.E. van der Wall, "Petrus Serrarius and Menasseh ben Israel: Christian Millenarianism and Jewish Messianism in Seventeenth-Century Amsterdam," in *Menasseh ben Israel and His World*, 164–90.
14. Jonathan Israel, *Diasporas within a Diaspora: Jews, Crypto-Jews, and the World Maritime Empires (1540–1740)* (Leiden: Brill, 2002), 406–14. Jonathan Israel, "Menasseh ben Israel and the Dutch Sephardic Colonization Movement of the Mid-Seventeenth Century (1645–1657)," in *Menasseh ben Israel and His World*, 139–63.

biographical works.[15] Collectively, the broad literature on Menasseh ben Israel has illuminated many dimensions of the life of one of the Amsterdam community's most prominent rabbis and representatives to the Christian world of learned scholars. Despite the significant work on Menasseh, however, there has been comparatively little systematic analysis of his biblical commentaries.[16] The absence of such studies is especially surprising in light of the fact that exegetical works represent some of his largest individual contributions to Jewish thought.

15. Cecil Roth, *A Life of Menasseh ben Israel: Rabbi, Printer, and Diplomat* (Philadelphia, PA: The Jewish Publication Society of America, 1934); Menahem Dohrman, *Menasseh ben Israel* [Hebrew]. (Kibbutz ha-Me'uchad, 1989); Lionel Ifrah, *L'Aigle d'Amsterdam: Menasseh ben Israel 1604–1657* (Paris: Honoré Champion Éditeur, 2001), and most recently Steven Nadler, *Menasseh ben Israel: Rabbi of Amsterdam* (New Haven, CT and London: Yale University Press, 2018).

16. To the extent that scholars remark upon the *Conciliador* in their studies of Menasseh, the text is often seen as an apologetic response to Uriel da Costa's heterodox challenge to rabbinic Judaism. See Henry Méchoulan, "Menasseh ben Israel," in *Moreshet Sepharad: The Sephardi Legacy*, ed. Haim Beinart (Jerusalem: Hebrew University Magnes Press, 1992), 2:318; Menahem Dohrman, *Menasseh ben Israel* [Hebrew], 42–44; Cecil Roth, *A Life of Menasseh ben Israel: Rabbi, Printer, Diplomat*, 85–87. However, as Noah Rosenbloom emphasizes, the beliefs of heterodox ex-conversos like da Costa, Spinoza, and others were not rooted in biblical contradictions. See Noah Rosenbloom, "Discreet Theological Polemics in Menasseh ben Israel's Conciliador," *Proceedings of the American Academy for Jewish Research* 58 (1992): 147–48. Rosenbloom is undoubtedly correct in this regard, and in fact one of the primary characteristics of Uriel da Costa's *Examination of Pharisaic Traditions* is an emphatically literal reading of biblical precepts, and a critique of the chasm he perceived between Scripture and rabbinic Judaism. See Uriel da Costa, *Examination of Pharisaic Traditions*, 5. Rosenbloom, who has written the only article-length study of the *Conciliador*, suggests as an alternative that the work is merely a printed collection of Menasseh's sermons, which is equally unsatisfactory. As evidence for the sermonic origins of the *Conciliador*, Rosenbloom cites the composition of the work in Spanish rather than Hebrew, but little else. Nevertheless, he views Menasseh's method of juxtaposing conflicting verses as merely a "skillful literary method to evoke the interest of his audience." Appended to his commentary on the Book of Daniel, *Piedra gloriosa*, Menasseh includes a list of works that he has published in Hebrew, Latin, and Spanish, and ones that he intends to print in the future. Among the latter, he lists "450 sermons in Portuguese." See Menasseh ben Israel, *'Even yeqarah. Piedra Gloriosa*, (Amsterdam, 1655) "Catalogo" [unpaginated]. Thus, Menasseh preached in Portuguese, not Spanish, and did not regard the *Conciliador* as the printed version of his sermons four years after the completion of the fourth and final volume of biblical reconciliations.

Between 1632 and 1651 Menasseh ben Israel published his *Conciliador, o de la conveniencia de los Lugares de la S. Escriptura, que repugnantes entre si parecen* [The Reconciler, or the agreement of verses in Sacred Scripture that appear contradictory].[17] The *Conciliador* is a massive attempt to reconcile hundreds of biblical contradictions involving thousands of verses, and to prove the complete infallibility of the Bible. While it was not at all uncommon for Jewish commentators to remark on individual contradictions and to affirm the perfection of the Bible, Menasseh's comprehensive and systematic effort to resolve all apparent inconsistencies in Scripture, cover to cover, was unprecedented in the medieval and early modern Jewish world. Over a period of nearly twenty years, spanning the majority of his career and adult life, Menasseh remained fixated by the Bible's internal inconsistencies. The second volume, the *Segunda parte del Conciliador*, was published in 1641, and focuses particularly on scientific, mathematical, chronological, and numerical inconsistencies and contradictions in the Bible. It is an ambitious effort to identify, catalogue, and – in theory – resolve all such contradictions and problems, with a special focus on the history of ancient Israel's judges and kings. While a fervent believer in the infallibility of Scripture, Menasseh's efforts to disentangle the mathematical and chronological quagmire of ancient Israelite judges and kings left him more – rather than less – unsettled. While Menasseh worked assiduously to craft a seamless chronology of ancient Israelite history, he repeatedly confessed his own inability to resolve these challenging mathematical and numerical problems. His efforts revealed more problems than they resolved, and brought these inconsistencies to the attention of many other Jews and Christians, including – perhaps – his community's most famous heretic, Benedict Spinoza. Studying Menasseh's writings reveals that doubts and concerns regarding the Bible's authority were making inroads not only on the fringes of this Jewish community, but at its very center. While the culmination of the seventeenth-century's exegetical revolution lay in the future – after Menasseh's lifetime – study of his writings provides

17. Menasseh ben Israel, *Conciliador, sive De convenientia locorum S. Scripturae, que pugnare inter se videntur. Esto es, Conciliador, o de los Lugares de la S. Escriptura, que repugnantes entre si parecen*. 4 vols. (Frankfurt and Amsterdam, 1632–1651).

background to the prominence and contentiousness of the mathematical and chronological inconsistencies in Scripture that would soon become one of the several strands of philological scholarship that Spinoza would employ in his critique of the Bible's sanctity and authority.

Part I of this chapter sets the stage for a study of Menasseh's project by examining the genre in which he wrote, and the assumptions that he shared with Christian writers who were equally devoted to proving the infallibility of the Bible by reconciling its contradictions. Yet in the *Segunda parte del Conciliador,* Menasseh has tunnel vision for a very particular type of contradiction: scientific, mathematical, and chronological inconsistencies. Part II explains this focus in terms of the broader mathematization of knowledge in the world and society in which Menasseh lived. In a time period where there was a growing demand for, and confidence in, mathematical knowledge, and in which mathematical knowledge was applied indiscriminately across disciplinary lines, Menasseh clearly recognized the dangerous implications that this could have for biblical studies. He was acutely aware of the potential for mathematics to shine a spotlight on the Bible's weak numerical underbelly. And nowhere, perhaps, was the Bible seen to be more vulnerable in the seventeenth century than in the apparent conflict between the miracle of Joshua and the changing understanding of the heavens – a problem that Spinoza accentuated enthusiastically, and that vexed Menasseh greatly. Menasseh and Spinoza lived in the same mathematizing world, though they occupied very different parts of it.

The tension between new ways of thinking about the heavens and scriptural texts was certainly important to Menasseh, but it was ultimately a small piece of a much larger and more challenging problem that he hoped to resolve: the pervasiveness of mathematical inconsistencies throughout the Bible, especially in the narratives of ancient Israel and Judah's judges and kings. Part III and Part IV of this chapter therefore explore Menasseh's efforts to disentangle the devilishly complicated chronological threads strewn throughout the different biblical books, in an ambitious – and ultimately futile – effort to prove the infallibility of the Bible by reconciling all of its mathematical contradictions. For although Menasseh devoted impressive energies to the task, he twice confesses the failure of his project and his inability to truly resolve these problems. This admitted "failure" provides a fitting bookend for a seventeenth-century project attempting to resolve mathematical contradictions. For as we shall see, Spinoza turns to the same problems that Menasseh was unable to resolve in his assault upon the authority of the Bible in the *Theological-Political Treatise.*

Part I: Biblical Contradictions and Infallibility: Jewish and Christian Contexts

On the first page of his opening volume of the *Conciliador,* Menasseh ben Israel made a grandiose statement about his contribution to Jewish biblical studies: "I present to you the conciliation of all of the places in Sacred Scripture that are apparently contradictory, a new work, and never developed by another of our *nacion*... At the end of having collected over several years all of the difficulties and texts that are contradictory at first glance, I resolved to reconcile them."[18] In making such a boastful claim, he was both right and wrong. On the one hand, Menasseh's claims about biblical infallibility have their parallel in Jewish-Muslim polemics, in which Muslim scholars alleged that the Torah had been corrupted in transmission (*tahrif*), deliberately falsified, that it contained theological impossibilities, and that it was littered with contradictory biblical verses. It was further alleged that the Jewish chain of transmission had been serially interrupted, so that there could be no certainty about the content of the text.[19] Among the most systematic in his textual critique of the Bible is Abu Muhammad 'Ali b. Ahmad b. Hazm (Ibn Hazm, b. 994 in Cordoba). Ibn Hazm analyzes over fifty passages from the Pentateuch illuminating a wide range of numerical, historical, and geographic inconsistencies, as well as statements that are theologically problematic (such as biblical anthropomorphisms) and conflict with teachings in the Qur'ān. Far more than most other ninth- and tenth-century scholars, Ibn Hazm draws attention specifically to contradictory verses: for instance,

18. Menasseh ben Israel, *Conciliador,* "Al Lector" [unpaginated].
19. For a survey of Islamic critiques of the Hebrew Bible, see Camilla Adang, *Muslim Writers on Judaism and the Hebrew Bible: From Ibn Rabban to Ibn Hazm* (New York and Leiden: Brill, 1996), 223–49. See also Hava Lazarus-Yafeh, *Intertwined Worlds: Medieval Islam and Bible Criticism* (Princeton, NJ: Princeton University Press, 1992), 19–49.

discrepancies in the narrative descriptions of manna in Exodus 16:31 and Numbers 11:7.[20] Ibn Hazm also argues that the Torah is textually corrupt and unreliable, and that the chain of transmission between Moses and the present had been interrupted at certain junctures.[21]

Jews responded to these allegations, and vigorously asserted the perfection and integrity of the Torah. Against Muslim claims that Ezra the Scribe falsified the text of the Bible when the Israelites returned from Babylonia (especially in the writings of Ibn Hazm), the Baghdadi Jewish philosopher Ibn Kammuna (d. 1285) deflected these allegations by emphasizing Ezra's piety and righteousness, which were beyond reproach, and would have inhibited him from tampering with the divine text.[22] Rabbi Solomon ibn Adret (1235–1310) wrote a detailed rebuttal of Ibn Hazm's critique of the Bible, the *Ma'amar al Yishmael* [Treatise against Ishmael],[23] that specifically addresses many claims made in Ibn Hazm's polemic. He emphasizes that the presence of many unflattering accounts about the Israelites and Patriarchs proves the authenticity of the Bible, since a forger would certainly have had no compunctions about removing these passages.[24] The Bible's authenticity is also evident from the agreement between diverse copies of the text possessed by many Jewish communities, and he defends the contiguity of the Jewish chain of transmission.[25] Throughout, his goal is to demonstrate the perfection of the Torah. In the fifteenth century, Shimon ben Zemaḥ Duran included a defense of the Torah's perfection against Muslim

20. Camilla Adang, *Muslim Writers on Judaism and the Hebrew Bible*, 237–48.
21. Camilla Adang, *Muslim Writers on Judaism and the Hebrew Bible*, 225–36, 241–48. This was a common motif in Islamic anti-Jewish polemics that was employed by a variety of ninth-century Muslim figures, including Abu Muhammad 'Abd Allah b. Muslim b. Qutayba (Ibn Qutayba, b. ca. 828), Abu Ja'far Muhammad b. Jarir al-Tabari (b. 839), and Abu Nasr Mutahhar b. Tahir al-Maqdisi (10th century).
22. Hava Lazarus-Yafeh, *Intertwined Worlds*, 71–72.
23. Camilla Adang, "A Jewish Reply to Ibn Hazm: Solomon b. Adret's Polemic Against Islam," in *Judíos y musulmanes en al-Andalus y el Magreb: Contactos intelectuales*, ed. Maribel Fierro (Madrid: Casa de Velázquez, 2002), 179–209. See also Harvey Hames, "A Jew amongst Christians and Muslims: Introspection in Solomon ibn Adret's Response to Ibn Hazm," *Mediterranean Historical Review* 25, no. 2 (2010): 203–19.
24. Camilla Adang, "A Jewish Reply to Ibn Hazm," 186–87.
25. Camilla Adang, "A Jewish Reply to Ibn Hazm," 188–92.

allegations of corruption and imperfection within his treatise *Keshet u-magen* (1438). Duran vigorously rebuts Muslim allegations against the integrity of the Bible, and insists that the use of the Old Testament by both Jews and Christians is proof that the text has not been tampered with or otherwise corrupted over the course of time, since it would be implausible to suggest that Jews and Christians collaborated to cover up supposed falsifications.[26]

It is also clear that there were important precedents in European Jewish society for Menasseh's effort to reconcile contradictory biblical verses.[27] To examine but one of many potential examples of earlier Jewish efforts, we may look briefly at Moses of Coucy's *Sefer Mitzvot Gadol* [Large Book of Commandments], the introduction to which presents a large number of these inconsistencies. Jeffrey Woolf has shown that Moses of Coucy's introduction should be set against the background of the 1240 Disputation of Paris and the debate over whether the Talmud was a heretical work. Woolf sees the introduction as a response to Nicholas Donin's allegation that the Talmud was an inauthentic rabbinic creation that violated the traditional basis for Jewish settlement in Christian lands.[28] To counter these claims, Moses of Coucy stressed that the Talmud was in fact divine, and that it was intimately connected to the Bible. Contradictory biblical verses played a key part of his strategy. He argued that without the Talmud, Jews would have no way of reconciling a variety of inconsistencies in the Bible: Numbers 3:39 states that the Levites numbered 22,000, their actual number is only 21,700; Exodus 13:6 says that you shall eat matzo for seven days, Numbers 16:8 says that

26. Shimon ben Zemaḥ Duran, *Keshet u-magen*, 16–17.

27. Although Ibn Hazm made contradictory verses a prominent component of his critique of the Bible, it is important to note that this particular element of his polemic did not evoke a response of any kind from contemporary Jews. In fact, Solomon ibn Adret's response more than two centuries later is the first systematic Jewish rebuttal of Ibn Hazm, and it does not address the question of biblical contradictions at all. See Camilla Adang, "A Jewish Reply to Ibn Hazm," 179–209.

28. Jeffrey Woolf, "Some Polemical Emphases in the 'Sefer Miswot Gadol,'" *The Jewish Quarterly Review* 89, no. 1–2 (1998): 85. Christian polemicists alleged that Jewish adherence to law based on the Talmud rather than the Bible deviated sharply from the Augustinian requirement that the toleration of Jews in Christendom required their adherence to biblical law and modes of life.

you shall eat matzo for six days; Exodus 12:19 says that no leaven shall be found in your house for seven days, while Exodus 12:15 states that only on the very first day you shall remove all leaven from your houses, and so on.[29] And Moses of Coucy was not by any means the only medieval Jewish reconciler of biblical inconsistencies.

Just a few years before the printing of Menasseh's first volume of the *Conciliador* in 1632, a Jewish work again raising the problem of biblical inconsistencies was printed in Amsterdam itself: Imanuel Aboab's *Nomologia o discursos legales* (Amsterdam, 1629), which highlighted the problems posed by several of these contradictions in order to accentuate the importance of Oral Law in Judaism for the correct understanding of the Bible and Jewish law. Many of the internal contradictions that appear in the writings of Moses of Coucy are reprised in the inconsistencies explored by Aboab, and appear as well in the first volume of the *Conciliador* – and Sina Rauschenbach compellingly suggests that Menasseh may have been inspired in part by Aboab's methodology.[30] As we shall see, Menasseh's efforts at resolving apparent contradictions in Scripture draw ubiquitously on the way individual discrepencies are reconciled in the Talmud, as well as in the writings of medieval Jewish exegetes including Abraham ibn Ezra, Rashi, Maimonides, David Kimḥi, Levi ben Gershon, Bahya ben Asher, Isaac Abravanel, Eliezer Ashkenazi, and many others.

29. Moses of Coucy, *Sefer Mitzvot Gadol* (Jerusalem: Mekhon Yerushalayim, 2002), 2–3. For Moses of Coucy, Oral Law also clarifies commandments in the Bible that are obscure or ambiguous, providing the necessary specific information that the Bible itself lacks. For instance, while the Bible prohibits impure birds, it is the Oral Law that describes exactly which birds may be consumed and which may not. See b. Ḥullin 59a. Within the first two volumes of the *Conciliador*, Menasseh repeatedly uses Oral Law in order to clarify scriptural inconsistencies. However, it is exceptionally rare for Menasseh to use contradictory verses in order to demonstrate the theological importance of Oral Law itself. See Menasseh ben Israel, *Conciliador*, vol. 1, p. 249. Menasseh identifies a grammatical inaccuracy in Genesis. He argues that there can be no error whatsoever in an infallible Bible, and therefore the Oral Law is necessary to make this apparent grammatical inconsistency religiously edifying.

30. Sina Rauschenbach, "Mediating Jewish Knowledge," 566 and Sina Rauschenbach, *Judentum für Christen: Vermittlung und Selbstbehauptung Menasseh ben Israels in den gelehrten Debatten des 17. Jahrhunderts* (Berlin and Boston: De Gruyter, 2012), 55–56. On the *Nomologia* itself, see Moisés Orfali, ed., trans. *Nomologia o discursos legales* [Hebrew] (Jerusalem: Mekhon Ben Tsevi, 1997) 13–51.

And yet there is also an important sense in which Menasseh *was* justified in claiming that he tread on virgin territory in the admittedly vast world of pre-modern Jewish exegesis. What was new about his work, what was "never developed by another of our *nacion*," was the *comprehensiveness* of the project, the effort to reconcile "*all* of the places in Sacred Scripture that are apparently contradictory, [my emphasis]" thus proving the complete infallibility and inerrancy of the Bible systematically. No earlier Jewish exegete composed an entire text devoted to reconciling biblical contradictions, let alone one that could compare to the four volumes that Menasseh produced over the course of his career. And no medieval Jewish exegete was as concerned about the implications of these contradictions as Menasseh. The distinctive characteristics of the *Conciliador* invite reflection on the ways in which Menasseh's contemporary world, the seventeenth-century Netherlands and Europe, led him to be especially concerned about biblical contradictions and the infallibility of Scriptures, and offered models that influenced how he thought and wrote about the Bible.

CHRISTIAN PERSPECTIVES ON BIBLICAL CONTRADICTIONS

For a Jewish scholar and ex-converso immersed in the Christian world of seventeenth-century Europe, nothing could be more normative than to compose a systematic reconciliation of biblical contradictions. Harmonies and synopses of the Gospels were ubiquitous in the Protestant world in which Menasseh lived, as attested by Martin Bucer's commentaries on the Synoptic Gospels (1526–1536), Andreas Osiander's *Evangelienharmonie* (1537), and John Calvin's *Commentary on the harmony of the three Evangelists: Matthew, Mark, and Luke* (1555).[31] Catholic Gospel harmonies also circulated in Menasseh's cultural milieu, such as *Evangelistarum quaternio* and the *Mysticae Ezechielis quadrigae*, both written by Jesuits in the southern Low Countries in the early seventeenth century.[32] These commentaries offer a close reading of the Gospels, with

31. Donald McKim, *Calvin and the Bible* (Cambridge: Cambridge University Press, 2004), 131–54.

32. Marijke H. de Lang, *De opkomst van de historische en literaire kritiek in de synoptische beschouwing van de evangelien van Calvijn (1555) tot Griesbach (1774)*. PhD Thesis, University of Leiden, 1993. De Lang distinguishes between "harmonies," which weave

a particular focus on their conflicting descriptions of similar events and teachings. The texts of each Gospel are considered alongside one another, followed by an effort to reconcile theological, factual, and genealogical contradictions. In order to resolve these inconsistencies, Christian scholars relied upon patristic writings, medieval exegetical works, alternative translations in the Septuagint, and references to rabbinic Jewish interpretations.

Throughout the seventeenth century, a wide range of Christian scholars recognized the ongoing popularity and significance of this type of biblical commentary. Amandus Polanus (1561–1610), one of the earliest and most significant systematic theologians of Protestant orthodoxy, provided a list in his *Theologiae syntagmae* (Hanover, 1609) of what he saw as being the most significant approaches to exegesis. Among several others, he included "the bringing together of the passage to be explained with the other passages that are different or even apparently contradictory, and their reconciliation."[33] Scholars with strikingly different theological and philosophical perspectives also appreciated the prominence of these approaches to reading the Bible, even if they did not approve of them. The seventeenth-century Cartesian biblical commentator Lodewijk Meijer sheds further light on the importance of harmonies of Scripture.[34] In his *Philosophia S[acrae] Scripturae Interpretes* [Philosophy as the Interpreter of Holy Scripture; Amsterdam, 1666], Meijer provides a curious definition of the verb "to interpret." One meaning of the term,

the conflicting narratives into a single, cohesive narrative , and "synopses," in which the conflicting verses are juxtaposed alongside one another for the reader to see, and are then analyzed. Most of the works listed above, and Menasseh's *Conciliador*, follow this second approach.

33. Lodwijk Meijer, *Philosophy as the Interpreter of Holy Scripture* (Amsterdam, 1666), trans. Samuel Shirley, ed. Lee C. Rice and Francis Pastijn (Milwaukee, WI: Marquette University Press, 2005), 219.

34. Meijer, who received his doctorate in philosophy and medicine at Leiden, viewed Descartes' philosophy as providing a way to circumvent the disagreements about Scripture that permeated the Christian world by dislodging biblical interpretation from the realm of theology to that of philosophy. Meijer has been seen as an especially radical proponent of Cartesian philosophy. The *Philosophia S[acrae] Scripturae Interpretes* received a hostile welcome even from academic Cartesians at Leiden. See Willem Frijhoff and Marijke Spies, eds. *Dutch Culture in a European Perspective*, 1:338–39. As well, see Jonathan Israel, *The Dutch Republic: Its Rise, Greatness, and Fall. 1477–1806* (Oxford: Clarendon Press, 1995), 913–16.

Meijer writes, is to explain what is obscure. "To interpret" may also refer to translators who make comprehensible in one language what was opaque in another language. Significantly, however, Meijer identifies another use of the verb "to interpret" in the context of biblical exegesis of his period: "The more common meaning of the verb 'to interpret' and the noun 'interpretation' is: 'one who brings together and reconciles parties who are at variance.'"[35] Benedict Spinoza mentions – and dismisses – this method of scholarship in his *Theological-Political Treatise.* After drawing his readers' attention to contradictory verses regarding the reigns of Israel's kings and the duration of the period between the Exodus and Solomon's Temple, Spinoza writes: "Many other discrepancies such as this are evident throughout the text, and I certainly do not need to review the maneuvers of those writers who try to reconcile them. The rabbis talk evident nonsense."[36] The harmonization of scriptural contradictions was prominent in the minds of significant Protestant theologians and radical skeptics alike, during the very years in which thousands of conversos settled in Amsterdam and converted to Judaism, and during which Menasseh began composing his *Conciliador.*

Reformed Protestant theologians regularly emphasized the necessity of reconciling all contradictions in Scripture, since the appearance of internal errors or contradictions threatened their understanding of the Bible as an infallible text. Only one year before Menasseh printed the first volume of the *Conciliador,* the English theologian John Mayer wrote that "Some books of Scripture are historicall, and therefore may not seeme to have been inspired, but they are also said to be inspired, because they who wrote them, were infallibly guided by the Spirit, that they could not erre in any thing, and for the choice of the things written by them, others being omitted."[37] Writing later in the seventeenth century, Matthew Poole commented on 2 Peter 1:21,

> For the prophecy came not in old time by the will of man: but holy men of God spake as they were moved by the Holy Ghost.

Poole insisted that the writers of Scripture were

35. Lodwijk Meijer, *Philosophy as the Interpreter of Holy Scripture,* 34–37.
36. Jonathan Israel, ed. *Theological-Political Treatise,* 135–36.
37. John Mayer, *A commentarie upon the New Testament* (London, 1631), 2:552.

> elevated above their own natural abilities... this may imply the illumination of their minds with the knowledge of divine mysteries, the gift of infallibility, that they might not err, of prophecy, to foretell things to come, and a peculiar instinct of the Holy Ghost, whereby they were moved to preach or write.[38]

Additionally, the Leiden *Synopsis purioris theologiae* (1625) states that "the writers [of Scripture] did not regard themselves as purely *pathetikos*, or passive, but also *energetikos*, or active, as those who applied both skill and mental activity and discourse and memory, arrangement and order and their own style (whence the difference in manner of writing among them)... presided over, however, perpetually by the Holy Spirit, who so guides and directs them, that they are preserved from all errors of mind, memory, language, and pen."[39]

Likewise, the English theologian Edward Leigh, in his work *A Treatise of Divinity* (1646), wrote that "the wonderfull consent, singular harmony and agreement of the Scriptures shewes that they came not from men but from God... If there seem any contrariety either in numbering of yeeres, circumstance of time and place, or point of doctrine, the fault is with our apprehension and ignorance, not in the thing it selfe, and by a right interpretation may easily be cleared."[40] Additionally, Benedict Pictet (1655–1724) included the complete harmony of all books and verses of Scripture in his list of proofs for the divinity of the Bible: "The first characteristic is to state nothing but the truth. Second, to reveal such mysteries as cannot arise from the human imagination, but which are nonetheless in accord with the natural ideas God has impressed upon the mind. Third, to direct our worship and our minds to the true God alone. Fourth, so to instruct the mind, as to satisfy and set at rest the most insatiable desire after knowledge. Fifth, to teach men by the most

38. Matthew Poole, *Annotations upon the Holy Bible* (London, 1683). Reissued in 3 vols., London: Banner of Truth, 1962, 3:921.
39. Richard A. Muller, *Post-Reformation Reformed Dogmatics*, 2:246–47. See also Donald McKim, ed. *The Westminster Handbook to Reformed Theology*, 136. The *Synopsis purioris theologiae* (Leiden Synopsis; 1625) is a collective statement of Reformed theology written following the Synod of Dort by Polyander, Walaeus, Thysius, and Rivetus.
40. Edward Leigh, *A Treatise of Divinity* (London, 1646), 18.

holy precepts to love God above all other things, and to renounce all iniquities. Sixth, to be always consistent with itself, and to exhibit no contradiction."[41] Thus, the assertions that the Bible was an infallible text, that Scriptures were free from human and divine error, and that the Bible was free from internal contradictions or inconsistencies, were on the tip of the tongue for numerous Protestant religious scholars during the seventeenth century.

The fixation on biblical contradictions evident in many of the Christian harmonies was driven by assumptions that were shared by Menasseh and Christian theologians of the sixteenth and seventeenth century. For many Christian scholars – and Menasseh – the systematic resolution of biblical contradictions was linked to the perfection and infallibility of the Bible. Scriptural contradictions and infallibility existed in a zero-sum game, where the presence of the former negated the latter. It was therefore essential to eliminate these contradictions in order to uphold the authority of the Bible. Like his Christian contemporaries, Menasseh viewed even miniscule contradictions in the Bible as threatening the integrity and authority of the text. After calculating that the Israelites ate manna in the desert for thirty-nine years and eleven months (based on data from Exodus and Joshua), Menasseh exclaims that "this being infallible, how does the third verse [Exodus 16:35] say that Israel ate manna for forty years?"[42] It was vital to resolve even such seemingly innocuous and trivial contradictions, which loomed improbably large in Menasseh's eyes.

Menasseh and many Christian theologians were convinced of Scripture's total infallibility. Yet in the seventeenth century this assumption was increasingly pressured from a number of directions. For instance, the total infallibility of the Bible was a core issue of debate between seventeenth-century Catholics and Protestants. Robert Bellarmine argued that church traditions existed prior to the canonical Bible, and that the biblical text was imperfect, insufficient, and obscure.[43] To a large degree, it was the Bible's complete infallibility that was also at stake in

41. Richard A. Muller, *Post-Reformation Reformed Dogmatics*, 2:270.
42. Menasseh ben Israel, *Conciliador*, 1:178.
43. Stephen Burnett, *From Christian Hebraism to Jewish Studies*, 206.

Protestant-Catholic debates about the antiquity of the Hebrew vowel points. If Catholic scholars were correct in arguing that the vowel points were a late (post-canonical) addition to the Hebrew text of Scriptures, then Bellarmine's view of Scripture as an imperfect text that was dependent on human traditions was correct, and Protestants could not rely on the Bible to be the main tool in its own interpretation. Furthermore, it was alleged that Jews themselves – the ostensible guardians of the Hebrew texts and its vowels – could have manipulated or falsified them to hide Christian truth.[44] Against these arguments, Protestant men of letters, such as Amandus Polanus and Johannes Buxtorf, insisted on the authentic antiquity of the vowel points based on extrabiblical Jewish texts such as the Talmud and the Zohar.[45] Polanus argued that the Hebrew text was reliable because it had been edited by the Men of the Great Synagogue.[46]

The total infallibility of the Bible was also disputed and questioned by a variety of Protestant movements that advocated more limited understandings of biblical infallibility and divine inspiration, including Arminians, Remonstrants, and Socinians. Leading figures like Hugo Grotius and Simon Episcopius, professor of theology at Leiden from 1612, attempted to define different levels of truth in Scripture against

44. Debate over the antiquity of the vowel points had a significant history prior to the Reformation, but was intensified by the theological valences of the issue for Protestants and Catholics. On the importance of Elijah Levita's *Sefer Masoret ha-Masoret* (1538), which argued that the vowel points were a late accretion that reflected authentic oral traditions, see Jordan Penkower, "New Considerations on Sefer Massoret ha-Massoret of Elijah Levita." For the reception and appropriation of Levita's arguments in Protestant-Catholic polemics, see Stephen Burnett, *From Christian Hebraism to Jewish Studies*, 203–39.
45. Richard Muller, *After Calvin: Studies in the Development of a Theological Tradition*, 146–48; Stephen Burnett, *From Christian Hebraism to Jewish Studies*, 211. There were learned Protestants who disagreed strongly with this approach. Joseph Scaliger pointed out to Buxtorf that the Zohar and Talmud were post-biblical compositions, and therefore could not be used to attest the antiquity of the vowel points. The Protestant scholar Louis Cappel in 1624 published his *Arcanum punctationis revelatum*, which decisively proved the lateness of the Hebrew vowel points against Buxtorf's arguments for ancient origins. Cappel assumed that the vowels were an obstacle to reconstructing the original text of Scripture based on ancient Aramaic and Syriac translations.
46. Stephen Burnett, *From Christian Hebraism to Jewish Studies*, 209.

the uniform infallibility and inspired nature of Scripture advanced by many Reformed scholars. Simon Episcopius argued that the revelation of the Old Testament was inferior to that of the New Testament, and Faustus Socinus argued that there were less important or consequential elements of the Bible in which the biblical authors could and did err.[47] Socinus and Episcopius insisted that the truth of the New Testament should be grounded not in doctrines of divine inspiration, as Reformed scholars argued, but on the "impeccably documented historical *veritas* of the New Testament reports."[48] These types of arguments specifically provoked the Reformed theologian Johannes Hoornbeeck to compose an extensive work, *Socinianismus confutatus,* defending the divine inspiration and infallibility of the *entire* biblical canon and the absence of any error whatsoever in the text. He insisted that there was nothing "minor" or "inconsequential" in Scripture where error would be acceptable, and that an error in part implied flaws in the whole. While some Christians, according to Hoornbeeck, based their beliefs about the limitations of divine inspiration on scriptural contradictions and inconsistencies, these were merely difficult passages that in no way could support the belief that the text of Scripture was fundamentally flawed. For Hoornbeeck, a Bible with flaws and internal contradictions could not be the basis for attaining salvation.[49]

Part II: Old Miracles and the New Philosophy

The infallibility of Scripture was also challenged by Protestant and Catholic thinkers who were sympathetic to the new astronomy of Copernicus and Galileo, the mechanistic model of the universe, and the importance of mathematically demonstrable knowledge for the study of nature.[50] This mathematization of knowledge was well underway in Europe long before Spinoza expressed his confidence in mathematical

47. Richard A. Muller, *Post-Reformation Reformed Dogmatics,* 2:306.
48. Kestutis Daugirdas, "The Biblical Hermeneutics of Socinians and Remonstrants in the Seventeenth Century," in *Arminius, Arminianism, and Europe: Jacob Arminius (1559/1560–1609),* 97–99.
49. Richard Muller, *Post-Reformation Reformed Dogmatics* 2:306–7.
50. Richard Blackwell, *Galileo, Bellarmine, and the Bible;* and Kenneth Howell, *God's Two Books.*

certainty and used it to subvert the miraculous claims in Joshua 10:12. As Galileo famously stated in *Il Saggiatore* (1610), "the universe ... which stands continually open to our gaze ... is written in the language of mathematics."[51] And it was the language of conclusive mathematics, rather than inherited traditions of the church, that would be decisive in evaluating the miracle in Joshua.

The implications of Copernicus's ideas, the new philosophy, and mathematics for the authority of the Bible were deeply contested in the decades before Menasseh wrote the *Segunda parte del Conciliador*. The Reformed pastor Philipp Lansbergen argued in his *Bedenckingen Op den Dagelijckschen, ende Iaerlijkschen loop van den Aerdt-kloot* [Considerations on the diurnal and annual motion of the earth; 1629] that the Bible's scientific information was both erroneous and contradictory. According to 1 Kings 7:23, for example, the ratio of the circumference of the circle to its diameter is 30/10, and 2 Chronicles 4:2 gives the relationship as 21/7. In fact, both biblical passages are incorrect; as Archimedes demonstrated, the real figure is 22/7.[52] On the basis of these types of inconsistencies and mathematical errors, Lansbergen emphasized that while he fully accepted the divinity and inspiration of Scripture and its usefulness for teaching morals and correct theological doctrines, in no way was the Bible's information about scientific and philosophical questions to be trusted.[53] Against these types of arguments, Gisbert Voet argued that philosophy and science must be entirely subordinated to theological doctrines, and that in fact biblical texts such as Psalm 104 contained profound truths related to the disciplines of history, politics, economics, geography, physics, astronomy, chronology, and navigation. Voet believed firmly in the notion of a "Mosaic and sacred physics" in which the Bible could serve as the foundation for scientific inquiry.[54] Voet could not accept arguments that Scripture could err in scientific

51. See the discussion of this famous metaphor in Stillman Drake, ed. *Essays on Galileo and the History and Philosophy of Science* (Toronto: University of Toronto Press, 1999), 50–62.
52. Kenneth Howell, *God's Two Books*, 146–49.
53. Kenneth Howell, *God's Two Books*, 149–50.
54. Kenneth Howell, *God's Two Books*, 169. Regarding the wider phenomenon of the search for a Mosaic or "pious philosophy" that could challenge and replace the appeal

matters, or that the authority of the Bible could be limited to only those doctrines pertaining to religion. Endless debates could ensue, he feared, about what parts of the Bible did or did not pertain to the spheres of religion or science. Furthermore, if the Bible's language was flawed or insufficient in the area of natural philosophy, this meant that Scripture was inherently false and deceptive, and could not be trusted on questions of central theological doctrines.[55] The controversy that took place in the Netherlands over Copernicus, Galileo, and the heliocentric universe is especially significant. Not only did it occur here earlier and more extensively than in many other corners of Europe; it was waged where Menasseh ben Israel lived.

Menasseh ben Israel lived in a world that increasingly gave priority to mathematics as the highest and most certain form of knowledge – even when it conflicted with Scripture. And this disturbed him in many ways, both small and large. I would like to begin with a small – but I believe instructive – example: Menasseh's take on Joshua 10:12. Decades before Spinoza would use this passage as a fulcrum to subvert the authority of the Bible and the idea of miracles, Menasseh ben Israel grappled with the miracle for very different – but related – reasons. Near the beginning of the second volume of the *Conciliador*, Menasseh juxtaposes verse 12: "Sun, stand still at Gibeon, and Moon, in the Valley of Aijalon," with verse 13: "The sun stopped in midheaven, and did not hurry to set for the whole day." Menasseh was ostensibly interested in the rather basic question of whether the miracle took place at night, or during the day. But he had a larger goal in mind. His real target was radical philosophical interpretations of Joshua that stressed the immutability of the laws of nature, and precluded their violation even temporarily. Within the medieval Jewish world, nobody was more closely associated with radical philosophical interpretations of Joshua than the talmudist and astronomer Levi ben Gershon (1288–1344), who denied outright than any celestial miracle had taken place above the ancient field of battle. Gersonides is well known for espousing an especially radical version of

to pagan philosophers, see Ann Blair, "Mosaic Physics and the Search for a Pious Philosophy in the Late Renaissance," *Isis* 91, no. 1 (2000): 32–58, esp. pp. 50–51.

55. Kenneth Howell, *God's Two Books*, 169.

Aristotle's metaphysics, in which God rigidly controls the celestial and sublunar realms according to fixed and immutable rules. Simply put, the universe runs and there is order in the world because God continually meditates upon the rules that keep it going. Furthermore, these rules can never be changed. To make any alteration would imply an imperfection in God's creation, and would cause utter chaos in the sublunar world. These laws are rooted in God's mind, but order is maintained by the emanations stemming from the Separate Intellects (and especially the Agent Intellect) that implement God's blueprints. Because of the importance of nature's immutability for Gersonides, miracles like the sun standing still posed a particularly sharp challenge. For Gersonides, miracles were the result of an individual achieving especially exalted intellectual perfection, activating information and knowledge that was emanating from the Active Intellect all along; there was no possibility that the sun could have ceased its movements in contravention to all the laws of the universe and nature. Indeed, it is clear that within Gersonides' universe any miracle must necessarily function within the boundaries of what is naturally already possible.[56]

Menasseh joined a long line of medieval Jewish commentators who emphatically criticized Gersonides' metaphysics. Between the late fourteenth and the fifteenth century, figures such as Ḥasdai Crescas, Shem Tov ibn Shem Tov, Isaac Arama, Isaac Abravanel, and others, lined up to pile scorn on his ideas.[57] Isaac Arama (1420–1494) comments on the miracle that takes place in Isaiah 38:7–8, "'This is the sign to you from the Lord, that the Lord will do this thing that he has promised: See, I will make the shadow cast by the declining sun on the dial of Ahaz turn back ten steps.' So the sun turned back on the dial the ten steps by which it had declined." According to Gersonides, this was simply the result of shifting clouds which caused a non-miraculous realignment

56. For an overview of Gersonides' metaphysics and his perspective on miracles, see Robert Eisen, *Gersonides on Providence, Covenant, and the Chosen People: A Study in Medieval Jewish Philosophy and Biblical Commentary* (Albany, NY: SUNY Press, 1995), esp. 13–38.

57. Regarding the line of Jewish scholars' criticism of Gersonides, see Menachem Kellner, "Gersonides and his Cultured Despisers: Arama and Abravanel," *Journal of Medieval and Renaissance Studies*, vol. 6 (1976): 269–96.

of the shadow on the sun dial. Arama dismisses this as "*divrei ruaḥ*," or nonsense. "Even more repulsive," Arama continues, "is what he [Gersonides] writes about the Sun at Gibeon," described in Joshua 10:12–13.[58] Abravanel went further, perhaps, describing Gersonides' rationalism as being an inexcusable offense to the Torah (*sholeh yad neged Torah*).[59] However, nobody before Menasseh ben Israel described Gersonides as a *heretic*. Menasseh was as incensed as Arama and Abravanel by the idea that miracles are the work of the Agent Intellect and cannot have any effect on celestial bodies such as the sun. But he goes much further than earlier commentators in denouncing those who hold such beliefs. Menasseh, after pointing to the fact that the Bible is full of miracles for which God is absolutely the proximate, most direct cause, announces: "and believing otherwise, giving this capability to another, *is a remarkable heresy* [my emphasis]."[60] This crucial phrase raises the stakes significantly in the debate about Gersonides' perspectives on miracles. Whereas some earlier commentators were content to reject Levi ben Gershon's interpretation of Joshua 10:12 as meaningless, Menasseh uses language inherited from the Catholic world in order to place extreme philosophical interpretations of this miracle beyond the boundaries of Judaism.

Was this mere rhetorical strategy? Was it simply a choice of words? Is the accusation of heresy *only* a lingering vestige of the Catholic world that echoed in the Portuguese Jewish community? Seen in the context of the Netherlands in the seventeenth century, Menasseh's invocation of "heresy" to describe radical philosophical interpretations of Joshua 10:12 indicates that there is something more here than mere semantics. Rather, it reflects the debates about the implications of natural philosophy for religious belief and the authority of Scripture that had begun to rage in the Netherlands during the 1620s and 1630s. The heliocentric model of the universe and its implications for biblical authority were – as we have seen – vigorously debated in Amsterdam and the Low Countries in the 1620s and 1630s, the decade or so before Menasseh wrote the

58. Isaak Arama, *Sefer Akedat Yitzhak* (Pressburg, 1849), 97–98.
59. Isaac Abravanel, *Perush al Nevi'im Rishonim*, 53–54.
60. Menasseh ben Israel, *Segunda Parte del Conciliador*, 14–16: "*. . . y creer otra cosa, dando esta facultad a otro, es notable heregia.*"

second volume of the *Conciliador.* During this period, lectures on the heliocentric model were given at the Amsterdam Athenium – the institution where Menasseh once attempted unsuccessfully to secure the position of Hebrew professor – [61] and it is also worth observing that there were vectors for the dissemination of these ideas within the Jewish community as well. Joseph Delmedigo, a peripatetic Jewish scholar known for his scientific and kabbalistic writings, was a former student of Galileo's who traveled to Amsterdam in 1626. Delmedigo's *Sefer Elim* which (among much else) records Galileo's astronomical discoveries, was actually printed by Menasseh ben Israel.[62] Thus clearly, Menasseh could have learned about the contentious, new mathematical model of the universe from any number of sources. It is likely that his unusually venomous reaction to radical philosophical interpretations of Joshua 10:12 was informed by these debates.

Part III: The Challenges of Biblical Chronology

While Menasseh was interested in the implications of new approaches to astronomy for the interpretation of Scripture, he was transfixed by mathematical problems nearer at hand: the ubiquitous numerical and chronological inconsistencies in the biblical narratives of ancient Israel's judges and kings. The central focus of the *Segunda parte del Conciliador* was the Jewish past, as Menasseh makes abundantly clear: "And as for the subject of this book, although it is not History, it is rooted in History, and divine history, and in the succession of Judges and leaders who for a period of 846 years held power among the Hebrews. On these questions many of the most distinguished and celebrated men have labored not a little, which this and past centuries have enjoyed."[63] Menasseh's task was

61. Dirk van Miert, *Humanism in an Age of Science: The Amsterdam Athenaeum in the Golden Age, 1632–1704*, trans. Michiel Wielema and Anthony Ossa-Richardson (Leiden: Brill, 2009), 247–53.
62. Tamar Rudavsky, "Galileo and Spinoza: Heroes, Heretics, and Hermeneutics," *Journal of the History of Ideas*, vol. 62, no. 4 (October, 2001): 613 and 618–19.
63. Menasseh ben Israel, *Segunda Parte del Conciliador o de la convivienca de los lugares de la S. Escriptura, que repugnantes entre si parecen* (Amsterdam, 1642). 'Epistola Dedicatoria.' "Y quanto al asumpto de la obra, puesto que no sea historia, es fundado en Historia, y sacra, y en la sucession de Juezes y Principes que por espacio de 846 anos obtuvieron

straightforward enough, or so it would appear: giving chronological and mathematical coherence to the lines of judges and kings who governed the biblical Israelites. Yet in the age of mathematization of knowledge, the numbers and data in the Bible could pose a most serious problem. What if the numbers do not compute? What if the errors or contradictions in the Bible's numerical and mathematical information could not be resolved? What implications might such perceived deficiencies have on the integrity – and the authority – of God's Word? Chronological inconsistencies in the biblical narrative posed an especially sharp challenge to Menasseh's assumptions about the integrity and infallibility of Scripture. Because of the numerical and mathematical nature of chronological contradictions, a persuasive resolution had to be mathematically coherent and account for all of the available data. However, Menasseh often found his efforts frustrated by the limited numerical information actually available in the Bible's accounts of Israelite rulers. If the chronology of the ancient judges and kings refused to cohere, then the assumption of biblical infallibility teetered on the brink of a dangerous precipice.

Menasseh was a voracious reader of Jewish and Christian literature, and many of the texts he read brought him in touch with humanist authors sensitive to the mathematical and chronological inconsistencies that permeate Scripture. In his treatise on original sin, the *Dissertatio de fragilitate humana ex lapsu Adami*, Menasseh offered a list of recommended readings on different subjects in Jewish literature. Commenting particularly on the most essential works of biblical scholarship produced by Jewish authors, he cited Sa'adia Gaon, Maimonides, David Kimḥi, Ibn Ezra, Rashi, Levi ben Gershon, Bahya ben Asher, Isaac Arama, Isaac Abravanel, Azariah de' Rossi, Moses Almosnino, and many others, writing that "These will be sufficient for explicating the Bible and theological questions."[64] Works such as these, Menasseh affirmed,

el ceptro entre el pueblo Hebreo. En cuyas questiones, no poco trabajaron los mas insignes y celebres varones, deque gozo este y los passados siglos."

64. Menasseh ben Israel, *Dissertatio de fragilitate humana ex lapsu Adami*, (Amsterdam, 1642), 134–35. "Hi suffecerint ad Bibliorum explicationem, & Theolgicas quaestiones." See also Menasseh ben Israel, *De la fragilidad humana, y inclinacion del hombre al peccado* (Amsterdam, 1642), 80.

"should never be set aside from one's hands,"[65] but rather, "the works of the aforementioned authors must always be kept by the headboard" of one's bed.[66] If Menasseh indeed read works such as Isaac Abravanel's biblical commentaries and Azariah de' Rossi's *The Light of the Eyes* before going to sleep, these volumes likely did not always engender restful dreams. Abravanel and de' Rossi, two of the most historically attuned sixteenth-century Jewish humanists, did much to accentuate the most pressing mathematical problems of biblical chronology, and little to resolve them. Their attention focused especially on those inconsistencies that perplexed and worried Menasseh most – chronological problems surrounding the ancient judges and kings of Israel and Judah.

Perhaps no Jewish author that Menasseh read disquieted him more than Isaac Abravanel, whose work on biblical chronology illuminated profound inconsistencies in the narratives of ancient Israelite judges. Abravanel's skeptical remarks about the Bible's chronology of these judges were centered on Judges 11:26, "Israel has been inhabiting Heshbon and its dependencies ... for three hundred years." This verse refers back to a conflict between the Israelites and Amorites that took place following the Exodus from Egypt. During Israel's period of wandering in the desert, the Israelites requested permission from King Sihon of the Amorites to pass through his lands. Sihon refused, and according to the biblical text initiated a battle with Israel at Jahaz. The Israelites successfully rebuffed Sihon's attack, and subsequently "Israel settled in all the towns of the Amorites, in Heshbon and all its dependencies."[67] Many generations later, Jephthah sent messengers to the king of the Amorites asserting that Israel had now been in control of Heshbon and its environs for three hundred years.[68]

Despite the fact that Jephthah stated quite plainly that Israel had held Heshbon for precisely three hundred years, Abravanel deeply distrusted this figure. Abravanel's commentaries on the books of Joshua, Judges, and 1–2 Samuel, which were completed following his flight to

65. Menasseh ben Israel, *Dissertatio de fragilitate humana*, 134–35.
66. Menasseh ben Israel, *De la fragilidad humana*, 80.
67. Numbers 21:25.
68. Judges 11:19–23.

Castille from the court of the king of Portugal in 1484, exposed a serious chronological problem.[69] When added together, the total number of years governed by all of the judges prior to Jephthah did not cohere with the three-hundred-year period between the Exodus and capture of Heshbon.[70] Abravanel, like many other Jewish and Christian readers of the Bible, knew that there were a bare handful of clear signposts for organizing a chronology of the judges and kings of ancient Israel: the three-hundred-year period between the Exodus and capture of Heshbon; and a total of 480 years between the Exodus and construction of Solomon's Temple. Yet he admitted that "it is appropriate to search for the details of this counting according to the literal meaning of the text and whether they agree with these [statements]... And I say that if we are inclined to the literal meaning of Scriptures, the dilemma increases greatly."[71] Abravanel calculated that there were in fact 348 years between the capture of Heshbon and Jephthah, and 576 years between the Exodus and Solomon's Temple, in complete contradiction to the Bible's clear chronological statements.[72] Even if Abravanel assumed that all periods of subjugation overlapped with the years governed by one judge or another, he was still left with only 268 years between the Exodus and the capture of Heshbon, a figure that likewise confounded the biblical information and stubbornly refused to cohere to the biblical framework of three hundred years between the Exodus and Jephthah. Not only did Abravanel's chronological investigations expose highly problematic inconsistencies; his "solutions" served only to throw additional fuel on the fire.

Whereas Menasseh insisted on the rigorous infallibility of the Bible's chronological information, Abravanel dismissed such expectations of rigorous mathematical coherence as foolish and beside the point:

> Just because Jephthah sent [ambassadors] to assert his right on the basis of three hundred years, we do not have to understand this literally. And this is because when Scripture says or testifies

69. Isaac Abravanel, *Perush al Nevi'im Rishonim* [Commentary on the Early Prophets] (Jerusalem: Hotsa'at Sefarim Torah ve-da'at, 1954/1955), 422.
70. Isaac Abravanel, *Perush al Nevi'im Rishonim*, 129.
71. Isaac Abravanel, *Perush al Nevi'im Rishonim*, 231.
72. Isaac Abravanel, *Perush al Nevi'im Rishonim*, 231.

> that something happened in such and such a way, it must be accepted precisely in the form described. However, this is not so in exchanges between some men and other men, and much less so in those of Israel with the gentiles, in which each man speaks in the manner he sees fit, just as here Jephthah – in order to secure the rights to his lands – sent ambassadors to testify that he had possessed them for many years, and he said three hundred, even though the truth was that it was 268 years.[73]

In other words, according to Abravanel, the statement specifying three hundred years between the Exodus and the Israelite capture of Heshbon was nothing more than a rhetorical strategy: "Jephthah did not say this to be precise, that there were no more and no less than three hundred years, but he said it because there were two hundred and sixty-eight years, and they favored the number of three hundred years."[74]

Menasseh, immersed in a world where many increasingly demanded mathematically sound knowledge, and in a Protestant milieu where debate about biblical infallibility and scriptural contradictions crescendoed, could not accept Abravanel's laxity toward mathematical and chronological inconsistencies in the Bible. For Menasseh, establishing the integrity and precision of Jephthah's statement was vital. His efforts

73. Menasseh ben Israel, *Conciliador* 2:33–34. "Y puesto que Iptah embio a dezir el derecho de la Prescripcion de 300 años, no por esso se deue entender eso puntualmente: y esto, porque quando la Escriptura dize, o textifica, aver sucedido una cosa de tal y tal modo, se deue entender, derechamente en la forma que se dize; mas no en las platicas que unos hombres tiened con otros, y mucho menos en las de Israél para con los gentiles, que en estas cada uno hablara en la forma que le estuviere bien, como aqui Iptah para asegurar el derecho de sus tierras embio a notificar la possession de muchos años, y dixo 300 aun que a la verdad eran 268." See also Isaac Abravanel, *Perush al Nevi'im Rishonim*, 232–33. Abravanel insists that earlier commentators upon the problem of Jephthah's 300 years insisted that this mathematical figure was an estimate or rhetorical expression not intended to be precise or infallible. Abravanel then affirms that his own approach is based on three *hakdamot*. His third *hakdamah* insists that there is a difference between Scripture's accounts of events that took place – which must have happened precisely as stated in the text – and what it reports about oral exchanges between men. Especially in cases of conversation between Israel and the nations, these exchanges may be shaped by the rhetorical needs of the situation and need not conform themselves to the precision that Scripture uses in its first-hand narration.

74. Isaac Abraanel, *Perush al Nevi'im Rishonim*, 233.

to produce a coherent portrait of biblical chronology were inconceivable without upholding the few clear numerical signposts given in Scripture – the three-hundred-year period between the Exodus and Jephthah, and the 480-year period until the construction of the Temple. Crucially, he insists that the Bible's chronological information was in fact rigorously accurate, "this being infallible." In order to demonstrate this to be so, Menasseh began by adding up the years governed by each judge. This, as Menasseh knew, did not get him very far: "[C]ontinuing through the years of each king until the fourth year of Solomon, they do not fit with the [biblical] count."[75] Like Abravanel, Menasseh discovered significant discrepancies between the totals reported in the Bible, and the sum of the individual periods assigned to each judge. He discovered that the judges who governed before Jephthah covered 348 years, instead of three hundred. Furthermore, he found that there were 188 years between Jephthah and the construction of the Temple, instead of 180. Summarizing his conclusions, Menasseh writes that: "adding the 388 years between the Exodus from Egypt and Jephthah and the 188 between Jephthah and the fourth year of Solomon's reign, the sum is 576 years. How then does the text say that the Temple was built 480 years after the Exodus from Egypt, since according to this count there were 576 years, and there is a difference of 96 years?"[76] The task of shaving nearly a full century from his calculations in order to prove the infallibility of the Bible made this problem challenging indeed.

Medieval exegetes used a number of strategies to try and close this gap. For instance, the rabbinic chronological text *Seder 'Olam* and the medieval talmudist and astronomer Levi ben Gershon tried to resolve the problem by selectively discounting some – but not all – of the periods of time in which Israel was ruled by a foreign power. Both *Seder 'Olam* and Levi ben Gershon exclude nearly all periods of foreign rule from the calculations, but include the eighteen years in which Israel was ruled by the Amonites in order to whittle the ninety-six year gap down to just three years.[77] Menasseh had great respect for these medieval authors,

75. Menasseh ben Israel, *Conciliador,* 2:30–31.
76. Menasseh ben Israel, *Conciliador,* 2:30–31.
77. Chaim Milikowsky, "Seder Olam: A Rabbinic Chronography," (PhD diss., Yale University, 1981), 286–92.

and was at least somewhat sympathetic toward their approaches. And yet despite the fact that they seemed to offer an easy resolution to these chronological problems, he remained dissatisfied. Perhaps he shared Isaac Abravanel's concern about the arbitrariness of their methods and the inherent mathematical flaws of their conclusions. As Menasseh writes, "And since they count some [years of foreign rule], why do they not count others? From which we are forced to conclude that they were not moved to this by any reason, but they lacked for their calculation the said number, which cannot be sufficient."[78]

For Menasseh, biblical chronological information that was truly infallible must cohere in a far more mathematically rigorous fashion. He demanded a resolution that was self-evidently true and irrefutable. He therefore excluded *all* periods of subjugation from his calculations, arguing that they were encompassed within the years assigned by the Bible to each judge. Adding the biblical data together, Menasseh calculated that the judges governed Israel for a total of 248 years prior to Jephthah, well below the three hundred years specified by Jephthah. Menasseh's solution was to (arbitrarily) distribute the remaining fifty-two years among three judges whose periods of governance were unspecified in the Bible: "we have three judges whose time is not specified, namely, Joshua, the elders . . . and Shamgar between Ehud and Deborah. We shall say therefore that Joshua governed twenty-eight years . . . that the elders followed for twenty years, and Shamgar four, which closes our number at three hundred." In the end, Menasseh's calculations were every bit as arbitrary as those of the medieval exegetes he critiqued. Following a decidedly circular logic, he insisted that Joshua, the elders, and Shamgar ruled fifty-two years because this was the difference between the total years governed by the known judges and Jephthah's figure of three hundred years.

How confident was Menasseh ben Israel in his resolution? Did Menasseh feel that he had achieved his stated goal, successfully proving the Bible to be infallible in its chronological information regarding judges of ancient Israel? Crucially, he confesses that "although in this way we have not achieved more insight than through reason [i.e., the mathematical calculations], it will be sufficient for us here in order to

78. Menasseh ben Israel, *Conciliador,* 2: 32–33.

discern that there is no fault in the authority of the Divine letters."[79] Thus, Menasseh himself was unconvinced that his mathematical solutions were persuasive enough to resolve the conflict posed by an apparent period of 576 years between the Exodus and construction of the Temple. Menasseh ben Israel fervently wanted his theological convictions about the Bible's infallibility to align with his commitment to mathematical certainty. However, he recognized that the chronological information available within the biblical text was insufficient, and he was forced to adopt a flawed, vulnerable methodology.

Part IV: One of the Greatest Problems That There Is in Scripture

Menasseh's ambitious goal – establishing the chronological order of rulers for a period of 846 years in the biblical past – required him to venture far beyond the years of the ancient judges, and to grapple with the even more challenging task of disentangling the chronology of the kings who ruled over the kingdoms of Israel and Judah. Menasseh understood all too well the immensity of this undertaking. In the conclusion he wrote to this volume, he observes that "all of the interpreters have greatly exerted themselves upon this point. And ultimately, Samotheus confesses that many learned men have perspired over this, since they were unable to find a solution to such a great problem."[80] Continuing, Menasseh adds that "in truth, this is one of the greatest [problems] that is to be found in the Sacred text." We can easily appreciate the alluring appeal that a strong resolution to these chronological problems would have over Menasseh. A robust solution would appeal to the demand for mathematically sound knowledge that was in great demand during this period, and it would demonstrate the unquestioned infallibility of the Bible as well. In the end, however, he repeatedly found himself challenged by the limited numerical and chronological information

79. Menasseh ben Israel, *Conciliador*, 2:35–36. "Aun que en esto no tenemos mas luz que la de razon, bastanos essa para juzgarmos, que en aquello, que no repugna la autoridad de las divinas letras."

80. Menasseh ben Israel *Conciliador* 2: 168. "Sobre cuyo punto, no poco an trabajado todos los interpretes, y al fin confiessa Samoteo, que muchos doctores sudaron en esto, pero q[ue] no pudieron hallar salida a difficuldad tan grande."

provided by the Bible, which again strained his ability to mathematically prove the internal consistency of Scripture, to reconcile its contradictions, and to demonstrate the infallibility of Holy Writ. In the last lines of his work, he would openly abandon the attempt for a future effort that never materialized.

It was another book which Menasseh kept by his bedside that left him disquieted regarding the chronology of ancient Israelite and Judean kings: Azariah de' Rossi's *The Light of the Eyes*.[81] Menasseh had long been familiar with this text, and cited it by name in the first volume of his *Conciliador*, quoting from the discussions of chronological and calendrical questions in Chapter 35 of Part III, "Words of Understanding."[82] In Chapter 34, de' Rossi observes that chronological inconsistencies in the Bible's information about the kingdoms of Judah and Israel posed a serious problem for his effort to arrive at a precise figure for the duration of Solomon's Temple:

> Know that when the length of the reigns of the kings of Israel is reckoned from the beginning of the reign of Jeroboam son of Nebat to the exile of Hoshea, on the basis of Scriptural exposition, a figure of 241 is reached… The corresponding period for the kings of Judah reckoned from the reign of Rehoboam to the sixth year of Hezekiah's reign, which was when Hoshea and Israel were exiled from their land, amounts to 261 years. Accordingly, when the years are reckoned on the basis of the reigns of the kings of Israel from the fourth year of Solomon until the destruction, there is a total of 410 years, but 430 when reckoned on the basis of the reigns of kings of Judah.[83]

While de' Rossi concedes that "you would be justified in saying that all [numbers] alike were divinely inspired," in practice he rejects this assertion. Instead, he gives priority to the figure of 430 years and the chronology of the Judean kings, contending that the information on the kings of Judah in 2 Chronicles and 1–2 Kings is more accurate than that for the kings of Israel.

81. Azariah de' Rossi, *The Light of the Eyes*, trans. Joanna Weinberg (New Haven, CT: Yale University Press, 2001).
82. Menasseh ben Israel *Conciliador* 1: 179.
83. Azariah de' Rossi, *The Light of the Eyes*, 436. See also David Cassel, ed. *Me'or Enayim* (Vilna, 1866), 296–97.

In addition to de' Rossi, the writings of Christian scholars also alerted Menasseh to the complexity and seriousness of the chronological problems in the Bible's information about the kings of ancient Israel and Judah. It is significant that Menasseh cited Samotheus's dark assessment about the prospects of ever resolving these chronological inconsistencies. Giovanni Maria Tolosani, writing under the alias Samotheus, composed the *Opusculum de emendatione temporum* (Venice, 1537), a detailed exploration of world history that provides extensive lists and discussions of ancient rulers and dynasties. Tolosani's *Opusculum* is precisely the type of text that could have incited the sorts of sentiments that provoked Menasseh to spend the better part of two decades attempting to prove the infallibility of the Bible. Take, for instance, the apparently glaring contradiction that preoccupied both Menasseh and Tolosani between 1 Kings 15:33, "In the third year of Asa King of Judah, Baasha son of Ahijah became king of all Israel in Tirzah, and he reigned for twenty-four years," and 2 Chronicles 16:1, which states that "In the thirty-sixth year of Asa's reign, Baasha King of Israel went up against Judah and fortified Ramah." The problem posed by these verses was clear to Tolosani as well as to Menasseh: if Baasha became king in the third year of Asa and reigned for twenty-four years, then it follows that he died in Asa's twenty-seventh year. It would therefore be manifestly impossible for Baasha to have fortified Ramah, or any other city, in Asa's *thirty-sixth* year. As Tolosani observes, "If Baashah reigned twenty-four years, and began to reign in the third year of King Asa, that is to say, at the end of the second year and the beginning of the third year, he could not have lived to the thirty-sixth year of Asa: but in the twenty-sixth year he actually died, as it says in 1 Kings 16[:8], where thus it is written: 'In the twenty-sixth year of King Asa of Judah, Elah son of Baasha became king [of Israel].' In addition, it says in the same place [1 Kings 16:23], in the thirty-first year of King Asa of Judah, Omri ruled over Israel for twelve years. Therefore, during the thirty-sixth year of King Asa, Omri ruled over Israel, and ten years before that Baashah died." Tolosani's merciless and frank conclusion is laden with implications for the authority and infallibility of the Bible: "thus, the text of 2 Chronicles 16 is confirmed to be erroneous."[84]

84. Giovanni Maria Tolosani, *Opusculum de emendationibus temporum* (Venice, 1537), 24–25.

Tolosani was equally incredulous regarding the biblical information about the overall durations of the kings of Israel and Judah – the topic on which Menasseh invoked the work of "Samotheus." As part of a larger genealogy of Jesus, Tolosani draws up a list of rulers over the Kingdom of Israel, and remarks upon the same chronological inconsistency that Menasseh encountered in de' Rossi's text.

> If the years of the kings of Judah following the death of Solomon are calculated, when the Kingdom of Israel began and was separated from Rehoboam, Solomon's son, until the end of the sixth year of Hezekiah, in which year the Kingdom of Israel ceased, 261 years are discovered in the kings of Judah, not counting the ten years which some thoughtlessly add to King Asa of Judah, which, nevertheless, Philo and the seventy interpreters later add to Amos, king of Judah, without his father [i.e., sole rule after co-regency], which was after the destruction of the Kingdom of Israel. But if the years of the Kingdom of Israel from Jeroboam until the ninth and final year of Hoshea are counted, 241 years are discovered, which are twenty years less than the aforesaid kings of Judah.[85]

According to the chronology of the Kingdom of Judah, there were 261 years between the beginning of the divided monarchy and the destruction of the Kingdom of Israel. However, according to the chronology of the Kingdom of Israel, this period lasted only 241 years. Elaborating on the severe challenges posed by this contradiction, Tolosani speculated that the discrepancy could have resulted from numerous origins, including mistakes in the biblical text's numerical information caused by scribal error during the course of its transmission, or the possibility that there were interregnums left unmentioned by Scripture during which Israel had no ruler. Tolosani was also open to considering whether some kings of Judah reigned simultaneously with their predecessors. If this were the case, chronologers might inadvertently have calculated twenty additional – and unnecessary – years in the duration of the Kingdom of Israel, when (hypothetically) these years might have been already accounted for in periods of coregency.

85. Giovanni Maria Tolosani, *Opusculum de emendationibus temporum*, 48.

Finally, it was possible that Scripture's accounts of the kings of Israel describe only portions of their reigns, and not their entirety.[86] Tolosani, in short, appreciated the magnitude of the problem at hand – to such an extent, in fact, that he regarded efforts to reconcile the sizeable discrepancy between the periods ruled by the dynasties of Israel and Judah with acerbic disdain. He quoted from Jerome's letter to Vitalis the Presbyter: "Reread all the books of both the Old and New Testaments. You shall discover both the conflict of many years and the full number between Judah and Israel, that is confused between both kingdoms, so that to waste time with questions of this sort seems not for the studious man, but for the idle man."[87]

Menasseh, of course, disagreed. However, no matter how strenuously he believed in the infallibility of the Bible, and despite his profound conviction of the inerrancy of the Bible's chronological and numerical information, Menasseh was ultimately unable to reconcile the discrepancy between the years ruled by kings of Israel and Judah. In the conclusion to the *Segunda Parte del Conciliador* – the ostensible culmination of his vast attempt to give chronological order to the judges and kings of the ancient Israelites – Menasseh disingenuously states that "it is not my intent, for now, to examine these opinions and air out this material, for it would take a very long discussion. However, if God will grant me life I hope to do this in a separate book on Chronology and the succession of the times."[88] In the end, Menasseh never did. Having presented the problem of whether the kings of Israel had ruled for 241 or 261 years, Menasseh merely provides a list of ancient and medieval authorities who support each of the two conflicting calculations. Menasseh's effort

86. Giovanni Maria Tolosani, *Opusculum de emendationibus temporum*, 48.

87. Giovanni Maria Tolosani, *Opusculum de emendationibus temporum*, 48. In addition to the *Opusculum* itself, Menasseh may have derived some of his information about Tolosani's assessment regarding the severity of these chronological problems from Azariah de' Rossi's *The Light of the Eyes*, which summarizes Tolosani's statements about the difficulty of reconciling the chronological contradictions regarding biblical Israel's kings and judges. See Azariah de' Rossi, *The Light of the Eyes*, 439–40.

88. Menasseh ben Israel, *Conciliador*, 2:168. "Averiguar agora estas opiniones y ventilar esta material no es por ora mi intento, por q[ue] pedia muy largo y dilatado discurso: pero si Dios me concediere vida, espero hazer esto en un libro a parte, de la Chronologia y serie de los tiempos."

to resolve "one of the greatest problems that there is in Scripture" thus opened a can of chronological worms far more complicated than he was prepared to disentangle in the *Conciliador.* With this problem more than any other, Menasseh found himself – and his entire project of biblical chronology – pressed up against the limits of the numerical and mathematical information provided by the Bible. Somewhat weakly, he concludes Volume 2 in the following manner: "What has already been said, and these charts, will be sufficient for now."[89]

Conclusion: The Reverberations of Jewish Biblical Chronology

As we have seen, Menasseh ben Israel makes constant reference to discussions of individual chronological inconsistencies in the Talmud, *Seder 'Olam,* and in the writings of medieval and early modern Jewish and Christian commentators. In particular, Menasseh's sensitivity to Scripture's numerical and chronological contradictions shows an appreciation of two earlier Jewish works in particular: Isaac Abravanel's *Commentary on Early Prophets,* and Azariah de' Rossi's *The Light of the Eyes.* In both of these texts, Menasseh found extensive discussions about the succession of ancient Israel's judges and kings that accentuated the difficulties encountered by the exegete with an acute sense of historicity and a desire to give clear chronological order to the biblical past. Menasseh ben Israel was not the first learned Jewish writer to systematically study the chronological inconsistencies of ancient Israel's judges and kings.

Nor was he the last. Chronological contradictions also played an important role in Spinoza's efforts to evaluate the Bible's claim to divine origins, and to identify biblical moral and religious precepts that were free from human corruption. Chronological inconsistencies were also a central part of Spinoza's argument that Ezra had acted as the redactor of the Bible, the compiler of various texts that contained similar – but often conflicting – accounts of ancient Israel's rulers, events, and narratives. Spinoza viewed numerical and chronological inconsistencies in the Bible as being especially poignant proof that the biblical texts were not

89. Menasseh ben Israel, *Conciliador,* 2:168.

a homogenous, single unit, but rather had been compiled from diverse documents. Ezra, Spinoza believed, "collected narratives from different writers, sometimes copying them out as they were, without examining them properly and setting them in order."[90] "We have only to notice," Spinoza insists, "that everything in these five books, commandments and histories alike, is narrated in a confused manner, without order and without respect for chronology, and that stories are repeated, sometimes in different versions."[91] This is the case not only in the Pentateuch, he asserts, but also in the later biblical texts that cover the period through the destruction of the first Temple.[92]

Like Isaac Abravanel and Menasseh ben Israel, Spinoza was impressed by the discrepancy between Scripture's statement that the Temple had been constructed 480 years after the Exodus, and his own totals from the information provided in the Bible: "At 1 Kings 6 it is said that Solomon built the Temple 480 years after the Exodus from Egypt; but from the chronicles themselves we extrapolate a larger number."[93] Adding up the years governed by each judge and king prior to the fourth year of King Solomon, in which the Temple was built, Spinoza calculated a period of 580 years. Even this figure, Spinoza writes, does not represent the totality of time between the Exodus and the Temple: "And still more time must be added to this: the generation following the death of Joshua in which the Hebrew state flourished until conquered by Cushan-rishathaim, which must have been many years... Likewise, we must add the number of years Samuel was judge, which is unclear in Scripture, and the duration of Saul's reign, which is also unclear."[94] Like Menasseh and other Jewish commentators, Spinoza observes that in 1 Samuel 13:1, it says "Saul was... years old when he began to reign, and he reigned for two years over Israel." His age is clearly omitted." Furthermore, according to 1 Samuel 27:7, David spent one year and four months among the Philistines while he was pursued by Saul. This left Saul an impossibly brief period of time – only eight months – in which to achieve his many

90. Jonathan Israel, ed. *Theological-Political Treatise*, 130.
91. Jonathan Israel, ed. *Theological-Political Treatise*, 132.
92. Jonathan Israel, ed. *Theological-Political Treatise*, 132–33.
93. Jonathan Israel, ed. *Theological-Political Treatise*, 133–34.
94. Jonathan Israel, ed. *Theological-Political Treatise*, 134.

wars and conquests.[95] These types of inconsistencies, Spinoza believed, stood as evidence for the origins of the Bible in multiple ancient texts that were no longer extant.

Spinoza's sharp awareness of, and disdain for, contradictory chronological information in the Bible should be understood against the backdrop of a time and place in which harmonizing biblical inconsistancies was a popular genre of Christian and Jewish exegesis. As has been noted, the efforts of Martin Bucer, Andreas Osiander, John Calvin, and Menasseh ben Israel stand as especially prominent examples of the genre in the sixteenth and seventeenth centuries. This approach to studying Scripture was recognized by commentators as diverse as Amandus Polanus, Edward Leigh, Benedict Pictet, Lodewijk Meijer, and Spinoza himself. There existed a myriad of texts, contexts, and communities in which Spinoza could have encountered questions about internal contradictions in the Bible.

However, as we shall see, Spinoza's comments about the reconciling of contradictory chronological verses suggest that he had specifically Jewish precedents in mind when he wrote about and confronted efforts to resolve the Bible's inconsistent information. Spinoza first considers 2 Kings 1:17, which describes how Jehoram son of Ahab (Ahaziahu's brother) became king of Israel during the second year of King Joram, son of Jehoshaphat of Judah. How then, Spinoza asked rhetorically, is it possible for 2 Kings 8:16 to hold that "In the fifth year of King Jehoram son of Ahab of Israel – [Joram] son of King Jehoshaphat of Judah became king?" The verses appear to state opposite and mutually exclusive orders of succession.[96] Spinoza observes that according to 2 Kings 1:18, the information about Jehoram was derived from the non-extant Annals of the Kings of Israel.[97] The information concerning Joram and Jehoshaphat, however, was based on a different ancient text. 2 Kings 8:23 plainly says that "The other events of Joram's reign, and all his actions, are recorded in the Annals of the Kings of Judah." Therefore, Spinoza saw this contradiction as vivid testimony to the conflicting information

95. Jonathan Israel, ed. *Theological-Political Treatise*, 134–35.
96. Jonathan Israel, ed. *Theological-Political Treatise*, 135–36.
97. 2 Kings 1:18 states that "The other events of Ahaziah's reign [and] his actions are recorded in the Annals of the Kings of Israel."

provided by the different textual sources upon which the Bible was based. Reflecting on this inconsistency, as noted above, Spinoza remarks that "Many other discrepancies such as this are evident throughout the text, and I certainly do not need to review the manoeuvres of those writers who try to reconcile them. The rabbis talk evident nonsense."[98] Evidently, Spinoza was reacting to discussions of internal biblical contradictions in specifically Jewish sources.

Next, Spinoza draws his readers' attention to another contradiction, also examined by Menasseh, regarding 2 Chronicles 22:2: "Ahaziahu was forty-two years old when he became king, and reigned in Jerusalem for one year." This verse clearly conflicts with 2 Kings 8:26, which says that Ahaziahu was twenty-two years old when he became king.[99] One of the resolutions Menasseh proposes to this problem is Levi ben Gershon's suggestion that the forty-two years mentioned in 2 Chronicles do not refer to Ahaziahu's actual age, but to the age of the dynasty of the house of Omri.[100] Spinoza has nothing but scorn for this proposition. He remarks that "some rabbis forge a fiction whereby these years have their beginning from the reign of Omri and not from the birth of Ahaziah[u]."[101] Again, Spinoza is responding to specifically Jewish efforts to reconcile biblical contradictions. In both cases, Spinoza focuses on verses and chronological inconsistencies discussed in Menasseh ben Israel's *Conciliador*. This does not necessarily mean that Spinoza is writing with the *Conciliador* in mind, although this is possible, and even probable.[102] However, it strongly suggests that at the very least Spinoza is drawing on themes, ideas, and methods of biblical commentary with which he was thoroughly familiar during his life in Amsterdam's Portuguese Jewish community, or which he continued to read following his expulsion.

98. Jonathan Israel, ed. *Theological-Political Treatise*, 135–36.
99. Menasseh discusses this problem in the *Conciliador*, 2:117–18. However, he confuses the fathers of Ahaziahu of Israel, who is descended from Ahab, and Ahaziah of Judah, who is descended from Joram. Compare – on the one hand – 2 Kings 8:18 and 2 Kings 8:26 for the succession in the Kingdom of Judah, and on the other hand 1 Kings 16:29 and 1 Kings 22:52 for the succession in the Kingdom of Israel.
100. Menasseh ben Israel, *Conciliador*, 2:118.
101. Jonathan Israel, ed. *Theological-Political Treatise*, 136.
102. At least one scholar has suggested that Spinoza read the *Conciliador* closely. See Steven Nadler, *Spinoza: A Life*, 100.

Modern scholars have linked Spinoza's biblical scholarship to contact, interaction, and intellectual exchange with numerous groups of religious radicals and freethinkers in the United Provinces and broader European society. However, as Jetze Touber has argued and reminded us, we should never lose sight of the ways in which traditionally-minded orthodox scholars, both Jewish and Christian, may have influenced and stimulated Spinoza's radical thought as well. In addition to the provocative and subversive works of Isaac La Peyrère, Thomas Hobbes, Hugo Grotius, and others, Spinoza also possessed on his bookshelves "perfectly orthodox" works such as Calvin's *Institutes of the Christian Religion*, Tremellius' New Testament, the Hebrew and Chaldean editions of the Bible printed by Johannes Buxtorf, and Constantijn l'Empereur's *Clavis Talmudica*. Furthermore, Spinoza enthusiastically *used* these works to make his arguments in the *Treatise*.[103] At the same time, Spinoza has never been studied as a reader of the Bible whose methods of scholarship were shaped in important ways by the ideas, models, and problems that occupied traditionally-minded Jewish readers of the Bible in his community. Within this Jewish community, discussions of contradictory verses in Scripture were commonplace. Already in the early 1630s, Menasseh's rabbinic colleague in Amsterdam, Saul Levi Morteira, wrote an eviscerating critique of contradictory verses in the New Testament, the *Preguntas que hizo un clerigo de Ruan* [Questions asked by a priest from Ruen]. Furthermore, the four volumes of Menasseh ben Israel's *Conciliador* were published in 1632, 1641, 1650, and 1651, meaning that these works had been in circulation for approximately twenty-four years when Spinoza was excommunicated. Amsterdam's rabbis were fixated by the notion of contradictory verses in the Bible, and made these passages the center of apologetic and polemical works. This unique Jewish culture of biblical studies in Amsterdam should be seen as having had its own part in shaping Spinoza's attitudes toward the Bible.

Study of the *Conciliador* alongside Spinoza's *Treatise* also suggests a need to reconsider the relationship between religious skepticism and orthodoxy in seventeenth-century Amsterdam. Many scholars have written about the depth and longevity of ex-converso religious skepticism,

103. Jetze Touber, *Spinoza and Biblical Philology in the Dutch Republic, 1660–1710* (Oxford: Oxford University Press, 2018), 59–63, 67–79.

and the reticence of many ex-conversos to accept rabbinic authority. Most studies of Sephardic religious uncertainty focus on the famous individuals on the margins of ex-converso society: Uriel da Costa, Juan de Prado, Daniel Ribera, and of course, Spinoza himself. However, the anxieties and doubts that Menasseh ben Israel clearly felt regarding the internal inconsistencies of Scripture demonstrate the significance of serious religious uncertainties at the very center of Amsterdam's ex-converso community as well. This is not to suggest that Menasseh clandestinely doubted the authority of the Bible, secretly believed that Scripture was flawed and imperfect, or harbored skeptical leanings about Jewish law similar to the ex-converso critics and discontents. On the contrary, the *Conciliador* shows that Menasseh was passionately committed to proving the Bible to be mathematically infallible. Nevertheless, Menasseh felt a certain degree of unease about his ability to confirm his beliefs through the study of ancient biblical chronology. Examination of the *Conciliador* demonstrates the impact of these anxieties on how the Bible was read at the center of Amsterdam's ex-converso community, and the unintended reverberations of orthodox Jewish thought on skeptical freethinkers on the fringes of the community, who could use what they saw as the errors of orthodoxy for their own purposes. Menasseh and Spinoza alike lived in a society where mathematically demonstrable knowledge was in high and growing demand, as was an awareness of its implications for the study of theology and biblical exegesis. From this milieu, both took an interest in the mathematical and numerical contradictions and inconsistencies in Scripture, and both absorbed an awareness of the vulnerability of the Bible's numerical and mathematical inconsistencies. While Menasseh and Spinoza ultimately traveled down vastly different roads and arrived at very different destinations, they shared a common starting point.

FOUR

Opening the Eyes of the *Novos Reformados*: Rabbi Saul Levi Morteira, Radical Christianity, and the Jewish Reclamation of Jesus, 1631–1660

> It shall be our primary aim to undeceive the *novos reformados* of today, those who believe in professing a most pure unity of God, totally denying the Trinity... And they should ask for the compassion of Almighty God, creator of the heavens and the earth, hoping that just as God directed them and opened their eyes to recognize and flee from their many errors, so too He shall teach them everything perfectly, fleeing from all of the abuses and knowing only the pure truth.[1]

1. Saul Levi Morteira, *Tratado da verdade da Lei de Moisés*. Escrito pelo seu próprio punho em Português em Amsterdao, 1659–1660. Edicao facsimilada e leitura do Autógrafo (1659), ed. H.P. Salomon (University of Coimbra, 1988), 527. "Seja o noso principal intento desenganar os Nouos Reformados de oje, os quais confiados em confesar hũa purissima unidade, de Deos, negando totalmente e terinidade... e que pesa misericordia ao sumo Deos, Criador do ceo e da terra, sperando que assim como os encaminhou e lhe abrio os olhos para conhoser e fugir de tantos erros em que estauaõ, que assim os insinará del todo perfetamente, fugindo de todos os abusos e conhesendo solamente a uerdade pura." I am very grateful to my colleague Dr. Rita Costa-Gomes at Towson University, who was generous with her time and provided valuable advice regarding the translation of several passages from Morteira's *Tratado*.

With this bold statement, Rabbi Saul Levi Morteira expressed a daring and exciting agenda that led him to write his *Tratado da verdade da lei de Moisés* [Treatise on the Truth of the Law of Moses], a magisterial work of more than four-hundred folio manuscript pages blending an apologetic defense of Judaism and the Hebrew Bible with a probing study of Jesus, Christianity, and the New Testament. A Venetian rabbi who immigrated to the Calvinist Netherlands and became a leading rabbi of Amsterdam's ex-converso community, Morteira expressed his excitement at the discovery of anti-Trinitarian Christian groups in his adopted homeland who – in his eyes – appeared to be moving tantalizingly close to the adoption of Jewish religious beliefs. Moving beyond the normal boundaries of Jewish self-censorship and restraint, Morteira addressed himself to these Christians in Portuguese in an effort to urge them even closer toward the "pure" truth of Judaism. Although some groups of radical Christians were rejecting much of traditional Christian belief, and came in his eyes to resemble Jews in some ways, Morteira knew that a gulf remained which separated radical Christian sects from the faith of his coreligionists. There was distance yet to be traveled on the road toward "perfect" observance of Judaism. In order to close the gap and persuade the *novos reformados* to adopt Jewish beliefs and practices, Morteira produced a highly nuanced – and sympathetic – portrait of Jesus that illuminated the fundamental Jewishness of Christianity's central figure. Morteira sought to locate the Judaic origins of Jesus's teachings, reconcile apparent contradictions within the New Testament, and depict Jesus as a loyal rabbinic Jew whose fidelity to the Law of Moses offered an edifying model for Dutch Christians to follow. Bravely writing this proselytizing work in a European vernacular language, rather than Hebrew, Morteira sought to urge the *novos reformados* even closer to Jewish practices.

This study locates Morteira within a major transformation in the Jewish discourse about Jesus and Christianity that developed between the late fourteenth and seventeenth centuries. During this period, the figure of Jesus became the focus of an unprecedented level of serious study and scholarship, and learned Jewish men of letters delved deeply into the history, beliefs, and teachings of one of the most divisive and controversial religious figures in Jewish-Christian relations. These efforts produced some of the most comprehensive and insightful Jewish treatments of Jesus in the pre-modern period. The Jewish scholars who poured over the Gospels and later Christian writings for information about Jesus – men such as Profet Duran, Shimon ben Zemaḥ Duran, Leon Modena, and Saul Levi Morteira – had diverse and often overlapping goals. Some are characterized more by their vituperative polemic, others by their conciliatory and ecumenical portrayals. Yet they are linked by a common denominator: whether devoted to combative religious polemics or to building bridges between Judaism and Christianity, all were committed to emphasizing the fundamental Jewishness of Christianity's founder. This pre-modern Jewish effort to "reclaim" Jesus has been attributed to factors rooted in the religious transformation of the medieval and early modern Jewish and Christian worlds. On the one hand, a growing interest in the historical underpinnings of religious identity led Jews and Christians alike to explore the original setting in which Jesus had lived and taught.[2] On the other hand, in the post-1391 late medieval Jewish world there was a sharp desire to attract forced converts and their descendants to cross back into the Jewish world. A serious understanding of Jesus and Christian doctrine was required to speak persuasively to these Iberian New Christians.[3]

2. The growing tendency to appeal to historical scholarship in the construction of communal religious identity during the period between the late fourteenth and seventeenth centuries has been illuminated particularly in Christian contexts. The significance of rival constructions of the ancient past in Protestant-Catholic debates at this time has been emphasized in Anthony Grafton and Joanna Weinberg, *I Have Always Loved the Holy Tongue*, 164–231. See also Debora Shuger, *The Renaissance Bible: Scholarship, Sacrifice, and Subjectivity*, 1–128. David Berger and Talya Fishman have emphasized the growing Jewish interest in the historical circumstances of Jesus's life and teachings within the same time period, and the particular influence of humanist practices of scholarship. See David Berger, "On the Uses of History in Medieval Jewish Polemic against Christianity: The Quest for the Historical Jesus," in *Jewish History and Jewish Memory: Essays in Honor of Yosef Hayim Yerushalmi*, ed. Elisheva Carlebach, John Efron, and David Myers (Hanover and London: Brandeis University Press, 1998), 25–40; and Talya Fishman, "Changing Early Modern Jewish Discourse about Christianity: The Efforts of Rabbi Leon Modena," in *The Lion Shall Roar: Leon Modena and his World*, ed. Robert Bonfil (Jerusalem: Hebrew University Magnes Press, 2003), 159–94.
3. The role of the converso phenomenon in stimulating new perspectives on Jesus and

This chapter builds on current scholarship studying the Jewish reclamation of Jesus, and adds to our understanding of its origins. I argue that Jewish encounters with Protestant Christian movements, ideas, and texts were pivotal in stimulating the reorientation and reshaping of Jewish perspectives on Jesus.[4] The case of Rabbi Saul Levi Morteira exemplifies the striking impact of the Protestant environment on Jewish attitudes toward Jesus. Morteira was an enthusiastic reader of the New Testament throughout his life, but over the course of the four decades he spent in Amsterdam his attitudes toward Jesus and Christianity changed dramatically. His early writings exhibit unmitigated hostility toward the New Testament and Christianity. However, later in life Morteira shifted to a new posture characterized by efforts to find common ground between the Hebrew Bible and New Testament, to locate Judaic origins of Jesus's teachings, to cast Jesus as a faithful and observant rabbinic Jew, and to reconcile contradictory verses within Christian Scriptures. This remarkable change was triggered by Morteira's encounter with radical Protestants in the Netherlands such as the *novos reformados* – the name he gave to the Socinians. Morteira believed that members of certain radical Christian movements were, in their efforts to dissociate from the Catholic Church, increasingly moving toward the adoption of beliefs scarcely distinguishable from those of Judaism. Therefore, in his later

Christianity is compellingly demonstrated in Talya Fishman, "Changing Early Modern Jewish Discourse about Christianity," 159–94.

4. In identifying the Protestant Reformation as a key factor in mapping the development of Jewish attitudes toward Jesus, this study builds upon Haim Hillel Ben-Sasson's series of influential articles in which he demonstrated a pronounced Jewish awareness of fifteenth- and sixteenth-century Christian reform movements. Certain Jewish observers were struck by the extreme biblicism and anti-Trinitarianism of these movements, and believed that these might foreshadow a dramatic narrowing of the gap between Judaism and Christianity, and even bring nearer the horizon of messianic redemption. See Haim Hillel Ben-Sasson, "Jewish-Christian Disputation in the Setting of Humanism and the Reformation in the German Empire," *Harvard Theological Review* 59, no. 4 (1966), 369–90; Haim Hillel Ben-Sasson, "The Reformation in Contemporary Jewish Eyes," *Proceedings of the Israel Academy of Sciences and Humanities*, vol. 4, 1969–1970 (Jerusalem: Ahava, 1971), 239–327; Haim Hillel Ben-Sasson, "Jews and Christian Sectarians: Existential Similarities and Dialectical Tensions in 16th-Century Moravia and Poland-Lithuania," *Viator* 4 (1973): 369–85.

writings, Morteira deliberately appealed to these Christians to move even closer to Jewish perspectives by crafting a depiction of Jesus that was far more moderate and conciliatory. Jesus's teachings were now seen as being syncretistic and symbiotic with Judaism, rather than antagonistic.

Following a brief biographical sketch of Morteira, Part I of this chapter examines the particular Christian Bible that Morteira employed in his study of Jesus, and the cultural and intellectual background that informed his choice. Part II demonstrates the dramatic transformation of Morteira's attitudes toward Jesus's teachings by examining his interpretation of identical New Testament passages in literary works separated by three decades. Part III surveys medieval Jewish textual sources that may have, in part, inspired Morteira's changing perspectives. Yet the reversal of Morteira's understanding of Jesus and the New Testament was not simply a function of a deeper engagement with medieval Jewish books and manuscripts. It depended on the specific environment of the seventeenth-century Netherlands. Therefore, Part IV illustrates the importance of Morteira's encounter with Socinianism in the reconfiguration of his posture toward the founder of Christianity. Tracing the arc along which Morteira's New Testament studies progressed allows us to appreciate how the ex-converso experience and the Protestant milieu of the Netherlands helped to shape and change Morteira's views about Jesus and his teachings. It enables us to see Protestant influences as part of the constellation of factors that led to the Jewish reclamation of Jesus in early modern Europe.

* * *

Scholarship on Morteira has burgeoned in the last generation, and Chapter 4 is indebted to the research of many scholars, including Henry Méchoulan, H.P. Salomon, Yosef Kaplan, and Miriam Bodian. The recent work of Marc Saperstein in particular has shaped our understanding of Morteira as a preacher and leader within the ex-converso community.[5]

5. See Yosef Kaplan's foundational study, "Rabbi Saul Levi Morteira's Treatise 'Arguments Against the Christian Religion,'" in *Studies on the History of Dutch Jewry*, ed. Jozeph Michman (Jerusalem: Hebrew University Magnes Press, 1975), 9–31; and Henry

Morteira was born in Venice, where he received his education and rabbinic training. Beyond this very little is known about his early life. Based on Rabbi Leon Modena's statement that he "cared for Morteira like a son," it has been suggested that Morteira was a student of Modena's.[6] However, Modena did not include Morteira in a list of his distinguished pupils, and does not mention him in his autobiography.[7] Morteira's historical footprints are more clearly defined after he left Venice and accompanied the ex-converso physician Elijah Montalto to Paris in 1612.[8] Montalto had obtained a dispensation from the prohibition against Jewish settlement in France, and served as a physician in the court of Marie de Medici until he died in 1616, when Morteira brought Montalto's body to the nearest Jewish cemetery: the Portuguese Jewish cemetery at Ouderkerk, a short barge ride from Amsterdam. Afterward, Morteira remained in the city as a preacher.[9]

In 1618 Morteira was appointed rabbi of the Beth Jacob congregation of Portuguese Jews. Three years later, he received a contract from the Talmud Torah confraternity of the Beth Jacob congregation worth 300 florins per year to provide Talmud, Bible, and Hebrew grammar classes for the community's youths.[10] In addition to his preaching and teaching duties, Morteira was also a prolific writer in Hebrew, Spanish, and Portuguese. His first extensive treatise, *Preguntas que hizo un clerigo de Ruan* [Questions posed by a priest from Rouen] was written in 1631.[11]

Méchoulan, "Morteira et Spinoza au carrefour du socinianisme," *Revue des études juives* 135 (1976): 51–65. See also Miriam Bodian, *Hebrews of the Portuguese Nation*, 72–75. Marc Saperstein, in *Exile in Amsterdam*, painstakingly analyzes Morteira's sermons and provides a careful examination of the role of Christians and Christianity in Morteira's preaching.

6. Saul Levi Morteira, *Tratado da verdade da Lei de Moisés*, xxxix–xl.
7. Marc Saperstein, *Exile in Amsterdam*, 6. Cf. Mark Cohen, et al. eds., *The Autobiography of a Seventeenth-Century Venetian Rabbi: Leon Modena's Life of Judah* (Princeton, NJ: Princeton University Press, 1988), 214n, 248n.
8. H.P. Salomon, ed. *Tratado da verdade da Lei de Moisés*, xl.
9. Marc Saperstein, *Exile in Amsterdam*, 3–8.
10. GAS 334 1051 Fol. 8b.
11. Saul Levi Morteira, *Preguntas que hizo un clerigo de Ruan de Francia a las quales respondio el exelente y eminentissimo senor H:R: Saul Levy Mortera, Doctor Celebre y Prophesor de la Divina Theologia y predicador de la Nacion Judaica en la Ynsigne y opulenta Ciudad de Amsterdam.* Mss. (Amsterdam, ca. 1631).

The *Preguntas* is Morteira's aggressive and venomous response to twenty-three theological questions that had been recently posed to him by Diego de Cisneros, a Portuguese Christian clergyman.[12] In addition, Morteira includes a rejoinder of 148 questions about the New Testament, drawn from his readings of the synoptic Gospels of Matthew, Mark, and Luke, the Book of John, Paul's Epistles to Romans, Corinthians, Galatians, Ephesians, and Hebrews, and the Epistles of Peter, John, and James.[13] Morteira's vituperative queries critique Christological interpretations of key Old Testament verses, identify contradictory statements in the Gospels, and insist that numerous New Testament authors misquote or misrepresent the language and intent of the Hebrew Bible's narrative.[14]

Toward the end of his life, in 1660, Morteira composed his *magnum opus*, the *Tratado da verdade da lei de Moisés*. Within the *Tratado*, Morteira would cast an image of Jesus that differed sharply from the dismissive attitude that characterizes his approach in the *Preguntas*. In the *Tratado* Jesus emerges not as a figure to be scorned, but as a loyal rabbinic Jew whose fidelity to Jewish law offered an edifying model for

12. H.P. Salomon, *Tratado*, LV.
13. On the dating of this work, see I.S. Revah, "Autobiographie d'un Marrane," *Revue des études juives* 119 (1961): 65–66. Revah shows that Cisneros reported receiving the completed version of Morteira's *Preguntas* in September, 1631, giving a *terminus ad quem* for the composition of the work. H.P. Salomon also dates the manuscript to 1631, indicating that Morteira received Cisneros' questions and composed his reply in the same year (H.P. Salomon, *Tratado*, LV). For a broader discussion of the reception history of the *Preguntas*, and further argument in favor of dating the text to 1631, see Carsten Wilke, "Questions d'un Prêtre de Rouen à un Rabbin d'Amsterdam: La réception multilingue et multiconfessionnelle d'un écrit clandestine de Saül Lévi Mortera," *La letter clandestine: revue d'information sur la littérature clandestine de l'âge classique*, no. 27 (2019): 141–69.
14. Marc Saperstein, *Exile in Amsterdam*, 20. Saperstein notes that Morteira's *Preguntas* was also the subject of intense study by later seventeenth-century scholars. The Mennonite theologian Daniel de Breen published a text in 1644 entitled *Amica Disputatio adversus Iudaeos continens Examen scripti judaici e lusitanico in latinum versi et responsum ad quaestiones inibi christianis propositas* [A Friendly Disputation Against the Jews, Containing an Analysis of Jewish Texts Translated from Portuguese into Latin, and a Response to the Questions Therein Posed to the Christians]. Around 1664, Johannes Cocceijus published a text under the name of *Judaicarum Responsionum et Quaestionum Consideratio* [A Consideration of the Jewish Answers and Questions].

Morteira's Dutch Christian contemporaries to follow. The seventy-one chapters of the treatise can be divided into two sections, with areas of overlap between the two. The first thirty chapters focus overwhelmingly on subjects such as the divinity of the Hebrew Bible, the continuity of the covenant between God and Israel, and God's ongoing providence over the Jews.[15] Morteira deals with questions of prophecy, false prophecy, and the relationship between prophecy and miracles. These chapters of the *Tratado* appear to have been written with Morteira's ex-converso coreligionists in mind.[16] After chapter thirty-one, the focus of Morteira's *Tratado* shifts discernibly to theological and historical questions regarding the New Testament and Christian exegesis, as well as to the relationship between different Christian movements in the Netherlands and throughout Europe. It is within the second half of the *Tratado* where Morteira's effort to reassert the Jewishness of Jesus is most extensively developed.

The significance of the *Tratado* has been widely acknowledged by scholars. In an article on one of Morteira's other polemical works, Yosef Kaplan identifies the *Tratado* as being "without a doubt" the most important of his apologetic works. Marc Saperstein likewise identifies the manuscript as "Morteira's most important single manuscript text." Recently, Miriam Bodian described the *Tratado* as being the most learned and nuanced pre-Enlightenment Jewish reflection on Protestant Christianity.[17] H.P. Salomon described the treatise as "the most exten-

15. One major exception to the thematic division of the *Tratado* is the discussion of Jewish and Christian approaches to Sabbath observance, examined extensively below, which is located in chapter eighteen.
16. Morteira's younger colleague, Rabbi Moshe Raphael d'Aguilar (d. 1679), read these chapters of the *Tratado* with great care and kept detailed notes on them. See the miscellaneous collection of Aguilar's manuscripts in *Tratado da immortalidade da Alma* in the Ets Haim Library (EH 48 A 11), Fol. 388–437. Regarding Aguilar's life and intellectual activities in the community, see Shlomo Berger, *Classical Oratory and the Sephardim of Amsterdam: Rabbi Aguilar's Tratado de la Retórica* (Hilversum: Verloren, 1996).
17. See Yosef Kaplan, "Rabbi Saul Levi Morteira's Treatise 'Arguments Against the Christian Religion'," 15; Marc Saperstein, *Exile in Amsterdam*, 27–28; Miriam Bodian "The Reformation and the Jews," in *Rethinking European Jewish History*, ed. Jeremy Cohen and Moshe Rosman (The Litmann Library of Jewish Civilization: Oxford and Portland, Oregon, 2009), 130–31.

sive and comprehensive book about the New Testament and all forms of Christian dogma produced by a Jewish author" in early modern Europe.[18] Salomon's critical edition, notes, and articles about the *Tratado* have illuminated the incredible array of Christian and Jewish authors whose writings Morteira voraciously consumed as he wrote about Jewish and Christian Scriptures. Salomon's studies of the *Tratado* have also drawn attention to intriguing sections of the text to raise the possibility of an influence of the manuscript on Spinoza.[19] Yet in many ways, we are only beginning to understand the dynamic ways in which Morteira plumbed the depths of Christian exegesis and Scriptures, his perspectives on diverse Christian movements both past and present, the significance of his writings for Jewish-Christian relations in the seventeenth-century Netherlands, and the relationship between Morteira's methods of scholarship and those of more recent, critical readers of the Bible. Studying both Morteira's earlier *Preguntas* and his *magnum opus* the *Tratado*, this chapter explores why Morteira was so preoccupied with the figure of Jesus, why he tried so vigorously to create bridges between Judaism and the teachings of Christianity's founder, and why the scholarly career of one of Amsterdam's leading rabbis was book-ended by two of the most sophisticated seventeenth-century Jewish commentaries on Christian Scriptures.

Part 1: Jewish Readers of Christian Bibles

In order to examine the conclusions that Morteira derived from his intensive study of the Christian Scriptures, it is important first to ask what edition of the Bible Morteira employed when he studied the New Testament. One of Morteira's rabbinic colleagues provides a suggestive clue. In 1671, Rabbi Jacob Judah Leon published an edition of the Book of Psalms that contained a literal translation, paraphrase, commentary, and footnotes.[20] In explaining the need for such a text to the *pio lector* (pious

18. H.P. Salomon, "Did Saul Levi Mortera Plagiarize Joseph Albo?," *Studia Rosenthaliana*, vol. 23, no. 1 (1989): 28.
19. See H.P. Salomon, ed. *Tratado*, cxiv–cxviii, where it is contended that Spinoza may argue against the authenticity of the New Testament in similar ways.
20. Yaacob Yehudah Leon, *Kadosh Hillulim. Las Alabanças de Santidad* (Amsterdam, 1671).

reader), Leon remarked upon the faults of the available Jewish Bibles commonly read within his community, and the alluring attractiveness of certain Christian Bibles. Leon believed that the Spanish translation of the 1553 Ferrara Bible prepared by Jewish and crypto-Jewish exiles from the Iberian Peninsula was overly committed to a rigid, literal translation of Scripture: "And as for our translation, approved in the past in Ferrara by the most eminent men of that century, which is the most common among us because it concurs with the truth of the Hebrew text: I do not find its precision sufficiently satisfying." The Ferrara Bible, in Leon's view, was so attentive to the "literal sense of the 'servile' letters, and of some ordinary adverbs, without taking notice of the style of the language or the various senses that each of these letters or even words could have, that many times . . . it corrupts the true sense of the intent of Sacred Scripture."[21] Many other Iberian Jews likewise complained about the linguistic deficiencies of the Spanish Ferrara Bible and other Jewish translations of the Bible into Spanish, and cited these as justification for their own editions of Scripture.[22] Yosseph Franco Serrano complained in 1695 that "some translate the Sacred Books into Spanish word for word from the Hebrew, thinking that they make its expressions and concepts easier to understand, and they [in fact] obscure them in such a way that in some cases it is not even possible for the expert in Divine Studies to understand by them the true intent of the Divine Word, having given them a sense extremely different from, and even directly opposed to what is expressed in the Hebrew."[23] Because of the Ferrara Bible's stylistic and linguistic deficiencies, Leon complained that certain members of the

21. Yaacob Yehudah Leon, *Las Alabanças de Santidad*, "Al Pio Lector." Regarding the Ferrara Bible, see Iacob M. Hassán, ed. *Introducción a la Biblia de Ferrara: Actas del Simposio Internacional sobre la Biblia de Ferrara* (Seville: CSIC, 1992). In particular, see Harm den Boer's contribution focusing on the editions of the Ferrara Bible printed by ex-conversos in Amsterdam: "La Biblia de Ferrara y otras traducciónes españolas de la Biblia," 251–96. See also Harm Den Boer, *La Literatura Sefardi de Amsterdam*.

22. Harm Den Boer, *La Literatura Sefardi de Amsterdam*, 40. The editors of the original 1553 Ferrara Bible apologize in their introduction for the "barbaro y estraño" style of the edition's Spanish, which resulted from the adoption of a rigidly literal approach to translating the Hebrew text. Menasseh ben Israel reprinted this claim in his *Biblia en lengua Espanola* (Amsterdam, 1630).

23. Yosseph Franco Serrano, *Los cinco libros de la sacra Ley* (Amsterdam, 1695), "Prohemio."

Jewish community turned to more aesthetically pleasing Bibles written by Christians. In particular, he noted, "that gentile who translated our Bible into the Spanish language, is more preferred among some of our people, his version being more attractive and pleasing."[24] The identity of "that gentile" to whom Leon refers is most likely the Spanish Reformed scholar and polemicist Cipriano de Valera. Valera's Spanish translation of the Old and New Testaments, based on Casiodoro de Reina's earlier version, was printed at Amsterdam in 1602.[25] Morteira certainly possessed a copy of the Valera translation, based on analysis of his biblical quotations and explicit references to Valera's text. In the *Tratado*, Morteira specifically refers to Valera's approach to translating certain words and passages into Spanish, and praises the fidelity of Valera's translation to the Hebrew original of the Old Testament.[26]

At first glance, the reasons for Morteira's preference for the Valera Bible seem to be straightforward: Spanish made the Valera Bible accessible to Morteira and other ex-conversos. However, Valera's use of Spanish cannot, of course, on its own explain Morteira's choice, given the presence of numerous Spanish translations of the Bible available in the middle of the seventeenth century. In the introduction to his translation, Valera offers a brief history of renderings of the Bible into Spanish and related languages: he mentions Vincente Ferrer's Valencian edition, and the Ferrara Bible, which he describes as "the Old Testament without the apocryphal books, printed in 1553 in Ferrara, word for word as it is in Hebrew, which is a great treasure of the Spanish language." Next, Valera notes Francisco de Enzinas Burgales' 1542 translation of the New Testament; Juan Perez's 1556 edition of the New Testament; the Bible of Casiodoro de Reina printed at Basel in 1569; the polyglot Complutensian Bible, organized by Francisco Ximenez; and many others.[27] Thus, Morteira potentially had access to numerous Spanish

24. Yaacob Yehudah Leon, *Las Alabanças de Santidad*, "Al Pio Lector." "Por cuya razon, aquel Gentil que tradujo en Espanol Idioma nuestra sagrada Biblia, cuya version por ser mas affectada y agradable, es mas acepta entre algunos de los nuestros."
25. Harm den Boer, *La literatura Sefardi de Amsterdam*, 40. See also A. Gordon Kinder, "Religious Literature as an Offensive Weapon," 233.
26. See for example Morteira, *Tratado*, 399 and 549.
27. Cipriano de Valera, ed. *La Biblia. Que es/ Los Sacros Libros del Vieio y Nuevo Testamento.*

Bibles when he wrote the *Tratado*. Why, then, did Morteira select Valera's translation of the Bible specifically?

Apart from Valera's use of Spanish, this edition of the Bible would have had particular appeal for Morteira for several further reasons. Certain Spanish-language Bibles appear to have been extremely difficult to acquire. Valera complains that it was impossible to find someone willing to part with their set of the extraordinarily popular Complutensian Bible for any sum of money.[28] Casiodoro de Reina's equally popular edition was apparently produced in a print run of only 2,600 volumes, which were exported over a wide geographic expanse "in such a way that today it can almost not be found if someone wishes to purchase it."[29] Part of Valera's motive in editing and reissuing the Reina Bible was to reach a numerically broader audience. Morteira may therefore have used the Valera Bible because it was eminently accessible, having been printed recently and in Amsterdam.

There were also cultural and religious grounds for Morteira's preference for the Valera Bible. First and foremost, both Cipriano de Valera and Casiodoro de Reina were members of the Order of Observantine Jeronomites, situated near Seville, who embraced Reformation ideas during the 1550s.[30] When the authorities in Spain became aware of their sympathies in 1557, Valera, Reina, and ten other members of the order fled to Geneva and formally became Calvinist Protestants.[31] In 1558 Valera moved to England, and between 1588 and 1602 he wrote numerous texts and polemical works against Spain and Catholicism. Valera's first

Segunda edicion (Amsterdam, 1602). "Al Christiano Lector a leer la sagrada Escriptura."

28. Cipriano de Valera, *La Biblia*, "Al Christiano Lector a leer la sagrada Escriptura." On the production and organization of the Complutensian Bible, see Jerry Bentley, *Humanists and Holy Writ*, 70–112.
29. Cipriano de Valera, *La Biblia*, "Al Christiano Lector a leer la sagrada Escriptura."
30. There was a strong tradition of sympathy for conversos, and even a tolerance toward Judaizing activity, within the Jeronomite Order and its members who administered the shrine to the Virgin Mary near Seville. See Gretchen Starr-Lebeau, *In the Shadow of the Virgin*. However, there is no evidence that Morteira himself was aware of this tradition.
31. A. Gordon Kinder, "Juan Perez de Pineda (Pierius): A Spanish Calvinist Minister of the Gospel in Sixteenth-Century Geneva," *Bulletin of Hispanic Studies* 53 (1976): 283–300.

work was entitled *Dos Tratados. El primero es del Papa... el Segundo es de la missa* [Two Treatises: the first on the Pope... the second on the Mass], in which he subverts the institutional foundation of Catholicism, the papacy, and its doctrine of the Eucharist. Morteira refers to the *Dos Tratados* while criticizing both Protestant and Catholic doctrines of the Host. In 1597, Valera also completed a meticulous translation into Spanish of Calvin's fifth and definitive edition of the *Institutes of the Christian Religion*, which Morteira also employs extensively throughout his writings.[32] The availability of Bibles and theological texts prepared in Spanish by committed opponents of Spain's Inquisition and Catholicism would have had an understandably strong appeal to Morteira and the sensibilities of many other ex-conversos. Like many New Jews in Morteira's Amsterdam, Valera writes that Casiodoro de Reina had to "travel to a land of liberty in order to speak and deal with matters relating to God."[33] Furthermore, if Morteira's aim was truly to "undeceive the *novos reformados* of today," urging them to accept Jewish beliefs and practices, then it made eminent sense for him to make his appeal using a Bible prepared by a Reformed Christian.

Morteira may have had a further reason for favoring Cipriano de Valera's version of the Bible. Valera implemented two important editorial changes in Reina's Bible. First, he sought to achieve greater fidelity to the Hebrew original by filtering out translations that had been taken from the Vulgate and the Septuagint, demonstrating his stated preference for an *ad fontes* approach to biblical studies. Second, Valera reorganized the canonical and apocryphal books of the Bible. Whereas Casiodoro de Reina grouped the deuterocanonical texts within the Old Testament, the Valera Bible was divided into three separate sections: Old Testament, New Testament, and Apocrypha; all deuterocanonical and apocryphal books of the Bible were segmented into a separate section. As Valera emphasized in the introduction to his Bible, "We have removed everything added by the seventy interpreters, or from the Vulgate, that is not found in the Hebrew text... Because our intent is not to translate that which men added to the word of God, but only that which God

32. A. Gordon Kinder, "Religious Literature as an Offensive Weapon," 223–35.
33. Cipriano de Valera, *La Biblia*, "Al Christiano Lector a leer la sagrada Escriptura."

revealed in his Holy Scriptures. We have also removed all annotations to the Apocrypha from within the Canonical books. For it is not good to make a comparison of the certain with the uncertain, the word of God with the word of man."[34] Translating the Bible in a way that segregated apocryphal works and references to them from the Old Testament text, and filtering out residual influences of the Septuagint and Vulgate, Cipriano de Valera's Bible was closer to the Jewish version of Scripture than any other Christian Bible written in Spanish. Little wonder, then, that Jacob Judah Leon affirmed that the translation of "*aquel gentil*," the Bible of Cipriano de Valera, was the "most accepted among some of our nation" – including Morteira.

Part II: From the *Preguntas* to the *Tratado*, 1631–1660

Morteira read his Valera Bible assiduously throughout his life. However, his interpretation of Christian Scriptures was far from static. Between his immigration to Amsterdam and his death forty years later, Morteira's attitudes toward the New Testament and Christianity underwent a significant shift and intellectual transformation that was the result of his immersion in the theological and social milieu of the Dutch Netherlands of the mid-seventeenth century. From the aggressively polemical and antagonistic perspective that typifies the *Preguntas*, Morteira shifts to positions that can be seen as offering a more moderate and conciliatory posture in the *Tratado*. To illustrate the shift in Morteira's attitudes toward the New Testament and Christianity, it is possible to compare his comments upon identical New Testament passages in the *Preguntas* and the *Tratado*. In the *Preguntas*, Morteira contrasts Matthew 11:29–30, "Take my yoke upon you… for my yoke is easy and my burden is light," with the strict laws of Matthew 5:21–38, which include prohibitions against murder, becoming angry, calling one's brother a "fool," phys-

34. Cipriano de Valera, *La Biblia*, "Al Christiano Lector a leer la sagrada Escriptura." "…avemos quitado todo lo anidido de los 70 interpretes, o de la vulgate, que no se halla en el texto Hebreo…. Porque nuestro intento no es trasladar lo que los hombres han anidido a la palabra de Dios, sino lo que Dios ha revelado en sus sanctas Escripturas. Avemos tambien quitado las acotaciones de los libros Apocryphos en los libros Canonicos. Porque no es bien hecho confirmar lo cierto con lo incierto, la palabra de Dios con la de los hombres."

ical adultery, and adultery in the heart.[35] Additionally, Christians are enjoined to "not resist," and "if someone strikes your right cheek, turn the other as well; and if anyone wants to sue you and take your coat, give your cloak as well; and if anyone forces you to go one mile, go also the second mile.[36] "I ask," Morteira writes, "according to these precepts who is there among all of the Christians who could be saved? And how do they have the temerity to call the Law of Moses a heavy law, [those] who have in their own [law] such heavy... precepts?" Morteira's interpretation of these same verses in the *Tratado* is substantially different. By 1660, Morteira was committed to the view that Jesus was a resolutely loyal follower of the Law of Moses, and that the laws described in Matthew are in fact appropriated from the Hebrew Bible itself. Morteira could easily find precedents in the Hebrew Bible for the prohibitions against murder, slandering one's neighbour, and physical adultery.[37] However, aligning the Christian prohibition of adultery in the heart and Jewish law was more difficult. There is no mention in Jewish law of adultery in the heart. Furthermore, Matthew 5:32 says that "anyone who divorces his wife, except on the ground of unchastity, causes her to commit adultery; and whoever marries a divorced woman commits adultery." "This too is found in the Law of Moses," according to Morteira, "which says explicitly, if she does not find favour in his eyes, if he found in her some dishonesty, he will write a writ of divorce for her."[38] Nevertheless, Morteira was fully aware of the tension between rabbinic law and the verse in Matthew. He knew that Judaism permitted a husband to divorce his wife for any number of further reasons, and also permitted her to remarry. In order to reconcile Jewish law with Matthew's position, Morteira states that "if he is permitted to divorce for less serious reasons than adultery," this is only so that the husband is not forced to

35. New Testament references throughout are cited according to the New Revised Standard Edition (NRSV) unless otherwise noted.
36. Morteira, *Preguntas*, Fol. 119–20.
37. Regarding the identification of Matthew 5:21–38 as fundamentally rooted in Hebrew models, see Anthony Grafton, *Joseph Scaliger: A Study in the History of Classical Scholarship* (Oxford: Clarendon Press, 1983–1993), 2:320. Joseph Scaliger insisted that Jesus's statement about turning the other cheek was based on a Hebrew proverb.
38. Morteira, *Tratado*, 319–20.

prove his suspicions of adultery, "because were he able to prove it the woman would deserve death." Therefore, "it is enough that it is known to the husband, and since the husband knows in his conscience that it is so, he has no obligation to give any reason."[39] Yet although "the exterior court [the *beit din*] is satisfied with his will," Morteira insists that "in his conscience" (*el fuero interior*) and before God, the husband sins by divorcing his wife without just cause. Morteira then cites Malachi 2:16, "For I detest divorce – said the Lord, the God of Israel." "And our Rabbis," Morteira adds, "assert that divorce is abhorrent to God, and that it also insults the man who marries the divorcée." Like Matthew, Morteira thus presents divorce as a double offence against both God and man. Again shifting from his original position, Morteira now concludes that "in this too there is no innovation," and that Jesus's teachings are entirely compatible with Jewish law.[40]

In the *Preguntas*, Morteira also examines Matthew 15:11, "It is not what goes into the mouth that defiles a person, but it is what comes out of the mouth that defiles."[41] This verse appears to contradict a cornerstone of Judaism's dietary restrictions, the prohibition in Leviticus 11:43–44 against contaminating the body and soul by eating certain creatures. Morteira dismisses Matthew 15:11, and wryly notes that given their doctrine of original sin – "Adam and Eve eating from the Tree of Knowledge" – it is highly disingenuous for Christians to claim that food does not render the soul impure.[42] Thirty years later Morteira revisited Mathew 15:11 in the *Tratado*, and arrived at very different conclusions. He remained concerned that this teaching violated the commandment

39. Morteira, *Tratado*, 319–20.
40. Morteira, *Tratado*, 319–21. While Matthew 5:32 permits divorce in cases of adultery, Morteira also notes that Luke 16:18 issues a blanket prohibition on divorce: "Anyone who divorces his wife and marries another woman commits adultery, and the man who marries a divorced woman commits adultery." Morteira writes that Luke, unlike Matthew, does not distinguish between licit and illicit divorce. Morteira gives legal priority to Matthew, however, because "what Luke wrote was from 'hearsay' and not from personal witness, as he himself says in the beginning of his Book." It was important for Morteira to emphasize this point because in his view only Matthew's prohibition against divorce bears any resemblance to rabbinic Jewish law.
41. Morteira, *Preguntas*, Fol. 122–23.
42. Morteira, *Preguntas*, Fol. 122–23.

in the Hebrew Bible which says, "you shall not defile your souls with any reptile that pulls itself along the ground." However, Morteira was now inclined to see Jesus as an assiduous follower of Jewish law, and was therefore concerned that Matthew 15:11 contradicted Jesus's teaching that "until heaven and earth pass away, not one letter, not one stroke of a letter, will pass from the law" (Matthew 15:18). Furthermore, Morteira writes, how do we reconcile the verse in Matthew with Acts 15:28–29, which says "'it appears good to the Holy Spirit and to us not to place upon you a burden except [this]: abstain from foods sacrificed to idols and from blood, and strangled animals?' All of these things enter through the mouth and are prohibited because they contaminate [the body]." Morteira reconciles the apparent contradictions by arguing that the verse in Matthew does not intend to make licit *all* prohibited foods, and should only be understood to have a relative significance: "in no way did he intend these words to make licit all foods prohibited in the Law; rather, what he says is that relatively speaking that which exits the mouth contaminates the soul more than what enters the mouth." Morteira finds similar statements in the Hebrew Bible, where God demands more than sacrifices, and places a greater premium on acts of charity: "it is not that God does not desire sacrifices at all ... but that God requires acts of charity *more* than sacrifices [my emphasis]."[43] Morteira in fact agrees with Matthew 15:19, "For out of the heart come evil intentions, murder, adultery, fornication, theft, false witness, slander." There is again no innovation in Jesus's teachings, according to Morteira. Matthew's laws merely echo those enacted by the Jewish sages.[44]

In both the *Preguntas* and the *Tratado*, Morteira also comments upon the critical New Testament verses describing the Last Supper, and Jesus's teachings regarding the bread and the wine:

> While they were eating, Jesus took a loaf of bread, and after blessing it he broke it, gave it to the disciples, and said, 'Take, eat; this is my body.' Then he took a cup, and after giving thanks he gave it to them, saying, 'Drink from it, all of you; for this is my blood of

43. Morteira, *Tratado*, 331.
44. Morteira, *Tratado*, 331.

> the covenant, which is poured out for many for the forgiveness of sins. I tell you, I will never again drink of this fruit of the vine until that day when I drink it new with you in my Father's kingdom.'
>
> – Matthew 26:26–29

In the early 1630s, Morteira's reading of the verse was dismissive. "I ask," Morteira writes, "whether these words are metaphorical, signifying the glory of heaven. This comparison cannot be demonstrated through reference to the fruit of the vine . . . and if they wish to understand these words literally, the difficulty is much greater. For it makes me laugh to think that there is new wine in the heavens."[45] Morteira's approach to Matthew 26:26–29 in the *Tratado* is again very different. Rather than dismissing them totally, Morteira now sees these passages as examples of important Jewish traditions. Morteira draws his readers' attention to the many linguistic and cultural similarities between Jesus's benedictions at the Last Supper and those commonly performed by ancient and modern Jews. First of all, Morteira writes that it was the practice of Jews in antiquity to commemorate important events and memories upon a glass of wine, just as Jesus did with his disciples, on Passover in particular and regularly at meals.[46] Furthermore, Morteira perceived that the specific language and style of Jesus's blessing and teaching at the Last Supper closely paralleled the Jewish blessings commonly recited. Regarding the verse, "I say to you that from now on I will not drink of the fruit of the vine until that day when we are reunited in the kingdom of my Father," Morteira writes: "Many Hebrew phrases are seen here, for the text does not say 'of this wine' but rather 'of the fruit of the vine.' Likewise, Jews say 'Blessed is the Lord our God king of the universe who created the fruit of the vine.'" Finally, Morteira locates a talmudic analogy to Jesus's statement that he will only drink wine again in the kingdom of heaven. Commenting on the verse of the Prophet Isaiah, "No eye has seen them [the wonders], O God, but You," Rabbi Joshua b. Levi says that this refers to the wine preserved in its grapes from the beginning of the creation of the world.[47]

45. Morteira, *Preguntas*, Fol. 123–24.
46. Morteira, *Tratado*, 785.
47. Morteira, *Tratado*, 787. Morteira is quoting from b. Sanhedrin 99a, where R. Joshua

As can be seen from these comparisons, in contrast to Morteira's polemic against Christianity in the *Preguntas*, his *Tratado* consistently identifies areas of common ground between Jewish and Christian Scriptures, resolves contradictory verses in the New Testament, and reinscribes important Christian traditions in a Jewish idiom. What are the origins of Morteira's radical change in attitudes toward Jesus, the New Testament and Christianity?

Part III: Medieval Precedents

In some respects, Morteira's changing attitudes toward Jesus and his teachings were rooted in medieval and early modern Jewish texts that he likely knew thoroughly: Profet Duran's *Kelimat ha-goyyim* [Reproach of the Gentiles; 1396], Shimon ben Zemaḥ Duran's *Keshet u-magen* [Bow and Shield], and Leon Modena's *Magen va-ḥerev* [Shield and Sword; 1643]. Collectively, these texts insist on the continuity of Jewish and Christian legal and moral precepts between the Hebrew Bible and the New Testament.[48] The phenomenon of large-scale conversion of Jews to Christianity in the times of Profet Duran, Shimon ben Zemaḥ Duran, and during the late fifteenth century created a population of former Jews who possessed an unprecedented familiarity with Christian theology, exegesis, and the New Testament. Efforts to recruit conversos back into the Jewish fold led certain rabbis to adopt new postures toward Christianity and its founder that were in some ways more moderate or nuanced than earlier Jewish polemics. Therefore, between the late fourteenth and seventeenth centuries, it became common for Spanish and Italian Jewish scholars to insist on the compatibility of doctrines in the Hebrew Bible and New Testament, especially in ex-converso contexts.

ben Levi interprets Isaiah 64:3, "Such things had never been heard or noted. No eye has seen [them], O God, but You, who act for those who trust in you." R. Joshua ben Levi's quote is in reference to the unknown nature of the Garden of Eden.

48. On Profet Duran, see Frank Talmage, ed. *The Polemical Writings of Profiat Duran*. On Shimon ben Zemaḥ Duran, see *Keshet u-Magen*. See also Prosper Murciano, ed. and trans., "Shimon ben Zemaḥ Duran: A Critical Edition." Phd diss., New York University, 1975. On Leon Modena's contributions to this topic, see S. Simonsohn, ed., *Magen va-herev* (Jerusalem, 1960), and Talya Fishman's discussion of all three texts in "Changing Early Modern Jewish Discourse about Christianity" 159–94.

Profet Duran, Shimon ben Zemaḥ Duran, and Leon Modena believed that Jesus and early Christians had followed Jewish law assiduously, and frequently based their analyses of Christianity on the presumption that Jesus desired to uphold the commandments rather than abrogate the Torah and the Oral Law. They could point to numerous New Testament passages that supported this position: in Matthew 5:17–19, Jesus states "Do not think that I have come to abolish the law or the prophets; I have come not to abolish but to fulfill... Therefore, whoever breaks one of the least of these commandments, and teaches others to do the same, will be called least in the kingdom of heaven."[49] Shimon ben Zemaḥ Duran quotes Jesus's statement that "until heaven and earth pass away, not one letter, not one stroke of a letter, will pass from the law,"[50] and along with Profet Duran he emphasized Jesus's instructions in Matthew 23:2–3, "The scribes and the Pharisees sit on Moses's seat; therefore, do whatever they teach you and follow it."[51] Both Profet and Shimon ben Zemaḥ Duran called attention to passages that show Jesus's followers observing the commandments of the Torah even subsequent to his death. They continued to observe the Laws of the Nazir, and kept rabbinic commandments regarding the washing of the hands.[52] These writers believed that Jesus himself was a committed follower of rabbinic law who urged his followers to similarly obey the commandments and the Pharisees. Morteira was clearly familiar with this tradition of thought, and similar sentiments can be found throughout the *Tratado*.[53]

However, it is Leon Modena's *Magen va-ḥerev* that provides one of the most striking examples of how a seventeenth-century rabbi sought to modify the Jewish discourse about Jesus and Christianity in order to establish common ground with New Christians. Like Profet and Shimon

49. See variations of these passages articulated in Profet Duran, *Kelimat ha-goyyim*, 24, Shimon ben Zemaḥ Duran, *Keshet u-magen*, 2v., and Leon Modena, *Magen va-herev*, 44.
50. Shimon ben Zemaḥ Duran, *Keshet u-Magen*, 2v.
51. Profet Duran, *Kelimat ha-goyyim*, 24–26., Shimon ben Zemaḥ Duran, *Keshet u-magen*, 3r.
52. Profet Duran, *Kelimat ha-Goyyim*, 26; Shimon ben Zemaḥ Duran, *Keshet u-Magen*, 3r. Profet Duran draws specific parallels between the Laws of the Nazir and Acts 21:21–26.
53. Morteira, *Tratado*, 317–18.

ben Zemaḥ Duran, Leon Modena believed strongly that Jesus had not intended to violate or abrogate rabbinic authority and the laws of the Hebrew Bible.[54] In addition, Modena attempted to show that notions such as the Trinity and original sin could be reinterpreted in a Jewish idiom.[55] He emphasized that: "Were we to believe that the Trinity were attributes of God and not external properties, we would not err." The mistake of Christians, as he saw it, was in "believing that the son alone had been incarnated, and not the Father or the Holy Spirit," which to the Venetian rabbi's eyes implied an unacceptable division and rupture in the essence of God.[56] Leon Modena hoped that this more conciliatory approach to cross-confessional dialogue would serve as a potential bridge back to Judaism for conversos and their descendants.[57]

Leon Modena also sought to find elements in the Christian notion of Adam's original sin that could serve as the basis for a discussion of the common ground shared by New Christians and rabbinic Jews. Modena regarded this doctrine as being at the core of Christianity, and initially offered numerous proofs in order to subvert this theological pillar.[58] Nevertheless, at the end of his discussion Modena writes that "the sin of the first man caused a turn to evil and the evil inclination, and from this perspective it is possible to say that it contaminated the soul."[59] When seen from this perspective, Modena believed that "we shall find common ground easily...for the truth is that subsequent souls from his line suffered from what he had lost...and it was difficult for them to do good acts, and their souls were closer to evil and further from righteousness on account of that sin." Therefore, Modena believed it quite legitimate to see original sin as the "*fonte di peccato*" (source of sin) found in all later souls.[60]

54. Leon Modena, *Magen va-herev*, 44.
55. Leon Modena, *Magen va-herev*, 25, 37. Talya Fishman, "Changing Early Modern Jewish Discourse about Christianity," 159, 174–78.
56. Leon Modena, *Magen va-herev*, 25–26.
57. Talya Fishman "Changing Early Modern Jewish Discourse about Christianity," 159, 177–83.
58. Leon Modena, *Magen va-herev*, 7–10.
59. Leon Modena, *Magen va-herev*, 11.
60. Leon Modena, *Magen va-herev*, 11.

Like Leon Modena's *Magen va-herev*, Morteira's *Tratado* was intended to strengthen the Jewish faith of Portuguese ex-conversos, and to encourage reluctant conversos hovering on the margins of Jewish society to convert to Judaism. Both texts blended an aggressive polemic against Christianity alongside an attempt to construct bridges toward establishing a conversation with New Christians. Morteira, like Modena, sought to identify an area of theological terrain shared by both Jews and Christians, and attempted to reformulate Christian traditions in terms that brought them closer to Jewish doctrines. Yet the *Tratado* also differs from previous Jewish treatments of Jesus and Christianity in certain respects. Whereas Profet Duran, Shimon ben Zemaḥ Duran, and Leon Modena wrote in Hebrew for a Jewish audience, Morteira's *Tratado* circulated in Spanish and Portuguese, and was explicitly intended for a Christian audience. Unlike earlier Jewish treatments of Jesus, Morteira's *Tratado* is colored to appeal to the sensibilities of a specifically Protestant audience, drawing as it does on the works of Reformed authors like John Calvin, Cipriano de Valera, and Hugo Grotius. Morteira's meticulous citation of these sources by author, title, and – frequently – chapter and section number conveys the impression that he expected the *Tratado* to be read by people intimately familiar with these works. Finally, the proselytizing aspirations of the *Tratado* distinguish Morteira's writings from these earlier Sephardi polemical and apologetic works.

Part IV: Morteira and the Socinians: The Discovery of Judaizing Christians

The existence of precedents within medieval Sephardic literature for Morteira's new way of thinking about Christianity and the New Testament in the *Tratado* helps us to understand the origins of Morteira's ideas. However, these precedents cannot on their own explain why Morteira decided to draw upon these particular traditions in the second half of the seventeenth century, and not earlier. It is also important to remember that although rabbis like Leon Modena and Saul Levi Morteira employed novel forms of theological discourse in their interactions with certain Christians, these moderate and nuanced perspectives on Christianity and its Holy Writ were by no means the default or normative position. They were adopted in response to particular – and often very different – historical contexts in Venice and Amsterdam. Much of Morteira's discourse about Christianity and Christian Scriptures was clearly oriented toward a reading public of Protestant Christians. The language, texts, ideas, and terms of reference are those of Protestant, and especially Calvinist theology, and would not have been part of the vocabulary and experiences of conversos in Iberia and Italy. The fact that Morteira's approach to thinking about Jesus and the New Testament changed so drastically during his forty years in Amsterdam is a historical phenomenon that requires an explanation rooted in the particular religious and cultural environment in which this change took place.

The reversal of Morteira's positions on Jesus and the New Testament was the result of his immersion in Dutch Protestant society, his encounter with representatives of numerous Protestant movements, including Calvinists, Socinians, and Quakers, and his mastery of key Protestant texts. This process was fundamentally gradual in nature. As Marc Saperstein demonstrates, even before Morteira had written the *Preguntas* he was already beginning to reflect on the enormity of the new Protestant theological landscape in which he lived. In a sermon delivered in 1623, he remarked on Lutherans and Calvinists who "have repudiated the Pope, and who have eyes like those of human beings, namely, Israel, meaning that they have come closer to the Jews and are no longer so similar to a beast. They have opened their eyes to flee from some of the rigidities that those who believe in the Pope still cling to."[61] Morteira shows himself to be clearly aware of reforms implemented by major Protestant movements, but at this point he was not well attuned to the voices of more radical Christians. This turn came somewhat later, as a result of an exchange with a Socinian. This encounter was sufficiently shocking to convince Morteira that these movements were shedding layers of Catholic dogma to such a degree that they were on the verge of accepting Jewish beliefs and practices. Ultimately, he would attempt to encourage them further down this road to Jewish observance.

Around 1635, Morteira writes that he met a Protestant Socinian scholar and enthusiastically engaged him in an amicable theological conversation. Morteira describes this encounter in the *Tratado*:

61. Marc Saperstein, *Exile in Amsterdam*, 242–46.

Here I am reminded of a discourse that took place more than twenty-five years ago with an old, very learned, and peaceful man who, while talking with me said that there was very little difference between us and them. I replied to him, how can you say this, when we believe in a most pure unity, and they believe in a Trinity? He responded that in no way did he believe in the Trinity, but rather that there is only one God, creator of all things, and that everything besides Him is created. I was astonished to hear him, for this was the first of these *novos reformados,* who are commonly called Socinians, with whom I had ever spoken in my entire life, nor had I taken notice of this belief! Thus, I asked if he was not a Christian, since he did not confess the Trinity. He said that yes, he was [a Christian], and that he believed in "that man" [Jesus] as a creation, and not as the creator, and that he was the most perfect being that God ever created. I asked if he believed in the Gospels, and he replied that he did. I immediately answered, how would he interpret what John says at the beginning of his [Gospel]: "In the beginning there was the Word, and the Word was with God." He replied that from here we prove that the Word was created, because John attempts to imitate in the beginning of his Gospel the manner in which Moses begins the Law. And just as Moses said, "In the beginning God created the heavens and the earth," and with this he wanted to say that the heavens and the earth were created in time at the beginning, and were not eternal... so too John wanted to say that the Word was created in time and the beginning, and was not eternal, and this Word was with God. I turned and asked him, according to this, how would he understand the ending of the verse: "And God was the Word?" He responded to me that this passage was falsified in the translation, because the original Greek says "And God was in the Word."[62]

62. Morteira, *Tratado,* 335–36. "Aqui me ocore à memoria hũ discurso que tiue hauera mas de 25 annos com hũ homen uelho, asas doctor e apasible, o qual discursando comigo me dise que poca diferenza hauia entre nós e elles. Repliquélhe eu como podia dizer isso, quando nós criamos hũa purissima unidade, e elles a terinidade? Respondeome que por nihum caso cria elle terenidade, se naõ que hauia hum so

Several decades ago, Henry Méchoulan was captivated by this striking passage and used it to speculate that Spinoza might have encountered Socinian ideas and individuals even before his excommunication from the Jewish community – through the vector of the community's leading rabbi, Morteira.[63] Here, Morteira's exchange with the Socinian suggests that the encounter with new (and unexpected) Christian movements in the Netherlands offers an important interpretive key for understanding the dramatic shift in the rabbi's attitudes toward Christianity and the New Testament from acerbic hostility to reconciliation. This possibility is reinforced by some of Morteira's remarks in the introduction to the *Tratado,* where he emphasizes his awareness of the profound religious transformations taking place among diverse Protestant movements in the Netherlands. Morteira lauds the *novos reformados* – the Socinians – for rejecting the "incarnation and corporeality, passion, and death of [the] single Prime Cause," and for "denying any sort of imagined plurality in the divine essence, neither knowing nor professing any God and creator except for the one Prime Cause of all things with no exception." Furthermore, according to Morteira, the *novos reformados* are critical and skeptical about parts of the Gospels themselves – an

Deos, criador de todas as cosas, e que todo for a delle heraõ criaturas. Admiréme de ouuilo, por que hera o primero destes Nouos Reformados que uulgarmente chamaõ susinianos com que ouese falado em minha uida, nem tinha noticia desta profisaõ. E assim lhe perguntej se naõ hera cristaõ, pois naõ confesaua a terinidade? Dise que si, que hera, e que cria naquelle homẽ como criatura, e naõ como criador, e que hera a mas sobrana criatura que Deos house criado. Perguntélhe se cria nos Euangelios. Diseme que si. Repliquej eu logo como declararia o que diz Joaõ no principio do seu: '*En principio hera la palaura, e la palaura hera acerca de Dios.*' Respondeo: 'Antes dahi prouamos que la palaura he criatura, por quanto Joaõ quis imitar no modo com que principiou seu Euangelio ao modo com que Mose principiou a Lej. E assim como dise Mose: '*En principio criou el Dio os ceos e a tera,*' e com isto quis dizer que em tempo e principio foraõ criados os ceos e a terra, e naõ abeternamente criou el Dio os ceos e a terra, assim Joaõ quis dizer que em tempo e principio e naõ abeternamente foj a palabra, e esta palabra hera cerca [de] Deos... Tornej a replicarlhe, conforme isso como entendia o que diz no fim do uerso: '*E Dios hera la palaura*?' Respondeome que este paso estaua falsificado na traducsaõ, por que no original grego dizia: '*E Dios hera em la palaura.*" Regarding Morteira's encounter with the Socinian and this passage in the *Tratado*, see also H. Méchoulan, "Morteira et Spinoza au carrefour du Socinianisme," *Revue des études juives* 135 (1976): 51–65.

63. Henry Mechoulan, "Mortera et Spinoza au carrefour du Socinianisme," 51–65.

extraordinary leap in his eyes. He observes that they "also destroy the words of the Gospels with clear arguments" in order to defend "their consciences and beliefs."[64] These passages vividly encapsulate Morteira's moment of epiphany when he discovered the existence of a Christian movement with which he could find an expanse of shared theological terrain: belief in an extreme unity of God, a shared rejection of the Trinity, skepticism regarding the divinity of Christ, and criticism of the Gospels. Morteira viewed these Christian groups as having made many strides closer to Jewish law. In their effort to separate themselves from Roman Catholicism, Morteira believed, these Christians were adopting doctrines virtually indistinguishable from those held by Jews themselves. While Morteira was somewhat familiar with the contours of Lutheran and Calvinist beliefs when he wrote the *Preguntas,* it is only after his encounter with the Socinian that we can see him preaching to a Jewish audience in the early 1640s, telling his listeners that:

> Many of them [Christians] have abandoned the glaring errors their predecessors embraced . . . They have abandoned the plurality that they introduced into the Godhead, they have restored the proper belief in the eternity of the Torah, they believe in the beneficence promised in the future to the Jewish people. They err only to some extent in the matter of the doctrine of the Messiah. In our time, these [Christians] have grown more numerous; every day truth points out the proper path, and their numbers increase.[65]

The encounter with Socinians in the Netherlands provoked the remarkable transformation and reorientation of Morteira's attitudes toward Jesus and the New Testament, and helped launch his attempt to persuade them to move even closer to Jewish beliefs and practices.

It should not surprise us that Morteira conveys a reasonably informed understanding of Socinian beliefs in the *Tratado*. From the late sixteenth

64. Morteira, *Tratado,* 3–7.

65. Marc Saperstein, *Exile in Amsterdam,* 250. See also p. 250, n. 61 where Saperstein suggests that this sermon may have been shaped by the conversation that Morteira had with the Socinian scholar.

century through the seventeenth century, the marshy polders of the United Provinces provided surprisingly fertile ground for Socinian ideas, as well as for the Portuguese Jewish community. Controversial Socinian works were printed throughout this period, both in Europe and in the Netherlands, during the same years when the Portuguese Jewish community was establishing itself in Amsterdam. There is evidence that as early as the last years of the sixteenth century, Faustus Socinus's writings were circulating in the northern Low Countries, and that Jacob Arminius – the early leader of the Remonstrant movement – recommended Socinus's writings to his pupils. The Rakovian Catechism itself was printed in Latin in 1609; and Conrad Vorstius, who was appointed to a chair at Leiden University, supervised the printing of Faustus Socinus's *De Auctoritate Sacra Scripturae* (Steinfurt, 1612), a controversial work claiming that the New Testament was authoritative solely on the basis of its historical credibility. Johannes Crell, a Socinian sympathizer and later Rector of the Socinian academy at Rakow, published a scathing critique of the Trinity in *De Uno Patre*, an edition of which was printed at Leiden in 1639. *De Vera Religione* (Rakov, 1630), the programmatic statement of mid-seventeenth-century Socinianism, was printed in Amsterdam in 1642.[66] Outright rejection of the Trinity, criticism of Christ's divinity, and belief that Jesus was simply "the most perfect being that God ever created" – positions that shocked and excited Morteira – were basic tenets of many Socinian works that circulated in the Netherlands, and beyond, during this period.

Socinianism became more visible during these years in other ways as well. The Remonstrant faction within the northern Netherlands was receptive and sympathetic to certain Socinian ideas, such as opposition to strict predestinarianism, anti-Trinitarianism, and skepticism regarding the divinity of Christ. Simon Episcopius, Arminius's successor at the head of the Remonstrant movement, wrote in his "Apology for the Remonstrant Confession of Faith" (Leiden, 1629) that the Trinity could not be founded on the *terra firma* of God's Word. Depending as it did on a long line of philosophical deductions and inferences, and

66. Sarah Mortimer, *Reason and Religion in the English Revolution: The Challenge of Socinianism* (Cambridge: Cambridge University Press, 2010) 15, 25, 31, 45, 47.

unknown to the original followers of Christ, the doctrine of the Trinity had to be rejected. Later, Episcopius insisted that close examination of the historical record revealed that parts of Trinitarian theology – such as the doctrine of eternal generation – were formulated during the Church Councils of the third and fourth centuries. They were thus unknown to the original followers of Jesus and the earliest Christians.[67] Stephanus Curcellaeus, Episcopius's successor and Rector of the Remonstrant Academy, insisted that Christianity was entirely viable without the doctrine of the Trinity. Hugo Grotius sought to undermine the doctrine of the Trinity by casting doubt on the authenticity of New Testament passages traditionally cited in support of the triune God. In his *Annotationes ad Novum Testamentum*, Grotius appealed to text-critical methods that recall the Gospel criticism Morteira encountered in his exchange with the Socinian. Instead of seeing 1 Timothy 3:16 ("great is the mystery of godliness: God was manifest in the flesh") as an allusion to the Trinity, as was traditional, he insisted that the text was a corrupt version of an original text that had made no mention of God whatsoever. Instead, Grotius and Crell both held that according to the *uncorrupted* original text, what was revealed and made manifest in the flesh was not God, but rather the Gospel message.[68]

Likewise, Morteira's claim that the *novos reformados* distance themselves from the "passion, and death of [the] single Prime Cause" reflects the direction of Socinian thought during this period. At first glance, the statement appears rather opaque. What could possibly be meant by a rejection of Jesus's "passion and death?" In all likelihood, Morteira is referring to well-known Socinian opposition to the traditional Christian belief – Protestant and Catholic – that Jesus suffered and died to redeem humanity from the indelible stain of original sin. Whereas orthodox Calvinist theologians frequently emphasized a strict theology of predestination, Socinus insisted that human nature had not been altered by Adam's sin – that humans had the freedom to act in a way that would assure their salvation. From this perspective, there was no need for Christ to mount the cross or suffer, except as a model of Christian conduct.[69]

67. Sarah Mortimer, *Reason and Religion in the English Revolution*, 18, 24, 149–54.
68. Sarah Mortimer, *Reason and Religion in the English Revolution*, 153–54.
69. Sarah Mortimer, *Reason and Religion in the English Revolution*, 15–16, 22.

Radical Christianity was in the air and water of the Netherlands, and whether through oral or written vectors it was perhaps inevitable that Morteira would come into contact with its notorious tenets.

Morteira found that he had much in common with his Socinian interlocutor – much more, indeed, than he had ever anticipated. However, Morteira and the Socinian were not in full agreement. They differed over the divinity of the Gospels as a whole, the eternality of Revelation, and the perfection of Christ. There were numerous religious doctrines observed by Protestants which Morteira viewed as unnecessary innovations upon the Hebrew Bible, presumptuous efforts to improve upon God's own Law. These violated God's commandment "You shall not add to that which I have commanded you, nor shall you diminish the commandments that the Lord your God enjoined to you."[70] A central purpose of the *Tratado* was to urge the *novos reformados* even closer to the adoption of Jewish doctrines, and to rely on the Hebrew Bible rather than the Gospels. Morteira declares that "Our principal intent is to undeceive the *novos reformados* of today, those who trust in professing a single, most pure unity of God, totally denying the Trinity." Morteira hoped that he could urge the *novos reformados* even closer to Jewish beliefs: "just as God directed them and opened their eyes to recognize and flee from their many errors," so too "He shall teach them everything perfectly, fleeing from all of the abuses and recognizing only the pure truth."[71]

Morteira's discussion of the Jewish and Christian Sabbath illustrates how he sought to "open the eyes" of the *novos reformados* even further, encouraging them to embrace the Sabbath according to Jewish law. Morteira strongly believed that the first Christians had observed the Jewish Sabbath. He knew from examining Luke 23:56, "On the Sabbath they rested according to the commandment," that immediately after Jesus's death his Apostles continued to observe the Jewish Sabbath.[72] Additionally, Juan de Pineda's *Monarchia Ecclesiastica* noted that Christian

70. Deuteronomy 4:2. The commandment to neither add to nor subtract from the Law in Deut 4:2 (and Deut 13:1) plays a significant role in Morteira's discussion of Catholic and Protestant departures from biblical law between ancient and modern times. See for instance the *Tratado*, 597.
71. Morteira, *Tratado*, 527.
72. Morteira, *Tratado*, 333.

Sabbath observance shifted to Sunday only in the year 154, after Pope Pius I experienced a dream in which an angel instructed him to commemorate the resurrection.[73] Reflecting on the considerable reforms implemented in Dutch Protestant society, and on the emphasis given to biblical precedents, Morteira was unable to understand how Calvinists, Socinians, and other Protestant movements had failed to return Christian Sabbath observance to its original Saturday commemoration. From his close reading of the *Institutes of the Christian Religion*, Morteira knew that Calvin extolled the significance of strict Sabbath observance, and located the Sabbath at the top of the hierarchy of biblical commandments. Inviting his readers to consult the *Institutes*, Book II.8 directly, Morteira observes that according to Calvin, God prioritized observance of the Sabbath more than any other commandment during biblical times. Paraphrasing Calvin's text closley, Morteira writes that "When He wished to tell His prophets that the religion would be destroyed, He complained that His Sabbaths had been profaned, violated, and were neither observed nor sanctified. If they did not serve God in this manner of work, there remained nothing through which He could be honored."[74] Furthermore, as Morteira emphasizes, even Calvin admits that the shift from Saturday to Sunday Sabbath was implemented as an ordinance of the church.[75] In light of Calvin's understanding of the importance of the Sabbath, Morteira was all the more shocked that Reformed Christianity had not yet shifted its Sabbath observance from Sunday back to Saturday: "What amazes me, is [that] the *Reformados*, who try to govern themselves in all matters according to Holy Scripture and abandon the ordinances of the popes, and especially those that are against it [biblical law], nevertheless in their reformations they did not reform the precept of the Sunday Sabbath."[76]

73. Morteira, *Tratado*, 139. Juan de Pineda, *Monarchia ecclesiastica, o Historia vniuersal del mundo* (Barcelona, 1606), 2:152.

74. Morteira, *Tratado*, 141–43. See John Calvin, *Institutes of the Christian Religion*, ed. John T. McNeill, trans. Ford Lewis Battles (Philadelphia, PA: The Westminster Press, 1960), 1:394–96.

75. Morteira, *Tratado*, 145. John Calvin, *Institutes of the Christian Religion*, 1:398–99. "Because it was expedient to overthrow superstition, the day sacred to the Jews was set aside; because it was necessary to maintain decorum, order, and peace in the church, another [day] was appointed for that purpose."

76. Morteira, *Tratado*, 139–40. See John Calvin, *Institutes of the Christian Religion*, 1: 394–96.

Morteira believed firmly that Jesus had indeed observed the Jewish Sabbath in accordance with rabbinic law. However, he was also very much aware of passages in the New Testament that contradict this position. Matthew 12:1, for instance, says that "At that time Jesus went through the cornfields on the Sabbath; his disciples were hungry, and they began to pluck heads of grain and to eat."[77] The verse seems to suggest that Jesus condoned the violation of the Sabbath, as the Pharisees themselves allege in Matthew 12:2. Nevertheless, Morteira writes: "It is not to be inferred from this that the observance of the Sabbath was annulled, because when they were rebuked, [Jesus] excused what they did [as] not harming the observance of the Sabbath, saying that since they were hungry it was licit, comparing it to the case of David when he ate the holy bread, or... to the labor the priests of the Temple did on the Sabbath, saying that it was greater than the Temple."[78]

Morteira found additional ways to reconcile this apparent contradiction in Cipriano de Valera's comments on Luke 6:1, which repeats Matthew's narrative of Jesus walking through the fields. Regarding the verse "One Sabbath while Jesus was going through the cornfields," Valera notes in the printed margins of his Bible that "Sabbath" refers not only to the weekly Sabbath, but also signifies days of rest during longer festivals. Morteira suggests that the text in Matthew refers to the second day of Passover rather than the weekly Sabbath. This is a crucial point for Morteira, because the second day of Passover was instituted by the rabbis as a supplemental fence or hedge around the law (*valado*) to ensure full compliance with the commandments, and not as a precept taken directly from the Law whose observance is mandatory. On the day that Jesus and his followers walked through the fields "it is not prohibited to pick grain in the field, except according to the fences of the sages," which exist only "so that nobody would go out to harvest their fields

77. Morteira may have been directed to this passage by Profet Duran, who cites it as proof that Jesus did not annul Jewish dietary laws. See Frank Talmage, *The Polemical Writings of Profiat Duran*, 25–26. Morteira focuses on the more germane topic of Sabbath observance engaged by this episode. The parable of Jesus and the corn fields is cited as proof that Jesus endorsed the abrogation of the Sabbath in the late thirteenth-century polemical anthology, *Sefer Nizzahon Vetus*. See David Berger, "On the Uses of History in Medieval Jewish Polemic," 28.
78. Morteira, *Tratado*, 331.

on the festival day, and they would enjoy the happiness commanded by God."[79] According to *biblical* law, in fact, it was fully licit to prepare one's own food, even during the first and last days of Passover: "[No work at all shall be done on them], only what every person is to eat, that alone may be prepared for you" (Exod 12:16). As Morteira observes, "There was thus no transgression against a precept of the Law, but only against a fence around the law."[80] Although Morteira was a leading rabbi who would have highly valued adherence to these rabbinic fences around the law, he trivializes the importance of these types of precepts in order to exonerate Jesus from any significant violation of Jewish law. Morteira's Jewish Jesus was intended to set an example for the *novos reformados*. If Jesus and the Apostles observed the Sabbath according to Jewish law, so too should the Socinians of his own day.

Conclusion: Morteira's *Tratado* in a European Context

When Morteira expressed his belief that certain Christian movements were approaching the acceptance of Jewish beliefs, and stated that he wrote the *Tratado* in order to "open their eyes" even further, he was not articulating an abstract idea or a distant hope. His anticipation and excitement were rooted in the present, and in the particular milieu of religious life in Amsterdam, the United Provinces, and northwest Europe. First, Morteira's belief that certain Christian movements were inching closer to Jewish beliefs and practices needs to be considered against the background of the religious culture of Amsterdam during the seventeenth century. Amsterdam during this period was a notorious haven for religious boundary crossing. Morteira would have been intimately familiar with the experiences of hundreds of Iberian conversos who returned to Judaism in this period. Additionally, Amsterdam's rabbis, merchants, and scholars were in regular correspondence with converso relatives who had not converted to Judaism, and communities in southern France that continued to practice Judaism in secret. In addition, Morteira would

79. Morteira, *Tratado*, 331–32. Rabbinic fences or hedges around the law were a point of contention in seventeenth-century Venice, as well as in Amsterdam. They were critiqued – anonymously – by the famous Italian rabbi Leon Modena. See Talya Fishman, *Shaking the Pillars of Exile: 'Voice of a Fool,' an Early Modern Jewish Critique of Rabbinic Culture*, 51–52, 100–102.

80. Morteira, *Tratado*, 333.

have also been aware of remorseful Ashkenazi Jews who had converted to Christianity and later returned to Judaism in Amsterdam. The earliest evidence of such conversions dates to the early 1640s – well after Morteira had written the *Preguntas*, and well before he began writing the *Tratado*. These episodes of conversion to Judaism in Amsterdam persisted long after Morteira's death, across the seventeenth and eighteenth centuries.[81] There were also Christians with no discernible Jewish past who adopted Judaism in Amsterdam during this period, or engaged in Judaizing practices. In early seventeenth-century England, John Thraske organized one of the first English Christian movements advocating the observance of Jewish laws ranging from those concerning the Sabbath to Passover. Morteira may have known about Hamlet Jackson, a follower of Thraske who converted to Judaism in Amsterdam in the early 1620s.[82] Morteira would certainly have known about figures like Samuel Fisher, the Hebrew-speaking English Quaker who traveled to Amsterdam in 1657 (three years before Morteira's death) and who attended Sephardic synagogue services regularly.[83] The Dutch messianist Peter Serrarius likewise attended Jewish prayers regularly, and ultimately became a fervent believer in the Jewish false-Messiah Shabbetai Zevi.[84] Johann Rittangel arrived in Amsterdam in 1642, and at various points appears to have practiced Roman Catholicism, Lutheranism, and Judaism. Rittangel shifted between religions so abruptly and frequently, nobody could be certain what his original faith had actually been.[85] Different types of

81. Elisheva Carlebach "'Ich will dich nach Holland schicken': Amsterdam and the Reversion to Judaism of German Jewish Converts," in *Secret Conversions to Judaism in Early Modern Europe*, ed. Martin Mulsow and Richard Popkin (Leiden and Boston: Brill, 2004), 52–61.
82. David Katz, *Philo-Semitism and the Readmission of the Jews to England, 1603–1655* (Oxford: Clarendon Press, 1982), 21–28. See also David Katz, "Jewish Sabbath and Christian Sunday in Early Modern England," in *Jewish Christians and Christian Jews: From the Renaissance to the Enlightenment*, ed. Richard Popkin and Gordon Weiner (Dordrecht and Boston: Kluwer Academic Publishers, 1994), 126.
83. Richard Popkin, "Can One Be a True Christian and a Faithful Follower of the Law of Moses? The Answer of John Dury," in *Secret Conversions to Judaism in Early Modern Europe*, 41–42.
84. Richard Popkin, "Can One Be a True Christian and a Faithful Follower of the Law of Moses?," 41.
85. Elisheva Carlebach "'Ich will dich nach Holland schicken': Amsterdam and the Reversion to Judaism of German Jewish Converts," 65–66.

conversion to Judaism and hybrid religious identities were frequent, and even commonplace, in Morteira's Amsterdam.

In addition, Morteira's specific interest in Protestant approaches to Sabbath observance should be seen within the context of developments in religious culture in England during the 1640s and 1650s, when a significant debate about how to correctly observe the Sabbath took place between Puritans contending for the exclusive authority of the Bible, and supporters of the "co-ordinate authority of the Church."[86] During this period there was also a significant shift in royal and ecclesiastic policy regarding Sabbath observance. David Katz has shown that royal authorities in the first half of the century sought to suppress popular support for assiduous Sabbath observance, but that during the Civil War, English authorities encouraged and even legislated the meticulous observance of the Lord's Day. Early English religious reformers tended to view strict Sunday Sabbath observance as a relic of Catholicism invented by human authorities. Henry VIII and Edward VI denounced "superstitious observance" of the Lord's Day; Elizabeth vetoed a bill for "the better and more reverent observing of the Sabbath day" in 1585, and again in 1601. In 1617, James I rebuked Puritans in Lancashire for "prohibiting and unlawful punishing of our good people for using their lawful recreations and honest exercises upon Sundays, and other Holydays, after the afternoon sermon or service." In 1618 James extrapolated this decree to the entire kingdom in the Declaration of Sports, which Charles I reissued in 1633.[87] However, during the two-decade period of the Civil War and Puritan rule between 1640 and 1660, official opposition to rigorous observance of the Sabbath ceased. Cromwell's attempt to reorganize Parliament, English law, and religious observance along biblical models encouraged much thought about how to properly observe the Sabbath. English Puritans, in an effort to emphasize the exclusive authority of the Bible, took the Fourth Commandment literally and seriously: "thou shalt not do any work, thou, nor thy son, nor thy stranger that is within thy gates."[88] This strict approach to Sabbath

86. David Katz, "Jewish Sabbath and Christian Sunday," 125.
87. David Katz, "Jewish Sabbath and Christian Sunday," 121–23.
88. David Katz, "Jewish Sabbath and Christian Sunday," 121.

observance persisted as a permanent feature of English religious life throughout seventeenth-century England, even after the Restoration.[89] During the same period, the strict observance of the Saturday Sabbath also emerged as an entrenched feature of certain English Protestant churches. In 1618, the same year that Morteira was appointed to lead the Beth Jacob congregation, John Thraske was punished for leading a Judaizing, Saturday-Sabbath observing sect. Subsequent movements led by Theophilius Brabourne, and especially by Henry Jessey, practiced a rigidly literal interpretation of the Fourth Commandment.[90] They meticulously ceased all work on Saturday, rather than Sunday. Morteira could very well have learned about these developments from his colleague, Rabbi Menasseh ben Israel, or from one of the numerous English religious sectarians who traveled to the Netherlands. Menasseh ben Israel not only spent two years in Cromwellian England, but was also a close personal acquaintance of Jessey.[91] Assiduous observance of the Fourth Commandment was thus much more visible and politically charged during the years in which Morteira wrote the *Tratado* than when he wrote the *Preguntas*. In this way, the trajectory of how English Protestants understood Sabbath observance across the seventeenth century can help us to understand the changes in Morteira's perspectives on Protestant Christianity and the New Testament.

Finally, Morteira's *Tratado* needs to be seen alongside the rising messianic crescendo in northwest Europe during the middle decades of the seventeenth century. The notion that certain Christian movements were approaching the acceptance of Jewish doctrines may have emerged from contacts between Sephardic Jews in Amsterdam and millennarian or messianic figures in England and the Low Countries. The French millenarian Isaac La Peyrère advocated the creation of a Jewish-Christian church that would suppress Catholic dogma and traditions, anticipate the arrival of the Jewish Messiah, and expect the imminent ingathering of the exiles in the Holy Land. La Peyrère believed that the Jewish Messiah and the king of France would rule the world from the rebuilt

89. David Katz, "Jewish Sabbath and Christian Sunday," 119.
90. David Katz, "Jewish Sabbath and Christian Sunday," 126–27.
91. David Katz, "Jewish Sabbath and Christian Sunday," 126–27.

Jewish capital of Jerusalem, and that the entire population of the world – Jews, Christians, and all others – would achieve salvation. La Peyrère wrote his work anonymously around 1643 under the title *Du rappel des juifs*, and printed it in 1655. Menasseh ben Israel may have possessed a manuscript copy of the text even earlier.[92] Adam Boreel, the Messianic Dutch Collegiant, provided the funding necessary for Rabbi Jacob Judah Leon's construction of a model of Solomon's Temple that was highly popular among Jews and Christians in Holland, and that was exhibited in England and German territories into the eighteenth century. Boreel, who in fact lived with Menasseh ben Israel for several months and learned Portuguese in order to communicate with him better,[93] also collaborated with Menasseh and Leon to produce an edition of the Mishnah with Hebrew vowel points. The fascination and commitment of Messianic Christians to symbols of Jewish messianism may also have played a significant role in stimulating Morteira's belief that certain Christians were approaching the acceptance of Jewish doctrines. If we understand Morteira's belief that certain Christian movements were increasingly adopting Jewish doctrines to be an expression of messianic excitement in and of itself, the context of European messianism in the second half of the seventeenth century emerges even more forcefully as a central framework within which the *Tratado* must be situated.[94]

92. Richard Popkin, *Isaac La Peyrère: His Life, Work, and Influence (1596–1676)* (Leiden and New York: Brill, 1987), 3, 13, 23, 60–61. See also Menasseh ben Israel, *The Hope of Israel*, 48–49, and Richard Popkin "Jewish Christians and Christian Jews," 62.
93. Menasseh ben Israel, *The Hope of Israel*, 82–83; Richard Popkin "Can One Be a True Christian and a Faithful Follower of the Law of Moses?," 35–36.
94. The question of whether Morteira's expectation of an imminent adoption of Jewish doctrines by Socinian Christians constitutes an expression of Jewish messianism, and the degree to which Morteira's *Tratado* as a whole is messianic in nature, requires further research. On the one hand, while Morteira does not explicitly eschew messianic positions, the only location in which he deals with an overtly messianic Jewish text is his discussion of Isaac Abravanel's *Ma'ayanei ha-yeshua* [Wells of Salvation]. Morteira uses the text to contrast the exalted status of the land of Israel under Jewish rule, compared with its arid and unproductive status under the rule of other nations. However, Morteira does not speculate about the prospective date of messianic redemption at any point in the *Tratado*, and in fact uses Abravanel's text only for historical information. On the other hand, the question of the messianic character of the *Tratado* depends greatly on how we interpret Morteira's excitement regarding the apparent movement of certain

Morteira's *Tratado* reflects an intimate familiarity with the religious dynamics of the Protestant Low Countries, and demonstrates a thorough mastery of Protestant theological texts. The transformation in Morteira's attitudes toward Christianity and the New Testament is rooted in the immersion of a Venetian rabbi in Dutch Protestant society for a period of more than four decades. The encounter between Morteira and the anonymous Socinian represents only the overture of this process. The *Tratado* represents its climax. Yet, as we shall see in the next chapter, Morteira's project of Jewish-Christian *rapprochement* had its limits, and the Jewish embrace of Jesus and Christianity could only go so far.

Christians closer to the adoption of Jewish beliefs. Leon Modena makes an explicit connection between the conversion of the nations to Judaism and the miracles that will occur at the Messiah's arrival. See *Magen va-herev*, 70–71. If we interpret Morteira to have had a similar position, then the messianic context of seventeenth-century Europe is especially important to understanding the *Tratado*.

FIVE

Polemic and Scholarship in Seventeenth-Century Amsterdam: Rabbi Saul Levi Morteira and the History of the New Testament

> Everything that is believed and practiced among the Christians was developed little by little, according to the times and events, made up by the popes and the councils.
>
> – Saul Levi Morteira, *Tratado da verdade da lei de Moisés*, 1659/1660[1]

To interpret Scripture, we need to assemble a genuine history of it and to deduce the thinking of the Bible's authors by valid inferences from this history, as from certain data and principles... Our historical inquiry must explain the circumstances of all the books of the prophets whose memory has come down to us: the life, character and particular interests of each author of each individual book, who exactly he was, on what occasion he wrote, for whom and in what language. Then the fate of each book: namely how it was first received and whose hands it came into, how many variant readings there have been of its text, by whose decision it was received among the sacred books, and finally how all the books which are now accepted as sacred came to form a

1. Morteira, *Tratado*, 132.

> single corpus. All this, I contend, has to be dealt with in a history of the Bible.
>
> – Benedict Spinoza, *Theological-Political Treatise*, 1670[2]

When Saul Levi Morteira wrote his *Tratado da verdade da lei de Moisés*, he was inspired and excited by his encounter with Socinians in the Netherlands who – he believed – had so distanced themselves from Catholicism and traditional Christianity that they were on the verge of adopting religious beliefs that were scarecely distinguishable from those of Judaism. Morteira fervently hoped to encourage them even further down this path, toward Jewish beliefs about God, the Sabbath, Passover, and other festivals, to "undeceive" them completely, "opening their eyes" to the "pure truth."[3] Before arriving in Amsterdam from Venice, Morteira could never have imagined the uniquely active space for religious dialogue, innovation, and interaction that he would discover in his adopted city. Yet despite this excitement, Morteira remained profoundly concerned about the efforts of Dutch Christians to attract converts from within the Portuguese Jewish community. In light of the Catholic past of Amsterdam's New Jews, their intimate familiarity with Christian religious traditions, and the ambivalence felt by many ex-conversos about their new faith, Morteira took these polemics and efforts at proselytizing seriously. He expressed this anxiety in the introduction to his *Tratado*, where he exclaimed that "the *reformados* say that he who denies the truth and divinity of the Gospels also denies the Law of Moses . . . I was furthermore motivated to undertake this labor having heard that this way of arguing and threatening has also been advanced among the Papists, as well as by a Portuguese Jesuit who, finding himself confronted with arguments, tried to finish off [the debate] by saying that if he denied the Gospels, he would also have to deny the Law of Moses. But denying the Law of Moses is not the same as denying the Gospels, since when

2. Jonathan Israel, ed. *Theological-Political Treatise*, 98–101.
3. Morteira, *Tratado*, 527. For an additional discussion of Morteira's encounter with Socinians, and its impact on his thought, see Benjamin Fisher, "Opening the Eyes of the *Novos Reformados*: Rabbi Saul Levi Morteira, Radical Christianity, and the Jewish Reclamation of Jesus, 1620–1660," *Studia Rosenthaliana* 44 (2012): 117–48.

the foundation crumbles so does the house. And denying the Law of Moses is nothing less than confessing oneself a *libertino*, without Law or divine precepts."[4] Morteira makes clear to his readers that "Ending this threat that I heard every day made by the *senhores* is what motivated my zeal and sentiment."[5]

Morteira's "zeal" led him to compose one of the most elaborate, systematic, and well-researched critiques of the New Testament written by a pre-modern Jew, and the methodology that he employed for "ending this threat" was historical scholarship.[6] As the quote above suggests, Morteira believed that the books of the New Testament, and Christian religious practice generally, developed over time, "little by little," reflecting the cultural practices and social mores of the ancient Mediterranean world and the decisions of leaders and institutions within the later church. During the sixteenth and seventeenth centuries, the terrain of historical scholarship became the battleground for the authenticity of religious beliefs, texts, practices, and institutions in the work of many scholars, including – among others – Cesare Baronio, Isaac Casaubon, and Matthias Flacius Illyricus. This chapter shows that Saul Levi Morteira was part of this world, and no less than any of these Protestant and Catholic scholars he appreciated the potency of historical scholarship as a polemical tool. I situate the *Tratado* and its author in this world, where the authority of sacred texts was increasingly assailed by historical methodology. Furthermore, this chapter provides essential context and foundation for understanding the origins of a

4. Morteira, *Tratado*, 3. For a discussion of Morteira's use of the term *libertino*, see Benjamin Fisher, "For God and Country: Jewish Identity and the State in Seventeenth-Century Amsterdam," in *Jewish Culture in Early Modern Europe: Essays in Honor of David B. Ruderman*, ed. Richard Cohen, et al. (Cincinnati and Pittsburgh: Hebrew Union College Press and University of Pittsburgh Press, 2014), 50–62. While there were certainly antinomian elements within Morteira's own community, it is clear from the extended discussion of the *Tratado* that Morteira is thinking of Quakers, a group well known among his contemporaries for its antipathy toward state and judicial authority.
5. Morteira, *Tratado*, 3.
6. Morteira's *Tratado* has also been identified as "the most elaborate, nuanced, and learned Jewish evaluation of the Protestant world in the pre-Enlightenment period." See Miriam Bodian, "The Reformation and the Jews," 130–31.

radical thinker who emerged from within Morteira's community, and who proposed subjecting the Hebrew Bible to the scrutiny of historical scholarship: Benedict Spinoza. Spinoza, the Portuguese Jew and author of the *Theological-Political Treatise,* called for historical inquiry into the texts of the Hebrew Bible, the motives and background of these texts' authors, and their transmission through the ages. Spinoza, targeting the Hebrew Bible, and Morteira, focusing on the New Testament, both believed that historical scholarship could pose insurmountable challenges and unresolvable problems to their opponents, though their goals could not have been more different. Together, they reflect and illuminate a methodological turn in the study of Scripture that would ultimately have a powerful and enduring impact on the authority of the Bible in early modern Europe.

In Part I of this chapter, I survey earlier medieval Sephardic Jewish approaches to reading the New Testament that Morteira knew, and upon which he drew. Morteira found in these texts ideas about the historical context of the New Testament and the relationship between Jewish and Christian Holy Writ that were compelling to him, and incorporated these into his own treatise. I examine the key passages and ideas used by these authors in order to appreciate Morteira's debt to them, and to illuminate Morteira's departure from earlier precedents. While some of Morteira's approaches were influenced by examples in medieval Jewish polemical literature, Morteira's uses of history were also profoundly shaped by the milieu of Dutch Protestantism, Italian humanist historiography, and Spanish Catholic scholarship. Part II and Part III explore Morteira's systematic historical approach to studying the New Testament. Morteira strongly believed that in order to achieve an accurate understanding of Christian Scriptures, it was necessary to situate Jesus's teachings within two contexts: the setting of the rabbinic Jewish traditions, texts, and languages prevalent in Jesus's society; and the Greco-Roman religious practices that presided in the region in late antiquity. Finally, Part IV investigates Morteira's accounts of the temporal and geographic origins of the Gospels. By showing his readers the importance of historical context for understanding Jesus's teachings, Morteira sought to dislocate Christian Scriptures from the sphere of theological inquiry to the discipline of historical analysis. Achieving this aim required a sophisticated, meticulous reading of Christian Scripture that was unlike most previous Jewish works of biblical scholarship.

This chapter also makes a broader argument about the role of religious polemics in transmitting and disseminating new ways of reading the Bible. Religious polemics in general have been studied as a significant source for examining the absorption of historicist notions by Jewish scholars in medieval Europe, and especially during the sixteenth and seventeenth centuries.[7] Morteira's *Tratado da verdade da lei de Moisés* in particular can be seen as a sensitive barometer for measuring the adoption of new genres of biblical exegesis and historical study into Jewish culture within the milieu of seventeenth-century Amsterdam. Morteira did not see these methods as appropriate to his study of the Hebrew Bible, but viewed them as essential to his efforts to interrogate and subvert Christianity and its Holy Writ. Therefore, it is specifically within his religious polemic that these ideas and theories are most fully developed. In this way, Morteira made a vast array of novel methods, texts, and ideas available to Jewish readers in his community. Heterodox Jewish figures like Spinoza would not have had to leave the Sephardic community of Amsterdam in order to be exposed to historicist ways of reading the Bible. Morteira showed his readers that it was possible to study Christian sacred texts as fundamentally historical artefacts in a way that was potentially transferrable, and he provided part of the historicist toolbox for doing so.

Part 1: Medieval Precedents

As we have seen, Profet Duran, Shimon ben Zemaḥ Duran, and Leon Modena's perspectives on Christianity and the New Testament were fundamentally reshaped by the need to interact with conversos, and by their profound familiarity with Christian texts and traditions. These Jewish writers adopted more nuanced depictions of Christian theology, presented Jesus as a diligently observant rabbinic Jew, and insisted that Jesus had not intended to abrogate any laws or commandments in the

7. For a survey of the development of Jewish historical approaches in New Testament scholarship and religious polemic, see David Berger, "On the Uses of History in Medieval Jewish Polemic, 25–40.

Hebrew Bible. Furthermore, Leon Modena identified several areas where he believed Jewish and Christian doctrines shared common ground. In addition, these writers also offered several precedents for the historical assumptions that Morteira would expand upon in the *Tratado*. Morteira's efforts to contextualize Jesus and the Gospels within the settings of the Greco-Roman and ancient rabbinic Jewish worlds emerged out of an interest in the content and history of the New Testament that developed among Sephardic and Italian Jews between the fourteenth and seventeenth centuries. *Kelimat ha-goyyim, Keshet u-magen,* and *Magen va-ḥerev* contain several suggestions that certain elements of Christian Scripture clearly reflect the language and customs common within Jesus's rabbinic Jewish social milieu. Profet Duran, as part of his polemic against the sacrament of the Eucharist, comments on Jesus's well-known statements at the Last Supper comparing the bread and wine to his flesh and blood. These teachings, he insists, do not hint at a new sacrament or a theological mystery. Rather, Jesus merely recited blessings over the bread and wine, "as is the custom of Israel," and asked his students to commemorate him with bread and wine whenever they ate.[8] Shimon ben Zemaḥ Duran echoes Profet Duran's assertion that Jesus's pronouncements regarding the bread and the wine, his flesh and his blood, were "blessings on the bread and the wine in accordance with the traditions of Israel."[9] Furthermore, Profet Duran provides an insightful analysis of New Testament accounts of Jesus's crucifixion, and the normative legal practices of ancient Jewish society. Duran found a major problem of legal procedure in the Christian belief that Jesus was executed on the first day of Passover. If Matthew 26:17–20 is correct and Jesus did in fact celebrate Passover prior to his execution, then he was crucified on the first day of Passover – an act that was entirely prohibited according to the laws observed by Jews at that time. Additionally, despite Christian assertions that Jesus was arrested one day and executed the next, regulations in the Mishnah plainly state that decisions in capital crimes could not be initiated and concluded in a single day.[10]

8. Profet Duran, *Kelimat ha-goyyim*, 36–37.
9. Shimon ben Zemaḥ Duran, *Keshet u-magen*, 4b.
10. Profet Duran, *Kelimat ha-goyyim*, 52.

Leon Modena also makes the Judaic context of Jesus and the New Testament an important theme in his discussion of Christian theology. Modena rejected popular but ahistorical polemics against Jesus that neglected this reality, writing that:

> Only from having studied our texts and their texts I established a principle, which according to my opinion is stable and true, as if I were a member of his [Jesus's] generation and sat with him. Know that among the Jews of this time, close to the end of the Second Temple, there were a number of sects, all of whom recognized the Torah of Moses, but some of them disputed its interpretation and commandments. There were Pharisees and Scribes, that is to say, our sages... Sadducees, Boethusians, Essenes, and a few others. Some of them are recorded in the *Yosippon,* and also Carlo Sigonio [*De republica Hebraeorum libri*]. And from all of these Jesus chose the true one and followed the cult of the Pharisees.[11]

In these texts, Morteira would also have encountered suggestions about the need to consider the polytheistic pre-history of the early Christian world, and the impact of pagan religious culture on the formation of the New Testament. Profet Duran believed that on the one hand the Apostles themselves continued to observe Jewish law; on the other hand, they desired to attract converts among the nations, and Jesus's followers believed that the burdensome laws of the Bible, the "yoke" of the Torah, would doom their efforts to failure. Therefore, they agreed that faith alone, "rather than the active commandments," would be sufficient for salvation. The significance of the pagan context for the development of the New Testament is even more explicit in the writings of Profet Duran's followers. In *Keshet u-magen,* Shimon ben Zemaḥ Duran alleges that Jesus's followers were astounded after his death by the fact that none of the prophecies foretold in Scripture were fulfilled during his life. Accordingly, "when his students saw that he had fallen into the hands of Israel without these prophecies having been fulfilled, which

11. Leon Modena, *Magen va-herev,* 63. Translated in Talya Fishman, "Changing Early Modern Jewish Discourse about Christianity," 166–67.

they had entirely expected, they began to invent the famous doctrines of their faith. First of all, that he came into being without aid of a man, for Miriam was impregnated as a virgin by the Holy Spirit, and remained a virgin after his birth nine months later."[12] The reason for the widespread acceptance of this claim was "because of what was widespread at the time, that women would be impregnated by gods. And it is written in *Sefer Korot Alexander* that his mother, Olympias, the wife of Phillip of Macedonia, King of Greece, conceived from Amon, a god, and gave birth to Alexander. The truth is that Olympias conceived from Kanitor who was King of Egypt, through magic, and Kanitor was driven away."[13] Leon Modena reiterates this idea in *Magen va-ḥerev,* while explaining the emergence of central Christian doctrines that (in his view) were not articulated by Jesus: "it is not shocking that the nations (gentiles, as they are called by the Christians) accepted the Christian doctrines over time. Because for the Christians, everything rests upon the foundational belief that the Holy Spirit impregnated a virgin who gave birth to the Lord, and for the nations this was not an unfamiliar narrative or idea. There were already many who believed that every day the gods Apollo, Mars, and others would copulate with mortal women, and that children were born from these unions of gods and man, and that sometimes they died or were killed afterwards."[14]

Part II: Jesus and the New Testament in a Rabbinic Context

Morteira's *Tratado* clearly bears the signs of close familiarity with earlier Sephardic and Italian approaches to reading the New Testament, but he also goes beyond these precedents. Historical questions are more central in Morteira's *Tratado* than in any earlier medieval Jewish reading of the New Testament. Morteira employs a more expansive library of non-Jewish texts, and he is more systematic in his argumentation and collection of evidence. Unlike earlier writers, Morteira reflects on historical problems raised by Protestant Christians themselves, in

12. Shimon ben Zemaḥ Duran, *Keshet u-magen,* 7b.
13. Shimon ben Zemaḥ Duran, *Keshet u-magen,* 7b. See also Prosper Murciano "Shimon ben Zemaḥ Duran: A Critical Edition," 26.
14. Leon Modena, *Magen va-herev,* 63. See also Talya Fishman "Changing Early Modern Jewish Discourse about Christianity," 167–68.

their theological and exegetical writings. Furthermore, whereas Profet Duran, Shimon ben Zemaḥ Duran, and Leon Modena wrote for a Jewish, Hebrew-reading audience, Morteira wrote in a European vernacular and self-consciously anticipated an educated Protestant Christian readership. More than once in the *Tratado*, Morteira affirms that his overall aim is to "undeceive the *novos reformados* [Socinians] of today, those who believe in professing a most pure unity of God, totally denying the Trinity."[15] In many respects, Morteira's methods of historical scholarship also reflect the growing importance of historicist perspectives in European New Testament scholarship during the late sixteenth and seventeenth centuries. Diverse Christian confessions sought to ground the legitimacy of their practices on historical grounds, and sparred with one another over the historical authenticity of their beliefs and institutions. Very often, these polemical aims are evident beneath the veneer of European Christian historical studies of Holy Scripture. During the 1550s, the Slavic Protestant Matthias Flacius Illyricus composed an immense, multivolume history of the church designed "to expose the pope as a usurper, the Vulgate as an inaccurate version of the Bible, and the Mass and monasticism as corruptions of true Christian life and worship."[16] Cardinal Cesare Baronio, in an effort to refute Illyricus, sought to demonstrate that in fact Catholicism and its institutions had their origins in the societies of Jesus and the Church Fathers.[17] Historical scholarship also enabled Hugo Grotius and other Christian scholars to reconcile apparent errors and inconsistencies in the New Testament, strengthening the coherence and integrity of the text.[18]

15. Morteira, *Tratado*, 527.
16. Anthony Grafton and Joanna Weinberg, *I Have Always Loved the Holy Tongue*, 171.
17. Anthony Grafton and Joanna Weinberg, *I Have Always Loved the Holy Tongue*, 171. We also have seen the polemical valence of debates over the Hebrew Bible's vowel points during the late sixteenth and seventeenth centuries in Chapter 3.
18. Debora Kuller Shuger, *The Renaissance Bible: Scholarship, Sacrifice, and Subjectivity*, 27–28. For instance, see the development of Christian interpretations of Matthew 27:9: "Then was fulfilled that which was spoken by Jeremiah the prophet: 'They took thirty pieces of silver, the price set on him by the people of Israel,'" which in fact does not resemble any passage in Jeremiah but rather refers to Zechariah 11:12–13, "So they weighed out my wages, thirty shekels of silver." Sebastien Munster and earlier exegetes attributed this inconsistency to authorial mistake or error of transmission. Erasmus

For sixteenth- and seventeenth-century men of letters such as Illyricus, Munster, Baronio, Scaliger, Casaubon, Grotius, Selden, and many others, studying the ancient history of the New Testament also meant appreciating the background of Jewish laws and traditions that shaped the way in which Jesus and his earliest followers saw the world.[19] Illyricus acknowledged that an accurate understanding of ancient Jewish beliefs and practices was crucial for Christian scholars because "Christ arrived at a time when the Jewish religion was still in some sense intact. Therefore he used certain ceremonies, especially those that God established through Moses."[20] In the seventeenth century, diverse readers of the New Testament likewise insisted on filtering key passages describing the Last Supper and the execution of Jesus through the lens of Jewish authorities and texts,[21] and they viewed the New Testament as having been composed in a Mediterranean world shaped by an intersection of Hellenic, Roman, and Jewish traditions and practices.[22] Whatever the theological chasm that separated Baronio from Casaubon and Bellarmine from Grotius, there was a shared belief that it was ancient Jewish texts and traditions that would help settle key arguments in Christian exegesis.[23] Some of Morteira's most important and innovative methods must be attributed to the historical approaches to studying the New Testament being used by his Christian contemporaries and predecessors. To be sure, Morteira and his Christian counterparts had

suggests that the text may be derived from a lost apocryphal text of Jeremiah. Grotius emphasizes that according to patterns of transmission of knowledge practiced by Jews in the ancient Near East, it is possible that the reference to Jeremiah in Matthew was based on an orally transmitted tradition. In Grotius's view, just because Matthew refers to a statement by Jeremiah that did not become canonical does not mean that it was not grounded in ideas and texts that may have circulated in ancient times.

19. Anthony Grafton and Joanna Weinberg, *I Have Always Loved the Holy Tongue*, 171. Debora Kuller Shuger, *The Renaissance Bible: Scholarship, Sacrifice, and Subjectivity*, 22–47. Jason Rosenblatt, *Renaissance England's Chief Rabbi: John Selden*, 192–200.
20. Anthony Grafton and Joanna Weinberg, *I Have Always Loved the Holy Tongue*, 189.
21. Debora Kuller Shuger, *The Renaissance Bible: Scholarship, Sacrifice, and Subjectivity*, 32–33, 42–43.
22. Debora Kuller Shuger, *The Renaissance Bible: Scholarship, Sacrifice, and Subjectivity*, 42–45.
23. Anthony Grafton and Joanna Weinberg, *I Have Always Loved the Holy Tongue*, 183, 188–89, 219.

divergent aims. Nevertheless, alongside these theologians and scholars, Morteira studied the Christian Scriptures against the background of ancient rabbinic Jewish texts that added further dimensions to the social contexts from which Jesus and the New Testament emerged. The milieu of religious and historical scholarship in sixteenth- and seventeenth-century northwest Europe played a crucial role in shaping Morteira's polemic, and in adding new methods to the repertoire of pre-modern Jewish biblical studies.

One of the most significant influences on Morteira's historical approach to studying the New Testament was his encounter with John Calvin's *Commentary on the Harmony of the Three Evangelists: Matthew, Mark, and Luke* (Geneva, 1553). Morteira read Calvin's *Harmony* meticulously, and paid particular attention to Calvin's efforts to resolve the challenging contradiction between accounts of the Last Supper found in the Gospels of Matthew and John. On the one hand, Matthew narrates that:

> On the first day of the Feast of Unleavened Bread, the disciples came to Jesus and asked, "Where do you want us to make preparations for you to eat the Passover?" He replied, "Go into the city to a certain man and tell him, 'The Teacher says: My appointed time is near. I am going to celebrate the Passover with my disciples at your house.'" So the disciples did as Jesus had directed them and prepared the Passover.
>
> – Matthew 26:17–18

At the same time, and in contradiction to Matthew, the Gospel of John states:

> Now it was the day of Preparation, and the next day was to be a special Sabbath. Because the Jews did not want the bodies left on the crosses during the Sabbath, they asked Pilate to have the legs broken and the bodies taken down.
>
> – John 19:31

How can it be, Calvin asked, that Jesus celebrated the Passover with the Apostles, as it says in Matthew, while according to John, Jesus was crucified *before* Passover had been observed by the rest of the Israelite population? Was it possible that Jesus had violated God's commandments pertaining to the observance of Passover? Calvin was unwilling to contemplate the possibility that Jesus had committed such a brazen violation of biblical Law: "He did not allow Himself to do anything in the rite that was against the Law's directions." It was only logical, then, for Calvin to also reject a popular approach to resolving this contradiction: that the Jews were so eager to kill Jesus that they arbitrarily delayed the holiday for a full day, enabling them to kill and bury Jesus before the start of their festival.[24] This, however, did nothing to bring Calvin any closer to resolving the problem of how Jesus and the Israelites celebrated Passover at different points in time.

Calvin was by no means the first Christian to wrestle with the challenging contradiction between John and Matthew regarding the dates of the Last Supper and execution. The twelfth-century theologian Rupert of Deutz and the fifteenth-century bishop Paul of Burgos (a Jewish convert to Christianity) argued that on occasions when Passover or another festival fell adjacent to the Sabbath, Jewish law permitted deferring the festival to the following day in order to obviate Jews from having to refrain from all work for two consecutive days. In the year Jesus died, according to John, the first day of Passover was to be followed by a "special Sabbath." Therefore, Jesus's Jewish contemporaries delayed their celebration of Passover until the day after Jesus's execution, while Jesus himself observed Passover on the precise day prescribed in Leviticus.[25] In order to resolve these seemingly contradictory New Testament verses, Calvin offers a very similar interpretation. He insists that Jewish legal texts permitted both the execution of Jesus and the correct observance of Passover by all parties. Like Paul of Burgos, Calvin emphasizes that rabbinic Jewish laws enabled a holiday to be deferred when it fell adjacent to the Sabbath, as was the case on the Passover preceding Jesus's

24. John Calvin, *A Harmony of the Gospels*, 3:126. Morteira, *Tratado*, 260–61.
25. Anthony Grafton and Joanna Weinberg, *I Have Always Loved the Holy Tongue*, 215–16. Debora Kuller Shuger, *The Renaissance Bible: Scholarship, Sacrifice, and Subjectivity*, 36–37. This debate was carried on in intense exchanges well into the sixteenth and seventeenth centuries. Scholars like Paul of Middleburg in the early sixteenth century, and Scaliger, Casaubon, and Baronio later in the century, continued to debate the chronology of the Last Supper and Crucifixion.

execution. While Jesus observed Passover on the correct day according to the letter of the Law, as John states, the rest of the Jewish population followed rabbinic law and observed it the following day, as Matthew holds. "It is certain," Calvin writes, "that the Jews themselves do not deny that on all occasions when the Sabbath and the day of Passover fall consecutively, they observe the rest from labor no more than one day of the two, and this was introduced by the Rabbis, from which it follows that Christ performing [the Passover observance] in another way from the one in common usage was doing nothing contrary to the law."[26] Rabbinic law thus provided Calvin with the hermeneutical key to the scriptural contradiction between Matthew and John, helping him to explain how both the Jews and Christ correctly observed Passover.

Morteira responded to Calvin's solution to the problem between John and Matthew, and in so doing intervened in a long debate within Christian society that had begun as early as the twelfth century and was an ongoing source of friction between scholars such as Scaliger, Casaubon, Bellarmine, and Baronio.[27] Morteira agreed with Calvin that rabbinic law provided the crucial background for correctly understanding the contradictory accounts of the Last Supper. However, Morteira strongly disagreed with Calvin's reading of the rabbis. Morteira is palpably incensed at Calvin's suggestion that the Mishnah and Talmud hold that on all occasions when the Sabbath and the day of Passover fall consecutively, Jews refrain from labor only for one of the two days.[28] Morteira insists that according to the evidence of the Mishnah – "the most ancient books present among our people, which follow the books of the prophets in chronology… and were finished in the time of the Second Temple" – it was common for there to be multiple, consecutive festival days.[29]

As an example, Morteira points to a discussion of circumcision

26. John Calvin, *A Harmony of the Gospels*, 3:126. Morteira, *Tratado*, 265, quotes and translates Calvin, paraphrasing slightly: "Sabese muito ben que por hũa obseruaçaõ antiga, que quando a Pasqua ou os outros dias de festa sucediaõ em sesta feira, os remitiaõ ao dia seguinte por que houera sido muito dificultoso ao pouo cesar da obra dois dias areo."

27. Anthony Grafton and Joanna Weinberg, *I Have Always Loved the Holy Tongue*, 218–26.

28. Morteira, *Tratado*, 266.

29. Morteira, *Tratado*, 266.

practices in tractate Shabbat of the Mishnah that shows how it would not be unusual for Jews to observe two, three, or even four days of consecutive rest.[30] Morteira explains that normally, male children are circumcised on the eighth day. However, if there is uncertainty about whether the child was born after sunset (i.e., the beginning of the next day), then the ceremony is deferred to the ninth day; if the uncertain birth coincides with the Sabbath, there is no circumcision until the tenth day; if the Sabbath is followed immediately by a festival, circumcision is performed after eleven days. If this Sabbath is followed by a two-day festival such as Rosh Hashanah, the ceremony is performed at twelve days. Morteira's extended discussion of circumcision practices shows that it was quite common in the Jewish calendar for there to be multiple festival days of rest that are observed consecutively, contrary to Calvin's suggestion. Thus, Morteira writes, the "problem of the Gospels is without resolution."[31]

Morteira also found a discussion regarding festival days that fell adjacent to the Sabbath in tractate Bava Metzi'a of the Mishnah.[32] Quoting from this passage, Morteira writes: "The festival day that falls on a Friday evening: you shall not cook on that day for the following day's Sabbath. You may cook only for the day of the festival, and you may eat what is left over on the Sabbath."[33] Ancient Jews thus had to observe the festival *and* the Sabbath consecutively. Furthermore, Morteira emphasized that

30. Morteira, *Tratado*, 266. Mishnah Shabbat XIX.5.

משנה מסכת שבת פרק יט
משנה ה
ה] קטן נמול לשמונה לתשעה ולעשרה ולאחד עשר ולשנים עשר לא פחות ולא יותר הא כיצד כדרכו לשמונה נולד לבין השמשות נמול לתשעה בין השמשות של ערב שבת נמול לעשרה יום טוב לאחר השבת נמול לאחד עשר שני ימים טובים של ראש השנה נמול לשנים עשר קטן החולה אין מוהלין אותו עד שיבריא

31. Morteira, *Tratado*, 268.

32. Morteira references a passage in Mishnah Ḥagigah; the actual passage he quotes, however, is found in Mishnah Bava Metzi'a II.1.

משנה מסכת ביצה פרק ב
א] יום טוב שחל להיות ערב שבת לא יבשל אדם בתחלה מיום טוב לשבת אבל מבשל הוא ליום טוב ואם הותיר הותיר לשבת ועושה תבשיל מערב יום טוב וסומך עליו לשבת בית שמאי אומרים שני תבשילין ובית הלל אומרים תבשיל אחד ושוין בדג וביצה שעליו .שהן שני תבשילין אכלו או שאבד לא יבשל עליו בתחלה ואם שייר ממנו כל שהוא סומך עליו לשבת

33. Morteira, *Tratado*, 268. "O dia de festa que sucedeo ser em sesta feira, naõ cosiniheráõ

the ancient Jewish law against cooking on a festival day for the adjacent Sabbath was rooted in God's specific instructions regarding the observance of Passover. This made the passage from Bava Metzi'a especially pertinent to the subject of Jesus's Last Supper. Exodus 12:16 says, "You shall celebrate a sacred occasion on the first day, and a sacred occasion on the seventh day; no work at all shall be done on them; only what every person is to eat, that alone may be prepared by you." If Jesus's last Passover fell adjacent to the Sabbath – as Calvin and the Gospels insist – then Jews would have been obliged to observe both days of rest meticulously, contrary to Calvin's assertions.[34]

Morteira offers one final challenge to Calvin's interpretation of the rabbis. He demonstrates from the Mishnah that the requirements Israelites were obliged to perform at the Temple on Passover would not have been modified under any circumstances whatsoever, even when the first day of Passover fell adjacent to the Sabbath: "we shall show how many times the celebration [began] on a Friday evening, and it was not deferred [*remetiaõ*] to the Sabbath that followed, as was falsely invented."[35] Under normal circumstances, Morteira writes, the Passover offering "is to be presented before the Lord the day after the first day of the feast of unleavened bread, for the verse says '*the priest shall elevate it on the day after the Sabbath*'... It was thus the custom and rule, as it says in the Mishnah in the aforesaid location, that on the evening of the first day of Passover... many people from the cities and countryside that were close to the location where the sheaf [*omer*] had to be presented gathered, so that the divine precept was celebrated publicly and ostentatiously."[36] Continuing, Morteira writes,

> What would happen if the first day of the festival fell on a Friday, and the second day was the Sabbath, on which it would be necessary to perform so much work, such as reaping, threshing, milling,

de proposito no dia de festa para o sabado. Por em cosinheráõ pelo dia de festa. J se sobejar, seruirá para [el] sabado."

34. Morteira, *Tratado*, 268. "...se sigue claro como o sol ser a soluçaõ de Joaõ Caluino fundada sobre o que naõ he..."
35. Morteira, *Tratado*, 268.
36. Morteira, *Tratado*, 269.

> sifting, and more. Because nobody can imagine that on account of the sanctity of the Sabbath this labour would be performed by fewer people than what would be done ordinarily, and that thus they would gather less [grain offering] than normal, all in order to perform less labour by as few people as possible. As the *aforismo* says (Ḥagigah II.3), 'On the Sabbath as much as on any other day of the week the offering of the sheaf is presented [at the Temple].[37]

Referring back to Calvin's suggestion that the Israelites could defer a day of rest that fell adjacent to the Sabbath, Morteira emphatically insists that this could never have taken place in ancient times, if the laws of the Mishnah and Talmud were truly observed: "Oh, if only Calvin were alive! How I would open his eyes and embarrass him at the same time with this testimony that he so confidently affirms that the Jews themselves confess and hold according to their ancient books."[38] Ancient Jews observed the Passover festival so meticulously that they would not defer these rituals, even for the sake of the Sabbath.[39] In this manner, Morteira showed that Calvin's solution to the contradiction between John and Matthew could not be substantiated by the Mishnah and Talmud's descriptions of the laws and customs of the society in which Jesus lived.

However, like Calvin, Morteira *did* believe that the Mishnah and Talmud could help readers achieve a better historical understanding of Jesus's teachings in certain parts of the Gospels. Morteira interprets numerous important New Testament passages using ancient rabbinic

37. Morteira, *Tratado*, 269. Morteira is referring to the discussions of the Festival of Weeks and other holidays that overlap with a Sabbath in Mishnah Ḥagigah II. 3–4.
משנה מסכת חגיגה פרק ב
משנה ג
ג.] בית שמאי אומרים מביאין שלמים ואין סומכין עליהם אבל לא עולות ובית הלל אומרים מביאין שלמים ועולות וסומכין עליהם
משנה מסכת חגיגה פרק ב
ד] עצרת שחל להיות בערב שבת בית שמאי אומרים יום טבוח אחר השבת ובית הלל אומרים אין יום טבוח אחר השבת ומודים שאם חל להיות בשבת שיום טבוח אחר השבת ואין כהן גדול מתלבש בכליו ומותרין בהספד ובתענית שלא לקיים דברי האומרין עצרת .אחר השבת
38. Morteira, *Tratado*, 269–70.
39. Morteira, *Tratado*, 269–70.

sources as the foundation required for understanding the Gospels correctly. Turning his attention to specific Christian theological doctrines based on the Gospels, Morteira writes that "As a result of being ignorant of phrases and terms that were spoken during those times, they [Christians] understand them differently than what was meant, and many times oppositely, from which it follows that they established mysteries and doctrines upon false foundations."[40] Matthew 16:19 and John 20:23 offer two such instances of Christian interpretations that require analysis in a rabbinic Jewish context. The first verse says, "I will give to you the keys to the kingdom of heaven; whatever you bind on earth will be bound in heaven"; the second verse narrates how Jesus breathed the Holy Spirit over his disciples and said to them, "If you forgive anyone his sins, they are forgiven; if you do not forgive them, they are not forgiven." Based on these verses, Morteira writes, Christian authorities "established schemes and entire worlds . . . From here they derive the purchase and sale of that which is in heaven [i.e., indulgences], and on earth, all of the authority of the pope, the release of souls from Purgatory . . . and all auricular confession."[41] Morteira, however, urges readers to consider these verses alongside the Mishnah and Talmud, contemporaneous texts that elucidate the social and cultural context of New Testament times. In Morteira's view, the notion that God appoints men on earth to adjudicate guilt and innocence and to establish laws should be seen as nothing more than the "ordinary speech and customs that were used in that time when [Jewish] sages bestowed the title of 'Rabbi' upon their students . . . and the authority to teach and decide regarding doubtful matters that are found in the word of God."[42] Furthermore, there are similarities between the statements of Matthew and John, and the conversation in tractate Sanhedrin of the Babylonian Talmud, where the

40. Morteira, *Tratado*, 286. "Por causa de inhorar as frasis e termos com as quais se falaua naquelles tempos, entenderaõ delles diferentemente do que saõ, e muitas ueses o contrario. Do que se seguio que fundaraõ misterios e dotrinas sobre fundamentos falsos."

41. Morteira, *Tratado*, 286. "Sobre as quais palauras se fundaraõ maquinas e mundos enteros, como he notorio. Daqui procede o uender e comprar quanto ha no ceo e na terra, toda autoridade do papa, tirar almas do purgatorio . . . toda a confisaõ auricular."

42. Morteira, *Tratado*, 286.

authority granted to Rabbah bar Ḥana when he moved from the Land of Israel to Babylonia is described: "*Insinará, insinará; julgará julgará; soltará os primogenitos, soltará* – May he render decisions? He may render decisions. May he issue legal decisions? He may issue legal decisions. May he exempt [blemished] first borns? He may exempt [blemished first borns]."[43] In Morteira's view, this passage teaches that "That which is taught on earth is approved by God in the heavens. The first-born animals that are released [i.e., exempted from being sacrificed in the Temple] on the earth are released also in heaven."[44] Deuteronomy 15:19–22 relates the commandment to the sacrifice of the first-born of Israelite flocks each year at the Temple in Jerusalem, in the absence of any disqualifying defects. Morteira's commentary on this passage in Sanhedrin affirms that learned sages would be required to discern a vast number of potential blemishes that disqualify an animal from being sacrificed to God, to decide whether these could be ameliorated, and to determine when an animal was acceptable to be sacrificed. The decisions of these men are validated by God "*nos ceos*," in the heavens, just as Jesus bestowed Peter with the keys to the kingdom of heaven. Furthermore, Morteira continues, "all Jewish ecclesiastic authority is based on these words, because it is certain that God left uncertain matters that are encountered in the study of the divine Law to the doctors and sages of the People, who would pass judgment in accord with the principles they learned about the divine will."[45] Morteira found a very similar statement in Calvin's *Harmony* which he felt lent strong support to this interpretation of rabbinic sources. Calvin writes that "the metaphor of keys fits well with the office of teaching."[46] For example, Christ says in Luke that the Scribes and Pharisees have the keys to the kingdom of heaven, since they are expositors upon the Law.

43. b. Sanhedrin 5a
מאי רשותא כי הוה נחית רבה בר חנה לבבל אמר ליה רבי חייא לרבי בן אחי יורד לבבל יורה יורה ידין ידין יתיר בכורות יתיר

Morteira must mean the passage immediately before Raba's question to R. Judah, since this passage says that the son *may not* rule on first-borns, whereas the text of Morteira's quote affirms that he may do so.

44. Morteira, *Tratado*, 287.
45. Morteira, *Tratado*, 287.
46. John Calvin, *A Harmony of the Gospels*, 2:187. Morteira, *Tratado*, 288.

"Thus," Calvin writes, "we see that the gates of life are opened for us in no other way than the Word of God."[47]

The notion of reading the New Testament against the background of ancient rabbinic Jewish texts to provide a multi-dimensional picture of the society in which Jesus lived was not new when Morteira wrote the *Tratado*. Calvin, and a number of other Christian scholars after him, had employed the same methodology in their study of the New Testament and of the history of the earliest Christians. Well before Morteira, Joseph Scaliger read the New Testament narratives of the Last Supper as a fundamentally Jewish event, the Passover observance. In *De emendatione temporum* (1582), Scaliger emphasized that Jewish sources describing the society and religious customs of the time are essential for understanding the form and meaning of Jesus's teachings, language, and customs. Scaliger used tractate Pesaḥim of the Babylonian Talmud, along with a Passover Haggadah, to draw connections between numerous details of Mark's narrative of the Last Supper and Jewish religious practices.[48] Scaliger believed that using the Talmud to illuminate the historical context of the Gospels revealed a startling insight about the history of central Christian theological doctrines: that the Church Fathers had drawn incorrect conclusions about the nature of the Eucharist based on Jesus's statements at the Last Supper. As Scaliger noted, "Among the Jews, at every feast or meal, when they sat down at the table, they broke bread and said a blessing on the table as they broke it, and they said 'Blessed be God, who brings forth bread from the earth', and they supped or dined. After the meal they took a certain cup which they called Cos Hillel, the cup of blessing... and all drank from it, saying a certain prayer. Then they recited a certain canticle from Psalms. And when they blessed the table, that was called the Eucharist, not the thanks they offered after eating." Only later did the Apostle Paul separate the Eucharist from the normal meal.[49]

Likewise, John Selden saw the Mishnah and Talmud as providing

47. John Calvin, *A Harmony of the Gospels*, 2:187. Morteira, *Tratado*, 288.
48. Anthony Grafton, *Joseph Scaliger: A Study in the History of Classical Scholarship*, 2:300–319.
49. Anthony Grafton, *Joseph Scaliger: A Study in the History of Classical Scholarship*, 2:320–22.

the central context for understanding Jesus's arrest and trial and the authoritative legal opinions and practices that guided the Sanhedrin.[50] In his efforts to distance contemporary and ancient Jews from the charges of deicide in his *De synedriis et Praefecturis Juridicis Veterum Ebraeorum*, Selden subjects the New Testament narratives of Jesus's trial and execution to the standards of what would have been normative within ancient rabbinic Jewish society. Several discrepancies between the narrative of the Gospels and the practices prescribed in rabbinic literature emerge that would exonerate the Sanhedrin, or at least significantly complicate the consensus on Jewish culpability in Jesus's execution. First, according to tractate Sanhedrin, the punishment for blasphemy – with which Jesus was charged – is stoning, to be administered by the first witness from a height great enough to kill the blasphemer. Second, Selden notes the traditional reluctance of the Sanhedrin to impose capital punishment at all, and points to Maimonides' famous dictum in the *Mishneh Torah*, which affirms that everyone may claim that "Because of me God created the world." Furthermore, there are juridical procedural problems that result from a comparison of Jesus's trial and execution with the legal traditions of those held responsible. Selden cites numerous rabbinic statutes requiring capital cases to be completed on the very day of the proceedings, if the verdict is acquittal. However, in cases of a guilty verdict the decision may not be imposed until the subsequent day. No capital case, therefore, could be considered on the eve of the Sabbath or a festival.[51] This would have greatly complicated, and even contradicted, the narrative in John 19:31 of Jesus's execution taking place on the eve of Passover *and* one day prior to the Sabbath. Morteira, as we have seen, also focused much attention on the contradictions and problems posed by this verse in John.[52]

50. Jason Rosenblatt, *Renaissance England's Chief Rabbi: John Selden*, 192.
51. Jason Rosenblatt, *Renaissance England's Chief Rabbi: John Selden*, 196–99.
52. As in the case of Joseph Scaliger, there is no direct reference to John Selden's *De synedriis* in the *Tratado*. Nevertheless, there is evidence for the circulation of Selden's literature in Jewish society, including among individuals with whom Morteira was in close correspondence. Leon Modena was sent a copy of Selden's *De Successionibus in Bona Defuncti, Ad Leges Ebraeorum* (1631) in 1634, and paid particular attention to citations of his own *Historia degli riti Hebraici* (1637; 1638). See Mark Cohen, et

Morteira's approach to reading Christian Scripture drew upon many of the methods employed by Profet Duran, Shimon ben Zemaḥ Duran, and Leon Modena. However, his use of the New Testament and its rabbinic parallels is much more detailed and extensive, and Morteira engages with exegetical and historical problems raised by Protestant Christians themselves, rather than just those arbitrarily selected by Jewish polemicists. Like Calvin, Scaliger, and Selden, Morteira offered a reading of the New Testament that appreciated its rabbinic Jewish historical context, and explicitly employed the Talmud and Mishnah as historical sources necessary in order to depict multiple dimensions of the society inhabited by Jesus and the first Christians. The assumptions and methods employed by prominent scholars in the Protestant world of the Dutch Netherlands thus played an important role in shaping and inspiring Morteira's systematic use of new methods of historical study, biblical exegesis, and religious polemic.

Part III: The New Testament and Its Greco-Roman Context

Morteira's sensitivity to the historical context in which the New Testament was composed extended beyond the significance of rabbinic texts, customs, and language. Many Christian scholars in the seventeenth century viewed the New Testament as a text shaped by the convergence of Hellenic, Roman, and Jewish traditions. Especially after 1580, biblical scholarship tended to regard the New Testament as a text that was fundamentally part of ancient Mediterranean society, and its customs and rituals as shared by other cultures in the region. Justus Lipsius's *De cruce* (1592) offers a comprehensive survey of different types of crucifixion practiced by the Romans, and their legal reasoning, in order to clarify the specific punishments inflicted on Jesus, and Grotius found passages in Livy and Philo that paralleled the way Pilate's soldiers mockingly dressed Jesus as a king, suggesting that this type of humiliation was typical for the cultures of the ancient world in which Jesus lived.[53]

al. (trans., eds.), *The Autobiography of a Seventeenth-Century Venetian Rabbi*, 170–71, 266–67.

53. Debora Kuller Shuger, *The Renaissance Bible: Scholarship, Sacrifice, and Subjectivity*, 43–44.

Grotius argued that ancient Egyptian practices of human and animal sacrifice were essential for understanding what it meant for Jesus to have been a "sacrifice for sins."[54] Morteira was also acutely attuned to the undertones of Greco-Roman religion and culture that influenced the teachings of Christian Scriptures, and provides extensive discussions about the ways in which Christian beliefs and practices were shaped by the surrounding religious cults of the ancient world. By contextualizing the development of Christianity in this manner, Morteira sought to claim Christianity's *Sacra Historia* for the discipline of secular history, removing the study of the Christian past from the realm of theological inquiry. In demonstrating the development of Christianity over time, and the indebtedness of Christian doctrine to earlier cultures and religious systems, Morteira sought to demonstrate the mundane historicity of Christian traditions, proving them to be unreliable as a source of theological and moral truth.

Vincenzo Cartari's *Le imagini con la spositione de i dei de gli antichi* (Venice, 1556) is one of the most significant sources that Morteira read, and provided valuable grist for his polemical mill.[55] Cartari was likely born around 1500 and lived into the last quarter of the sixteenth century. Not much is known about his early life. It appears that he was born into a Ferrarese family with links to the ruling Estense family. Cartari was certainly part of the circle of Alfonso II d'Este and aspired to patronage from the Estense in support of his scholarship. Cartari also spent significant time in Venice, particularly in order to coordinate the production of images for the second edition of the *Imagini*.[56] Cartari's text offers a systematic survey of Roman cults and religious practices, and is organized according to the deities worshiped in ancient times. Intellectually, Cartari appears to have been a mid-level scholar. While he certainly read many classical authors first-hand and quotes them directly throughout his text, Cartari was not especially innovative in terms of the content

54. Debora Kuller Shuger, *The Renaissance Bible: Scholarship, Sacrifice, and Subjectivity*, 54–55.

55. Vincenzo Cartari, *Le imagini de i dei degli antichi. Nelle quali si contengono gl'idoli, I riti, le cerimonie, et altre cose appartenenti alla religione degli antichi con la loro Espositione*, ed. Caterina Volpi (Padua, 1603), 60–62.

56. Volpi, *Le imagini*, 7–8.

of this work. He relies very heavily upon the writings of more notable humanist scholars such as Alessandro Napolitano, Pietro Appiano, Celio Calcagnini, and especially Lilio Gregorio Giraldi.[57] Giraldi's *De Deis Gentium* (Basilea, 1548) is, in fact, probably the source for much of Cartari's treatise.[58] Nevertheless, the *Imagini* was immensely popular and was reprinted in at least fifteen editions during the second half of the sixteenth century and the first fifteen years of the seventeenth century. The work was translated into English and French, and two editions of the *Imagini* were printed in Latin. The chief significance of Cartari's *Imagini* is often located in its systematic dissemination and popularization of Roman antiquities and religious practices in the vernacular.[59] Furthermore, numerous sixteenth-century artists and sculptors referred directly to the *Imagini* for literary information on the visual appearance of Roman religious icons, with the result that Cartari's text has been considered required reading for modern interpreters of certain artistic works.[60]

It would be logical to assume that Morteira first encountered the *Imagini* in Venice. However, in the *Tratado*, Morteira draws his readers' attention to "an Italian book called 'Images of the gods of the ancients' composed by Vicenzo Cartari, printed in Lyon."[61] It is therefore possible that Morteira first read the *Imagini* in French sometime after 1612, when he traveled to Paris with the ex-converso physician Elijah Montalto.[62] Morteira used the *Imagini* to demonstrate that many doctrines articulated in the New Testament, and developed by later Christians based on the New Testament, had significant parallels and antecedents in the religious culture of the Roman world in which Jesus and the earliest Christians lived. Morteira begins with one of the foundational claims of Christianity: the doctrine of the Virgin Birth, rooted in the narratives

57. Volpi, *Le imagini*, 15–16.
58. Volpi, *Le imagini*, 17.
59. Volpi, *Le imagini*, 1–5.
60. Volpi, *Le imagini*, 1–5.
61. Morteira, *Tratado*, 148.
62. The French edition of Cartari's work was published at Lyon, France, in 1581 as *Les images de dieux ancièns*. Regarding Morteira's journey with Montalto, see Saul Levi Morteira, *Tratado da verdade da Lei de Moisés*, xl–xli.

of Matthew 1:18–20 and Luke 1:26–35, which describe how Mary and Joseph became aware that her pregnancy was through the Holy Spirit. While he believed that many accounts in the New Testament "imitate" or "copy" the example of the Hebrew Bible, Morteira writes that "there are also other accounts never heard nor preached among the Jews," for which "it [was] necessary for their disciples to look for refuge with the gentiles [i.e., pagans], among whom they were well received, flattering them."[63] These pagans did not find the "impossibilities" of the Christian accounts at all surprising, since many similar themes and stories were already preached and believed among them – "as we shall prove from their own accounts."[64] First of all, Morteira writes, it was entirely unremarkable for the pagans to hear that a woman had conceived a child without a man, but rather had been impregnated by a god: "For the gentiles [i.e., pagans], who say that their gods impregnate women every day, it does not surprise them, and they accept it because it mimics their teachings."[65] For instance, Morteira writes that "Folio 141 deals with the different figures that the gentiles [i.e., pagans] give to Jupiter, the greatest of their gods." Morteira continues: "The many stories that are read about Jupiter give cause to the depictions [of Jupiter] in many manners, because they hold that he transforms himself ordinarily in diverse forms in order to enjoy his lovers, such as when he changed into a white bull in order to steal Europa," and "into an eagle in order to take Agarimede," among many others.[66] The pagans further believe that children are born from these unions between gods and mortals. Morteira quotes Cartari's discussion of how children were born from Jupiter's frequent trysts, and that Jupiter transformed into a serpent and impregnated his daughter, Prosperina, who later gave birth to Bacchus.[67] Furthermore, Josephus, in the *Jewish Antiquities* (18:4) relates a story during the reign of the Emperor Tiberius regarding a woman named Paulina and a young man named Decius Mundus, who was greatly enamoured with her. Paulina rejected all of the man's advances and gifts, and even those offered to the

63. Morteira, *Tratado*, 148.
64. Morteira, *Tratado*, 148.
65. Morteira, *Tratado*, 148.
66. Morteira, *Tratado*, 148–49. Volpi, *Le imagini*, 189.
67. Morteira, *Tratado*, 149. Volpi, *Le imagini*, 469.

priests of the goddess Isis, to whom she was very devoted. As part of a conspiracy to lure Paulina into a union with Decius, the eldest priest of Isis told her that the God Anubis was very attracted to her, and wished to lie with her. Paulina was flattered by this offer, told her husband, and received his consent. Instead of Anubis, however, Paulina was tricked into spending the night with Decius Mundus.[68]

From his reading of Josephus and Cartari, Morteira derived two important conclusions. First, narratives about deities consorting with mortal women were not thought to be imaginary or allegorical, but rather were taken as true accounts (*historias verdaderas*) throughout the pagan world. The priest's story did not appear to Paulina to have been the product of his imagination, but rather was something commonly believed to be practiced by all of the gods: "Neither the youth, nor the priests, nor Paulina, nor her husband, nor her neighbours had difficulty believing the story."[69] Second, from the accounts that Morteira presents in the *Tratado*, it is easy to understand how the pagans received the Gospels' teachings about the Virgin Birth in Matthew and Luke. The idea that the Holy Spirit impregnated Mary, in Morteira's view, sought to "mimic and imitate" the very beliefs already held by the ancients.[70]

In addition to the Virgin Birth, Morteira draws upon Cartari's *Imagini* to place New Testament accounts of Jesus's death in a context of pre-existing pagan religious beliefs and customs. Morteira was especially fascinated with parallels between the ancient Egyptian cult of Apis and Christian beliefs about the Passion.[71] Morteira urges his readers "to see what the author cited above said in the *Imagines de los Dioses*... which deals at length with the reasons why the Egyptians worshiped an ox."[72] Cartari writes that "they were not content only with a figure [representation], but desired that the animal be living, which, of course, would only be for a few years, after which they bury it in the spot where it died. After this, the people express great emotions and mourn... tearing their

68. Morteira, *Tratado*, 149. Flavius Josephus, *Jewish Antiquities*, trans. William Whiston, ed. Brian McGing (Ware, UK: Wordsworth Editions, 2006), 780.
69. Morteira, *Tratado*, 150.
70. Morteira, *Tratado*, 150.
71. Volpi, *Le imagini*, 60–62. Morteira, *Tratado*, 152–53.
72. Morteira, *Tratado*, 153.

clothes and hair, suspending the administration of justice, until another [ox] is found. For not every cow or calf... was suitable to be the God Apis."[73] Cartari also relates that in the Egyptian city of Memphis, Apis was known to have appeared several times. As a result, the populace marked these days with elaborate celebrations.[74] "Who," Morteira asks, "is amazed that a people, who believe and practice this, would believe with great ease that a woman can be impregnated by a god, since they believe and confess to a cow," and that they "introduce among themselves mourning and crying [rituals], tearing their clothes and pulling out their hair for the death of their god, as they [Christians] do in the time of the Passion?"[75] Thus, when Christians composed the New Testament, the idea of a god dying, followed by elaborate mourning rituals, was by no means foreign to the regions from which Christianity emerged.

Furthermore, Morteira believed that the popular belief that a god could die was widespread in the ancient Mediterranean world, well beyond the borders of Egypt. For example, the prophet Ezekiel inveighed against the deplorable spiritual situation of the Israelites, and describes witnessing a series of theological abominations in the Temple that included visual depictions of forbidden creatures and the worship of celestial spheres.[76] Morteira describes one offence that Ezekiel observed: "He brought me (that is to say, the Spirit of the Lord) to the entrance of the north gate of the House of the Lord, and there were women seated bewailing Tammuz." Who, or what, Morteira wondered, was this Tammuz? Morteira found a reference to Tammuz in the *Guide for the Perplexed* (3:29) where Maimonides writes that he had:

> ...found written in an occult book of the ancient idolators that there was a great prophet named Tammuz who taught and persuaded a certain king to serve and adore the seven planets and the twelve signs of the Zodiac. The king ordered him killed most cruelly. On the night of his death, all the images of the idols in the land and skies gathered together in the Temple of Babylonia,

73. Morteira, *Tratado*, 153.
74. Morteira, *Tratado*, 153.
75. Morteira, *Tratado*, 153.
76. Ezekiel 8:1–17.

> which was dedicated to the Golden Image, which was the image of the sun, and this image was suspended between the heavens and the earth. It then fell within the Temple, and all the idols began to mourn for Tammuz, and they explained the passion and martyrdom that Tammuz the prophet had suffered. Because of this, all the idols were crying out, and lamenting all the night.[77]

Thus in the ancient land of Israel and Babylonia as well, Morteira found evidence of belief in the death and martyrdom of deities. Reading in the marginal notes of Cipriano de Valera's translation of the Bible, Morteira also discovered accounts linking the cult of Tammuz to religious beliefs in ancient Greece. Valera wrote: "Tammuz: Adonis, friend of Venus."[78] Returning to Cartari's *Imagini,* Morteira looked up the passage on Adonis and learned that "because of the death of Adonis, the friend of Venus, certain days were kept as sacred and were called '*Festas de Adonis,*' (Festivals of Adonis) and on those days women all over the city placed images similar to dead bodies at the top of certain beds prepared for this, and these were of people who had died recently. Weeping, they took these [images] to the gravesites. This, according to Plutarch, was done in Athens in memory of the tears that Venus wept for the death of Adonis, her lover. And in the land of the Argives... women go weeping for Adonis in a certain chapel not far from the Temple of Jupiter."[79]

Morteira also knew that Calvin – in his commentary on Ezekiel – cited

77. Morteira, *Tratado,* 154. "Diz pois Rebi Mose de Egipto na terzera parte do *More,* capitolo 29, no comento deste paso, que achou escrito nhum libro dos cultos dos antigos idolatras, que oue hum grande profeta chamado Tamuz que insinando e persuadindo a hum rej que seruise e adorase aos sete estrellas erantes e aos 12 sinos, o mandou o tal rej matar com cruelisima morte. E na noite de sua morte se ajuntaraõ todas as imagines dos idolos que hauia na terra ao templo de Babilonha a la imagine doiro, que hera a imagine do sol, e esta imagin estaua pendente entre os ceos e a terra. E em taõ cajo dentro templo e se puseraõ todas as imagines a redor delle, e elle lhe contaua a paxaõ e o martirio que hauia pasado Tamuz o profeta; pello que todas as imagines estiueraõ chorando e endechando toda a noite." See Maimonides, *Guide for the Perplexed,* trans. Shlomo Pines (Chicago and London: University of Chicago Press, 1963), 519–20.
78. Cipriano de Valera, *La Biblia,* Fol. 236. Morteira, *Tratado,* 154.
79. Vincenzo Cartari, *Le Imagini de i Dei degli Antichi,* 480–503. See esp. 501. Morteira, *Tratado,* 154–55.

Jerome, who agrees that Tammuz is Adonis. However, Jerome disagrees with Maimonides that this form of idolatry could have been prevalent in the land of Israel, since the Jews were not in naval communication with Athens and Asia Minor, where this particular religious cult flourished. Rather, for Jerome, the idolatry spoken of in Ezekiel is the cult of Osiris, the Egyptian God.[80] Thus, Jerome believes that the idolatry described by Ezekiel is of Egyptian rather than Greek origins. Either way, for Morteira the essential point is that the Christian practice of worshiping a dead god had deep origins in the religious cults of the pre-Christian ancient world: "for this reason almost all of the Epistles are dedicated to the Greeks, and there is an entire Gospel entitled '*conforme os Egipcianos*,' as Jerome writes in his prologue to the Gospels.[81] Thus, when [the Christians] sought to proselytize and persuade them [pagans] to accept the Messiah that they preached had come to [save] them, they sought to imitate and mimic the doctrines of the Greeks and copied from Apis or Osiris, for it was all one doctrine, only an alteration of names was introduced to the weeping and lamentations." For the pagan audience of the first Christians, "there was little difficulty since they were already introduced and accustomed [to these practices]," such as the celebration of the Passion, self-flagellation, and conspicuous crying.[82]

By using Cartari's *Imagini*, Morteira was thus able to reconstruct a detailed historical genealogy of ancient beliefs about the death and martyrdom of deities, and a plausible explanation for the reception of Christian belief in a pagan environment.

Part IV: New Testament Origins

In addition to investigating the cultural and social context that shaped the composition of the New Testament, Morteira also investigated Christian sources and reports concerning the time and place in which the

80. Morteira, *Tratado*, 155.
81. Morteira is referring to the early Christian non-canonical Gospel of the Egyptians, popular in Egypt during the second century and known only from quotations by Clement of Alexandria. See Ron Cameron, *The Other Gospels: Non-Canonical Gospel Texts* (Philadelphia, PA: The Westminster Press, 1982), 49ff. It appears that Morteira knew about non-canonical Christian literature from second- and third-hand sources.
82. Morteira, *Tratado*, 155.

different books of the New Testament had been composed. Exploring the provenance of Christianity's Holy Writ was an essential part of Morteira's broader project to demonstrate the role of human intervention and historical development in the emergence of what would later coalesce into the canon of Christian Scriptures.

As he had in his treatment of the Greco-Roman background of New Testament doctrines, Morteira mined the works of sixteenth-century authors for information about the origins of the Gospels. In order to find grist for his polemical mill, Morteira read traditional Catholic literature against the grain. This subversive approach to reading was common among religious dissidents and heterodox thinkers in the sixteenth and seventeenth centuries, both Christian and Jewish. Carlo Ginzburg provides an example of this in his famous study of the sixteenth-century Italian miller and accused heretic Menocchio, who developed strikingly unorthodox doctrines by combing popular religious texts and travel literature and reading them subversively. Menocchio was an eclectic and creative reader who held a variety of unorthodox beliefs: he rejected the authority of priests and the pope; he denied the divinity of Jesus; criticized the Gospels and most of the sacraments; and believed that the world had its origins in a mass of primordial cheese and worms.[83] Menocchio mined a wide range of innocuous and traditional works, such as *The Rosary of the Glorious Virgin Mary* and *The Travels of Sir John Mandeville,* for information that would confirm his unorthodox views.[84]

Subversive readings of traditional texts were also prominent among circles of secret Jews in sixteenth- and seventeenth-century Spain. As Yosef Hayim Yerushalmi demonstrated, the crypto-Jew Fernando Cardoso meticulously searched through the writings of the Church Fathers, biblical commentaries, and scientific works in order to learn about Jewish beliefs and practices. He found discussions about Jewish history, for

83. Carlo Ginzburg, *The Cheese and the Worms: The Cosmos of a Sixteenth Century Miller,* trans. John and Anne Tedeschi (New York: Penguin Books, 1982), 4, 9–10, 12–13, 18–22.
84. See Carlo Ginzburg, *The Cheese and the Worms,* 24–26, 28–29, and especially 33–41, 49, 69 where Ginzburg specifically discusses the filter through which Menocchio read his texts, and the ways in which he selectively played with the meaning of different passages.

example, in the writings of the French scholar Jacques Gaffarel, and was able to glean information about the Talmud, and the Jewish tradition that the world would exist for 6,000 years, from texts written by the sixteenth-century French Hebraist Gilbert Genébrard. Reading Sixtus of Siena's *Bibliotheca sancta*, Fernando Cardoso discovered passages from the Talmud in Latin, as well as in the original Hebrew. And he was able to access parts of one of Judaism's most influential legal codes, the *Mishneh Torah*, through the astronomical writings of a Jewish convert to Christianity.

Morteira was an accomplished subversive reader of traditional Catholic texts. The first text Morteira studied was Juan de Pineda's *Monarchia Ecclesiastica* (Barcelona, 1606). The *Monarchia Ecclesiastica* was first printed at Saragossa in 1576, and was later reissued at Barcelona in 1588 and 1606. The treatise comprises five volumes focusing on the interwoven sacred and secular histories of church institutions and figures. In the face of Protestant critiques of Roman Catholicism and the papacy, Juan de Pineda sought to demonstrate the eternality of the papacy as a Christian institution, its perfect blending of monarchical, aristocratic, and popular forms of government, and the continuity of the institution between Creation and the present. In order to achieve this aim, Pineda traces the chronological history of Christian institutions across a 3,970-year period. Recognizing that the numeric and historical information in Scripture is incomplete, Pineda supplements his data with Philo's *Breviarum de Temporibus*, which purports to give a complete chronology of the Persian, Babylonian, Greek, and Roman monarchies.[85] Pineda

85. This methodology is very close to the approach adopted by Azariah de' Rossi in his own efforts to establish an understanding of biblical chronology based both on the information provided by Scripture as well as on the writings of Philo and Josephus. The *Breviarum de Temporibus* was in fact a forgery of Annius of Viterbo. See Azariah de' Rossi, *The Light of the Eyes*, 415. Regarding Annius of Viterbo more generally, see Anthony Grafton, "Traditions of Invention and Inventions of Tradition in Renaissance Italy: Annius of Viterbo," in *Defenders of the Text: The Traditions of Scholarship in an Age of Science, 1450–1800* (Cambridge, MA: Harvard University Press, 1991), 76–103; and Joanna Weinberg, "Azariah de' Rossi and the Forgeries of Annius of Viterbo," in *Associazione Italiana per lo Studio del Giudaismo: Atti del Congresso IV*, ed. Fausto Parente and Daniela Piattelli (Rome, 1987), 23–47.

thus uses the firm dates of profane history in order to establish a clear picture of biblical chronology.[86]

By the time Morteira completed the *Tratado da verdade da lei de Moisés* in 1660, he had long harbored suspicions about the origins and authorship of the Book of John. Already in 1635, in his intriguing encounter with a Socinian scholar, Morteira had specifically asked how he would interpret John 1:1, "In the beginning was the Word, and the Word was with God, and the Word was God." As we have noted, the Socinian replied that "from here we prove the word was created, because John in the beginning of his Gospel mirrors the way Moses begins the Book of Genesis." "Thus," Morteira reported, "the man argued that the Word is in time and has a beginning and is not eternal." Morteira pressed him further regarding the ending of the verse, "and the Word was God," which seems to contradict this statement, indicating the eternality of the text. To this, as we have seen, Morteira's interlocutor "replied that this text was falsified in the translation [of the Vulgate], because in the original Greek it says 'and God was with the Word.'"[87]

Perhaps inspired by this encounter and discussion, Morteira made a concerted effort to gather information about the nebulous origins of the Gospel of John and many other New Testament books. Morteira believed that Pineda's *Monarchia Ecclesiastica* substantiated his suspicions, providing several conflicting accounts regarding the origins of the Book of John. Working his way through the treatise, Morteira discovered one account which related that Jesus and a disciple ascended a jagged mountain on the Isle of Patmos, and following intense fasting and prayers the Gospel was dictated and written on scrolls.[88] In the same chapter, however, Pineda also described an alternative foundation narrative, according to which the Book of John was composed at Ephesus at the urging and request of the bishops in Asia.[89] Elsewhere, in the *Monarchia Ecclesiastica,* Morteira read that "many very learned Christians" hold the text to have been composed in opposition to the Ebionite sect

86. Juan de Pineda, *Monarchia ecclesiastica*. "El Autor a los Lectores" and "Prefacion de la Monarchia Ecclesiastica."
87. Morteira, *Tratado,* 129–30.
88. Juan de Pineda, *Monarchia ecclesiastica,* 2:74–75; Morteira, *Tratado,* 130–31.
89. Juan de Pineda, *Monarchia ecclesiastica,* 2:75. Morteira, *Tratado,* 131.

in Second Temple times. Ebionites believed Jesus to have been entirely human in nature, not divine, and John wrote his Gospel in order to combat this belief. "A fine way indeed to agree and get muddled up with heresy and heretics," Morteira writes, "by creating texts and Scriptures according to his taste!"[90] The *Monarchia* also contains an additional narrative about the Emperor Julian digging within the Temple compound. After coming upon a cave, a single person was lowered down and found a tree growing amidst a watery lake. Upon this tree the Book of John was discovered.[91] Reflecting on John, Morteira writes that "although this Gospel more than any other seeks to deify a mortal man... they do not know upon what authority he was authorized to teach such a scandalous doctrine... and thus this author [Juan de Pineda] says in one instance the book came from the heavens, and in another that it came from the land and was made against the Ebionites, at the request of the Bishops of Asia in Ephesus; another time it was discovered in waters below the earth."[92] "The Papists," Morteira stated with a heavy finality, "do not know how to resolve the origins [of this text], and invent one thousand fables, one contradicting the other."[93]

Morteira next turned his attention to Sixtus of Siena's *Bibliotheca Sancta* (Venice, 1566) in his efforts to cast historically grounded aspersions on the origins of the New Testament. The *Bibliotheca Sancta* is divided into eight books, the first of which addresses the division and authority of the Bible, verse and chapter partitions, and the differences between canonical, deuterocanonical, and apocryphal texts. The second book offers a historical and alphabetical directory of writers and texts mentioned in the Bible but no longer extant, while the third book catalogues the variety of modes of biblical exegesis that have been employed by commentators. The fourth book is an encyclopaedic survey of individuals who have written significant commentaries on the Bible.

90. Juan de Pineda, *Monarchia ecclesiastica*, 2:146. "El error de los Ebionitas, q[ue] Christo fue puro ho[m]bre y no Dios, co[n]tra el qual error escriuio de directo S. Iuan su Euangelio, dizie[n]do, en las primeras palabras, q[ue] Christo fue y es Dios eterno." Morteira, *Tratado*, 131.

91. Juan de Pineda, *Monarchia ecclesiastica*, 2:252. Morteira, *Tratado*, 132.

92. Morteira, *Tratado*, 132.

93. Morteira, *Tratado*, 130.

The fifth book offers a collection of analyses by the Church Fathers on Old Testament passages, and the sixth book performs a similar survey of the New Testament. The seventh and eighth books of the *Bibliotheca Sancta* present the arguments made by ancient and modern "heretics" against the Old and New Testaments, respectively, and refute these allegations.[94] Sixtus's writings stood the test of time, with ten editions of the *Bibliotheca Sancta* printed between 1566 and 1742.[95] Morteira's use of Sixtus's *Bibliotheca Sancta* may seem unusual at first glance, given the fact that Morteira first became familiar with Sixtus while writing the sharply polemical manuscript defending the Talmud from Sixtus's attacks, *Respuesta a las objecciones con que el Sinense injustamente calunia al Talmud* (Mss. Amsterdam, 1648). Nevertheless, Morteira may have had other reasons for favoring the *Bibliotheca Sancta* as a source in the *Tratado*: he may have been aware of Sixtus's confrontational history with the Inquisition in Naples and Rome. During two inquisitorial proceedings which took place in the spring of 1552 and between June 1552 and November 1553, witnesses testified that many elements of Sixtus's sermons contained heterodox, and potentially Protestant leanings. Sixtus expressed doubts regarding the efficacy of good works, the sacrament of penance, the absolute requirement of auricular confession, and the nature of purgatory. In one interrogation session, he also stated that Jesus was the *adopted* son of God.[96] It may be the case that Morteira saw Sixtus's heterodox and Protestant leanings as being similar to those of

94. On the *Bibliotheca Sancta* see John Warwick Montgomery "Sixtus of Siena and Roman Catholic Biblical Scholarship in the Reformation Period," *Archiv fur Reformationsgeschichte* 54 (1963): 225–28. There has been debate about whether Sixtus of Siena was a converted Jew, as Montgomery and many others have held. Ulderico Parente, in "Sul preteso giudaismo di fra Sisto da Siena davanti all'Inquisizione Romana (1551–1553)," in *Le inquisizioni cristiane e gli ebrei* (Rome: Accademia nazionale dei Lincei, 2003), 375–405, convincingly argues that this was not the case. Not only did Sixtus's interests in rabbinic and Jewish topics develop only late in life, but all attestations to Sixtus's Jewish ancestry substantially postdate his death.
95. Fausto Parente, "Quelques contributions a propos de la biographie de Sixte de Sienne et de sa (pretendue) culture juive," in *idem*, *Les juifs et l'église romaine a l'époque moderne* (Paris: Honoré Champion, 2007), 205–32. Montgomery, "Sixtus of Siena and Roman Catholic Biblical Scholarship," 216–20.
96. Ulderico Parente "Sul preteso giudaismo di fra Sisto," 392–96.

other Spanish Protestant exiles whose writings he also favored, such as Cipriano de Valera and Casiodoro de Reina. Furthermore, the writings of heterodox Christian and Protestant writers provided Morteira with a common idiom for his discussions and polemic with Christians in the Netherlands. It therefore made a good deal of sense for Morteira to comb Sixtus of Siena's *Bibliotheca Sancta* for historical information to subvert Christian convictions regarding the origins and authorship of the New Testament.

In his search for information that would help place Christian Scriptures in a historical context that proved they were composed and edited by human beings, Morteira relies mostly on the seventh book of Sixtus's *Bibliotheca Sancta*, "Objections of the Heretics against the Catholics." Just as Morteira used the *Monarchia Ecclesiastica* to cast doubts on the origins of the Book of John, now he used the *Bibliotheca Sancta* to subvert Christian certainty regarding the origins and authenticity of the Gospel of Matthew: "The Gospel in the name of Matthew is not his, the Manicheans and Anabaptists demonstrate, and especially Faustus the Manichean, to whom it appears uncertain whether Matthew wrote any Gospel, because there are various opinions in Ecclesiastic writings about the time in which he wrote."[97] On the one hand, Eusebius argues in his *Chronicon* that Matthew is the very first Apostle to write his text, and that it was written in Judea when Peter ruled the church from Antioch. On the other hand, Irenaeus contends in *Adversus haereses* (III.1) that the Gospel dates to a significantly later period, when Peter and Paul evangelized together in Rome.[98]

97. Morteira, *Tratado*, 206. See Sixtus of Siena, *Bibliotheca Sancta*, 566. "Obiectiones Haereticorum." "1. Iam primum omnium quòd Euangelium Matthaei nomine inscriptum, ipsius Matthaei Euangelistae non sit, tam Manichaei quàm Anabaptistae nonnullis, sed plane contemnendis argumentis ostendere nituntur. atque in primis Faustus Manichaeus sic ait."

98. Morteira, *Tratado*, 206. Sixtus of Siena, *Bibliotheca Sancta*, 567. "Obiectiones Haereticorum." "3. Redditur etiam incertum, an Mathaeus Euangelium aliquod scripserit. quia de tempore, quo Matthaeus illud scripserit varia inter scriptores Ecclesiasticos sentential est. Eusebius Caesariensis in Chronicis refert, Mathaeum primum omnium scripsisse Euangeliu[m] in Iudaea, dum Petrus Antiochenam regeret Ecclesiam, anno tertioImperij Caligulae. Irenaeus verò libro tertio aduersus Haereses capite primo, tradit Matthaeum scripsisse Euangeliu[m] cum Petrus & Paulus Romae Euangelizarent."

Morteira also learned from Sixtus that the Church Fathers were skeptical about the authenticity and origins of numerous other parts of the Gospels. Luke 22:39–44, for instance, describes how Jesus began to sweat blood during an encounter with an angel while praying on the Mount of Olives. In his *Dialogi contra Pelagianos*, Jerome writes that the narrative of the angel appearing before Luke is found only in some of the early Greek and Latin manuscripts – certainly not in all, or even most. Likewise, Hilary demonstrates that the narrative about Jesus sweating blood is questionable: "we certainly should not ignore that in many Greek and Latin manuscripts there is no mention of the Angel who came nor of the sweating of blood."[99] Through the *Bibliotheca Sancta* Morteira also encountered certain passages in John that were questioned both by Church Fathers in late antiquity and by more recent commentators. John 8:1–11, for example, narrates how Jesus encountered an adulterous woman in the Pharisaic courts. Jesus challenges any individual who is without sin to condemn the woman and cast the first stone, in accordance with Jewish law, but no one volunteers to indict her. Sixtus and Morteira observe that Eusebius, in the third book of his *Historia Eclesiastica*, writes that the second-century Christian figure Papias of Hierapolis "encountered a certain story about an adulterous woman who was accused by the Jews that was in a Gospel called 'according to the Hebrews.'[100] These words show that not only in the time of Papias,

99. Morteira, *Tratado*, 210. Sixtus of Siena, *Bibliotheca Sancta*, 579. "De lucae Euangelio Haeresis IIII." "Tertium indiciu[nt] ex quibusdam verbis Hieronymi deducitu, quod is in libro secundo aduersus Pelagianos significare videtur, Historiam Angeli apparetis in horto ad Christi consolationem, quae Lucae 22. Cap. habetur, in vetutis Ecclesiae exemplaribus non fuisse, ait enim Hieronymus eo in libro: In quibusdam codicibus tam Graecis quàm Latinis inuenitur scribente Luca: Apparavit ei Angelus de coelo, confortans eum. haud dubium, quin Dominum Saluatorem. Quae verba si in omnibus ecclesiae exemplaribus fuissent, non oportuerat Hieronymum dicere, *in quibusdam codicibus ea verba legi, sed in omnibus*. Hilarius autem libro x de Trid. non solum Angeli consolationem, sed & historiam Christi sanguine sudantis in Euangelio non haberi, multo apertius affirmat his verbis: *Nec sane ignorandum nobis est, & in Graecis & in Latinis codicibus coplurimis, vel de Aduenient Angelo, vel de sudore sanguine nihil scriptum reperiri. Ambigentibus igitur utrum hoc in libris varijs aut desit, aut superfluum sit, incertum hoc nobis relinquitur de diuersitate librorum.*

100. Ron Cameron, *The Other Gospels*, 83. Another non-canonical New Testament text, the Gospel of the Hebrews, is one of the Jewish-Christian texts most frequently cited

but also much later, this narrative was not in the Book of John, but certainly [was in] the apocryphal Gospel 'according to the Hebrews.'"[101] As Epiphanius suggests, it is indeed quite possible – and even likely – that this story was at some point transferred to the Book of John from the Gospel "according to the Hebrews."[102] In addition to these ancient interpreters of Scripture, Morteira and Sixtus were also aware that the Anabaptists "complain about many matters added to the Gospel of John, and among others the narrative of the adulterous woman."[103]

Reading further in the *Bibliotheca Sancta,* Morteira learned that ancient scholars and Anabaptists also disputed the authenticity of the story regarding the crippled individuals lying by the healing pool in John 5:19. This passage describes a pool in Jerusalem located near the Temple and surrounded by five colonnades, where numerous ill people lay, and where Jesus heals a person who had been paralyzed for thirty-eight years. Anabaptists hesitated to accept this narrative as authoritative

by leading figures in the early church. It is known from fragmentary citations in the writings of Papias of Hieropolis, Hegesippus, Clement of Alexandria, Cyril, Origen, and Jerome, among many others. See also James R. Edwards, *The Hebrew Gospel and the Development of the Synoptic Tradition* (Grand Rapids, MI and Cambridge, UK: Eerdmans, 2009), xviii–xxxiv, 1–10. Edwards shows that, in fact, the narrative in Eusebius refers to a woman guilty of a number of sins, whereas John 7–8 refers specifically to an adulterous woman. Nevertheless, the point of interest for Morteira and Sixtus of Siena – whether the story about the sinful or adulterous woman was interpolated into the Gospel of John at a later point in time – remains a topic of serious scholarship. Sixtus and Morteira are correct, however, in pointing to the paucity of references to John 8's adulterous woman in eastern Christian texts. Prior to the twelfth century, no Greek Church Father comments upon this passage.

101. Morteira, *Tratado,* 211.
102. Morteira, *Tratado,* 211.
103. Morteira, *Tratado,* 211. Sixtus of Siena, *Bibliotheca Sancta,* 583. "4. Post quem Anabaptistae multa in eode[m] Euangelio superaddita conqueruntur: ac inter alia Mulieris adulterae in adulterio deprehensae historiam, octauo Ioannis capite scriptam. qua[m] olim in hoc Euangelio minimè fuisse multi vestuti Patres testantur. in primis verò Eusebius libro tertio hist. Ecclesiae cap. 39. loquens de Papia, haec habet. *Papias historiam quondam subiungit de muliere adultera, quae accusata est à Iudaeis apud Dominum. habetur autem in Euangelio, quod dicitur secumdum Hebraeos scripta ista parabola.* Quae verba ostendunt, non solùm Papiae temporibus, sed multò post, historiam hanc non fuisse in Euangelio Ioannis, sed in Euangelio quodam apocrypha secundum Hebraeos."

because there is no mention of any such pool or resting spot in the Old Testament. "Nor [is it described] by Josephus," Morteira elaborates, "the diligent historian and writer of Jewish antiquities," who was especially assiduous in commenting on matters related to Solomon, Zerubabel, and Herod. Furthermore, Morteira finds it implausible that Josephus would have neglected to mention such a significant demonstration of divine compassion. According to Sixtus, some writers have suggested that the pool was located within the "*atrio*" of the Temple itself. Morteira, however, writes that in all the descriptions of Temple architecture in the Book of Kings, and in the "sacred annals," there is not any mention of the pool, nor in the books of Esdras, which describes the Temple's exterior and interior in particular.[104]

Morteira concludes his systematic textual analysis of the New Testament books with a critical examination of Christian disputes regarding the Book of the Apocalypse. Although attributed to the Apostle John, Morteira discovered competing theories of authorship that gave him deep reservations about the authenticity of the text. The notion that John the Apostle was not actually the author of this book of Holy Writ was based on the fact that in all of the Greek manuscripts it is attributed to the revelation of "John the Theologian." However, Papias of Hieropolis, in his book entitled *Explanations of the Sayings of the Lord*, distinguishes between two different Johns: one who was an Apostle and another who authored the Book of the Apocalypse, and was called John Presbyter.

104. Morteira, *Tratado*, 211–12. Sixtus of Siena, *Bibliotheca Sancta*, 583. "5. Atque eiusdem audacis commentum Anabaptistae fuisse dicunt historiam illam de languid ad probaticam piscinam iacente, quam locus in quo Ioannes eam factam fuisse scribit, omnino reddit falsitatis supectam: tum quia in veteri Testamento nihil quicquam de hac piscine, cum quinque porticibus memoratur, tum quia Iosephus Hebraicarum antiquitatum, ac praesertim trium Templi constructionum, sub Salomone videlicet, Zorobabel, & Herode diligentissimus scriptor, nihil vel de piscine, vel de aqua frequenter, ac diuinitus ab Angelo turbata scribit. nec verisimile est Iosephum plus nimio Hebraeis suis fauentem, praetermissurum fuisse tam insignem diuinae bonitatis erga suam patriam fauorem, qui in caeteris leuioris moment, & quae minus ad Urbis suae decorum, & gloriam facere viderentur, usque ad superfluitatem scripserit, sit antae rei miraculum suoque potissimum tempore, & in suo natali solo fuisset... Quidam eam piscinam in atrio temple fuisse scribunt, cum tame[n] id, neque in libris regum, neque in libris sacroru[m] Annalium aut Esdrae, in quibus describitur tam prioris quam posterioris Templi structura, legatur."

Eusebius suspected that Papias was correct in this assumption, since "some men in Asia write that there are in Ephesus two graves, and each one is called the tomb of John."[105] In addition, Eusebius perceived distinctly different styles of writing in the Gospel of John and the Book of the Apocalypse. He writes that "The Apocalypse is not only not by John the Apostle, but we can prove it with clear reasons by the style of the Scripture, and by the differences of the phrases and ways of speaking in one book and the other, that is in the Gospel of John and in the Apocalypse, and also by the fact that John in writing the Gospel did not make mention or give a sign of his own name." By way of contrast, the John who wrote the Book of the Apocalypse "mentions his name almost every third word, repeating many times, I am John, I am John, as if he had not written a Gospel for us."[106] Even among those ecclesiastic writers who identify a single author of the Gospel of John and of the Apocalypse, there are divergent accounts regarding the time and place in which the final book of the New Testament was composed. Irenaeus writes at the end of his *Memoria* that the Apocalypse was composed late in the reign of the emperor Domitian. Likewise, Eusebius in his *Chronicon* and Jerome in his *De viris illustribus* hold that the Apocalypse was written on the Isle of Patmos by John in the fourteenth year of Domitian's fifteen-year reign. However, Epiphanius, Bishop of Salamis, and other early Church Fathers insist that the Apocalypse dates to the reign of Claudio Nero, almost forty years before.[107]

In this manner, Morteira sought to show that ostensibly canonical

105. Morteira, *Tratado*, 216–17.

106. Morteira, *Tratado*, 217.

107. Morteira, *Tratado*, 217. Sixtus of Siena, *Bibliotheca Sancta*, 601. "Principio etiam atque etiam constat, Apocalypsim non esse Ioannis Apostoli ex operis inscription, quae in omnibus Graecis codicibus habetur... id est, *Reuelatio Beati Ioannis Theologi*, hunc autem Theologum longè alium fuisse à Ioanne Euangelista, Papias Ioannis auditor testatus est, scribens in libris quos VERBORUM COMINICORUM attitulauit, duos fuisse Ioannes, alterum Apostolorum, alterum verò extra Apostolorum numerum, quem distinction quadam facta, Ioannem Presbyterum appellauit... Ex ipso Scripturae stylo, tum quia utriusque Voluminis, Euangelij scilicet Ioannis, & Apocalypseos phrasis ac dicendi modus sit diuersus, tum quia Ioannes, qui Euangelium scripsit, nusquam in Euangelio suo, nominis fui mentionem fecerit, ac... signauerit nominatim: hic autem, qui Apocalypsim scripsit, tertio ferme verbo nominis fui mentionem facit, illud saepè repetens: ego Ioannes: ego Ioannes."

books of Christian Scriptures were of doubtful origins, uncertain authorship, and unclear date. Through Sixtus of Siena, Morteira accessed a significant reservoir of information about ancient and contemporary Christian heterodox beliefs that were crucial to his efforts to historicize central Christian symbols, traditions, and texts, thus laicizing Christian sacred history, dislodging it from the realm of the divine into the sphere of the mundane.

Religious Polemic and the Study of History – Between Morteira and Spinoza

Religious polemic offered Saul Levi Morteira a setting wherein he could experiment with new methods of historical analysis and a new library of Christian texts, and thus offer new varieties of biblical exegesis to a Jewish reading public. Religious polemic in general, and the *Tratado* in particular, functions as an especially sensitive barometer for measuring the Jewish absorption of historical methodologies, libraries of texts, and ways of thinking about the past. In his study of the New Testament Morteira could fully develop his argument that the central religious texts, traditions, and teachings of Christianity had to be understood through a systematic historical analysis. Morteira applied himself to this challenge in a way that was unprecedented within European Jewish society. He insisted that Christian Holy Writ, composed in a rabbinic Jewish society and shaped by the religious traditions of the Greco-Roman world, must be studied in light of the formative texts and traditions of these cultures: the Talmud and Mishnah, Josephus, Jerome, Eusebius, Irenaeus, and numerous other Patristic sources. Morteira combed popular and little-known texts alike from the libraries of sixteenth- and seventeenth-century Italian and Spanish literature for information about the origin and authorship of the New Testament. He made great use of the writings of Sixtus of Siena, Vincenzo Cartari, and Cipriano de Valera, where he found numerous, conflicting reports on the locations, dates, and authors connected with the writing of the Gospels. These texts helped Morteira become sensitive to the individual writing styles of specific authors of different New Testament texts, as well as attuned to the temporal distance of certain authors from Jesus and the texts of the New Testament. Not all accounts of Jesus's life in the Gospels were the product of direct historical witness by their authors. The framework of a polemic against Christianity afforded Morteira an opportunity to think historically about one culture's Sacred Scripture in a way that he would certainly have avoided in the contemplation of Judaism and its sacred texts.

The potential for traditional genres of religious literature to serve as incubators for new and even radical ideas has been recognized by scholars of early modern European history. The deeply religious scholars of Alan Kors' history of atheists and atheism in seventeenth- and eighteenth-century France offer a case in point. Theologians, missionaries, philosophers, and travelers made vast numbers of potentially subversive ideas and texts available to a broad, educated reading public through their profoundly conservative debates: they made the existence of atheist communities – both ancient and modern – common knowledge across Europe; they disseminated the doctrines of ancient atheist philosophers; and in their theological polemics, committed Christians exposed the "atheistic" tendencies of each other's arguments.

Kors demonstrates how the work of European missionaries around the globe helped to undermine the confidence of many Christians in proofs of the existence of God based on universal consent: the argument that every society known throughout history had articulated a belief – however incomplete, inaccurate, or erroneous – in a deity or being superior to themselves.[108] Jean de Léry, a French Calvinist and future Genevan pastor, lived with the Carib Aboriginals in Brazil for one year, and reported that "if there is a nation which is without God, and which lives without God in the world, it is truly they." Antoine Biet, a priest from Sainte Geneviève de Senlis, traveled to French Guyana where he was father *superieur* of the local missionaries, and wrote about the local native population and their disbelief in God. In the 1660s, the Dominican missionary Jean-Baptiste du Tertre wrote from the Antilles that he had met enslaved blacks who were genuinely atheist. Meanwhile, in New France, the Jesuit Paul Le Jeune encountered indigenous peoples in Cape Bréton who – he reported – lacked any knowledge of God, or even linguistic terms for holy or divine beings that were superior to

108. Alan Kors, *Atheism in France*, 135–50.

humans. Not only did missionary travel reports make known the existence of large numbers of apparently atheistic communities, they also made it clear that these individuals led virtuous, ethical lives. Alexandre de Rhodes, a Jesuit missionary in Tonkin, wrote in 1651 that Confucian beliefs were highly conducive to "forming good morals," even though they were devoid of any notion of God.

The study of ancient Greece and Rome by philosophers and theologians also helped bring potentially atheistic ideas of antiquity to the surface of contemporary European culture. Fierce debates about whether different schools of ancient thought were atheistic or not made an extensive literature of potentially subversive philosophy easily accessible to European readers. Savants like Anton Reiser and Theophil Spizelius, for instance, wrote sharply differing histories of atheistic movements in antiquity that gave detailed descriptions of philosophical and religious arguments that were inimical to, or prohibited by, current belief. They then traced the reception of these ideas by modern "atheists," including Machiavelli, the *Politiques* of the French religious wars, naturalists like Aretin, Politien, and Cremonius, and many others. Ralph Cudworth's *True Intellectual System of the Universe* and Johann Franz von Buddeus's *Theses theologicae de atheismo* were also widely consulted histories of atheistic philosophy.[109] In their polemical assault on ideas that seemingly lead by implication to atheism, or were judged to be atheistic outright, Cudworth and Buddeus made a vast swath of atheistic belief accessible to educated readers across Europe.[110] Historical studies of atheistic thought reinforced what European missionaries and travelers had been reporting throughout the sixteenth and seventeenth centuries: that there was little reason to be confident in "universal consent" as a reliable proof for the existence of God. Communities of virtuous people had existed in ancient and modern times within a framework of disbelief and atheism, and – Kors argues – would emerge in eighteenth-century Europe upon the foundation of these "orthodox" sixteenth- and seventeenth-century Christian theological and philosophical texts.

109. Ralph Cudworth, *The True Intellectual System of the Universe* (London, 1678). Johann Franz von Buddeus, *Theses theologicae de atheism* (Jena, 1717).
110. Alan Kors, *Atheism in France*, 231–43.

The third vector for the dissemination of atheist doctrines in "traditional" literature was the intense polemic between Aristotelian and Cartesian theologians. Convinced that they alone had produced irrefutable proofs of God's existence, each side believed the other to have espoused doctrines so flimsy and unconvincing that they bordered on atheism – or at least that they would lead to atheism, were it not for the existence of better proofs. On the one hand, profoundly religious Cartesian theologians assailed Aristotelian demonstrations of God's existence and perfection, which were based on the fallible and unquestionably limited information perceived by the senses. As the Cartesian Nicolas Poisson explained, the "fatal flaw" of scholastic theology was its assumption that intellectual knowledge was acquired exclusively by means of the senses. In the realm of religious and spiritual knowledge, this led to the grievous error of subordinating knowledge of God to the flawed and fallible corporeal world. If the scholastics were in fact correct, and the Cartesians wrong, he believed that no authentic – or even "incoherent" – idea of God could possibly be achieved.[111] On the other hand, Jean Vincent, an Aristotelian priest and member of the Congregation of Christian Doctrine, insisted that by pinning their efforts to prove God's existence on the ability of the mind to perceive or conceive of something perfect and infinite, Cartesian theologians were condemning themselves to an impossible endeavor. Vincent was troubled by the idea that one should proceed from "methodological doubt" before demonstrating the existence of God through elaborate proofs, and was especially perturbed by the idea that Christians would be left hanging in this state of suspended disbelief due to the limitations of the human mind. The mind, he insisted, could not possibly conceptualize something infinite.[112]

In the same way that seventeenth- and eighteenth-century theologians, missionaries, travelers, and clerics made a vast literature of subversive doctrines accessible to the reading public of early modern France, Saul Levi Morteira's *Tratado da verdade da lei de Moisés* made new methods of historical analysis, an expansive library of Christian

111. Alan Kors, *Atheism in France*, 349–50.
112. Alan Kors, *Atheism in France*, 312.

texts, and new varieties of biblical exegesis available to a Jewish reading public. Morteira's *Tratado* is from many perspectives a deeply traditional, "orthodox" treatise that serves as a platform for the reiteration of numerous medieval philosophical and theological beliefs: the ongoing providence of God over Israel; Israel's election and ongoing status as God's chosen People; the unique qualities and divinity of the Law of Moses and Israel's Revelation at Sinai; the link between the People of Israel and the Holy Land; the superiority of Moses's prophecy over all other prophets'; the belief that Jesus did not intend to change or abrogate the Law; and many others. And yet, from the perspective taken in this chapter we have seen that the profoundly conservative *Tratado* served as an incubator for historicist ways of reading Christianity's Holy Scriptures that – within Jewish society – were extremely innovative, and that were shaped by Morteira's encounter with Protestant scholarship, humanist historiography, and European theological texts. The *Tratado* served as a clearing house for numerous cutting-edge European approaches to studying the past, applied them in a serious way to dissecting the New Testament, and made these methods available to the members of Morteira's community in a vernacular language.

In any discussion about historicist approaches to reading the Bible, as well as about Amsterdam, and the ex-conversos, Spinoza looms as a towering figure who must at some point be addressed. Morteira's relationship with Spinoza has always been clouded by a certain degree of obscurity, and many scholars have sought to discover points of contact between the two figures – beyond, of course, Morteira's role in Spinoza's excommunication.[113] Regarding Morteira's 1652 reference to "experts in books of metaphysics" who regularly sat at his table and studied with him, Marc Saperstein speculates that "[o]ne imagines that in the category of 'experts in books of metaphysics,' he would have included the twenty-year old Baruch Espinosa."[114] Much attention has also focused on the possibility that Spinoza attended Morteira's society for Bible study, the *Keter Torah* [Crown of Torah], which was founded in 1643. Forty years later, the Portuguese Jewish poet Daniel Levi de Barrios described

113. H. Méchoulan, "Morteira et Spinoza au carrefour du Socinianisme," 51.
114. Marc Saperstein, *Exile in Amsterdam*, 8.

the circumstances of the society's establishment and the importance of its activities:

> The Crown of the Law, from the year 1643 in which it was founded, has never ceased to burn in the academic bush, with the learned doctrines that the most wise Saul Levi Morteira wrote, who dedicated his intellect to the rulings of wisdom, and the quill of his hand to speculation against Atheism and in defence of religion. Thorns [*Espinos*] are they that in the fields [*Prados*] of impiety, desire to shine with the fire that consumes them.[115]

Several historians have cited this passage for its cryptic reference to the participation of Spinoza and Juan de Prado in the meetings of the *Keter Torah.*[116] Recently, scholars attempting to identify additional links between Morteira and Spinoza have also pointed to established links between their families. Michel de Espinosa, for instance, was a leading figure within Morteira's Beth Jacob congregation before the amalgamation of Portuguese synagogues in 1639.[117] Whether or not Spinoza and Prado did in fact study with Morteira at the *Keter Torah*, Morteira may have had these types of heterodox Portuguese Jews in mind when he wrote, at the end of his introduction to the *Tratado*, that: "In no way is denying the Law of Moses the same as denying the Gospels, because if the foundation falls, the entire structure falls; and denying the Law of Moses is nothing other than confessing oneself to be a *libertino* without Law or divine precepts, since these come from no other source."[118]

We may never prove with absolute certainty that Morteira and Spinoza knew each other closely, although there probably was a relationship between them of some kind. However, the fact remains that

115. Daniel Levi de Barrios, *Triumpho del govierno popular*, 61–62. "La CORONA DE LA LEY, desde el ano de 5403 [1643] en que se fundo, nunca ha dexado de arder en la carca Academica, con las doctrinales hojas que escrivio el Sapientissimo Saul Levi Mortera, entregando su intelecto al dictamen la Sabiduria, y su pluma a la mano de la Especulacion, contra el Atheismo, en defensa de la Religion. *Espinos* son los que en *Prados* de impiedad, dessean luzir con el fuego que los consume."
116. I.S. Revah, *Spinoza et le Dr. Juan de Prado* (Paris: Mouton & Co., 1959), 27; Steven Nadler, *Spinoza: A Life*, 90; Marc Saperstein *Exile in Amsterdam*, 8–9.
117. Steven Nadler, *Spinoza: A Life*, 90; Saperstein, *Exile in Amsterdam*, 8–9.
118. Morteira, *Tratado*, 7.

Benedict Spinoza was born in Amsterdam's Portuguese Jewish community, was educated in its schools, and interacted with its members. He was part of the social, religious, and cultural fabric of the time and place in which he lived. He knew the beliefs, values, and biases of Amsterdam's community and its leaders. In short, before Baruch Espinosa became Benedict Spinoza he was an unremarkable member of the ex-converso community in Amsterdam, born into a well-respected and reasonably well-off family. These simple facts point to a significant question that is frequently overlooked in the study of Spinoza's ideas about the Bible: to what degree did Spinoza's formative experiences within this specific environment contribute to his intellectual development? Logically, it would be a reasonable initial hypothesis to venture that Spinoza's life in Amsterdam's ex-converso community stimulated ideas, provided models, and exposed problems that he would write about later in life. In fact, it would be far more historically problematic if this were *not* the case, and Spinoza was utterly uninfluenced by the milieu in which he lived. Such a seemingly counter-intuitive conclusion would require a robust historical explanation. Nevertheless, the fact that Spinoza lived within a Portuguese Jewish community in which the Bible served as the central text for education, religious culture, and rabbinic scholarship has never been investigated as a part of the essential background for understanding the development of his approach to thinking about and studying the Bible. Portuguese Jewish scholars and rabbis in Spinoza's Amsterdam introduced novel genres of biblical exegesis into the Jewish repertoire, engaged and confronted conservative and radical Christian approaches to reading Scripture, and – as we have just seen – thought about the historical background of Scripture in new way. The unique Jewish culture of biblical studies in Amsterdam should be seen as having had its own part in shaping Spinoza's attitudes toward the Bible.

The famous seventh chapter of Spinoza's *Theological-Political Treatise*, "On the Interpretation of Scripture," outlines the principles of historical inquiry that Spinoza saw as critical to achieve an accurate understanding of the meaning and significance of different parts of the text: "I hold that the method of interpreting Scripture does not differ from the [correct] method of interpreting nature, but rather is wholly consonant with it. The [correct] method of interpreting nature consists above all in constructing a natural history, from which we derive the definitions of natural things... Likewise, to interpret Scripture, we need to assemble a genuine history of it and to deduce the thinking of the Bible's authors by valid inferences from this history, as from certain data and principles."[119] Several elements were critical to constructing a historical portrait of the context in which Scripture was composed. The language of the ancient world was significant for both Morteira and Spinoza, who writes that: "This history of the Bible must include: the nature and properties of the language in which the biblical books were composed and which were spoken by their authors."[120] In addition, Spinoza saw it as essential to construct a biographical picture of the authors of separate parts of the biblical text in order to understand their unique approaches to writing, and he insisted upon the need to produce a genealogy of biblical texts that would show how they had meandered their way through history to the present: "The historical inquiry must explain the circumstances of all the books of the prophets whose memory has come down to us: the life, character, and particular interests of the author of each book. Then the fate of each book: namely how it was first received and whose hands it came into, how many variant readings there have been of its text, by whose decision it was received among the sacred books, and finally how all the books which are now accepted as sacred came to form a single corpus."[121] In addition, just as Morteira sought to study the New Testament against contemporaneous texts such as the Mishnah, Talmud, and Josephus, so too Spinoza desired to produce a catalogue of the ancient texts mentioned in the Bible in order to produce a more multi-dimensional picture of the society in which the Bible was composed. This presented a serious problem which, as Spinoza himself confesses, was impossible to overcome.[122]

In Chapter Eight of the *Theological-Political Treatise* Spinoza also discusses the question of ambiguous origins and authorship of the biblical texts in a way that recalls Morteira's discussion of the uncertain

119. Jonathan Israel, ed. *Theological-Political Treatise*, 98.
120. Jonathan Israel, ed. *Theological-Political Treatise*, 100.
121. Jonathan Israel, ed. *Theological-Political Treatise*, 101.
122. Jonathan Israel, ed. *Theological-Political Treatise*, 109.

provenance of New Testament texts. In this chapter, Spinoza's intent was to show that: "the Pentateuch and the books of Joshua, Judges, Ruth, Samuel and Kings were not written by the persons after whom they are named. The question is then asked whether they were written by several authors or by one, and who they were." Spinoza regarded the authorial ambiguity of the Bible's texts as being one of the chief obstacles to writing a "history of the Bible," but believed what little evidence there was to be sufficient to "remove our prevailing theological prejudices."[123] In a manner similar to Morteira's use of Sixtus of Siena, Spinoza combed the Bible and medieval Jewish sources for evidence of uncertain authorship and origins. Ibn Ezra also raised the possibility of later authors either editing or interpolating text into the Pentateuch in his comments on Genesis 12:6: "Abram passed through the land as far as the site of Shechem, at the terebinth of Moreh. The Canaanites were then in the land." Spinoza read this as a sign that a reader had edited the text after the Canaanites had been expelled from the land. Throughout the Pentateuch, the writer, author, or compiler refers to Moses in the third person, except – Spinoza interjects – in the case of the Decalogue, which is narrated in the first person. Furthermore, the last verses of Deuteronomy describe additional topics about which Moses could not have known: his burial place, the completion of the thirty-day mourning period the Israelites observed, and the early leadership of Joshua.[124]

Spinoza's writings speak to contact with a wide variety of texts, traditions, and individuals across numerous groups within Dutch and broader European society during the middle decades of the seventeenth century. Nevertheless, Spinoza did not need to leave the Portuguese Jewish community to be exposed to historical ways of thinking about Scripture. Menasseh ben Israel's struggle with the chronological inconsistencies of the Bible, and the incompatibility of biblical information regarding the reigns of biblical Israel's kings and prophets, represents one source of this mode of thought. Saul Levi Morteira's *Tratado da verdade da lei de Moisés* represents another. Although the *Tratado* was written after Spinoza's expulsion, the manuscript reflects a long-term engagement

123. Jonathan Israel, ed. *Theological-Political Treatise*, 118.
124. Jonathan Israel, ed. *Theological-Political Treatise*, 119–21.

with texts, people, and ideas that we know extended well back into Morteira's earlier decades. Morteira's encounter with the Socinian in the 1630s, and their discussion of the origins of the Book of John, is the most poignant example of this process. It is possible, and even probable, that the historicist ideas of the *Tratado* circulated orally earlier than they were put to pen. Morteira's *Tratado* illustrates the potential of using a deeply conservative theological text to make strikingly novel – and potentially subversive – historicist methods of studying Sacred Scriptures accessible to educated readers in the Portuguese Jewish community in which Spinoza lived. Morteira's *Tratado* employed these methods toward, from a Jewish perspective, "conservative" ends – a systematic, erudite deconstruction of central Christian texts and doctrines. Nevertheless, in a broader sense the *Tratado* provided its readers with a veritable manual of how to embed one community's Sacred Scriptures within the cultures and societies of the ancient world where they were composed.

EPILOGUE

Jewish Biblical Studies in Amsterdam: Spinoza's Origins and the Horizon of Modernity

> "Despite being steeped in the common beliefs about the Bible from childhood on, I have not been able to resist my conclusion."[1]
>
> – Benedict Spinoza

Scarcely one week after Spinoza's death in The Hague on February 21, 1677, the notary Willem van den Hove inventoried the late philosopher's possessions, which were to be sold at public auction. Spinoza was clearly not a man of great means at his death, and taking stock of his relatively meagre possessions was not a tremendously effortful exercise. Apart from a small handful of silver accoutrements, much of the inventory consists of unremarkable and very basic household items: pillows and sheets, coats, undergarments, a few small tables, a modest chest for books, and instruments in various states of repair. His library was another story. Approximately 160 books are listed in the inventory, recorded across ten manuscript pages not by the notary, but by the prominent Amsterdam bookseller Jan Riewertsz, Spinoza's publisher and friend, whose education and experience in the book trade was essential for cataloguing and accurately recording Spinoza's personal library.[2] The titles of the

1. Jonathan Israel, ed. *Theological-Political Treatise*, 136.
2. A.K. Offenberg, "Spinoza's Library: The Story of a Reconstruction," *Quaerendo*, vol. 3, Issue 4 (1973): 309–21; Jacob van Sluis and Tonnis Musschenga, *De Boeken van Spinoza*

collection are a testament to the breadth of Spinoza's erudition and interests, which crossed religious, geographic, and linguistic boundaries. From Spanish and Portuguese *belles lettres,* to classical literature in Greek and Latin, to the Hebrew Bible and New Testament in a variety of formats, as well as a wide array of philosophical, scientific, political, and medical treatises, Spinoza's collection of texts provided a gateway into many intellectual worlds. Studying the books that Spinoza kept on his shelves can be revealing and rewarding, and can illuminate at least some of the origins of the ideas and insights he developed. It can also help map him, culturally, onto the terrain of Dutch and Jewish societies and their reading habits during this period.

Many of the materials on Spinoza's shelves confirm what historians have suspected and compellingly argued: the crucial importance of Spinoza's engagement with leading – and provocative – seventeenth-century religious and political ideas. Perhaps no text in Spinoza's collection was more provocative than Isaac La Peyrère's *Praeadamita.*[3] Richard Popkin has drawn attention to the fact that Peyrère's treatise forcefully presents the argument against complete Mosaic authorship of the Pentateuch, and enthusiastically embraces and promotes the arguments made by Joseph Scaliger that the ancient histories and traditions of Egypt, Greece, Babylonia, and China all vastly exceed in antiquity the chronology that the Bible attributes to world and human history. On these grounds, Peyrère argues that the Bible may therefore be a record only of *Jewish* history, telling the story only of an isolated part of humanity in a particular region of the world, and that this account was written not exclusively by Moses, but by additional and unknown hands. While Popkin ultimately concludes that Spinoza was only "a very partial disciple" of Peyrère, he nevertheless points out that Peyrère's writings circulated in Amsterdam during the very years just prior to Spinoza's excommunication from the Portuguese Jewish community, suggesting that the work was read – and rejected – by at least one of Amsterdam's leading rabbis, Menasseh ben

(The Hague: Bibliotheek der Rijksuniversiteit Groningen, 2009). All references to the literature in Spinoza's library in the following discussion come from the "Boeken van Spinoza" unless otherwise noted.

3. Jacob van Sluis and Tonnis Musschenga, "Boeken van Spinoza," 40.

Israel, and raising the possibility that Peyrère's biblical criticism could have served as a jumping-off point for Spinoza and as an essential part of the intellectual historical context from which Amsterdam's most famous Jewish heretic emerged.[4]

Other scholars have emphasized different elements of Spinoza's library as being formative in the development of his radical critique of the Bible and the religio-political order. Unlike Popkin, Jonathan Israel rejects the possibility that Spinoza was influenced by Peyrère "or by any internal heretical tendencies within Amsterdam Sephardic Judaism of the mid-1650s."[5] Instead, Israel accentuates the critical role of René Descartes and Dutch Cartesianism, which were also heavily represented in the books that Spinoza kept close at hand. The inventory of Spinoza's books includes Descarte's *La Géométrie* (1637), *Meditationes de prima philosophia* (1641; 1654), and the *Principia Philosophica* (1650), among several other works.[6] Debates about Cartesian philosophy raged in Dutch academic and political circles during the middle decades of the seventeenth century, and Israel argues that it was the radical Dutch thinker Franciscus van den Enden (1602–1674) who turned Spinoza's attention toward the more extreme domains of these controversies.[7] Van den Enden was the figure that many of Spinoza's earliest biographers, including Colerus and Maximilien Lucas, remembered as being the formative force in the development of this extreme Cartesianism, and as Spinoza's teacher in mathematics, Greek, and Cartesian philosophy.[8] Tammy Nyden, who also accentuates van den Enden's significance, positions Spinoza and his fully developed ideas as being an integral

4. Richard Popkin, *Isaac La Peyrère*, 42–60; 80–94.
5. Jonathan Israel, *Radical Enlightenment*, 168–69. Regarding the argument that Spinoza was powerfully shaped by heretical or heterodox tendencies within the Amsterdam Portuguese Jewish community, see Yirmiyahu Yovel, *Spinoza and Other Heretics: The Marrano of Reason* (Princeton, NJ: Princeton University Press, 1989). Yovel offers a "typology" of intellectual and psychological characteristics that typified the ex-conversos as a society, especially in the seventeenth-century Western Sephardi diaspora. Among others, the tendency toward heterodoxy and "transcendence of revealed religion" is emphasized.
6. Jacob van Sluis and Tonnis Musschenga, "Boeken van Spinoza," 30–40.
7. Jonathan Israel, *Radical Englightenment*, 160–61.
8. Jonathan Israel, *Radical Enlightenment*, 168.

component of a specifically Dutch "Radical Cartesianism." This movement, as she defines it, weaves together elements of leading philosophers and political thinkers such as Thomas Hobbes, Niccolo Machiavelli, Pieter De la Court, and Descartes. Nyden argues – ambitiously – that many of Spinoza's most important ideas can be traced to this movement. He certainly *owned* key books by many of these authors: Thomas Hobbes' *De Cive*, the collected works of Machiavelli printed in five volumes, the *Politicke discoursen* of Johan and Pieter De la Court, and – as we have seen – the many writings of Descartes himself, are all to be found in the inventory.[9] Nyden demonstrates that Spinoza's assessments of the merits of popular governing bodies versus aristocratic and monarchical modes of government can be traced to this movement, as well as can his efforts to "secularize" and naturalize morality, taking philosophical and moral judgements out of the hands and authority of theologians.[10]

Developments in early modern science have also been cited as key factors in shaping Spinoza's perspectives and helping to coalesce his radical approaches to reading and thinking about the Bible. Jonathan Israel has stressed the degree which the new philosophy of the seventeenth century fundamentally shaped the way in which Spinoza thought about nature, as well as Scripture. Spinoza's convictions that the Bible needed to be approached with the same tools, methods, and mindset brought to the study of nature meant that traditional religious beliefs about miracles and providence needed to be severely adumbrated if not discarded altogether.[11] Nature's laws permit no alteration or temporary hiatus, and are eternally inviolable – as was emphasized in Chapter 3, where Spinoza's objections to the miracle in Joshua 10 were made abundantly clear. We need not look far down Spinoza's bookshelf to discover clues about where he may have encountered these types of ideas. The works of the Calvinist minister Philip Lansbergen (1561–1632) are especially well represented in Spinoza's collection: Lansbergen's *Cyclometria* (1616), his

9. Jacob van Sluis and Tonnis Musschenga, "Boeken van Spinoza," 32–33 and 72.
10. Tammy Nyden-Bullock, "Radical Cartesian Politics: Velthuysen, De la Court, and Spinoza," in Wiep van Bunge, ed. *Studia Spinozana*, vol. 15 (1999): 35–67. See aslo Tammy Nyden-Bullock, *Spinoza's Radical Cartesian Mind* (New York: Continuum Studies in Philosophy, 2010).
11. Jonathan Israel, *Radical Enlightenment*, 244–45.

Preparatory exercise of the restored astronomy, book 1: on the motion of the sun (1628), and a Latin edition of the *Reflections upon the daily and annual course of the earth* could all be found on the shelves of the book closet that was catalogued in the posthumous inventory of his possessions.[12] Of these works, the *Reflections*, in particular, was especially significant for Dutch society. The first defense of the Copernican system to be published in Dutch and accessible to an audience of non-specialists, the *Reflections* offered emphatically naturalistic explanations for biblical miracles, such as the narrative in Joshua 10, and did more than any other work to popularize Copernicus's views in the northern Low Countries. The presence of this work on Spinoza's shelf is at the very least highly intriguing and very suggestive of his connections with this particular world of thought.

Many other connections between Spinoza's thought and his books could be raised here – not least the likely influence of Hugo Grotius's *De satisfactione Christi* (1617), a treatise that would have been a valuable resource for a learned scholar interested in the historical study of Scripture, as well as in the arguments of radical, anti-Trinitarian Christians.[13] Ostensibly a refutation of Faustus Socinus's arguments about Jesus Christ, the Crucifixion, and the Atonement, Grotius's arguments were seen as so tenuous by his contemporaries that many wondered if it was indeed a half-hearted, false refutation actually meant to advance a Socinian agenda.[14] In order to show that Jesus's sacrifice for humanity was a form of judicial "substitution" – punishment of another person in place of the actual offender – and that this was a common practice among many peoples throughout history, Grotius presents an almost anthropological comparison between the redemptive function of Jesus's crucifixion and similar practices among ancient societies that are often so gruesome that they created more problems than they solved: the Phoenicians, who sacrificed men to their god Moloch; the people of Carthage, who allegedly burned two hundred noble children

12. Jacob van Sluis and Tonnis Musschenga, "Boeken van Spinoza," 47–51.
13. Deborah Shuger, *The Renaissance Bible: Scholarship, Sacrifice, and Subjectivity*, 54–88. Jacob van Sluis and Tonnis Musschenga, "Boeken van Spinoza," 34.
14. Jonathan Israel, "Grotius and the Rise of Christian 'Radical Enlightenment,' *Grotiana* 35 (2014): 23.

in order to make amends with their deity; the Egyptians, who allegedly sacrificed people of particular beauty; and the Persians, who were said to have buried men alive. The *De satisfactione* thus would have offered Spinoza a telling model of the power of history to "naturalize" revelation, sacred texts, and beliefs in the miraculous and supernatural, seizing them from the authority of theologians and claiming them for the realm of philosophers and students of history – a central goal of the *Theological-Political Treatise.*

While many of the books in Spinoza's collection thus point toward connections with the Christian world that were essential for the development of his ideas and his philosophical system, there are numerous others that link Spinoza with the Portuguese Jewish community into which he was born. One of the Bibles catalogued after his death, the *Biblia en lengua espagnola* translated by Casiodoro de Reina and Cipriano de Valera, is the same version of Scripture that Saul Levi Morteira used for his discussions of the New Testament, and which – according to Jacob Judah Leon – was one of the favored versions of Scripture among many members of the community. Given the popularity of the Reina-Valera Bible in the Portuguese Jewish community, it is possible – and even likely – that it was acquired earlier than those that are listed alongside it, which are either in Latin or intended for very sophisticated and advanced scholars: the 1569 Syriac New Testament edition of Immanuel Tremellius, and Johannes Buxtorf's large format Hebrew Bible with Masoretic notes, the Aramaic *targum,* and rabbinic commentaries.[15] A folio copy of Maimonides' *Guide for the Perplexed,* a Passover Haggadah, an edition of Leon Ebreo's *Dialoghi d'Amore,* and an edition of Joseph Delmedigo's *Sefer Elim* all speak to an engagement with and interest in medieval and early modern Jewish thought. The presence of Jacob Judah Leon's *Sefer Tavnit Heikhal* (Amsterdam, 1650) and Menasseh ben

15. On Tremellius, see Kenneth Austin, *From Judaism to Calvinism: The Life and Writings of Emmanuel Tremellius* (Aldershot: Ashgate, 2007) and, regarding his Syriac New Testament, Robert J. Wilkinson, "Emmanuel Tremellius' 1569 Edition of the Syriac New Testament," *Journal of Ecclesiastical History,* vol. 58, no. 1 (January 2007): 9–25. Regarding Buxtorf's scholarship and publications of Hebraica, see Stephen Burnett, *From Christian Hebraism to Jewish Studies;* Jacob van Sluis and Tonnis Musschenga, "Boeken van Spinoza," 16, 21, 24, 27.

Israel's *Esperanza de Israel* (Amsterdam, 1650) represents literary links connecting Spinoza to the community that ejected him from its midst just a handful of years after these works were first published. The recent research of Warren Zev Harvey, Carlos Fraenkel, Steven Nadler, and many others has enriched our understanding of Spinoza's engagement with medieval Jewish philosophical traditions generally, and especially with the writings of Maimonides – whose *Guide for the Perplexed* was located on Spinoza's shelf, was cited explicitly, and was regularly consulted. As a result, there is now a deeper appreciation of the similarities – and differences – between Spinoza's and Maimonides' views about prophecy, intellect, imagination and the relationship between philosophy and revelation, as well as between Scripture and the study of the natural world.[16]

Much may be learned from the study of those books that Spinoza chose to keep on his personal shelves, which indeed deserve further research and more systematic exploration. Yet as helpful and revealing as Spinoza's book inventory may be, we must also be cautious in its use. Such book lists do not necessarily give a precise indication of when Spinoza came into possession of a given work. Nor – in the absence of his personal *marginalia* – does the mere presence of a book on his shelf indicate his esteem for the text, positive or negative. Furthermore, the list of works on his shelves can never be assumed to encompass the full range of his reading material and interests, and reflects nothing of the importance of personal relationships, conversations, meetings, and all other non-textual settings where ideas are discussed and transmitted. In addition, books that are *absent* from Spinoza's collection should also be of great interest to us. Their absence – and the possible reasons for it – may be instructive, offering insights about Spinoza, his reading habits, his background, and beliefs. One salient feature of Spinoza's library stands out especially: the near-complete absence of talmudic and rabbinic literature. Apart from the presence of the few medieval and early modern Jewish texts listed above, Spinoza possessed only a small handful of books that touched on topics related to rabbinic Judaism: a book on the

16. Steven Nadler, ed. *Spinoza and Medieval Jewish Philosophy* (Cambridge: Cambridge University Press, 2014).

computation of the Jewish calendar: *Sefer She'erit Yosef* (Salonika, 1568); and a text described as *"Een Rabbinsch Mathematisch Boeck."*[17] Spinoza also possessed Constantijn L'Empereur's *Halikhot Olam, sive Clavis Talmudica* (Amsterdam, 1634), a translation of a fifteenth-century Spanish Jewish text which has been described as an "introduction to Talmud," and which offered a survey of the contents of the Talmud, explanations of the literary formulas used in rabbinic literature, and outlines on how to determine the solutions to unresolved rabbinic discussions.[18]

Not a single volume of Talmud, Mishnah, or Midrash is to be found within the inventory of Spinoza's books. Given Spinoza's prejudices and disdain for the rabbis, this is perhaps understandable. But it is still surprising and notable, given that Spinoza composed his sharp and biting polemic against Jewish beliefs and practices without, apparently, possessing a deep understanding of the central religious texts read throughout the Jewish world. Rabbinic literature is not only absent from Spinoza's shelves; it is also absent – or nearly so – from the body of the *Theological-Political Treatise* itself. Only in a few instances do the rabbis of the Talmud appear in the *Treatise* – and even these fall within a very limited scope that only serves to accentuate their broader absence. In Chapter 2 of the *Theological-Political Treatise*, Spinoza develops his understanding of prophets and prophecy, defining explicitly what prophecy *is* – a particularly "vivid power of imagination," a "moral certainty," and variable depending on the nature and background of different prophets. Prophecy explicitly does *not* offer knowledge that is certain. Because

17. Jacob van Sluis and Tonnis Musschenga, "Boeken van Spinoza," identify this "*Rabbinsch Mathematisch Boeck*" as the *Sefer Shevile Emunah* [Paths of Faith] of the fourteenth-century Meir Aldabi. On this work, see Resianne Fontaine, "An Unexpected Source of Meir Aldabi's *Shevile Emuna*," *Zutot*, vol. 4, Issue 1 (2004): 96–100. Aldabi's encyclopedic text ranges widely, covering religious, philosophical, and scientific topics including the creation of the world, astronomy, the creation of humans, God and His attributes, anatomy, religious observances, the soul, and the world to come. It is not clear, however, on what grounds the association between this book and the "*Rabbinsch Mathematisch Boeck*" is made. The title does not appear on the original inventory list and Offenberg does not mention it in his classic article.
18. Peter T. Van Rooden, *Theology, Biblical Scholarship, and Rabbinical Studies in the Seventeenth Century: Constantijn L'Empereur (1591–1648), Professor of Hebrew and Theology at Leiden* (Leiden: Brill, 1989), 128–29.

it requires confirmation from God, it is in all ways inferior to natural knowledge, which needs no such additional affirmation; and, it is often contradictory.[19] To illustrate the potentially contradictory nature of prophecy, and the tenuous claims to truth that it possesses, Spinoza offers an example from Tractate Shabbat of the Babylonian Talmud – one of the very few occasions where he cites the Talmud carefully and directly: "The rabbis who handed down to us the books of the prophets (the only ones now extant) found the opinions of Ezekiel to be so much in conflict with those of Moses (as we are told in the treatise Shabbat chapter 1, folio 13, page 2) that they almost decided not to admit that book among the canonical books, and would have completely suppressed it if a certain Hananiah had not taken it upon himself to explain it." How Hananiah achieved this remarkable feat – Spinoza writes – is unclear: "Did he write a commentary that happens to have perished, or had he the audacity to change the actual words and statements of Ezekiel and embellish them at his own discretion?"[20] It is important to note that the rabbis make their appearance in this discussion not regarding matters of Jewish law or ritual practice, but rather as witnesses to the formation of the Bible and as authorities on the Jewish canon of Scripture.

Rabbinic interpreters of Scripture come on stage again later in Chapter 10, when Spinoza works his way to questions concerning the Book of Ecclesiastes. At this juncture, Spinoza makes clear that his broader goal is to demonstrate the crucial role of the rabbis in setting the scriptural canon – making the editorial decisions that shaped the contents of the Jewish Bible and excluded many other worthy books: "The Pharisees themselves plainly tell us as much in the Talmud," Spinoza observes, "for in the treatise Sabbath [ch. 2, folio 30, p. 2] 'Rabbi Jehuda, speaking in the name of Rab, said: the learned sought to suppress the Book of Ecclesiastes, because its words are not consistent with the Law [of Moses].' 'But why did they not withdraw it? Because it begins with the law and ends with the Law.'" Spinoza also draws attention to another passage [ch. 1, folio 13, p. 2] which states, "'Remember that man for his generous spirit, whose name was Neghunja, the son of Hiskia; for

19. Jonathan Israel, ed. *Theological-Political Treatise*, 27–28.
20. Jonathan Israel, ed. *Theological-Political Treatise*, 39–40.

without him the Book of Ezekiel would have been discarded, because its words contradicted the words of the Law.'" On the basis of this evidence, Spinoza concludes that those "learned in the Law" must have convened a council "to determine what kind of books should be received as sacred and which should be excluded." This created severe problems for those who wished to dogmatically accept the authority and status of the canonical Bible, or so Spinoza hoped: "Anyone desirous of being sure about the authority of them all, must go through the entire deliberative process afresh seeking justification for each of them," a process that Spinoza knew to be impossible, therefore leaving major questions about the status of Scripture permanently open and unresolved, and the luster of the biblical canon permanently tarnished.[21] Again, Spinoza calls upon the rabbis only as exegetes, and as (problematic) witnesses to the process of canonization, rather than as the major authorities on Jewish law, ritual practice, and belief.

Why is the role of rabbinic literature so attenuated in the *Treatise*? Why does Spinoza appear to not have a fuller appreciation for the role that rabbinic authorities and texts played in the Jewish world of the time? Although proving a negative proposition conclusively is difficult, and sometimes even impossible, Spinoza did leave clues in his own writings that offer revealing insights. In Chapter 9 of the *Theological-Political Treatise,* as we have already seen, Spinoza offers an extensive list of contradictory mathematical and chronological information found within the Bible, as part of his effort to demonstrate that the text is a composite of several different works woven together by an editor – Ezra. Midway through the chapter, Spinoza provides a fascinating, almost autobiographical detail about his background: "I say nothing here that I have not long been pondering deeply, and despite being steeped in the common beliefs about the Bible from childhood on, I have not been able to resist my conclusion."[22] This crucial statement may serve as a hermeneutical key for unpacking and exploring an additional dimension of Spinoza's background that has received little attention: the connection between Spinoza as a reader and interpreter of the Hebrew Bible and

21. Jonathan Israel, ed. *Theological-Political Treatise,* 154.
22. Jonathan Israel, ed. *Theological-Political Treatise,* 134.

the culture of biblical studies in the community where he was born and raised. The children of ex-conversos raised in Amsterdam – such as Spinoza – certainly were "steeped in the common beliefs about the Bible" during their childhoods.

Scripture, as has been discussed, was the central focus of the curriculum for children and adults alike, and the community's educational institutions were shaped by a blend of New Christian, Dutch, Spanish, and medieval Jewish perspectives. For most students in the community, formal education was centered on comprehensive study of the entire biblical corpus, the translation of biblical texts, and practice chanting the weekly readings from the prophets. Some students did encounter Jewish legal and theological texts, but these subjects were deferred to the very end of the educational process, which not all children were destined to reach. Life, the need to learn a trade, pressure to join the family business, lack of money, and lack of talent could all impede a student from reaching this stage. The community thus raised generations of children whose expertise was virtually guaranteed to be in the Bible, rather than in Talmud and legal thought. Adult education likewise was frequently centered on the Bible. A hypothetical member of Selomoh de Oliveira's confraternities in the last quarter of the seventeenth century attending regular meetings would have been immersed in discussion and debate about the Bible, but would rarely have systematically studied texts from rabbinic literature.

Appreciating the specifically Bible-oriented approach to education in the community is important for several reasons. First, it helps us to see biblically-oriented religion and culture in Amsterdam as being a phenomenon with wide resonance in the community. It was not the exclusive preserve of elite scholars, though they too demonstrate a strong proclivity toward producing sophisticated works of biblical scholarship. Second, it helps us to better understand the relationship between the theoretical library of translated Jewish texts prepared for ex-conversos at printing presses in Venice and Amsterdam, and what was actually read within the Portuguese Jewish community. While the variety of Spanish and Portuguese texts available from these presses and within the communal library was quite extensive, editions of the Bible were among the texts most frequently purchased and pulled from the shelves for educating ex-conversos and their descendants. Study of the texts that were used in classrooms and confraternities provides insight into the strategies of religious education that were employed in the Jewish education of former conversos and their children within this community. Finally, appreciating the Bible-centered curriculum and culture of the Portuguese Jewish community offers important context for the emergence of Spinoza from within this community. It helps us understand how Amsterdam's most famous Jewish heretic became "steeped in the common beliefs about the Bible *from childhood on*" [my emphasis], and why the adult Spinoza still needed an introductory guide to rabbinic literature on his book shelf. The general lack of rabbinic literature on the shelves of Spinoza's library, and the contents of his writings, can be attributed in part to the focus on Scripture in the educational system and culture of the community where he was raised. For while Spinoza and most of his contemporaries would have received little if any formal instruction in Jewish law and its central texts, they would have explored Scripture meticulously and deeply within and beyond the walls of their classrooms. Spinoza's background within the Jewish community thus helped to lay the groundwork for profound insights in biblical scholarship, but created a blind-spot regarding the rabbinic literature that guided the observance of early modern Judaism across Europe at this time.

As has been shown, the biblical focus in Portuguese Jewish schools was the product of a theological outlook in which the Bible played a pivotal role in the achievement of salvation. The connection between the observance of biblical doctrines, engaging in Bible study, and achieving salvation was widely held by members of the community, including Menasseh ben Israel, Saul Levi Morteira, Daniel Levi de Barrios, and others. Menasseh repeatedly made claims about the link between Bible study and salvation in the editions of Scripture that he printed for the community, and he stressed in his *Conciliador* that the active observance of biblical commandments and teachings was the foundation of both Jewish *and* Christian efforts to attain salvation. Morteira, approaching the question from the vantage point of a study of the New Testament, utilized a commentary on Galatians to make a similar point: that the "justification" and salvation of Jews depended on the rigorous observance of biblical commandments, and that many (though not all) Christians had erred, misinterpreting Paul's teachings and believing that there was no longer any need for the commandments. Appearing in lengthy theological works, personal editions of Scripture, historical writings, and other varieties of literature, the link between Scripture and salvation appeared frequently in the seventeenth-century thought of this community. This is perhaps unsurprising, given the importance of personal salvation in the Catholic world in which the ex-conversos had lived, the centrality given to the Bible in the efforts of Dutch Protestants to secure their personal salvation, and the fact that many *conversos* were accustomed to thinking of Judaism as a biblically-oriented religion, regarding the Law of Moses as the central focus of their own personal efforts to attain salvation.

What is surprising is that the link between Scripture and salvation is also made by one of the concept's most unlikely proponents: Benedict Spinoza, in the *Theological-Political Treatise*. In Chapter 7, in the context of his explanation of the importance of reading the Bible with his rigorous methodology, modeled on the study of nature, Spinoza writes:

> And since true salvation and happiness consists in our intellect's genuine acquiescence [in what is true] and we truly acquiesce only in what we understand very clearly, it most evidently follows that we can securely grasp the meaning of Scripture in matters necessary for salvation and happiness. Consequently, there is no reason why we should be concerned to the same extent about the rest, given that for the most part we are unable to grasp it by reason or the intellect and it is therefore something more curious than useful.[23]

Spinoza clearly associates the Bible – or at least part of it – with the goal of attaining some form of "salvation," although this undoubtedly meant something vastly different for Amsterdam's infamous Jewish heretic than it did for his erstwhile, more orthodox coreligionists – as Steven Nadler has shown.[24] As we have seen, many groups and individuals in

23. Jonathan Israel, ed. *Theological-Political Treatise*, 111.

24. Steven Nadler, *Spinoza's Heresy: Immortality and the Jewish Mind* (Oxford: Clarendon Press, 2001), 94–132. Whereas contemporaries like Menasseh ben Israel believed firmly in ideas about personal salvation, participation in the post-mortem world to come, and eternal reward and punishment, Nadler demonstrates that Spinoza denied

seventeenth-century Europe isolated those areas of the Bible that were absolutely crucial for salvation, and were therefore rigidly incorruptible. Even among this company, the area of biblical terrain that Spinoza included as crucial for salvation was paltry. He refuses "to grant that because Scripture contains the divine law, it has always preserved the same points, the same letters, and the same words."[25] While the text of the Bible itself had been irreversibly transformed through the vicissitudes of historical transmission, he also insisted that "the meaning, which alone entitles any text to be called divine, has come down to us uncorrupted, even though the words in which it was first expressed are deemed to have been frequently altered." This unadulterated layer of meaning allowed for a very few eternally true principles that were key for salvation – another term that Spinoza defined very differently from his contemporary Jewish acquaintances: "that God exists, that He provides for all things, is omnipotent, and has decreed that the pious will fare well and wrongdoers badly, and that our salvation depends on His grace alone. For Scripture everywhere manifestly teaches these things, and thus must always have taught them."[26] Similarly, Spinoza continues, there are also moral principles in the Bible that derive from this "universal foundation," and are therefore equally pristine and part of the path to salvation: "to defend justice, assist the poor, not to kill, [and] not to covet other men's property."[27]

To judge by the number of times Spinoza makes this connection between Scripture and salvation, it is not a superficial statement of little import. Elsewhere, he defends the Bible against those "impious persons" who believe that Scripture is "thoroughly flawed and corrupted and

these concepts in any traditional sense. Spinoza specifically discounts the immortality of the soul, and the "immortality of the mind" that he does grant differs starkly from that of earlier Jewish and Christian theologians. Spinoza's immortality, according to Nadler, is based on an individual's acquisition of perfect ("adequate"), atemporal knowledge identical with God's. Spinoza, as Nadler writes, believes that "the more of these ideas we accumulate the more we participate in eternity now, and the more of us remains after the death of the body and the end of the durational aspect of ourselves" (122).

25. Jonathan Israel, ed. *Theological-Political Treatise*, 170.
26. Jonathan Israel, ed. *Theological-Political Treatise*, 170.
27. Jonathan Israel, ed. *Theological-Political Treatise*, 170.

lacks authority... one can do nothing to help such people." In contrast, Spinoza insists that he "must demonstrate that, in so far as the Bible teaches what is requisite for obedience and salvation, it could not have been corrupted," and that "anything adulterated or spurious could only have occurred in the remaining material."[28] The basic ideas examined here – the link between Scripture and salvation, and the immunity of the core parts of the Bible that contain the essential doctrines, were eminently traditional in the Jewish community where he was raised, and the Dutch world in which he lived. The direction that Spinoza took these ideas, and his conclusions, were eminently *atypical*, non-traditional, and revolutionary. However, exploring the popularity of these ideas in the community in which Spinoza was born helps us to better understand why Spinoza turned to these ideas as his starting points in the first place, and to appreciate why he thought of the traditional relationship between Scripture and salvation as an effective medium for advancing his radical agenda.

Menasseh ben Israel's approach to thinking about the Hebrew Bible belonged to a world that was becoming increasingly preoccupied with knowledge that could be proven mathematically, and his *Conciliador* embodies the nexus between this turn in European culture and Jewish approaches to reading the Bible. Scientific discoveries and mathematical revelations created exegetical problems for many Jewish and Christian thinkers in the seventeenth century, who responded in different ways: some attenuating the terrain of the Bible that was considered infallible, others defending every grain of sand, insisting that every letter of Scripture was divinely inspired and unerring. In a world where the mathematically derived, heliocentric model of the universe that conflicted with the Bible excited powerful passions, and vigorous opposition, Menasseh set out to prove the complete mathematical infallibility of the Bible – that there were no numerical, arithmetic, and mathematical contradictions or inconsistencies in Scripture. As we have seen, Menasseh ben Israel's world was also Benedict Spinoza's world. Spinoza grew up in a Dutch world where debates about the implications of scientific discoveries and radical philosophical positions for the Bible were increasingly

28. Jonathan Israel, ed. *Theological-Political Treatise*, 164–65.

vigorous, and in a Jewish world where Menasseh's four enormous tomes on biblical contradictions had circulated for over two decades before Spinoza's expulsion from the community. Menasseh and Spinoza were indeed of one world, but they were on opposite sides of it. We see that Spinoza shared the interests and concerns of his more traditionally minded contemporary, and took interest in the questions and problems that preoccupied the orthodox members of his community. Yet though they began tilling the same garden, the fruits of their labors could not have been more different. Whereas Menasseh sought to prove the *absence* of any biblical mathematical contradictions, Spinoza gleefully seized these problems as exemplifying his broader arguments about the nature of the Bible, magnifying them to the highest possible degree and forcing them into the limelight. Menasseh's anxiety about whether he had in fact reconciled the Bible's mathematical inconsistencies and contradictions, and his obsession with biblical contradictions overall, stands as a sort of silent testimony to his fear of the doubts that Spinoza would ultimately bring to light with such disastrous effect himself. At a time when orthodox and radical Dutch and European scholars alike were testing and probing the boundaries between mathematic and scientific truths and biblical infallibility, Spinoza went further still – pushing the claims of science to what were seen as extreme conclusions. The salient point remains, however: Spinoza's methods, interests, and authorial choices are set in relief by comparison to the broader culture of biblical studies in which he was raised, and from which he cannot be separated.

Also illuminating the focus on Scripture in the Portuguese Jewish community was the ongoing importance of the New Testament to religious scholars – an echo of their experiences as New Christians. Christian Scripture, exegesis, and theology were familiar to many of the ex-converso members of Morteira's congregation, and references to these appeared frequently in his sermons. Morteira's interest in Christianity and the New Testament led him to spend much of his adult life engrossed in the study of the Gospels, and his encounter with radical Christian movements, such as the Socinians, and his appreciation of more mainstream reforms implemented by orthodox Calvinists, led to a fundamental transformation in his beliefs about Christianity and its holy texts – from an early and inveterate hostility to a far more conciliatory tone. He came to believe that there were fundamental connections between the doctrines taught by the Gospels and the Hebrew Bible, and that Jesus was a faithful rabbinic Jew. He also attempted to resolve certain contradictory passages in the New Testament. Morteira believed that many Christians in the Netherlands had made such strides in distancing themselves from Catholicism that they were in fact on the verge of adopting Jewish doctrines. Stimulated by his encounter with the Socinians, Morteira sought to show *reformados* and *novos reformados,* Calvinists and Socinians, the path to correct, Jewish perspectives on the observance of the Sabbath. Morteira's *Tratado* is thus representative of an exceedingly rare literary genre: pre-modern Jewish literature written in a European vernacular language in order to urge Christians closer to the practices and beliefs of Judaism.

We have also noted the absorption of historical approaches to studying sacred texts among orthodox members of the Jewish community from which Spinoza emerged. Morteira's hopes to "open the eyes" of the Socinians included an effort to contextualize certain Christian texts and beliefs historically, showing that to be correctly understood they needed to be viewed through the lens of biblical law and Second Temple Jewish society. He gradually came to see the Last Supper as an example of Second-Temple era Passover observance, and, instead of exemplifying Jesus's defiance of the Pharisees, through Morteira's reinterpretation the parable of Jesus in the cornfields becomes a paradigmatic example of how Christianity's central figure continued to perform the biblical commandments assiduously. Morteira subjected Christian texts, beliefs, and practices to the microscope of historical critique, in an effort to deprive them of theological legitimacy by dragging them through the mud of history.

Concerned about efforts of Christians to proselytize among members of his community, Morteira produced an extensive historicist study of the New Testament. In the course of this work, he demonstrated his familiarity with some of the newest and most sophisticated approaches to biblical and historical scholarship in seventeenth-century Europe. He contextualized numerous New Testament passages within the settings of Greco-Roman and rabbinic Jewish customs and beliefs, and argued that there was profound ambiguity regarding the authorship of different New Testament texts that cast shadows over the authenticity of these works. Based on a close examination of the writings of leading sixteenth- and seventeenth-century Catholic authorities, and the diverse beliefs of early Christian movements, Morteira believed he could show that figures unknown had interpolated texts into the Gospels long after they had ostensibly been written. He believed he could show that Christianity's sacred Scriptures had been deliberately crafted to appeal to the sensibilities of ancient Greeks and Egyptians, mirroring their existing beliefs and religious practices. Morteira's historical study of the New Testament provides further background that is crucial for understanding the emergence of Spinoza from within Amsterdam's Portuguese Jewish community. It shows the degree to which leading members of this community were engaged with avant-garde biblical scholarship during this period, and raises the possibility that many of the historicist tools that Spinoza would later employ were already in use within the very community where he was raised.

Amsterdam's People of the Book seeks to capture a significant moment in the development of modern approaches to thinking about the Bible. Menasseh ben Israel and Saul Levi Morteira lived in an age when the Bible's aura of perfection was being gradually subverted by studies in biblical chronology, debates over the antiquity of the vowel points, ancient Near Eastern historical studies, and the beginnings of critical biblical scholarship by figures like Spinoza and Richard Simon. Menasseh, Morteira, and Spinoza were clearly engaged in very different activities: Menasseh used literary and exegetical genres that were traditional in Jewish and European society to defend the infallibility of the Hebrew Bible and the integrity of Scripture's chronological information. He feared that the incoherence of biblical chronology threatened the Bible's status as an infallible text. Morteira subjected the New Testament to a rigorous historical critique by exposing the Greek, Roman, and rabbinic Jewish substrata that lurked beneath the surface of the Gospels. By emphasizing the debt of Christian texts and beliefs to ancient religious cultures in the Mediterranean world, Morteira sought to dislocate the New Testament from the realm of theological study, and place it in the domain of historical analysis. Spinoza capitalized on methods of scholarship, reading practices, ideas, and assumptions shared by many within his community, pushed them to new limits, more radical than anything his conservative contemporaries could have imagined, and applied these strategies to the Hebrew Bible. What links Menasseh and Morteira – and Spinoza – is a shared understanding of historical study as a potent weapon for supporting the beliefs of one's coreligionists, or subverting those of one's opponents. By the end of the seventeenth century an exegetical revolution had taken place, as well as a scientific one. Menasseh and Morteira did not drive this exegetical revolution, nor would they have been pleased by it. They do, however, reflect the changes taking place in European society at this time, demonstrating the anxieties that surfaced about the authority and status of the Biblical text, and the historicist tools that could be used to support – or subvert – it.

* * *

European Jewish Society, Scripture, and the Horizon of Modernity

In conclusion, we can reflect on the significance of the Hebrew Bible in the Portuguese Jewish community of seventeenth-century Amsterdam, and the place of the Bible in modern Jewish religious movements. Can the movement of the Bible toward the center of Jewish religious culture in Amsterdam be related to the prominent religious and cultural space occupied by the Bible in a variety of European Jewish communities during the eighteenth and nineteenth centuries? Or was the centrality of the Bible in Jewish religious culture, education, and rabbinic scholarship in Amsterdam a limited phenomenon driven exclusively by the particular experiences of the ex-conversos? Despite a variety of significant differences between the political and religious environment of seventeenth-century Amsterdam, the world of the Jewish and European Enlightenments of the eighteenth century, and the experiences of Jewish emancipation and assimilation in the nineteenth centuries, it does appear that there are certain similarities. The movement of the Bible toward the center of Jewish religious culture, education, and scholarship was not completely restricted to Amsterdam's ex-conversos. Between the seventeenth and nineteenth centuries, Jewish acculturation to Christian religious values in a variety of settings contributed to the growing importance of the Bible in diverse aspects of Jewish life and society.

David Ruderman has demonstrated a similar phenomenon among eighteenth- and nineteenth-century Jews in England, connected to their encounter with English Protestant religious values.[29] Through the study of what he has called the "Englishing" of Jewish culture, Ruderman depicts the transformation of Jewish culture in England that resulted from the decline of multilingualism in the community and growing patterns of assimilation. At a basic level, the decline of Hebraic literacy among English Jews led to the adoption of the English Authorized Version of Scripture as the Jewish community's main portal into the biblical text.[30] In addition, Ruderman sees at this time a general decline in religious knowledge, observance, and esteem for rabbinic literature in general among English Jews.[31] These changes led Jews to reformulate their traditional texts in new languages, and to adopt new reading practices and literary genres.[32] In this environment, English Jews produced a range of manuals for religious instruction and observance, as well as catechisms for children's education, that were "quite blatantly biblical in orientation."[33] David Levi's *A Succinct Account of the Duties, Rites, and Ceremonies of the Jews* (1782) – "the standard English guide to Jewish practice for almost four decades"[34] – constantly emphasizes the biblical basis for Jewish beliefs and practices. Levi devotes only ten pages of the work to discussion of the Talmud, and although there are ninety pages on the Mishnah, this section is mostly a historical account of ancient Judaism until the time of Judah the Prince. The legal content of the Oral Law is subordinated to the historical narrative.[35] Likewise, Jewish catechisms produced in England during this period were heavily biblical in their orientation, and Ruderman sees this phenomenon too as the

29. David Ruderman, *Jewish Enlightenment in an English Key: Anglo-Jewry's Construction of Modern Jewish Thought* (Princeton, NJ and Oxford: Princeton University Press, 2000).
30. Ruderman, *Jewish Enlightenment in an English Key*, 219–20.
31. Ruderman, *Jewish Enlightenment in an English Key*, 261–62.
32. Ruderman, *Jewish Enlightenment in an English Key*, 215.
33. Ruderman, *Jewish Enlightenment in an English Key*, 261–62.
34. Ruderman, *Jewish Enlightenment in an English Key*, 246.
35. Ruderman, *Jewish Enlightenment in an English Key*, 245–46.

product of Jewish engagement with the Protestant religious culture of their Christian contemporaries.[36]

Ruderman's findings regarding the influence of Protestant religious culture on Jewish biblicism support Yosef Kaplan's arguments about Karaism in early eighteenth-century Amsterdam. Kaplan demonstrates that there was a resurgence of antinomian tendencies in the Portuguese community during the early eighteenth century, characterized by reticence to follow the rabbinic commandments in the Oral Law, and that those with such tendencies self-identified as "Karaites." Although there was in fact real contact between seventeenth-century Lithuanian Karaites and a few Amsterdam Jews during the early seventeenth century, Kaplan shows that these were quite limited, brief in duration, and of no lasting impact. It is unlikely that the early eighteenth-century Karaites were influenced by actual Karaites or medieval Karaite literature.

Instead, Kaplan demonstrates that eighteenth-century Sephardi "Karaites" in Amsterdam were influenced by literature about Karaites written by Christian Hebraists that circulated in Protestant northwest Europe at this time. The *sola scriptura* perspectives of Protestants led to sympathetic tendencies toward Karaites who also denied the divine inspiration of post-biblical texts and traditions, including the Talmud. Interest in Karaites and their literature flourished in late seventeenth-century Holland. Levinus Warner, who lived in Istanbul between 1645 and 1654, returned to the University of Leiden with seventy-nine Karaite works and dozens of manuscripts. Above all, Amsterdam's "Karaites" were influenced by Richard Simon, whose portrayal of Karaism as the most enlightened form of Judaism circulated widely in English translations produced in 1650, 1707, and 1711.[37] As Kaplan observes, this group of Amsterdam Sephardi "Karaites" made one of the earliest organized efforts within early modern Judaism "to give organized expression to their deviant views" and to create a separate, parallel religious framework for their members. Unlike the individual heretics who sought to

36. Ruderman, *Jewish Enlightenment in an English Key*, 255–56, 258–59.
37. Yosef Kaplan, "Karaites in Early Eighteenth-Century Amsterdam," in *Sceptics, Millenarians, and Jews*, ed. David Katz and Jonathan Israel (New York: Brill, 1990), 199, 214–24.

extricate themselves from the Jewish community, this group desired to give a "different positive content to its Judaism."[38]

There is also a self-conscious emphasis on the role of the Bible in Jewish culture and education among proponents of the Jewish Enlightenment (*maskilim*) across Europe during the eighteenth and into the nineteenth century. As Shmuel Feiner has shown, Moses Mendelssohn and early *maskilim* who attempted to promote cultural reform selected a translation of the Pentateuch with a systematic commentary as the starting point for their efforts.[39] Mendelssohn saw this project as promising to act as a counterweight to the emphasis on Talmud in Jewish education, and raise the profile of Bible study among his coreligionists by making Scripture available to them in high German.[40] Naphtali Herz Wessely, who participated in the preparation of the section on Leviticus, likewise perceived an urgent need to shift the focus of Jewish education from Talmud to Bible. He observed the traditional approach to Jewish education, and remarked that:

> They send their children to school at the age of four or five, to teachers of Bible, without even taking note that they speak with a stammering tongue, and sometimes do not even know how to read properly... and they will teach these tender children the word of God in their one way for a year or more, and when that time is up, will inform their parents: your children have already succeeded in learning Mishnah and Talmud, so it is no longer fit to teach them Bible... and most of them, when they grow up, will cast off the yoke of Talmud, and as they turn aside from it, nothing will remain with them, neither Torah nor the elements of the Jewish faith. [41]

At a time when German Christians were attempting to justify the relevance of the Bible in the modern world by investing the text with new meaning demonstrating its reasonableness, its conformity with natural

38. Yosef Kaplan, "An Alternative Path to Modernity," 19–20.
39. Shmuel Feiner, *The Jewish Enlightenment*, trans. Chaya Naor (Philadelphia: University of Pennsylvania Press, 2002), 127–30, 139.
40. Shmuel Feiner, *The Jewish Enlightenment*, 128.
41. Shmuel Feiner, *The Jewish Enlightenment*, 129.

philosophy and mathematics, and its ongoing importance in education,[42] Mendelssohn's circle of collaborators endeavored to produce a major Jewish Bible translation that they hoped would serve vital educational purposes in their own community. The "mania" of Germans for pedagogy and the preparation of a Bible that was useful for educational purposes was shared by Mendelssohn and other early *maskilim*.[43]

The movement of the Bible toward the center of education, religious culture, and scholarship is also evident in late eighteenth- and nineteenth-century France. As Jay Berkovitz has shown, French *régénérateurs*, proponents of the "regeneration" of French Jewry through the modernization of its morals, religious beliefs, and education sought to mitigate the role of Talmud and rabbinic literature in these facets of Jewish life, and to raise the profile of Scripture. The *régénérateurs* viewed these changes in Jewish society and thought as necessary in order to make Jews and Judaism not only compatible with demands of the modern state, economy, and citizenship, but also virtually indistinguishable from the French Christian society in which they lived.[44] In the area of education, French Jews attempting to create a school system that would prepare their children for participation in French economic and cultural life stressed greater emphasis on the study of the Bible, and

42. Jonathan Sheehan, *The Enlightenment Bible: Translation, Scholarship, and Culture* (Princeton, NJ and Oxford: Princeton University Press, 2005), 118–220. However, note the significant difference between the exegetical principles that Mendelssohn followed compared with the approach of the scholars who wrote what Sheehan describes as the "Enlightenment Bible." Whereas Mendelssohn defined his approach to translation as "the profundity of the literal meaning," his late eighteenth-century German contemporaries frequently held literal translation in disdain, preferring to compose paraphrases or poetic compositions that could more easily inscribe rational, moral, and aesthetic values into the biblical text. On Mendelssohn's methods, see David Sorkin, *Moses Mendelssohn and the Religious Enlightenment* (Berkeley: University of California Press, 1996), 65–66. See also Edward Breuer, *The Limits of Enlightenment: Jews, Germans, and the Eighteenth-Century Study of Scripture* (Cambridge, MA: Harvard University Press, 1996), 151–78. Breuer shows the full extent to which Mendelssohn's methods and his reliance on a litany of medieval Jewish authorities "flew in the face" of how his German contemporaries thought Bible scholarship should be performed.
43. Jonathan Sheehan, *The Enlightenment Bible*, 132.
44. Jay Berkovitz *The Shaping of Jewish Identity in Nineteenth-Century France* (Detroit, MI: Wayne State University Press, 1989), 14–16, 248.

Michel Berr (1781–1843), the first Jew to practice in France as a barrister, produced a new French translation of the Bible emphasizing morality that was adopted in many French-Jewish schools. Whereas previously the overwhelming emphasis in children's education had been on Talmud, Jewish schools in France now tended to prioritize exploration of the Pentateuch.[45] As part of this overall effort, leading Jewish scholars such as Samuel Cahen (1796–1862) produced sophisticated Bible translations modeled on Mendelssohn's *Bi'ur*, featuring medieval French and Spanish "literalist" biblical interpreters as companion texts.[46] The emphasis on Bible in schools and synagogues was not simply an exercise in making Scripture accessible to French Jews; rather, it was an important part of legitimating Judaism within France, "a rendering of the public cult in the national language."[47]

The movement of the Bible toward the center of Jewish religious and cultural life thus took place in a wide array of times and places, including many beyond those presented here. In some cases, this movement toward the center was the product of carefully considered programs of transformation and reform, as Kaplan, Feiner, and Berkovitz have shown in their studies of Dutch, German, and French Jewish societies during the eighteenth and nineteenth centuries. In contrast, Ruderman has shown that in England, the reflective aspects of Anglo-Jewry's experience of Enlightenment and modernity were not the product of a conscious program of reform and transformation, but rather of a variety of processes. The decline of bilingualism and multilingualism deprived Anglo-Jewry of access to rabbinic Jewish texts in their original languages, as well as to Spanish and Portuguese translations that were printed during the sixteenth and seventeenth centuries. This, along with assimilation, acculturation, and exposure to English models of religious culture led to a greater emphasis on the Bible in Jewish religious culture and education.

In view of the growing importance of biblical education and scholarship in a variety of modern Jewish communities, can the movement of the Bible toward the center of Jewish education and rabbinic scholarship

45. Jay Berkovitz, *The Shaping of Jewish Identity in Nineteenth-Century France*, 174–75, 180.
46. Jay Berkovitz, *The Shaping of Jewish Identity in Nineteenth-Century France*, 142.
47. Jay Berkovitz, *The Shaping of Jewish Identity in Nineteenth-Century France*, 175.

in Amsterdam be viewed as modern, or at least as an incipient departure from tradition? Is there a fissure that divides "traditional" Jewish society and its prioritization of Talmud study from the ex-conversos and certain Jewish thinkers in the eighteenth and nineteenth centuries who sought to give far greater emphasis to Bible study?

Many historians have turned their attention to questions regarding the relationship of medieval Sephardi and ex-converso thought to modern Jewish society. Yosef Hayim Yerushalmi concluded that the ex-conversos "stand out as perhaps the first modern Jews" on the grounds that Iberian New Christians were immersed in European theological, philosophic, and scientific learning before they became New Jews, and had greater access to European universities than any other pre-modern Jewish community. Furthermore, Yerushalmi affirms that "the secular culture of many Dutch and Italian Jews anticipated the Berlin Haskalah of the eighteenth century."[48] Some scholars, such as José Faur and Richard Popkin, have attempted to locate an especially pronounced proclivity among individuals with converso backgrounds toward skeptical tendencies in the study of science and Scripture.[49] There has also

48. Yosef Hayim Yerushalmi, *From Spanish Court to Italian Ghetto*, 44–48. Note, however, Yerushalmi's later statement that "In general we may regard the ends to which this literature [in European vernacular languages] was addressed and the method it applied as the reverse of those which were later to characterize the Berlin Haskalah. For if the disciples of Mendelssohn employed Hebrew as a means to spread secular enlightenment among the Jews of Germany, here the secular Spanish and Portuguese vernaculars were being used to spread Jewish enlightenment among the returning Marranos." Yosef Kaplan, in contrast to Yerushalmi, has argued that the access of conversos and ex-conversos to non-Jewish educational institutions does not represent a significant breaking point with the traditional Jewish world, and that in fact relatively few Jews attended Dutch universities for any extended length of time. See Kaplan, "Sephardi Students at the University of Leiden," in *An Alternative Path to Modernity*, 196–210. Kaplan has also observed that Isaac Orobio de Castro attempted to shut the door on his university past, rather than seeking to mold Jewish religious culture around it. See Yosef Kaplan, *From Christianity to Judaism*, 149–50.

49. José Faur, *In the Shadow of History: Jews and Conversos at the Dawn of Modernity* (Albany: State University of New York Press, 1992); Richard Popkin, *Isaac La Peyrère: His Life, Work, and Influence*. See David Ruderman's critique of this position in *Jewish Thought and Scientific Discovery in Early Modern Europe*, 276–85. As Ruderman emphasizes, the converso origins of skeptical individuals like Isaac La Peyrère and Francisco Sanchez is by no means certain; and even if we grant this, it is difficult to

been significant debate about the contributions of medieval Sephardi Jewish science and philosophy to the Haskalah, and the role of Menasseh ben Israel's arguments for the readmission of Jews to England on later eighteenth-century discussions about Jewish rights in Germany.[50]

On the other hand, Yosef Kaplan has characterized Amsterdam's ex-conversos as having created a Jewish society that for all of its unique characteristics remained deeply traditional. The Portuguese Jews, though profoundly shaped by the world of Iberian and European society and culture, lacked an ideology of change and transformation and did not see their cosmopolitan background as a model for reorganizing the wider Jewish world. Thus, Kaplan remarks that "the impression one gets from studying the thought of the members of the Western Sephardi diaspora in the seventeenth century is rather that the values brought from the Iberian peninsula served most of them as a means of bolstering the authority and legitimacy of the Jewish tradition."[51] In many respects, their cultural orientation looks to the sixteenth and seventeenth centuries, rather than forward to the eighteenth century: physicians within

attribute their skepticism directly to this background, which stands in such contrast to that of the majority of learned figures in the ex-converso community.

50. Regarding the challenges of linking the heritage of medieval Sephardi Jews and ex-conversos with the development of the Jewish Enlightenment, see *Sepharad in Ashkenaz: Medieval Knowledge and Eighteenth-Century Enlightened Jewish Discourse*, ed. Resianne Fontaine, Andrea Schatz, and Irene Zwiep (Amsterdam: Koninklijke Nederlandse Akademie van Wetenschappen, 2007). See especially Shmuel Feiner, "From Renaissance to Revolution: The Eighteenth Century in Jewish History," 1–10, which attempts to show the centrality of medieval Sephardi philosophical works as models for maskilic thought and activity. However, see also David Ruderman, "The Impact of Early Modern Jewish Thought on the Eighteenth Century: A Challenge to the Notion of the Sephardi Mystique," 11–22. Ruderman argues convincingly that although *maskilim* viewed medieval Sephardi scholars as heroes and models, the actual scientific and philosophical content of their texts was far less useful and up-to-date than the works of seventeenth-century Italian Jews.

Regarding the textual afterlife of Menasseh ben Israel's *Esperanca de Israel* (Amsterdam, 1650) and its reception within Mendelssohn's circle, see David Sorkin, *Moses Mendelssohn and the Religious Enlightenment*, 108–15 and Shmuel Feiner, *The Jewish Enlightenment*, 123–25. The standard work on the seventeenth-century debate about the readmission of Jews to England is David Katz, *Philo-Semitism and the Readmission of the Jews to England, 1603–1655*.

51. Yosef Kaplan, "An Alternative Path to Modernity," 13.

the community do not appear to have been influenced by the scientific revolution, and their society prioritized the maintenance of Jewish law as a framework for day-to-day life. As many scholars have shown, ex-converso Jews were voracious consumers of sixteenth-century Spanish belles-lettres and learned writings. On this basis, Kaplan concludes that there is "a clear line of separation between the world of the Sephardi Jews of Amsterdam in the seventeenth century and the Jewish world in the second half of the eighteenth century."[52]

In many ways, the biblical culture constructed by Amsterdam's Portuguese Jews resists being compartmentalized within the binary model of traditional and modern Jewish societies. Rather, it is a phenomenon that straddles and transcends definitions of modernity and traditionalism. In some respects, the biblical culture of Amsterdam's ex-conversos helped to build a society that Kaplan sees as being located firmly within the pre-modern world: their biblical scholarship defended the infallibility of the Bible and its authority as the basis for social and religious organization; it helped to define their identity as Jews and polemically distinguished them from Christians; it confirmed their faith in divine providence, and their messianic hopes. Amsterdam's Jews focused on the Bible in scholarship and education because of medieval Sephardi Jewish traditions, their New Christian past, and religious models in Protestant society – not because of a conscious desire to shift the emphasis of Jewish religious culture from Talmud to Bible.

Nevertheless, there are also compelling reasons to see the biblically-oriented Jewish culture in Portuguese Jewish Amsterdam as connected in some ways to Jewish communities that prioritized biblical culture and scholarship in the eighteenth and nineteenth centuries. The central role of the Bible in seventeenth-century Amsterdam's Portuguese Jewish society was a phenomenon that became even more pronounced later on in other settings, such as France, Germany, and England, where the Bible loomed ever larger as a religious and cultural resource, also in part because of acculturation to the values of the surrounding society. The movement of the Bible toward the center of Portuguese Jewish society in Amsterdam is significant not because it was self-consciously copied

52. Yosef Kaplan, "An Alternative Path to Modernity," 13–16.

or imitated by later Jewish communities, but because it reflects shared processes of acculturation to Christian religious practices that took place in diverse settings and times and which ultimately had a dynamic influence on Jewish religious practices in these environments. The reasons why many modern Jewish communities began to turn single-mindedly toward the Bible, instead of to rabbinic literature, can be best explained and understood by exploring and understanding the setting and circumstances of the place it happened first: the Portuguese Jewish community of Amsterdam, and the factors that drove its members to so resolutely become "people of the book."

Bibliography

Primary Sources

Note: Manuscripts are listed as "MS," with their catalog numbers at the Ets Haim/Montezinos Library (EH) in Amsterdam, and at the Amsterdam Municipal Archive (GAS).

Aboab, Imanuel. *Nomologia o discursos legales.* Amsterdam, 1629.

Aboab, Samuel. *Sefer ha-zikhronot.* Jerusalem, 2001.

Aboab da Fonseca, Isaac. *Parafrasis comentado sobre el Pentateuco.* Amsterdam, 1681.

Abravanel, Isaac. *Perush al Nevi'im Rishonim.* Jerusalem, 1954/1955.

Aguilar, Moshe Raphael d'. Miscellanious Manuscripts. MS EH 48 A 11.

Asher, Bahya ben. *Kad ha-kemah.* Jerusalem and New York: Mishor, 2006.

Athias, Isaac. *Fortificaccion de la ley de Moseh,* MS EH 48 C 6.

Barrios, Daniel Levi de. *Triumpho del govierno popular.* Amsterdam, 1683.

Bass, Shabbetai. *Sifte Yeshenim.* Amsterdam, 1679/1680.

Ben Israel, Menasseh. *Conciliador o de la conveniencia de los Lugares de la S. Escriptura que repugnantes entre si parecen.* 4 volumes. Amsterdam and Frankfurt, 1632–1651.

———. *'Even yeqarah. Piedra Gloriosa.* Amsterdam, 1655.

———. *De la resurreccion de los muertos.* Amsterdam, 1636.

———. *Thesouro dos denim que o povo de Israel he obrigado saber e observar.* Amsterdam, 1645–1647.

———. *De fragilidad humana, y inclinacion del hombre al peccado.* Amsterdam, 1642.

———. *The Hope of Israel.* Edited by Henry Méchoulan and Gérard Nahon, translated by Richenda George. Oxford and New York: The Littman Library of Jewish Civilization, 1987.

———. *Humas de Parasioth y Aftharoth.* Amsterdam, 1627.

Calvin, John. *A Harmony of the Gospels Matthew, Mark, and Luke.* Edited by A.W. Morrison, translated by David W. Torrance and Thomas F. Torrance. 3 volumes. Edinburgh: The Saint Andrews Press, 1972.

Cameron, John. *A tract of the soueraigne iudge of controuersies in matters of religion.* Oxford, 1628.

Cartari, Vincenzo. *Le imagini de i dei degli antichi. Nelle quali si contengono gl'idoli, I riti, le cerimonie, et altre cose appartenenti alla religione degli antichi con la loro Espositione.* Padua, 1603.

Costa, Uriel da. *Examination of Pharisaic Traditions. Exame das tradições phariseas.* Edited by H.P. Salomon and I.S.D. Sassoon. Leiden and New York: Brill, 1993.

———. *Exemplar humanae vitae.* Translated by John Whiston. London, 1740.

Coucy, Moses of. *Sefer Mitzvot Gadol.* Jerusalem, 2002.

Duran, Profet. *Sefer Ma'aseh Efod.* Jerusalem, 1969/1970.

Duran, Shimon ben Zemaḥ. *Keshet u-magen.* Jerusalem, 1969.

Gershon, Levi ben. *Perush ha-Nevi'im.* Edited by Yaakov Leib Levi. Jerusalem, 2008.

Guggenheimer, Heinrich, ed. *Seder Olam: The Rabbinic View of Biblical Chronology.* Jerusalem: Jason Aronson, Inc., 1998.

Horowitz, Shabbetai Sheftel. *Sefer Vave ha-Amudim.* Amsterdam, 1648.

Josephus, Flavius. *Jewish Antiquities.* Translated by William Whiston. Edited by Brian McGing. Ware, UK: Wordsworth Editions, 2006.

Leigh, Edward. *A Treatise of Divinity Cconsisting of Three Books.* London, 1646.

Leon, Jacob Judah. *Retrato de Templo de Selomo.* Middleburg, 1642.

———. *Tratado de la Arca del Testamento.* Amsterdam, 1653.

———. *Tratado de los Cherubim.* Amsterdam, 1654.

———. *Las Alabanças de Santidad.* Amsterdam, 1671.

Mayer, John. *A commentarie upon all the epistles of the apostle Saint Paul.* London, 1631.

Meijer, Lodwijk. *Philosophy as the Interpreter of Holy Scripture.* Amsterdam, 1666. Edited by Lee C. Rice and Francis Pastijn, translated by Samuel Shirley. Milwaukee, WI: Marquette University Press, 2005.

Morosini, Giulio. *Via della fede mostrata agli ebrei.* Rome, 1683.

Morteira, Saul Levi. *Tratado da verdade da lei de Moisés.* Escrito pelo seu próprio punho em Português em Amsterdao, 1659–1660. Edicao facsimilada e leitura do Autógrafo (1659). Edited by H.P. Salomon. University of Coimbra, 1988.

———. *Tratado de la verdad de la ley de Moseh.* MS CU X893 M841.

———. *Preguntas que hizo un clerigo de Ruan de Francia a las quales respondio el exelente y eminentissimo senor H:R: Saul Levy Mortera, Doctor Celebre y Prophesor de la Divina Theologia y predicador de la Nacion Judaica en la Ynsigne y opulenta Ciudad de Amsterdam.* MS EH 48 D 38.

Murciano, Prosper. "Shimon ben Zemaḥ Duran: A Critical Edition." PhD Dissertation, New York University, 1975.

Oliveira, Selomoh de. *Sefer har ha-zeitim.* 3 volumes. Amsterdam, 1673–1698. Mss EH 47 B 12–14.

Pardo, David and Salom ben Yosseph. *Mahzor. Orden de Ros Asanah y Kipur.* Amsterdam, 1630.

Parker, T.H.L., ed. *Calvin's Commentaries: The Epistles of Paul the Apostle to the Galatians, Ephesians, Philippians, and Colossians.* Grand Rapids, MI: Eerdmans, 1965.

Perkins, William. *A reformed Catholike: or, A declaration shewing how neere we may come to the present Church of Rome in sundrie points of religion.* London, 1597.

Poole, Matthew. *Annotations upon the Holy Bible.* Volume 2. New York, 1853.

———. *Synopsis Criticorum aliorumque sacrae scripturae interpretum et commentatatorum, summo studio et fide adornata.* Volume 2. London, 1669–1676.

Rossi, Azariah de'. *The Light of the Eyes.* Edited and translated by Joanna Weinberg. New Haven, CT and London: Yale University Press, 2001.

Serrano, Yosseph Franco. *Los cinco libros de la sacra Ley*. Amsterdam, 1695

Spinoza, Benedict de. *Theological-Political Treatise*. Edited by Jonathan Israel, translated by Michael Silverthorne and Jonathan Israel. New York: Cambridge University Press, 2007.

Termos de Talmud Torah e de Ets Haim. MS GAS [Gemeente Amsterdam Stadsarchief] 334, no. 1051.

Termos de Ets Haim. MS GAS 334, no. 1052.

Tarcagnota, Giovanni. *Delle Historie del mondo*. Venice, 1573.

Tolosani, Giovanni Maria. *Opusculum de emendationibus temporum*. Venice, 1537.

Valera, Cipriano de, ed. *La Biblia. Que es/ Los Sacros Libros del Vieio y Nuevo Testamento*. Amsterdam, 1602.

Secondary Sources

Adang, Camilla. *Muslim Writers on Judaism and the Hebrew Bible: From Ibn Rabban to Ibn Hazm*. Leiden and New York: Brill, 1996.

———. "A Jewish Reply to Ibn Hazm: Solomon b. Adret's Polemic Against Islam," in *Judíos y musulmanes en al-Andalus y el Magreb: Contactos intelectuales*, ed. Maribel Fierro. Madrid: Casa de Velázquez, 2002, 179–209.

Albert, Anne Oravetz. "Post-Sabbatian Politics: Reflections on Governance among the Spanish and Portuguese Jews of Amsterdam, 1665–1683." PhD Dissertation, University of Pennsylvania, 2008.

Altmann, Alexander. "Eternality of Punishment: A Theological Controversy within the Amsterdam Rabbinate in the Thirties of the Seventeenth Century." *Proceedings of the American Academy for Jewish Research* 40 (1972): 1–88.

Aptroot, Marion. "Yiddish Bibles in Amsterdam," in *The Bible in/and Yiddish*, ed. Shlomo Berger, 42–60. Amsterdam: Menasseh ben Israel Institute, 2007.

Austin, Kenneth. *From Judaism to Calvinism: The Life and Writings of Emmanuel Tremellius*. Aldershot, UK: Ashgate, 2007.

Backus, Irena. *Historical Method and Confessional Identity in the Era of the Reformation (1378–1615)*. Leiden and Boston: Brill, 2003.

Bentley, Jerry. *Humanists and Holy Writ: New Testament Scholarship in the Renaissance.* Princeton, NJ: Princeton University Press, 1983.

Berger, David. "On the Uses of History in Medieval Jewish Polemic: The Quest for the Historical Jesus," in *Jewish History and Jewish Memory: Essays in Honor of Yosef Hayim Yerushalmi*, ed. Elisheva Carlebach, John Efron, and David Myers, 25–39. Hanover and London: Brandeis University Press, 1998.

Berger, Shlomo. *Classical Oratory and the Sephardim of Amsterdam: Rabbi Aguilar's Tratado de la Retórica.* Hilversum: Verloren, 1996.

Berger, Yitzhak. *The Commentary of Rabbi David Kimhi to Chronicles: A Translation with Introduction and Supercommentary.* Providence, RI: Brown University Press, 2007.

Berkovitz, Jay. *The Shaping of Jewish Identity in Nineteenth-Century France.* Detroit, MI: Wayne State University Press, 1989.

Blackwell, Richard. *Galileo, Bellarmine, and the Bible.* London: University of Notre Dame Press, 1991.

Blair, Ann. "Mosaic Physics and the Search for a Pious Philosophy in the Late Renaissance," *Isis* 91, no. 1 (2000): 32–58.

Bodian, Miriam. *Hebrews of the Portuguese Nation: Conversos and Community in Early Modern Amsterdam.* Bloomington and Indianapolis: Indiana University Press, 1997.

———. *Dying in the Law of Moses: Crypto-Jewish Martyrdom in the Iberian World.* Bloomington and Indianapolis: University of Indiana Press, 2007.

———. "The Reformation and the Jews," in *Rethinking European Jewish History*, ed. by Jeremy Cohen and Moshe Rosman, 112–32. Oxford and Portland, OR: The Litmann Library of Jewish Civilization, 2009.

Boer, Harm den. *La literatura sefardi de Amsterdam.* Alcala, 1995.

———. "La Biblia de Ferrara y otras traducciones españolas de la Biblia entre los sefardíes de origen converso," in *Introducción a la Biblia de Ferrara: Actas del Simposio Internacional sobre la Biblia de Ferrara*, ed. Iacob M. Hassán, 251–96. Seville, 1991.

Bonfil, Robert. *Rabbis and Jewish Communities in Renaissance Italy*, trans. Jonathan Chipman. New York and Oxford: Oxford University Press, 1990.

Breuer, Edward. *The Limits of Enlightenment: Jews, Germans, and the*

Eighteenth-Century Study of Scripture. Cambridge, MA: Harvard University Press, 1996.

Burnett, Stephen. "German Jewish Printing in the Reformation Era (1530–1633)," in *Jews, Judaism, and the Reformation in Sixteenth-Century Germany*, ed. Dean Phillip Bell and Stephen Burnett, 503–27. Leiden and Boston: Brill, 2006.

———. "Christian Hebrew Printing in the Sixteenth Century: Printers, Humanism, and the Impact of the Reformation." *Helmantica: Revista de Filología Clásica y Hebrea.* Volume 51, no. 154 (January–April, 2000): 13–42.

———. *From Christian Hebraism to Jewish Studies: Johannes Buxtorf (1564–1629) and Hebrew Learning in the Seventeenth Century.* Leiden: Brill, 1996.

Cameron, Ron. *The Other Gospels: Non-Canonical Gospel Texts.* Philadelphia, PA: The Westminster Press, 1982.

Carlebach, Elisheva. "'Ich will dich nach Holland schicken': Amsterdam and the Reversion to Judaism of German Jewish Converts," in *Secret Conversions to Judaism in Early Modern Europe*, ed. Martin Mulsow and Richard Popkin, 51–69. Leiden and Boston: Brill, 2004.

Chajes, J.H. *Between Worlds: Dybbuks, Exorcists, and Early Modern Judaism.* Philadelphia: University of Pennsylvania Press, 2003.

Cohen, Mark, et al. eds. *The Autobiography of a Seventeenth-Century Venetian Rabbi: Leon Modena's Life of Judah.* Princeton, NJ: Princeton University Press, 1988.

Colberg, Shawn. "Human Action and the Possibility of Reward: Cajetan on Grace, Justification, and Merit." *Journal for the History of Modern Theology* 17, no. 1 (2010): 1–33.

Dan, Joseph. "Menasseh ben Israel: Attitude Towards the Zohar and Lurianic Kabbalah," in *Menasseh ben Israel and His World*, ed. Yosef Kaplan and Henry Méchoulan, 199–206. Leiden and New York: Brill, 1989.

Daugirdas, Kestutis. "The Biblical Hermeneutics of Socinians and Remonstrants in the Seventeenth Century," in *Arminius, Arminianism, and Europe. Jacobus Arminius, 1559/60–1609*, ed. Th. Marius van Leeuwen, Keith D. Stanglin, and Marijke Tolsma, 89–114. Leiden: Brill, 2009.

Dohrman, Menahem. *Menasseh ben Israel* [Hebrew]. Kibbutz ha-Me'uchad, 1989.

Dunn, James. *Jesus, Paul, and the Law: Studies in Mark and Galatians.* Louisville, KY: Westminster/John Knox Press, 1990.

———. "The Incident at Antioch (Gal. 2:11–18)." *Journal for the Study of the New Testament* 18 (1983): 3–57.

Dweck, Yaacob. *The Scandal of Kabbalah: Leon Modena, Jewish Mysticism, Early Modern Venice.* Princeton and Oxford: Princeton University Press, 2011.

Ecker-Rozinger, Neta. "Universalistic Tendencies in Rabbi Eliezer Ashkenazi's Teachings," PhD Dissertation, University of Haifa, 2010.

Edwards, James R. *The Hebrew Gospel and the Development of the Synoptic Tradition.* Grand Rapids, MI and Cambridge, UK: Eerdmans, 2009.

Eire, Carlos M.N. *From Madrid to Purgatory: The Art and Craft of Dying in Sixteenth-Century Spain.* Cambridge: Cambridge University Press, 1995.

Eisen, Robert. *Gersonides on Providence, Covenant, and the Chosen People: A Study in Medieval Jewish Philosophy and Biblical Commentary.* Albany, NY: SUNY Press, 1995.

Faur, José. *In the Shadow of History: Jews and Conversos at the Dawn of Modernity.* Albany, NY: SUNY Press, 1992.

Feiner, Shmuel. "From Renaissance to Revolution: The Eighteenth Century in Jewish History," in *Sepharad in Ashkenaz: Medieval Knowledge and Eighteenth-Century Enlightened Jewish Discourse,* ed. Resianne Fontaine, Andrea Schatz, and Irene Zwiep, 1–10. Amsterdam: Koninklijke Nederlandse Akademie van Wetenschappen, 2007.

———. *The Jewish Enlightenment,* trans. Chaya Naor. Philadelphia: University of Pennsylvania Press, 2002.

Fisher, Benjamin. "For God and Country: Jewish Identity and the State in Seventeenth-Century Amsterdam," in *Jewish Culture in Early Modern Europe: Essays in Honor of David B. Ruderman,* ed. Richard Cohen, et al. Cincinnati and Pittsburgh: Hebrew Union College Press and University of Pittsburgh Press, 2014, 50–62.

———. "Opening the Eyes of the *Novos Reformados*: Rabbi Saul Levi

Morteira, Radical Christianity, and the Jewish Reclamation of Jesus, 1620–1660." *Studia Rosenthaliana* 44 (2012): 117–48.

———. "From Boxes and Cabinets to the Bibliotheca: Building the Jewish Library of the Ex-Conversos in Amsterdam, 1620–1665." *European Journal of Jewish Studies* 13 (2019): 43–76.

Fishman, Talya. *Shaking the Pillars of Exile: Voice of a Fool, an Early Modern Jewish Critique of Rabbinic Culture.* Stanford, CA: Stanford University Press, 1997.

———. "Changing Early Modern Jewish Discourse about Christianity: The Efforts of Rabbi Leon Modena," in *The Lion Shall Roar: Leon Modena and his World,* ed. David Malkiel, 159–94. Jerusalem: Hebrew University Magnes Press, 2003.

———. *Becoming People of the Talmud: Oral Torah as Written Tradition in Medieval Jewish Cultures.* Philadelphia: University of Pennsylvania Press, 2011.

Frijhoff, Willem and Marijke Spies. *Dutch Culture in a European Perspective. 1650: Hard-Won Unity.* Assen, The Netherlands: Royal Van Gorcum; New York: Palgrave Macmillan, 2004.

Funkenstein, Amos. *Theology and the Scientific Imagination from the Middle Ages to the Seventeenth Century.* Princeton, NJ: Princeton University Press, 2007.

Galasso, Cristina. "Religious Space, Gender, and Power in the Sephardi Diaspora: The Return to Judaism of New Christian Men and Women in Livorno and Pisa," in *Sephardi Family Life in the Early Modern Diaspora,* ed. Julia Lieberman, 101–28. Hanover and London: University Press of New England; Waltham, MA: Brandeis University Press, 2011.

Gannet, Cinthia and John Brereton, eds. *Traditions of Eloquence: The Jesuits and Modern Rhetorical Studies.* New York: Fordham University Press, 2016.

Geiger, Abraham. *Leon da Modena, Rabbiner zu Venedig (1571–1648), Seine Stellung zur Kabbalah, zum Thalmud und zum Christenthume.* Breslau, 1856.

Ginzburg, Carlo. *The Cheese and the Worms: The Cosmos of a Sixteenth Century Miller,* trans. John and Anne Tedeschi. New York: Penguin Books, 1982.

Goldish, Matt. "Hakham Jacob Sasportas and the Former Conversos." *Studia Rosenthaliana* 44 (2012): 149–72.

Grafton, Anthony and Joanna Weinberg. *I Have Always Loved the Holy Tongue: Isaac Casaubon, the Jews, and a Forgotten Chapter in Renaissance Scholarship*. Cambridge, MA and London, England: The Belknap Press of Harvard University Press, 2011.

———. *Joseph Scaliger: A Study in the History of Classical Scholarship*. Volume 2, Historical Chronology. Oxford, 1993.

———. *Defenders of the Text: The Traditions of Scholarship in an Age of Science, 1450–1800*. Cambridge, MA and London, England: Harvard University Press, 1991.

———. "Joseph Scaliger and Historical Chronology: The Rise and Fall of a Discipline." *History and Theory* 14, no. 2 (May, 1975): 156–85.

Graizbord, David. *Souls in Dispute: Converso Identities in Iberia and the Jewish Diaspora, 1580–1700*. Philadelphia: University of Pennsylvania Press, 2004.

Grendler, Paul. *Jesuit Schools and Universities in Europe, 1548–1773*. Leiden and Boston: Brill, 2018.

Hacker, Joseph. "The Intellectual Activity of the Jews of the Ottoman Empire during the Sixteenth and Seventeenth Centuries," in *Jewish Thought in the Seventeenth Century*, ed. Isadore Twersky and Bernard Septimus, 95–135. Cambridge, MA: Harvard University Press, 1987.

Halévy, Michael Studemund, ed. *Die Sefarden in Hamburg: zur Geschichte einer Minderheit. Teil 2*. Hamburg: Helmut Buske Verlag, 1997.

Hames, Harvey. "A Jew amongst Christians and Muslims: Introspection in Solomon ibn Adret's Response to Ibn Hazm." *Mediterranean Historical Review* 25, no. 2 (2010): 203–19.

Hamm, Berndt. "What Was the Reformation Doctrine of Justification?," in *The German Reformation: The Essential Readings*, ed. C. Scott Dixon, 56–90. Oxford: Blackwell Publishers, 1999.

Hassán, Iacob M., ed. *Introducción a la Biblia de Ferrara: Actas del Simposio Internacional sobre la Biblia de Ferrara*. Seville, 1992.

Hazard, Paul. *The Crisis of the European Mind: 1680–1715*. New York: NYRB Classics, 2013; 1935.

Heller, Marvin. *The Sixteenth-Century Hebrew Book: An Abridged Thesaurus.* Leiden and Boston: Brill, 2004.

Howell, Kenneth. *God's Two Books: Copernican Cosmology and Biblical Interpretation in Early Modern Science.* Notre Dame, IN: University of Notre Dame Press, 2002.

Idel, Moshe. "Kabbalah, Platonism and Prisca Theologia: The Case of R. Menasseh ben Israel," in *Menasseh ben Israel and His World,* 207–19, ed. Yosef Kaplan and Henry Méchoulan. Leiden and New York: Brill, 1989.

Ifrah, Lionel. *L'Aigle d'Amsterdam: Menasseh ben Israel 1604–1657.* Paris: Honoré Champion Éditeur, 2001.

Israel, Jonathan. *Diasporas within a Diaspora: Jews, Crypto-Jews, and the World Maritime Empires (1540–1740).* Leiden and Boston: Brill, 2002.

———. *Radical Enlightenment: Philosophy and the Making of Modernity 1650–1750.* Oxford: Oxford University Press, 2001.

———. "Grotius and the Rise of Christian 'Radical Enlightenment,' *Grotiana* 35 (2014): 19–31.

———. *The Dutch Republic: Its Rise, Greatness, and Fall. 1477–1806.* Oxford: Clarendon Press, 1995.

———. "Menasseh ben Israel and the Dutch Sephardic Colonization Movement of the Mid-Seventeenth Century (1645–1657)," in *Menasseh ben Israel and His World,* ed. Yosef Kaplan and Henry Méchoulan, 139–63. Leiden and New York: Brill, 1989.

———. "Spain and the Dutch Sephardim, 1609–1660," *Studia Rosenthaliana* 12, no. 1–2 (1978): 1–61.

Kanarfogel, Ephraim. *Jewish Education and Society in the High Middle Ages.* Detroit, MI: Wayne State University Press, 1992.

Kaplan, Yosef. "Amsterdam, the Forbidden Lands, and the Dynamics of the Sephardi Diaspora," in *The Dutch Intersection: The Jews and the Netherlands in Modern History,* ed. Yosef Kaplan, 33–62. Leiden: Brill, 2008.

———. "An Alternative Path to Modernity," in *An Alternative Path to Modernity: The Sephardi Diaspora in Western Europe,* ed. Yosef Kaplan, 1–28. Leiden and Boston: Brill, 2000.

———. "Bom Judesmo: The Western Sephardi Diaspora," in *Cultures of the Jews: A New History*, ed. David Biale. New York: Schocken Books, 2002.

———. "Sephardi Students at the University of Leiden," in *An Alternative Path to Modernity: The Sephardi Diaspora in Western Europe*, ed. Yosef Kaplan, 196–210. Leiden and Boston: Brill, 2000.

———. "The Intellectual Ferment in the Spanish-Portuguese Community of Seventeenth-Century Amsterdam," in *Moreshet Sepharad: The Sephardi Legacy*, ed. Haim Beinart, 289–314. Jerusalem: Hebrew University, 1992.

———. "Karaites in Early Eighteenth-Century Amsterdam," in *Sceptics, Millenarians, and Jews*, ed. David Katz and Jonathan Israel, 196–236. Leiden and New York: Brill, 1990.

———. *From Christianity to Judaism: The Story of Isaac Orobio de Castro*, trans. Raphael Loewe. Oxford and New York: Oxford University Press, 1989.

———. "From Apostasy to Return to Judaism: The Portuguese Jews in Amsterdam," in *Binah: Studies in Jewish History, Thought, and Culture*, ed. Joseph Dan, 199–217. New York: Praeger, 1988.

———. "Rabbi Saul Levi Morteira's Treatise 'Arguments Against the Christian Religion'," in *Studies on the History of Dutch Jewry I*, ed. Jozeph Michman, 9–31. Jerusalem, 1975.

Katz, David. "Jewish Sabbath and Christian Sunday in Early Modern England," in *Jewish Christians and Christian Jews: From the Renaissance to the Enlightenment*, ed. Richard Popkin and Gordon Weiner, 119–30. Dordrecht and Boston: Kluwer Academic Publishers, 1994.

———. "Menasseh ben Israel's Christian Connection: Henry Jessey and the Jews," in *Menasseh ben Israel and His World*, ed. Yosef Kaplan and Henry Méchoulan, 117–38. Leiden and New York: Brill, 1989.

———. *Philo-Semitism and the Readmission of the Jews to England, 1603–1655*. Oxford: Clarendon Press, 1982.

———. *Tradition and Crisis: Jewish Society at the End of the Middle Ages*. New York: Syracuse University Press, 1961.

Kellner, Menachem. "Gersonides and his Cultured Despisers: Arama and Abravanel." *Journal of Medieval and Renaissance Studies*, Volume 6 (1976): 269–96.

Kinder, Godron A. "Religious Literature as an Offensive Weapon:

Cipriano de Valera's Part in England's War with Spain." *Sixteenth Century Journal* 16, no. 2 (1988): 223–35.

———. "Juan Perez de Pineda (Pierius): A Spanish Calvinist Minister of the Gospel in Sixteenth-Century Geneva." *Bulletin of Hispanic Studies* 53 (1976): 283–300.

Kors, Alan. *Atheism in France, 1650–1729: The Orthodox Sources of Disbelief.* Princeton, NJ: Princeton University Press, 1990.

Lang, Marijke H. de. *De opkomst van de historische en literaire kritiek in de synoptische beschouwing van de evangelien van Calvijn (1555) tot Griesbach (1774).* Leiden: Brill, 1993.

Lawee, Eric. *Isaac Abarbanel's Stance Toward Tradition: Defense, Dissent, and Dialogue.* Albany, NY: SUNY Press, 2001.

Lazar, Moshe, ed. *Biblia de Ferrara.* Biblioteca Castro, 1996.

Lazarus-Yafeh, Hava. *Intertwined Worlds: Medieval Islam and Bible Criticism.* Princeton, NJ: Princeton University Press, 1992.

Leone Leoni, Aron di. *The Hebrew Portuguese Nations in Antwerp and London at the Time of Charles* V *and Henry* VIII. Jersey City, NJ: KTAV, 2005.

——— and Siegfried Herzfeld, "The *Orden de oraciones de mes arreo* (Ferrara, 1555) and a *Bakasah* composed by Abraham Usque." *Sefarad* 62 (2002): 99–124.

Levy, B. Barry. *Fixing God's Torah: The Accuracy of the Hebrew Bible Text in Jewish Law.* New York: Oxford University Press, 2001.

Lieberman, Julia. "Childhood and Family among the Western Sephardim in the Seventeenth Century," in *Sephardi Family Life in the Early Modern Diaspora,* ed. Julia Lieberman, 129–76. Hanover and London: University Press of New England; Waltham, MA: Brandeis University Press, 2011.

———. "Adolescence and the Period of Apprenticeship among Western Sephardim in the Seventeenth Century," in *El Prezente: Studies in Sephardic Culture* 4 (2010), ed. Tamar Alexander, Yaakov Bentolia, and Eliezer Papo.

———. "'Jonen Dalim,' Auto Alegórico de Miguel (Daniel Leví) de Barrios," in *From Iberia to Diaspora: Studies in Sephardic History and Culture,* ed. Yedida K. Stillman and Norman Stillman, 300–315. Leiden and Boston: Brill, 1999.

———. "Academias Literarias y de Estudios Religiosos en Amsterdam en el Siglo XVII," in *Los Judaizantes en Europa y la Literatura Castellana del Siglo de Oro,* ed. Fernando Díaz Esteban, 247–60. Madrid: Letrúmbo S.L., 1994.

———. "Educational Institutions among the Western Sephardim in the Seventeenth Century," [forthcoming].

McGrath, Alister. *Iustitia Dei: A History of the Christian Doctrine of Justification.* Cambridge: Cambridge University Press, 2005.

McKim, Donald. *Calvin and the Bible.* Cambridge: Cambridge University Press, 2004.

———. *The Westminster Handbook to Reformed Theology.* London and Leiden: Westminster John Knox Press, 2001.

Méchoulan, Henry. "Menasseh ben Israel: lecteur du docteur Juan Huarte de San Juan dans 'De la fragilidad humana' et 'Esperanza de Israel.'" *Revue des études juives* 163, no. 34 (2004): 463–74.

———. "Menasseh ben Israel," in *Moreshet Sepharad: The Sephardi Legacy,* ed. Haim Beinart, volume 2, 315–35. Jerusalem: Hebrew University Magnes Press, 1992.

———. *Hispanidad y Judaismo en Tiempos de Espinoza. Edicion de La Certeza del Camino de Abraham Pereyra.* Salamanca: Ediciones Universidad de Salamanca, 1987.

———. "Morteira et Spinoza au Carrefour du Socinianisme." *Revue des études juives* 135 (1976): 51–65.

Miert, Dirk van. *Humanism in an Age of Science: The Amsterdam Athenaeum in the Golden Age, 1632–1704,* trans. Michiel Wielema and Anthony Ossa-Richardson. Leiden: Brill, 2009.

Milikowsky, Chaim. "Seder Olam and Jewish Chronography in the Hellenistic and Roman Periods." *Proceedings of the American Academy for Jewish Research* 52 (1985): 115–39.

Miller, Peter. "The 'Antiquarianization' of Biblical Scholarship and the London Polyglot Bible (1653–57)." *Journal of the History of Ideas* 62, no. 3 (July, 2001): 463–82.

Montgomery, John Warwick. "Sixtus of Siena and Roman Catholic Biblical Scholarship in the Reformation Period." *Archiv fur Reformationsgeschichte* 54 (1963): 214–34.

Mortimer, Sarah. *Reason and Religion in the English Revolution: The*

Challenge of Socinianism. Cambridge: Cambridge University Press, 2010.

Muller, Richard. *Post-Reformation Reformed Dogmatics: The Rise and Development of Reformed Orthodoxy, ca. 1520–1725*. Volume 2, Holy Scripture. Ada, MI: Baker Academic, 2003.

———. *After Calvin: Studies in the Development of a Theological Tradition*. New York and Oxford: Oxford University Press, 2003.

Mulsow, Martin and Jan Rohls, eds. *Socinianism and Arminianism: Antitrinitarians, Calvinists, and Cultural Exchange in Seventeenth-Century Europe*. Leiden and Boston: Brill, 2005.

Nadler, Steven, ed. *Spinoza and Medieval Jewish Philosophy*. Cambridge: Cambridge University Press, 2014.

———. *A Book Forged in Hell: Spinoza's Scandalous Treatise and the Birth of the Secular Age*. Princeton, NJ: Princeton University Press, 2011.

———. *Spinoza's Heresy: Immortality and the Jewish Mind*. Oxford: Clarendon Press, 2001.

———. *Spinoza: A Life*. Cambridge and New York: Cambridge University Press, 1999.

Nyden-Bullock, Tammy. *Spinoza's Radical Cartesian Mind*. New York: Continuum Studies in Philosophy, 2010.

———. "Radical Cartesian Politics: Velthuysen, De la Court, and Spinoza," in *Studia Spinozana,* ed. Wiep van Bunge. Volume 15 (1999): 35–67

Offenberg, A.K., "Dirk van Santen and the Keur Bible: New Insights into Jacob Judah (Arye) Leon Templo's Model Temple." *Studia Rosenthaliana* 37 (2004): 401–22.

———. "Spinoza's Library. The Story of a Reconstruction," *Quaerendo,* vol. 3, Issue 4 (1973): 309–21.

———. "Jacob Jehuda Leon (1602–1675) and His Model of the Temple," in *Jewish-Christian Relations in the Seventeenth Century: Studies and Documents,* ed. J. van den Berg and Ernestine van der Wall, 95–115. Dordrecht: Kluwer Academic Publishers, 1988.

Orfali, Moisés. ed., trans. *Nomologia o discursos legales* [Hebrew]. Jerusalem: Mekhon Ben Tsevi, 1997.

Parente, Fausto. "Quelques contributions à propos de la biographie de Sixte de Sienne et de sa (prétendue) culture juive," in *Les juifs et l'église romaine à l'époque moderne*, ed. Fausto Parente, 205–32. Paris: Honoré Champion, 2007.

Parente, Ulderico. "Sul preteso giudaismo di fra Sisto da Siena davanti all'Inquisizione Romana (1551–1553)." *Le inquisizioni cristiane e gli ebrei* (2003): 375–405.

Pavur, Claude SJ., ed., trans. *The Ratio Studiorum: The Official Plan for Jesuit Education.* St Louis, MO: The Institute of Jesuit Sources, 2005.

Penkower, Jordan. "New Perspectives on Sefer Massoret ha-Massoret of Elijah Levita. The Lateness of the Vowel Points and Criticism of the Zohar." *Italia* 8 (1989): 7–73.

———. "Ya'akov ben Hayim u-tsemihat mahadurat ha-mikra'ot ha-gedolot." 2 volumes. PhD Dissertation, Hebrew University of Jerusalem, 1982.

Popkin, Richard. "Can One Be a True Christian and a Faithful Follower of the Law of Moses? The Answer of John Dury," in *Secret Conversions to Judaism in Early Modern Europe*, ed. Martin Mulsow and Richard Popkin, 33–50. Leiden and Boston: Brill, 2004.

———. *Isaac La Peyrère: His Life, Work, and Influence (1596–1676).* Leiden and New York, Brill, 1987.

Rauschenbach, Sina. "Mediating Jewish Knowledge: Menasseh ben Israel and the Christian *Respublica literraria.*" *The Jewish Quarterly Review*, vol. 102, no. 4 (Fall 2012): 561–588.

———. *Judentum Für Christen: Vermittlung und Selbstbehauptung Menasseh ben Israels in den gelehrten Debatten des 17. Jahrhunderts.* Berlin and Boston: De Gruyter, 2012.

Ravid, Benjamin. "'Contra Judeos' in Seventeenth-Century Italy: Two Responses to the 'Discorso' of Simone Luzzatto by Melchiore Palontrotti and Giulio Morosini," *AJS Review* 7/8 (1982/1983): 301–351.

Revah, I.S. *Spinoza et le Dr. Juan de Prado.* Paris, 1959.

Rooden, Peter T. van. *Theology, Biblical Scholarship, and Rabbinical Studies in the Seventeenth Century. Constantijn L'Empereur (1591–1648), Professor of Hebrew and Theology at Leiden.* Leiden: Brill, 1989.

Rosen, Edward. "Was Copernicus' Revolutions Approved by the Pope?" *Journal of the History of Ideas* 36, no. 3 (July-Sept, 1975): 531–33.

Rosenblatt, Jason. *Renaissance England's Chief Rabbi: John Selden*. New York and Oxford: Oxford University Press, 2006.

Rosenbloom, Noah. "Discreet Theological Polemics in Menasseh ben Israel's Conciliador." *Proceedings of the American Academy for Jewish Research* 58 (1992): 143–91.

Roth, Cecil. *A Life of Menasseh ben Israel: Rabbi, Printer, Diplomat*. Philadelphia, PA: The Jewish Publication Society of America, 1934.

Rudavsky, Tamar. "Galileo and Spinoza: Heroes, Heretics, and Hermeneutics." *Journal of the History of Ideas*, vol. 62, no. 4 (October, 2001): 611–31.

Ruderman, David. "The Impact of Early Modern Jewish Thought on the Eighteenth Century: A Challenge to the Notion of the Sephardi Mystique," in *Sepharad in Ashkenaz: Medieval Knowledge and Eighteenth-Century Enlightened Jewish Discourse*, ed. Resianne Fontaine, Andrea Schatz, and Irene Zwiep, 11–22. Amsterdam: Koninklijke Nederlandse Akademie van Wetenschappen, 2007.

———. *Jewish Enlightenment in an English Key: Anglo-Jewry's Construction of Modern Jewish Thought*. Princeton and Oxford: Princeton University Press, 2000.

———. *Jewish Thought and Scientific Discovery in Early Modern Europe*. New Haven, CT and London: Yale University Press, 1995.

Salomon, H.P. "Did Saul Levi Mortera Plagiarize Joseph Albo?" *Studia Rosenthaliana*, vol. 23, no. 1 (1989): 28–37.

Sánchez, Carlos José Hernando. "La cultura nobiliara en el virreinato de Nápoles durante el sigolo XVI." *Historia Social* 28 (1997): 95–112.

Saraiva, António José. *The Marrano Factory: The Portuguese Inquisition and its New Christians, 1536–1765*, ed. and trans. H.P. Salomon and I.S.D. Sassoon. Leiden and Boston: Brill, 1991.

Saperstein, Marc. *Exile in Amsterdam: Saul Levi Morteira's Sermons to a Congregation of New Jews*. Cincinnati, OH: Hebrew Union College Press, 2005.

———. "Christianity, Christians, and "New Christians" in the Sermons of Saul Levi Morteira." *Hebrew Union College Annual* 70–71 (1999–2000): 339–43.

———. "Saul Levi Morteira's Treatise on the Immortality of the Soul." *Studia Rosenthaliana* 25, no. 2 (1991): 131–48.

Saraiva, Antonio José. "Antonio Vieira, Menasseh ben Israel, et le cinquieme empire." *Studia Rosenthaliana* 6 (1972): 25–57.

Sasson, Haim Hillel ben. "Jews and Christian Sectarians: Existential Similarities and Dialectical Tensions in 16th-Century Moravia and Poland-Lithuania." *Viator* 4 (1973): 369–85.

———. "The Reformation in Contemporary Jewish Eyes." *Proceedings of the Israel Academy of Sciences and Humanities*, vol. 4, 1969–1970 (Jerusalem, 1971): 239–327.

———. "Jewish-Christian Disputation in the Setting of Humanism and the Reformation in the German Empire." *Harvard Theological Review* 59, no. 4 (1966): 369–90.

Scholberg, Kenneth. "Miguel de Barrios and the Amsterdam Sephardic Community." *The Jewish Quarterly Review* 53, no. 2 (October, 1962): 120–59.

Scholem, Gershom. *Sabbatai Sevi: The Mystical Messiah, 1626–1627*. Princeton, NJ: Princeton University Press, 1973.

Sclar, David. "Books in the Ets Haim Yeshivah: Acquisition, Publishing, and a Community of Scholarship in Eighteenth-Century Amsterdam." *Jewish History* 30 (2016): 207–32.

Sheehan, Jonathan. *The Enlightenment Bible: Translation, Scholarship, and Culture*. Princeton and Oxford: Princeton University Press, 2005.

Shuger, Debora Kuller. *The Renaissance Bible: Scholarship, Sacrifice, and Subjectivity*. Berkeley: University of California Press, 1994.

Simonsohn, S., ed. *Magen va-herev*. Jerusalem, 1960.

Sorkin, David. *Moses Mendelssohn and the Religious Enlightenment*. Berkeley: University of California Press, 1996.

Spoelder, J. *Prijsboeken op de Latijnse School. Een studie naar het verschijnsel prijsuitreiking en prijsboek op e Latijnse scholen in de Noordelijke Nederlanden, ca. 1585–1876*. Amsterdam and Maarssen: Apa-Holland Universiteits Press, 2000.

Stampfer, Shaul. "Ḥeder Study, Torah, and Social Stratification," in *Families, Rabbis, and Education: Traditional Jewish Society in Nineteenth-Century Eastern Europe*, ed. Shaul Stampfer, 145–66. Oxford, 2010.

Starr-Lebeau, Gretchen. *In the Shadow of the Virgin: Inquisitors, Friars, and Conversos in Guadalupe, Spain*. Princeton, NJ: Princeton University Press, 2003.

Swetschinski, Daniel. *Reluctant Cosmopolitans: The Portuguese Jews of Seventeenth-Century Amsterdam*. London: The Littman Library of Jewish Civilization, 2000.

Talmage, Frank. "Keep Your Sons from Scripture: The Bible in Medieval Jewish Scholarship and Spirituality," in *Apples of Gold in Settings of Silver: Studies in Medieval Jewish Exegesis and Polemic*, ed. Barry Dov Walfish, 151–71. Toronto: Pontifical Institute for Medieval Studies, 1999.

———, ed. *The Polemical Writings of Profiat Duran: The Reproach of the Gentiles and 'Be not like unto thy fathers.'* [Hebrew] Jerusalem: Zalman Shazar Center and Dinur Center, 1981.

Teller, Adam. "The Laicization of Early Modern Jewish Society: The Development of the Polish Communal Rabbinate in the Sixteenth Century," in *Schoepferische Momente des europaische Judentums in der fruhen Neuzeit*, ed. Michael Graetz, 333–49. Heidelberg: C. Winter, 2000.

Touber, Jetze. *Spinoza and Biblical Philology in the Dutch Republic, 1660–1710*. Oxford: Oxford University Press, 2018.

Turniansky, Chava. "La pedagogia dell'insegnamento della Bibbia nell'Europa orientale," in *La lettura ebraica delle scritture*, ed. Sergio Garcia, 329–47. Bologna, 1995.

Van der Wall, Ernestine G.E. "Petrus Serrarius and Menasseh ben Israel: Christian Millenarianism and Jewish Messianism in Seventeenth-Century Amsterdam," in *Menasseh ben Israel and His World*, ed. Yosef Kaplan and Henry Méchoulan, 164–90. Leiden and New York: Brill, 1989.

Vermij, Rienk. *The Calvinist Copernicans: The Reception of the New Astronomy in the Dutch Republic, 1575–1750*. Amsterdam: Edita, 2002.

Voet, Leon. *The Plantin Press (1555–1589): A Bibliography of the Works Printed and Published by Christopher Plantin at Antwerp and Leiden*. 6 volumes. Amsterdam: Van Hoeve, 1980–1983.

———. *The Golden Compasses: A History and Evaluation of the Printing and Publishing Activities of the Officina Plantiana at Antwerp*. 2 volumes. Amsterdam: Van Hoeve, 1969–1972.

Volpi, Caterina, ed. *Le imagini degli dèi di Vincenzo Cartari*. Edizioni de Luca, 1996.

Weinberg, Joanna. *Azariah de Rossi's Observations on the Syriac New Testament: A Critique of the Vulgate by a Sixteenth-Century Jew*. London, Turin: Warburg Institute Studies and Texts, 2005.

Wilke, Carsten. "Questions d'un Prêtre de Rouen à un Rabbin d'Amsterdam: La reception multilingue et multiconfessionnelle d'un écrit clandestine de Saül Lévi Mortera," in *La letter clandestine: revue d'information sur la littérature clandestine de l'âge classique*, no. 27 (2019): 141–69.

Wilkinson, Robert J. "Emmanuel Tremellius' 1569 Edition of the Syriac New Testament." *Journal of Ecclesiastical History*, vol. 58, no. 1 (January, 2007): 9–25.

———. "Azariah de' Rossi and the Forgeries of Annius of Viterbo," in *Associazione Italiana per lo Studio del Giudaismo: Atti del Congresso IV*, ed. Fausto Parente and Daniela Piattelli, 23–47. Rome, 1987.

Woolf, Jeffrey. "Some Polemical Emphases in the 'Sefer Miswot Gadol.'" *The Jewish Quarterly Review* 89, no. 1–2 (1998): 81–100.

Yerushalmi, Yosef Hayim, *From Spanish Court to Italian Ghetto. Isaac Cardoso: A Study in Seventeenth-Century Marranism and Jewish Apologetics*. Seattle and London: University of Washington Press, 1981.

———. *The Re-education of Marranos in the Seventeenth Century*. Cincinnati, OH: University of Cincinnati Press, 1980.

Yovel, Yirmiyahu. *Spinoza and Other Heretics. The Marrano of Reason*. Princeton, NJ: Princeton University Press, 1989.

Index

1 Timothy 3:16, 194

Abas, R. Selomoh, 91
Abendana de Britto, Isaac Hayim, 58n100
Aboab da Fonseca, Isaac, 3, 7–8, 42n53, 43n57, 44, 57–58, 63, 76; *Parafrasis comentado sobre el Pentateuco* (Paraphrased commentary upon the Pentateuch), 7
Aboab, Imanuel: *Nomologia o discursos legales*, 136
Aboab, Isaac: *Menorat ha-Ma'or*, 61
Aboab, Samuel, 64: *Sefer ha-zikhronot*, 63
Abraham ben Mordecai Jaffe: *Levushim*, 57
Abram (Bible), 251
Abravanel, Isaac, 11, 14, 136, 146–47, 149–54, 161; *Commentary on Early Prophets*, 160; *Ma'ayanei ha-yeshua* (Wells of Salvation), 202n94
Abravanel, Samuel, 56–58
Aby Yetomim Confraternity, 36n28, 71
Academia, 89
Active Intellect, 146–47. *See also* Agent Intellect *and* Separate Intellects.
Acts: 10:9, 113; 15:28–29, 183; 21:21–26, 186n52
Adam (Bible), 95, 182, 187, 194
Adonis: *Festas de Adonis* (Festivals of Adonis), 231–32. See also Tammuz.
Adret, R. Solomon ibn (Rashba): *Ma'amar al Yishmael* (Treatise against Ishmael), 134, 135n27
Adultery, 181–83, 182n40
Agarimede, 228
Agent Intellect, 146–47. *See also* Active Intellect *and* Separate Intellects.
Ahab (Bible), 162, 163n99
Ahaziah of Judah (Bible), 162n97, 163n99
Ahaziahu of Israel (Bible), 162–63
Albert, Anne Oravetz, 41, 41n53
Aldabi, Meir: *Sefer Shevile Emunah* [Paths of Faith], 260n17
Alexander, 212
Alexandre de Rhodes, 245
Alfonso II d'Este, 226
Almosnino, Moses, 149
al-Tabari, Abu Ja'far Muhammad ibn Jarir, 134n21
Altaras, Moses: *Libro de Mantenimiento de la Alma* (Book on the care of the soul), 10
Amon (god), 212

Amonites, 153
Amorites, 126, 150
Amos, king of Judah (Bible), 158
Amstel, 28, 112
Amsterdam Athenium, 148
Anabaptists, 238, 240
Annius of Viterbo, 234n85
Anno mundi, 15
Anticlericalism, 96, 98
Antilles, 244
Antioch, 112–14, 238
Antitrinitarianism, 168, 170n4, 192–94, 213, 257
Anubis, 229
Apis, Egyptian cult of, 229–32
Apocrypha, 179–80, 236, 240
Apollo, 212
Apostles, 13, 113, 195, 198, 211, 215
Appiano, Pietro, 227
Arabic, 13
Arama, Isaac, 146–49
Aramaic, 8, 9, 13 43n57, 55, 60, 67, 142n45, 258
Archimedes, 144
Aretin (Pietro Aretino), 245
Argives, 231
Aristotelian theologians, 245–46
Aristotle: metaphysics, 146
Ark of the Covenant, 7
Arminians, 16, 122–23, 142
Arminius, Jacob, 88n5, 122, 193
Ars moriendi (the art of dying), 95, 96n25
Asa, King of Judah (Bible), 157–58
Ashkenazi Judaism, 51, 59, 62–63, 198; pietists, 60
Ashkenazi, Eliezer, 12, 136
Astronomy, 17, 143–44, 148
Atheism, 107–9, 248; history of, 244–46
Athens, 231–32
Atias, Yomtob: *Libro de Oracyones de Todo el año* [Book of Prayers for the Whole Year], 35n28
Atonement, 257
Athias, David Israel, 58n100
Athias, Isaac: *Fortificaccion de la ley de Moseh* [Strengthening of the Law of Moses], 88–89, 123; *Thesoro de preceptos* [Treasury of Precepts], 9
Auricular confession, 221, 237

b. Pesaḥim, 57–58, 223
b. Sanhedrin, 57, 221–22, 224; 99a, 184n47
Ba'ale Tesubah, 65
Baasha, son of Ahijah (Bible), 157
Babylon, 134, 221, 254; Temple of Babylonia, 230–31
Bacchus (god), 228
Baptism, 95
Barcelona, 234
Barnabas (Apostle), 113
Baronio, Cesare, 15, 207, 213–14, 216n25, 217
Barrios, Daniel Levi de, 50, 65, 67–68, 70n137, 70–71, 76, 79, 89, 91, 123, 247, 264; *Triumpho del govierno popular* (Triumph of Popular Government), 65
Baruch, Abraham, 44, 54–56, 58
Basel, 67, 122, 177
Bass, Shabbetai, 44n63, 51–56, 59, 61–63; *Sifte Yeshenim*, 51
Belillos, Daniel, 56–58, 70–71
Bellarmine, Cardinal Robert, 17, 141–42, 214, 217
Belmonte, Mosseh (Moses ben Benjamin), 65, 72
Ben-Sasson, Haim Hillel, 170n4
Berger, David, 169n2

Berkovitz, Jay, 275–76
Berlin Haskalah, 277
Berns, Andrew: *The Bible and Natural Philosophy in Renaissance Italy*, 11
Berr, Michel, 276
Beth Israel Congregation, 32
Beth Jacob Congregation, 31–33, 35, 36n28, 54, 172, 201, 248
Beth Joseph, 53
Beza, Theodor, 122
Bible of Alcalá, 12
Bible of Antwerp, 12
Bible of London, 12
Bible of Paris, 12
Biblical scholarship: aura of perfection, 270; authority of Bible, 100, 125, 127–28, 131–32, 141, 144–45, 147, 158, 165, 200, 208, 236, 262, 267, 279; authorship of biblical texts, 11, 144, 205, 250–51; biblical contradictions, 26, 135–37, 139–44, 149, 156; biblical (in)fallibility, 16–17, 20–21, 25, 131, 133, 136–37, 139–44, 151–58, 267, 270, 279; chronological inconsistencies, 148–57, 160–63, 165, 251, 270; controversy over antiquity of the vowel points, 99n36, 213n17; critique of biblical chronology, 15; exegesis, 185, 209; exegesis for a Jewish reading public, 243; history of transmission, 166; (im)perfect transmission of text, 85, 100, 133–35, 141–42; implications of scientific discoveries, 268; mathematical contradictions in Bible, 127–28, 131–33, 155, 158, 267; naturalization of miracles, 258; origins of, 249–50; unreliability of prophetic knowledge, 125
Biet, Antoine, 244
Bishops of Asia, 236
Bodian, Miriam, 29, 34n24, 42, 95n21, 96n25, 171, 174
Boethusians, 211
Bonfil, Robert, 41
Book of the Apocalypse, 241–42. *See also* John (Book).
Boreel, Adam, 202
Brabourne, Theophilius, 201
Brazil, 36, 244
Breuer, Edward, 275n42
Brun, Antoine, 1
Bucer, Martin, 121, 123, 162; commentaries on the Synoptic Gospels, 137
Burgales, Francisco de Enzinas: 1542 translation of the New Testament, 177
Burnett, Stephen, 56
Buxtorf, Johannes, 67, 142, 164, 258; *Mikra Gedolah*, 67

Cahanet, Sara, 37
Cahen, Samuel, 276
Calcagnini, Celio, 227
Calvin, John, 87, 98, 114–15, 120, 122–23, 188, 196, 215–20, 222–23, 225; commentary on Ezekiel, 231; *Commentary on the harmony of the three Evangelists: Matthew, Mark, and Luke*, 137, 215; *Harmony of the Gospels*, 222; *Institutes of the Christian Religion*, 97, 164, 179, 196
Calvinism, 16–17, 95, 122–23, 178, 189, 192, 196, 269; theology of, 188, 194
Cameron, John, 100–101
Camus, Jean Pierre, 75
Canaanites, 251
Cape Bréton, 244

Cappel, Louis: *Arcanum punctationis revelatum*, 142n45
Cardoso, Fernando (Isaac), 29n5, 64, 95n21, 233–34
Cartari, Vincenzo, 228, 243; *Le imagini con la spositione de I dei de gli antichi*, 226–27, 229, 230–32
Cartesianism, 138n34; in the Netherlands, 255–56; philosophy, 256; theologians, 245–46
Carthage, 257
Casaubon, Isaac, 13, 207, 214, 216n25, 217
Castille, 151
Catholicism, 13, 16–17, 27–28, 47, 96–99, 103, 178–79, 192, 199–201, 206, 269; Iberian, 95; origins of, 213; the Pope, 179, 189, 213, 233–34; Roman, 99, 103, 192, 199, 234; rituals, 28; salvation, 95, 112, 265; soteriology of, 97; Spanish, 96; theological values of, 75; understanding of sacraments, 14
Cephas (Peter), 112–15, 222, 238; Epistles of, 173
Charles I (King), 200
Cherubs, 7
China (antiquity), 254
Christian Hebraists, 11
Christianity, 4, 14, 22–23, 74–75, 96, 167–72, 180, 187–88, 209; historical analysis of texts, 225; in Jewish idiom, 124; interpretations of Matthew 27:9, 213; justification, 20, 114–18, 120–21; messianic, 201–2; pagan roots of, 229–30, 232; passion and death, 191, 194, 229–30, 232; radical, 194; role of Bible, 25, 85; role of saints, 95; salvation in, 111, 264–65; theology of, 185, 210, 220; valorization of poverty, 75
Chronicles, Books of: 2 Chronicles, 157, 163; 4:2, 144; 16, 158; 16:1, 157; 22:2, 163
Cicero: *Orationes*, 47; *Pro Milone*, 47
Circumcision, 95n21, 99, 103–4, 217–18
Cisneros, Diego de, 112, 173
Cisneros, Francisco Ximenes de, 177. See also Complutensian Bible.
Claudio Nero, 242
Clement of Alexandria, 232, 239n100
Clement VIII: Bible of 1592, 13
Cocceijus, Johannes: *Judaicarum Responsionum et Quaestionum Consideratio* (A Consideration of the Jewish Answers and Questions), 173n14
Colerus, 255
Complutensian Bible, 177–78. *See also* Ximenez, Francisco.
Confession, 95
Confucianism, 245
Congregation of Christian Doctrine, 246
Constantinople, 5
Conversos, 2, 4, 6–7, 9–10, 18–19, 22–23, 26, 28–29, 80–83, 87–89, 94–98, 111–12, 120, 128, 130n16, 137, 165, 168–69, 171–72, 174, 176–77, 179, 185, 187, 206, 227, 247, 249, 255n5, 263–65, 268, 271–72, 277, 278n49, 279; Christian–Jewish integration, 3–4, 10, 18, 64, 73, 178, 185, 188, 198–99; education of, 42, 264; skepticism of science, 277
Copernicus, 15, 17, 127, 143–45;

defense of Copernican system, 257
Cordier, Mathurin: *Colloquiorum scholasticorum libri quatuor,* 47
Cordoba, 133
Cos Hillel, 223
Costa, Uriel da, 19–20, 27–28, 34, 82, 87, 96, 107, 110, 123, 129, 130n16 165; *Examination of Pharisaic Traditions,* 105–6, 130n16; excommunication from Hamburg and Venice, 104; *Exemplar Humanae Vitae,* 27, 104, 106
Council of Trent, 13
Count-Duke of Olivares, 6
Crell, Johannes, 194; *De Uno Patre,* 193
Cremonius (Cesare Cremonini), 245
Crescas, Hasdai, 146
Cromwell, Oliver, 200
Crucifixion, 210, 257; chronology of, 216n25; Roman practices of, 225
Crusades, the, 60
Crypto-Jews, 28, 95, 277n48
Cudworth, Ralph: *True Intellectual System of the Universe,* 245
Curcellaeus, Stephanus, 194
Cyril (of Alexandria), 240n100
d'Aguilar, Moshe Raphael, 2, 49, 56–58, 77–78, 174n16; *Tratado da immortalidade da alma,* 79n159; *Tratado de la retórica divide en ocho libros que cology de los megores autores griegos y latinos,* 79n159
Daniel de Breen: *Amica Disputatio adversus Iudaeos continens Examen scripti judaici e lusitanico in latinum versi et responsum ad quaestiones inibi christianis propositas* (A Friendly Disputation Against the Jews, Containing an Analysis of Jewish Texts Translated from Portuguese into Latin, and a Response to the Questions Therein Posed to the Christians), 173n14
David (Bible), 109–10, 161, 197
De la Court, Johan, 256
De la Court, Pieter, 256
De Lang, Marijke H., 137n32, 138
De Vera Religione, 193
de' Rossi, Azariah, 12, 14–15, 149–50, 156–58, 234n85; *The Light of the Eyes,* 150, 156, 159–60.
Deborah (Bible), 154
Decalogue. *See* Ten Commandments.
Decius Mundus, 228–29. *See also* Anubis *and* Paulina.
Delmedigo, Joseph: *Sefer Elim,* 148, 258
den Boer, Harm, 6, 62, 176
"*Derasiot,*" 76–77
Descartes, René, 126, 138, 255–56; *La Géométrie,* 255; *Meditationes de prima philosophia,* 255; *Principia Philosophica,* 255
Deuteronomy, 251; 4:2, 74, 195n70; 10:2, 102; 10:4, 102; 13:1, 74, 76, 195n70; 15–25, 117; 15:19, 222
Dias Fatto, Benjamin ben Jacob, 72
Dikduk Rashi, 53
Divine law, 222, 269
Divorce, 181–82
Domitian (Emperor), 242
Donin, Nicholas, 135
Drusius, Johannes, 97

du Tertre, Jean-Baptiste, 244
Duke of Lerma, 5
Dunn, James, 113
Duran, Profet, 92–93, 119–20, 169, 186, 188, 197n77, 209, 211–12, 225; *Kelimat ha-goyyim* (Reproach of the Gentiles), 185, 210; *Sefer Ma'aseh Efod*, 92, 94
Duran, Shimon ben Zemah, 120, 134, 169, 186, 188, 209–12, 225; *Keshet u-magen* (Bow and Shield), 135, 185, 210–11

Early modern science, 256
Ebionites, 236
Ebreo, Leon: *Dialoghi d'Amore*, 258
Ecclesiastes, 261; 4:1–2, 109; 11:9, 109; 12:7, 109
Ecker-Rozinger, Neta, 12
Eden. *See* Garden of Eden.
Edward VI, 200
Edwards, James R., 240n100
Egypt (antiquity), 12, 23, 150, 153, 161, 212, 226, 229–30, 232, 254, 258; idolatry in, 232
Ehud (Bible), 154
Eire, Carlos, 95
Elah, son of Baasha (Bible), 157
Elizabeth (Queen of England), 200
England, 178, 200, 202, 272, 276, 279; biblical orientation of English Jews, 272–73; Christian movements of, 199; Civil War, 200; "Englishing" of Jewish culture, 272; readmission of Jews, 278; under Cromwell, 201
Ephesus, 235, 242
Epiphanius, 240
Episcopius, Simon, 142–43, 194; "Apology for the Remonstrant Confession of Faith," 193
Epistles, 232
Erasmus, 213; *Annotations upon the New Testament*, 97; *Formulae familliaries*, 47
Esdras, Books of, 241
Espinosa, Michel de, 248. *See also* Spinoza, Benedict.
Essenes, 211
Estense family, 226. *See also* Alfonso II d'Este.
Eternal generation, 194
Eternal reward and punishment, 87, 106, 265n24
Ethiopic, 13
Ets Haim Confraternity, 37, 46, 58n100; library of, 174
Eucharist, 95, 179; incorrect conclusions on nature of, 223; Jesus's pronouncement on, 210
Europa (Greek myth), 228
Eusebius, 240n100, 241, 243; *Chronicon*, 238, 242; *Historia Eclesiastica*, 239
Evangelistarum quaternion, 137
Eve (Bible), 182
Ex-conversos. *See* conversos.
Exodus from Egypt, timeline of, 150–55, 161
Exodus, 139, 141; 10:16, 111; 12:15, 136; 12:16, 198, 219; 12:19, 136; 13:6, 135; 16:31, 134; 16:35, 141; 34:27–28, 102;
Ezekiel (Book), 262
Ezekiel (Prophet), 230, 231–32, 261
Ezra the Scribe, 134, 160–61, 262

Faro, Joshua, 57
Faur, José, 277
Faustus the Manichaean, 238

Feiner, Shmuel, 274, 276, 278
Ferdinand (King of Spain), 4
Ferrara Bible (1553), 6, 56, 62n112, 71, 176
Ferrer, Vincente: Valencian Bible, 177
Festival of Weeks, 220n37
Fifth Lateran Council, 15
Fisher, Samuel, 199
Fishman, Talya, 94, 169n2
Five Scrolls (Megillot), 63
Fonte di peccato (source of sin), 187
Fraenkel, Carlos, 259
France, 198, 201, 244, 246, 275, 279; biblically focused Jewish education in, 276; Jewish emphasis on morality in education in, 275–276; King of, 201; translation of Bible, 276
French Guyana, 244
Funkenstein, Amos, 126

Gabbai, 33–34, 38–39, 43, 48
Gaffarel, Jacques, 234
Galasso, Cristina, 46n67
Galatians, 121, 264; 2:11–17, 112; 2:16, 87–88, 115–16, 3, 120; 3:10, 111, 117
Galileo, 17, 126–27, 143, 145, 148; *Il Saggiatore*, 144
Gaon, Sa'adia, 149
Garden of Eden, 185n47
Geiger, Abraham, 104
Gemara, 46, 53
Gemilut Hasadim [Society for the Performance of Charitable Acts], 65–69, 71
Genébrard, Gilbert, 234
Genesis, 15, 136n29, 235; 12:6, 251
Geneva, 122, 178, 244
Geonim, 50
Germany, 25, 55, 202, 277–79; biblically focused Jewish education in, 274–75
Gershon, Levi ben (Gersonides), 136, 145–46, 149, 153; rationalism of, 147
Ginzburg, Carlo, 233
Giraldi, Lilio Gregorio: *De Deis Gentium*, 227
Givat Sha'ul, 72–73
Góis, Damão de, 4
Goldish, Matt, 81
Gomes, Rabbi Jacob, 38n45, 44
Gospels, 7, 22–23, 107n58, 137–38, 169, 173, 190–92, 194, 210, 215–16, 218–21, 223–24, 232, 236, 238, 242–43, 248, 268, 270; authenticity of, 241; criticism of, 192; divinity of, 195, 206; non-canonical Gospel of the Egyptians, 232n81; non-canonical Gospel of the Hebrews, 239n100; origins of, 208
Grafton, Anthony, 126, 169
Greco-Roman world, 210, 232, 245, 254; impregnation of women by gods, 228; influence on Christianity, 226; popularization of antiquities, 227; religious practices of, 208;
Greek, 12, 45, 47–48, 190, 232, 235, 239, 241, 254, 256; manuscripts in, 239
Gregorian reform of 1582, 15
Grotius, Hugo, 13, 24, 48, 142, 164, 188, 213–14, 225; *Annotationes ad Novum Testamentum*, 194; *De satisfaction Christi*, 257–58

Hagigah 2:3, 220
Hague, the, 253
Hakdamot, 152n73

Halakhah, 9, 19, 53, 58, 61, 65, 81–84, 216–17
Halevy, Moses Uri, 31
Hamburg, 35, 80–81, 103–4
Hananiah, 261
Harvey, Warren Zev, 259
Hazard, Paul, 125
Hebrew, 12, 172
Heders, 59–60
Hegesippus, 240n100
Heliocentric universe, 127, 145, 147–48, 267
Henry VIII, 200
Herera, Abraham Cohen, 37
Heresy (Heretics), 147, 233, 236, 255
Herod (the Great), 241
Heshbon, 150–52
Hezekiah (Bible), 156, 158
Hilary, 239
Hiram (Bible), 128
Hiskia (Bible), 261. *See also* Hezekiah.
Historiography, 207, 213, 223; as a weapon, 271; humanist, 208; new method of, 209, 246–47, 252
Hobbes, Thomas, 164; *De Cive*, 256
Holy Spirit, 211–12, 221, 228–29
Honen Dalim, 3, 65–69, 91
Hoornbeeck, Johannes: *Socinianismus confutatus*, 143
Horowitz, Isaiah, 49
Horowitz, Shabbetai Sheftel, 50–51, 53–54, 59, 61, 63; *Sefer Vave ha-Amudim*, 49; *Vave ha-Amudim*, 52
Hoshea (Prophet), 156, 158

ibn Ezra, Abraham, 97, 136, 251
ibn Hazm, Abu Muhammad 'Ali ibn Ahmad, 133–34, 135n27
ibn Kammuna, 134
ibn Qutayba, Abu Muhammad 'Abd Allah ibn Muslim, 134n21
ibn Tahir al-Maqdisi, Abu Nasr Mutahhar b., 134n21
Immortality of the soul, 9n25 104–6, 108–9, 266n24; in the Bible, 109
Imposta board, 33
Incarnation, 97, 100, 191
"Incident at Antioch," 113–14
Irenaeus, 243; *Adversus haereses*, 238
Isabella (Princess), 4
Isaiah (Book), 86; 38:7–8, 146; 64:3, 184
Isaiah (Prophet), 76, 184
Isis (god), 228–29
Islam, 96; anti-Jewish polemics, 134n21
Isle of Patmos, 235, 242
Israel, Jonathan, 36, 127, 255–56
Israel, Kingdom (Land) of, 104, 155–59, 202, 231–32
Istanbul, 273
Italy, 11–12, 31, 41, 45, 61, 64, 189; Inquisition in Naples and Rome, 237; Talmud Torah schools in, 61

Jackson, Hamlet, 199
Jacob ben Hayyim ibn Adoniyah: 1525 Rabbinic Bible, 11
Jahaz, 150
James (Epistles), 173; 121: 2:14, 118, 121–22; 2:26, 119
James I (King), 200
Jehoram, son of Ahab (Bible), 162
Jehoshaphat (Bible), 162
Jephthah (Bible), 150–54
Jeremiah (Prophet), 213n18, 214
Jeroboam (Bible), 156

Jerome, 159, 232, 239, 243; *De viris illustribus*, 242; *Dialogi contra Pelagianos*, 239
Jerusalem, 6, 163, 202, 222, 240
Jessey, Henry, 201
Jesuit schools, 44, 45n65, 46
Jesus, 13–15, 23, 87, 100, 113, 116, 119–20, 122, 158, 168–71, 173, 181–86, 189–90, 192, 194–97, 208–12, 214–17, 219, 221–26, 235, 237, 240, 243, 247, 257; and adulterous woman in Pharisaic courts, 239, 240n100; crucifixion, 257; defense of sacrifice, 257; divinity of, 22, 192–94, 233; execution of, 214, 224, 229; historical understanding of, 220; in Roman world, 227; Jewish polemic against, 26; Jewish reclamation of, 170–71, 174–75, 188, 198, 203, 269; rejection of Jewish culpability in death of, 14n41, 224; sweating blood narrative, 238–39; turning the other cheek, 181n37
Jewish-Christian *rapprochement*, 170n4, 185–87, 189, 192, 198, 201–3, 206, 269, 272; in Amsterdam, 199
John (Apostle), 216–17, 239, 241–42
John (Book), 173, 190, 236, 240, 242; 1:1, 235; 7–8, 240; 8:1–11, 239; 19:31, 215, 224; 20:23, 221; authenticity of, 240; origins of, 235. *See also* Book of the Apocalypse.
John the Presbyter, 241–42
Joram (Bible), 162–63
Joseph (New Testament), 228
Joseph de Faro, 44, 77
Joseph Senior Coronel, 89
Josephus, 228–29, 234n85, 240–41, 243, 250; *Jewish Antiquities* 18:4, 228
Joshua (Bible), 251; miracle of, 144–45, 256
Joshua (Book), 141, 150, 250; 10, 256; 10:11, 127; 10:12–13, 126–27, 132, 144–45, 147–48, 154
Judah the Prince, 272
Judah, Kingdom of, 155–58
Judaism, ancient rabbinic world, 210, 214: charge of deicide, 224; legal practices, 13; norms of, 224; texts of, 220, 223
Judaism: ancient life, 14; authority of tradition, 278; biblically oriented education, 263, 265, 276–77, 279; competition in education, 46; depiction of Christian theology, 209; dietary laws, 10, 64, 113, 115, 182, 197n77; Dutch influence, 43; Enlightenment in, 274, 276; Holy Land, 247; identity, 18, 20; importance of Talmud, 94; intellectual life, 25; interpretation of Christian texts, 117–20; justification, 120–21, 123, 265; medieval traditions, 25; Oral Law, 42, 136, 185, 272; Orthodox scholarship, 21; particularism, 74, 247; rabbinic, 28, 30–31, 82, 130n16, 221; resolving polemics in Christian exegesis, 214; role of Bible, 85, 93–94; salvation in, 20, 93–95, 99, 264; settlement in Christendom, 135; traditions against capital punishment, 224; weakening rabbinic authority, 41, 165
Judaizers, 96, 178n30
Judea, 238
Judges (Book), 250; 11:26, 150
Julian (Emperor), 236

Jupiter (god), 228; Temple of, 231

Kabbalah, 37, 129, 148
Kanarfogel, Ephraim, 60n103
Kanitor, King of Egypt, 212
Kaplan, Yosef, 29n5, 171, 174, 273, 276, 277n48, 278–79
Karaism: in Amsterdam, 273; in Lithuania, 273
Karo, Joseph: *Shulhan Arukh*, 9, 53, 57–58, 61; *Beit Yosef*, 57–58
Katz, David, 200
Katz, Jacob, 59n102
Kesis, 198
Keter Sem Tob (Crown of the Good Name), 50, 89
Keter Torah, 247–48
Kimhi, David, 136, 149
Kings, Books of, 157, 241, 250; 1 Kings 6, 161; 1 Kings 7:23, 144; 1 Kings 15:33, 157; 1 Kings 16:23, 157; 1 Kings 16:29, 163; 1 Kings 22:52, 163; 1 Kings 23, 128; 2 Kings 1:17, 162; 2 Kings 1:18, 162; 2 Kings 8:16, 162; 2 Kings 8:18, 163; 2 Kings 8:23, 163; 2 Kings 8:26, 163
Kors, Alan, 244–45
Kozodoy, Maud, 92
Krakow, 58

l'Empereur, Constantijn: *Clavis Talmudica*, 164; *Halikhot Olam, sive Clavis Talmudica*, 260
Ladino, 9, 43n54, 44
Lansbergen, Philipp: *Bedenckingen Op den Dagelijckschen, ende Iaerlijkschen loop van den Aerdt-kloot* [Considerations on the diurnal and annual motion of the earth], 144; *Cyclometria*, 257; *Preparatory exercise of the restored astronomy, book I: on the motion of the sun*, 257; *Reflections upon the daily and annual course of the earth*, 257
Last Supper, 183–84, 210, 214, 219, 223, 269; as Jewish event, 223; contradiction of, 215–16, 220; chronology of, 216n25
Latin, 12, 45, 47–48, 227, 234, 254, 258; manuscripts in, 239
Law of Moses, 19, 27–28, 58, 72, 85, 96, 98, 101, 103n49, 107n58, 120, 168, 181–83, 195, 197–98, 206–7, 216, 248, 261–62, 265, 279; divinity of, 247
Lawee, Eric, 11
Laws of Nazir, 186
Leiden, 122, 142; Synopsis of 1625, 115, 140; University of, 138n34, 193, 273
Leigh, Edward, 98–99, 101, 162; *A Treatise of Divinity*, 140
Leon, Jacob Judah, 7, 57–58, 63, 176–77, 180, 202, 258; Book of Psalms, 175; *Sefer Tavnit Heikhal*, 259
Léry, Jean de, 244
Levi, David: *A Succinct Account of the Duties, Rites, and Ceremonies of the Jews*, 272
Levita, Elijah, 11; *Sefer Masoret haMasoret*, 142
Leviticus, 216, 274; 11:43–44, 182; 17:10–14, 105n53
Levush, 57–58
Levy, B. Barry, 12
Libertines, 107n58, 128, 248
Libro de oraciones de todo el anno... traducydo del Hebrayco de verbo a verbo [Book of prayers for the entire year...translated word for word from the Hebrew], 9
Lieberman, Julia, 45n65
Lipsius, Justus: *De cruce*, 225

Liuros de mes [Books of the month], 35
Liuros de taniot [Books of fasts], 35
Liuros de tefilla [Books of prayers], 35
Livorno, 80–81
Livy, 225
London, 80–81, 91, 97
Lope de Vara, 96–97
Lucas, Maximilien, 255
Luke (Book): 1:26–35, 227; 16:18, 182n40; 22:39–44, 238; 23:56, 195
Luke (Evangelist), 222, 229, 239
Luther, Martin, 13, 87, 115, 120–23
Lutheranism, 189, 192, 199; books of, 97
Lyon, 227

Machiavelli, Niccolò, 245, 256
Mahamad, 34, 40, 65, 79, 82
Mahzor, 91
Maimonides, 136, 149, 232; *Guide for the Perplexed*, 230, 258–59; *Mishneh Torah*, 3, 61, 224, 234
Maimuni, 53
Malachi 2:16, 182
Manicheans, 238
Manuel I (King), 4–5
Marburg, 122
Marie de Medici, 172
Mark (Evangelist); narrative of Last Supper, 223
Marranos. *See* Crypto-Jews.
Mars (god), 212
Mary (mother of Christ), 228–29
Maskil el Dal, 69
Maskilim, 274–275, 278n50
Mathematization of knowledge, 126, 128, 132, 143, 149, 152, 165, 267; certainty of, 155; privilege of mathematics, 145
Matthew (Book): 75, 120, 213n18; 1:18, 227; 5:17–19, 186; 5:21–38, 180; 5:32, 181n40, 182; 5:43–44, 75; 11:29–30, 180; 12:1, 196; 12:2, 197; 15:11, 182; 15:18, 183; 15:19, 183; 16:9, 221; 23:2, 186; 26:17–20, 210, 215; 26:26–29, 183–84; (doubtful) origins of, 238
Matthew (Evangelist), 213, 216–17, 229, 238; narrative of Jesus and the corn fields, 197n77, 269
Matthias Flacius Illyricus, 207, 213–14
Mayer, John, 139; *A commentarie upon all the epistles of the apostle Saint Paul*, 115
Méchoulan, Henry, 86n2, 171, 191
Mehizah, 49–50
Meijer, Lodewijk, 162; *Philosophia Sacrae Scripturae Interpretes* (Philosophy as the Interpreter of Holy Scripture), 138–39
Memphis, 230
Men of the Great Synagogue, 142
Menasseh ben Israel, 2, 20–21, 57, 63, 67, 72, 88, 91, 102–4, 106, 110–11, 124, 128, 141, 146–47, 150–58, 161–62, 201–2, 251, 254–55, 266n24, 270–71, 277
Menasseh ben Israel, works of: *Biblia en lengua Espanola*, 176n22; *Conciliador* (Reconciler), 7, 85, 90, 100–101, 107, 123, 130n16, 131, 133, 136–39, 156, 160, 163–65, 264, 267; *De la resurreccion de los Muertos* [On the Resurrection of the Dead], 86n2, 107–9; *Dissertatio de fragilitate humana ex lapsu Adami*, 149; *Esperanza de Israel*, 259, 278;

Humas de Parasioth y Aftharoth, 89, 123; *Nishmat Hayyim,* 129; *Piedra Gloriosa* [Glorious Stone], 86n2, 130n16; *Segunda parte del Conciliador,* 131–32, 144–45, 148, 159–60; *Thesouro dos denim que o povo de Israel he obrigado saber e observer* [A Treasury of Precepts that the People of Israel should Know and Observe] 10
Mendelssohn, Moses, 12, 274–75, 277n48, 278; *Bi'ur,* 276
Menocchio, 233
Messiah, 12, 192, 201, 232
Messianic Dutch Collegiant, 202
Messianism, 170n4, 202; crisis of, 81; in northwestern Europe, 201
Mezuzah, design of, 104
Midrash, 69, 79, 260
Milano, Isaac, 35
Minha, 41
Mi-qetz, 30
Miriam (Bible), 211
Mishnah, 9, 49–51, 61, 93, 210, 217, 219–21, 224–25, 243, 250, 260, 272, 274; Bava Metzi'a tractate, 218–19; Hagigah tractate, 218; Shabbat tractate, 217, 261;
Mishpatim, 103n48
Mizrahi, Rabbi Elijah: *Dikdukei Rashi,* 53n89
Modena, Leon, 120, 169, 172, 188, 198n79, 202n94, 209–10, 225; *Historia degli riti Hebraici,* 224; *Magen va-herev* [Shield and Sword], 185–87, 210, 212
Moloch (god), 257
Montalto, Elijah, 32n12, 172, 227
Montgomery, John Warwick, 237n94
Mordechai de Crasto, 44
Morocco, 80
Morosini, Giulio (Samuel Nahmias): *Via della fede* [The Way of Faith], 45, 61
Morteira, R. Saul Levi, 8n25, 22–24, 30, 32, 32*n*12, 43–45, 51n87, 57, 63 ,72, 75, 77–79, 91, 103, 106n56, 107n58, 111, 116–23, 168–71,179, 185, 193, 196–97, 200, 208, 211, 214–15, 217–22, 224–26, 228, 230–32, 234, 236–42, 250–51, 258, 264, 268, 270–71; attitudes towards Christianity, 191–92; role in Spinoza's excommunication, 247; "the Socinian," 189–92, 194–95, 203, 235, 251
Morteira, R. Saul Levi, works of: "Do Not Add to His Words" (sermon), 73–74; *Preguntas que hizo un clerigo de Ruan* [Questions posed by a priest from Rouen], 112, 116, 164, 172–73, 175, 180, 182–84, 189, 192, 199, 201; *Repuesta a las objecciones con que el Sinense injustamente calunia al Talmud,* 237; *Tratado da verdade da lei de Moisés* [Treatise on the Truth of the Law of Moses] 7, 167n1, 168, 173–75, 177–78, 180–92, 195, 198–207, 209–10, 212–13, 223, 227, 235, 237, 243, 246–48, 251–52, 269
Mosaic philosophy and sacred physics, 144n54
Moses (Bible), 99, 102, 134, 186, 190, 214, 235, 251, 261; authorship of Torah, 211, 254; superiority of, 247
Moses of Coucy, 136; *Sefer Mitzvot Gadol* [Large Book of Commandments], 135
Mount of Olives, 239

Munster, Sebastien, 213n18, 214
Musschenga, Tonnis, 260n17
Mysticae Ezechielis quadrigae, 137

Nadler, Steven, 44n61, 127, 259, 265, 266n24
Nahmanides, Moses, 80
Nahon, Gérard, 86n2
Naples, 237
Napolitano, Alessandro, 227
Naturalism (philosophy), 11, 265; nature's immutability, 146
Nebat, 156
Neghunja (Bible), 261
Netherlands, 1–2, 5, 18–22, 36–37, 42, 49, 62, 87, 95, 97, 122, 128–29, 137, 145, 147, 168, 171, 174–75, 180, 201–2, 238, 269, 273; collapse of Dutch Brazil, 36; Dutch Protestant society, 23–25, 170, 189–96, 203, 206, 208, 225, 265; pedagogy in, 45–49; 1625 *school-reglement* (school order), 45
Neve Salom Congregation, 31–33
New Testament, 7, 13, 15, 20, 22, 24, 27, 89, 96–97, 103, 107n58, 112, 119–21, 143, 159, 168, 170–71, 173–75, 180, 182, 207–8, 210–11, 215, 220–21, 223–25, 227–28, 235–37, 241–42, 247, 250, 254, 258, 268; Greco-Roman origins, 14, 225, 233, 243, 270; historical analysis of, 23, 269–71; Jewish origins, 14; origins of, 214, 238, 242–43; resolution of contradictions, 269; social context of composition, 232; Syriac, 11
Novos reformados. See Socinianism.
Numbers (Book): 3:39, 135; 11:7, 134; 16:8, 135
Nyden, Tammy, 256

Oliveira, R. Selomoh de, 65–66, 67n129, 68–69, 263; *Sefer har ha-zetim* [Book of the Mount of Olives], 68
Olympias, 212
Omri (Bible), 157, 163
Oporto, 103
Or Zarua, R. Isaac, 60
Order of Observantine Jeronomites, 178
Origen (of Alexandria), 239n100
Original sin, 95, 182–83, 186–87, 194
Orobio de Castro, Isaac, 89, 277n48
Osiander, Andreas, 162; *Evangelien-harmonie*, 137
Osiris, cult of, 232
Ouderkerk, 172
Oudewater, 122
Ovid: *Metamorphoses*, 48

Padua, 122
Paganism, 211, 228
Palache, Samuel, 32
Papias of Hierapolis, 239; *Explanations of the Sayings of the Lord*, 241
Parashah, 41, 78
Pardo, David, 91, 123
Pardo, Joseph, 31–32, 45
Pardo, Josiahu, 66
Parente, Ulderico, 237n94
Paris, 32n12, 172, 227; 1240 Disputation of, 135
Parnassim, 33–34, 38–40, 43, 48, 50, 78
Passover, 23, 53, 69, 184, 197–99, 206, 210, 215–17, 219–20, 223–24, 269; Haggadah, 223, 258
Patriarchs, 134
Paul (Apostle), 223, 238, 265

Paul (Gospels), 98, 111–16, 118, 121, 123; Epistles, 111–12, 173
Paul Le Jeune, 244
Paul of Burgos, 216
Paul of Middleburg, 216*n*25
Paulina, 228–29. *See also* Decius Mundus
Pauline Teachings, 87
Penance, 95, 237
Penkower, Jordan, 11
Pentateuch, 28–29, 38–39, 43–44, 51–52, 57, 60–61, 65, 71, 89, 108, 133, 161, 251, 274, 276
Pereyra, Tomás Rodrigues (Abraham Israel Pereyra), 1, 3–4, 6, 10, 37
Perez, Juan: 1556 edition of the New testament, 177
Perkins, William, 99–101
Persians, 258
Peter (Apostle). *See* Cephas.
Peter (Gospel): 2 Peter 1:21, 139
Peyrère, Isaac La, 164, 277n49; biblical criticism, 255; *Du rappel des juifs*, 201; *Praeadamita*, 254
Pharisees, 120, 186, 197, 211, 222, 261, 269
Philip III (King), 5
Philip IV (King), 1
Philistines, 161
Phillip of Macedonia, King of Greece, 212
Philo, 158, 225, 234n85; *Breviarum de Temporibus*, 234n85
Phoenicians, 257
Phylacteries, design of, 104
Pictet, Benedict, 140, 162
Pilate, 215, 225
Pineda, Juan de: *Monarchia Ecclesiastica*, 195, 234–36, 238
Pinto, Gil Lopes (Abraham de Pinto), 37
Pirkei Avot (Book), 9, 69
Plantin Bible, 71
Plantin Printing Press, 70
Plantin, Christophe, 70
Plutarch, 231
Poisson, Nicolas, 246
Polanus, Amandus, 162; *Theologiae syntagmae*, 138, 142
Politicke discoursen, 256
Politien (Agnolo Ambrogini), 245
Politiques, 245
Polyander, Johannes, 140n39
Polytheism, 211
Poole, Matthew, 101, 139
Pope Pius I, 196
Popkin, Richard, 254, 277
Portugal, 4–6, 19, 27–28, 73, 76, 83, 87, 94–96, 123, 151; expulsion of Jews from (1496), 4; Inquisition (1536), 5–6
Prado, Juan de, 19, 82, 165, 248
Predestination, 122, 194; opposition to, 193
Prime Cause, 191, 194
Proof of God's existence, 246
Prophecy, 127–28, 261
Prophets (Book), 11, 27, 29, 38, 43, 44, 51–53, 55, 60–61, 63, 65, 67–68, 71, 89, 99, 108, 120
Prosperina, 228
Protestantism, 13, 16–17, 19, 23; biblicism of, 97; Catholic debates, 169; in England, 201; Reformed, 87; religious reforms, 47; theology of, 26, 99, 202; understanding of sacraments, 14
Psalms (Book), 57–58, 66–67, 109, 223; 6:6, 110; 19, 98; 19:7, 20, 71; 19:8, 116; 104, 144
Purgatory, 96, 221, 237

Puritans, 200

Quakers, 128, 189, 199, 207n4

R. Bahya ben Asher, 136, 149; *Kad ha-kemah* (Vessel of Flour), 102
R. Jacob ben Asher: *Turim*, 61
R. Jehuda, 261
R. Joshua ben Levi, 184
Rabbah bar Hana, 221
Rabbinic fences around the law, 197n79
Rabbis, the, 217
Rakovian Catechism, 193
Ramah, 157
Rashi, 29, 38, 44, 52, 67, 136, 149; commentary on the Pentateuch, 53–55, 57–58, 60
Ratio Studiorum, 46–47
Rauschenbach, Sina, 86n2, 129, 136
Redemption, 100
Reformados, 196, 206, 269
Reformation, 23, 95, 170n4, 178, 196
Régénérateurs, 275
Rehoboam, 156, 158
Reina, Casiodoro de, 238, 258; 1569 Bible of (Basel), 177–79,
Reina-Valera Bible, 258
Reiser, Anton, 245
Remonstrants, 15–16, 88n5, 122–23, 142, 193
Renaissance, 12
Restoration, 200
Revah, I.S., 173n13
Ribera, Daniel, 165
Riewertsz, Jan, 253
Rittangel, Johann, 199
Rivetus, Andreus, 140n39
Roman and Hellenic world, 13; social practices, 14
Rome, 237–38
Rosenbloom, Noah, 130n16
Rosh Hashanah, 91, 218
Rosh Hodesh, 39, 48
Ruderman, David, 272–73, 276, 277n49, 278n50
Rupert of Deutz, 216
Ruth (Book), 250

Sabbath observance, 174, 195, 197, 206, 215–20, 224, 269; shifting of Christian Sabbath, 195–96; Jewish, 196, 198; Protestant, 200; royal policy of, 200; on Saturday, 201; on Sunday, 200
Sacraments, 95
Sacred texts as historical artefacts, 209, 226, 269; within Christian sacred history, 243
Sadducees, 107–9, 211
Safed, 5, 65
Sallustius, 48
Salom ben Yosseph, 44, 91, 123
Salom, R. Joseph (Josef), 32, 38–39, 43, 91
Salom, Selomoh, 56–57
Salomon, H.P., 171, 173n13, 174–75
Salonika, 5, 12
Salvation, 85–87, 100, 102, 106, 110, 115, 122, 194, 266; and Scripture, 88, 90–96, 98–100, 103–4, 108, 111–12, 117, 119, 121, 123–24, 264–66; based on faith, 120, 123
Samotheus. *See* Tolosani, Giovanni Maria.
Samuel (Bible), 161
Samuel (Books of), 110, 150, 250; 1 Samuel 13:1, 161; 1 Samuel 27:7, 162
Sanchez, Francisco, 277n49

Santa Companhia de dotar orphas e donzelas pobres, 32
Saperstein, Marc, 8n25, 171, 174, 189, 192, 247; *Exile in Amsterdam*, 172n5,
Saragossa, 234
Sasportas, R. Jacob, 19, 80–81, 84
Saul (Bible), 161–62
Scaliger, Joseph, 13–16, 24, 142n45, 181n37, 214, 216n25, 217, 224n52, 225, 254; *De emendation temporum*, 223; use of Talmud, 223
Scholberg, Kenneth, 60n135
Scientific Revolution, 279
Sclar, David, 58n100
Second Temple, 113, 211, 217, 236, 269
Seder 'Olam, 153, 160
Seder Mo'ed, 58n100
Sefer Korot Alexander, 212
Sefer Nizzahon Vetus, 197n77
Sefer She'erit Yosef, 260
Selden, John, 14n41, 24, 214, 223–25; *De Successionibus in Bona Defuncti, Ad Leges Ebraeorum*, 224n52; *De synedriis et Praefecturis Juridicis Veterum Ebraeorum*, 224
Self-flagellation, 232
Selomo (Bible), 105
Separate Intellects, 146. *See* also Active Intellect.
Sephardic Judaism, 6, 31, 35, 37, 45–46, 51–52, 188, 199, 210, 277, 279; approaches to New Testament, 208, 212; diaspora, 32, 84, 255n5, 278; hereticism in, 255; in Amsterdam, 201, 209; Karaites, 273; medieval philosophy, 278; religious uncertainty, 165;
Septuagint, 12, 15, 138, 179–80
Serrano, R. Yosseph Franco, 43n57, 176; *Los cinco libros de la sacra Ley* [The Five Books of the Holy Law], 8
Serrarius, Peter, 199
Seville, 178; Shrine to the Virgin Mary, 178n30
Shamgar (Bible), 154
Shechem, 251
Sheehan, Jonathan: "Enlightenment Bible," 275n42
Shelah Lekha, 78
Shem Tov, Shem Tov ibn, 146
Shuger, Debora, 13
Sigonio, Carlo: *De republica Hebraeorum libri*, 211
Sihon (Bible), 150
Simon, Richard, 270, 273
Sinai, 101; revelation at, 247
Single spiritual community, 86
Sixtus of Siena, 240n100, 241–43, 251; *Bibliotheca*, 234, 236–40
Socinianism, 23, 128, 142, 167–68, 170–71, 188–90, 191, 194–96, 198, 202n94, 206, 213, 257, 268–69; Academy at Rakow, 193
Socinus, Faustus, 143, 194, 257; *De Auctoritate Sacra Scripturae*, 193
Sola Scriptura, 99, 273
Solomon (Bible), 109, 128, 153, 158, 240; Temple of, 6–7, 127, 139, 151, 153, 155–56, 161, 202, 219–20, 222, 230–31, 236, 241
Song of Songs (Book), 9
Spain, 1–6, 19, 32, 36–37, 64, 73, 80, 83, 87, 94–95, 97, 123, 178, 233; Catholic scholarship in, 208; Expulsion of Jews from (1492), 4, 29n5; Inquisition, 36, 97, 179; religious culture in, 96
Spinoza, Benedict (Baruch), 19, 21, 26,